THICKER'N THIEVES

CHARLES STOKER

Foreword by Steve Hodel

Thoughtprint Press
Los Angeles, California

Copyright © 2011 by Thoughtprint Press
Los Angeles, California
Published in the United States of America
Visit our Web site at www.thoughtprintpress.com
ISBN-978-0-9830744-9-6

All rights reserved. Except as permitted under the U.S. Copyright Act of 1976, no part of this publication may be reproduced, distributed, or transmitted in any form or by any means, or stored in a database or retrieval system, without the prior written permission of the publisher.
A hardcover edition of this book was originally published in 1951 by the Sidereal Company, Santa Monica, California

THE REPRINTING OF THIS BOOK IS DEDICATED TO THE MEMORY OF

CHARLES F. STOKER

IN RECOGNITION OF HIS DEDICATED SERVICE AND SACRIFICE TO
THE CITIZENS OF LOS ANGELES, CALIFORNIA

TO MY AUNT

EVELYN P. COATS

— who gave so much

CONTENTS

FOREWORD xi
THE LOW COMEDIAN 1
THICKER'N THIEVES 19
MOBSTER COPPERS 31
LAW - A DECEPTIVE WHORE 41
MY FIRST ARREST 58
I MEET RUDY WELLPOTT 63
ALONG COMES BRENDA 68
SERGEANT ELMER V. JACKSON-HERO? 78
THE CIRCLE CONSTRICTS 85
ANOTHER FEMME FATALE 103
FINALE FOR BRENDA 116
ANGEL CITY ABORTION RING 133
IT'S FRAME-UP TIME 145
GRAND JURY PREVIEW 159
VICE AND POLITICS 169
CONSPIRATORIAL LADY 183
GRAND JURY 209
THE ENEMY GLOATS 231
THE SMEAR TECHNIQUE 239
A TRICK DONE WITH MIRRORS 265
CONDUCT UNBECOMING OFFICERS 286
COPS AND ROBBERS 313
"LOVE SENDS ITS LITTLE GIFT OF ROSES" 325
LOOKING BACKWARD- AND FORWARD 334
SEQUEL 368

Los Angeles Times July 8, 1949

Grand Jury Chief Fears for Life of Stoker After He Testifies Again

Foreman Lawson Calls Him 'Real Informer in Case'

BRIEF MEETING—"They're only using you to get at me," Sgt. Charles Stoker mumbles to Policewoman Audre Davis, who made damaging statements to grand jury against Stoker in Police Department inquiry. "I don't know what to do, Charlie," she replied.

Sgt. Charles Stoker, central figure in the ever-widening vice inquiry, "should be under guard" to forestall his being "found dead on the curb within five days," Grand Jury Foreman Harry A. Lawson warned yesterday. Also enlivening yesterday's session was a judge's opinion that District Attorney's aides should attend the panel's hearings.

Lawson's comment was made after Stoker completed his interrupted testimony by giving the jury new leads for officer graft and corruption in the Police Department.

At the adjournment until next Tuesday morning Lawson said:

"Stoker is the real informer in this case. Brenda Allen is just peanuts compared to what he has given us. He should be under guard. If he continues to name names and situations like he did today he will be found dead on the curb within five days."

Reports at a recess session that grand jury and the prosecutor's office believed discussions by veniremen concerning the exclusion of District Attorney's representatives from sessions.

Confronted by telephone, Presiding Superior Judge Robert H. Scott is understood to have pointed out to jurors that under the State Penal Code, attaches of the prosecutor's office "may" attend sessions. This is taken by District Attorney's aides to mean that they cannot be barred.

Excluded From Room

Some jurors had wanted to know if witnesses in the vice investigation could be questioned by the jury in the absence of men from the prosecutor's office. During the conference with Judge Scott, Asst. Dist. Atty. John Barnes and his colleagues were excluded from the jury room.

> "Stoker is the real informer in this case. Brenda Allen is just peanuts compared to what he has given us. He should be under guard. If he continues to name names and situations like he did today he will be found dead on the curb within five days."
>
> Harry A. Lawson
> 1949 Grand Jury Foreman

Foreword

LAPD detective, Charles Stoker. Hundred-to-one, you've never heard the name. NYPD detective, Frank Serpico. Hundred-to-one you have!

Well:

"Twenty-years before SERPICO there was STOKER!"

This book, THICKER'N THIEVES – THE FACTUAL EXPOSE *Of Police Pay-Offs, Graft, Political Corruption and Prostitution in Los Angeles and Hollywood,* was written by LAPD Sgt. Charles Stoker during two of Los Angeles' most politically volatile years – 1948-1950.

His book was originally published by the *Sidereal Company*, Santa Monica, California, in April, 1951.

Due to the original limited print run, a copy of THICKER'N THIEVES (in any condition) is almost impossible to locate. This morning, November 26, 2010, I made a search of the Internet and discovered that a mere seven (7) copies are available for purchase-*worldwide*. The prices range from $200-$500, with five of the editions priced over $400.

Reproduced below is the original text summary found on the 1951 jacket copy. Written sixty-years ago, and forged out of the heat and headlines of that day, as real-time, daily breaking news stories, it best captures the essence and spirit of *The Stoker Story*.

Thicker'N Thieves front and back flaps:

> This is the full, fearless expose by former vice-squad officer, Charles Stoker, of the shocking and unbelievable graft and corruption which prevail in the city government of Los Angeles.
>
> In writing this story, and in his long fight to have it published—most publishers considered it "too hot to handle"—the highest compliment paid to

Stoker was the frequent remark, "publish this book and it will cost you your life!"

Few men in his position in any city have ever had the courage to do what Stoker has done in this startling book. Here is an underworld—crime—racket story out of real life...with the true identity of those who play a part in it.

Here you can read how a Main Street street-walker, Marie Mitchell, zoomed to national fame as Brenda Allen—L.A.'s notorious vice queen—with the help and protection of the "city fathers" in cahoots with the underworld. You can "listen in" on the wire-tap recordings of Brenda getting her instructions from the high brass on the police force...you won't believe the conniving, crime-full corruption that cost Stoker his job when he finally trapped call-house madame, Brenda Allen. You remember the headlines proclaiming: "STOKER WAGES 1-MAN VICE CRUSADE?" This is a vital part of that crusade. This is a story that should be read with the lights on. If you can't read—it should be read to you!

THICKNER'N THIEVES is the first definitive, factual account of the Hollywood and Los Angeles underworld, told by Charles Stoker, former vice-squad officer and police sergeant who saw it from the inside and wrote many pages of its ignoble history on police blotters and in the city courts.

The Stoker Story is devoid of analysis, rationalization, deduction and philosophy. It is rather the breathtaking account of a police officer who ran into the political-underworld buzzsaw which is part and parcel of every big city.

Where corrupt police officers, venal politicians and office-holders claimed to have been fighting the underworld, Stoker fought it personally, furiously and with everything at his command to the point where he was framed and fired for "CONDUCT UNBECOMING AN OFFICER" because he testified to the facts before the 1949 Los Angeles Grand Jury.

Aside from being a cold steel account of what transpired within the Los Angeles Police Department during his tenure as an officer, this is the highly human story of young Texan, Stoker.

All men claim to have the courage of their convictions, but after you have read this book ask yourself whether or not you would have had the fortitude to go through this curtain of fire to uphold your ideals of honesty and integrity in city government.

Stoker was not only fighting individuals. He was fighting an underworld organization with all the money and "angles." Added to that, he was fighting the concentrated might of a highly organized and powerful city administration which had the help of a district attorney's office in its attempt to assuage and soften the impact of...The Stoker Story.

For all who read all or part of the newspaper accounts bearing on the activities of those involved, THICKER'N THIEVES is the down-to-earth, factual hook-up of political-police graft and corruption in the third largest metropolis in the nation!

A Little History

The fact that Sgt. Stoker has little to no name recognition TODAY would lead one to believe that sixty-years ago, he was just a blip on the radar screen. Maybe a disgruntled rogue cop that had his fifteen minutes of fame then sank below the surface?

The historical truth is quite the contrary.

Sgt. Charles Stoker and his real-time expose of political and police corruption dominated the headlines *for two full years*. In 1948 and 1949, Stoker appeared in more than *six-hundred separate print articles*, most of which were lead *Front Page* stories.

Stoker's testimony before the 1949 Grand Jury provided direct inside information on vice payoffs, bribe-taking and extortions *as they occurred. Real time graft that went all the way up the ladder to LAPD's top-cops.* Sgt. Stoker held back nothing, providing the grand jury with the corrupt officers' names, dates and specifics.

LAPD aided by the Mayor and the DA's Office fought back HARD. They used every available smear tactic in a full frontal assault on Stoker—the Whistle-Blower. "He's in league with gangsters." "It's an election ploy to try and take down our 'Honest Mayor Bowron.'" "Communists backers are supporting Stoker" etc.

When nothing stuck, they fired him for CUPO, *Conduct Unbecoming a Police Officer*. His crime? "Failing to obtain formal permission from the Department before testifying in front of the 1949 Grand Jury."

But, I will let Sgt. Stoker speak for himself on these points as he presents the factual chronology as it unfolded, month-by-month.

Thicker'N Thieves is not a polished police procedural as found in a Michael Connelly novel. Nor will his pages read like the practiced prose of ex-LAPD Sgt. Joseph Wambaugh. Unlike Wambaugh, Stoker had no degree in English Lit.

But, what he did have was a Ph.D. in *street smarts*. That coupled with a need to be absolutely honest and direct made for a powerful historical recording of two-years that changed the course and direction of the *Los Angeles Police Department forever*.

Stoker the Crusader, by exposing the graft and corruption, reset LAPD's moral compass. Chief Bill Parker, the Reformer, appointed in July 1950 would hold the ship on course for the next sixteen years.

I have two main reasons for wanting to make Sgt. Stoker's book available to ALL.

First, because it sets the record straight and provides us with a *printed program* of who did what and how. No spin, no deception, no subterfuge. As an insider, and active participant, Stoker simply tells it like it is. Mostly, without editorial, as if he were writing a "Just the Facts" police report.

My second reason for wanting to bring the *Stoker Story* into the present has to do with what I believe to be the book's *historical uniqueness and importance. Thicker'N Thieves* was written for and meant to be read by John and Jane Q. Citizen.

This book was not authored by a writer or historian who is trying to *recreate* the language and events from some sixty-years past.

Charley Stoker is a real-life 1940s police-sergeant working Hollywood Vice speaking directly to *The People*, in the idiom of his day.

His book is written without pretense or affectation. Like many of the men of his day, Stoker comes off both homophobic and chauvinistic; his world is obviously black-and-white. Good vs. Evil. You are either honest or a crook. You're a cop "on-the-take"—or clean.

One of the most dramatic historical revelations in the book comes from the dialogues he presents in—the *Stoker-Parker Conversations*.

Then Inspector, Bill Parker had just been assigned by interim Chief Worton to head the newly established, Bureau of Internal Affairs.(BIA) Incredibly, *Parker lays out to Stoker, confidential details of what he knows to be a "cop setup" which included everything from the shakedown of Main Street bars up to and including a police murder of two black prostitutes by two LAPD on duty vice-cops, going on to tell Stoker, "I can prove it."* Pay close attention to Stoker's assessment and early profile of Inspector Bill Parker in *Chapter 17, Grand Jury*—it's dead-on and riveting!

Stoker doesn't just call-out and name LAPD's corrupt gangster-cops; he also informs Angelenos which of the command staff are the "Good Guys."

In his chapter, *Looking Backward—And Forward*, he lists five of the high-command informing the public that, "Inspectors Jack Donahoe, Anthony Collins and Lee German along with Deputy Chiefs Thad Brown and Arthur Hohmann *have the respect and confidence of police personnel.*"

Stoker's early description of his mental state gives us a good sense of where he was coming from and headed. Here's how he described it at the time:

"Most of the tortuous mental travail was physically akin to
chasing a dozen snakes under a field full of autumn leaves."

He talks to us in cop terminology: "square apples," "juice," "boat-rides," "tank jobs" and "B-Girls." Riding with Stoker on his undercover vice operations we learn about: "masquerading," "resorting," "Black and Tan," "The Negro Belt," "Little Brother" and "programmed raids."

He takes us in and out of 1940s L.A. nightclubs and restaurants, now long gone: *The House of Murphy, The Brown Derby, Dave's Blue Room, Slapsie Maxie's, and the Piccadilly.*

In this reprinting of *Thicker'N Thieves* I have changed *nothing*. None of the original text has been altered or edited. The book reads exactly as it was printed in 1951.

I have made a few *additions*. The original printing contained no photographs. I have included a "Line-Up" so readers can put real faces to the many "players." The only other additions are a contents table and an index.

I will close with Sgt. Stoker's own words from an early chapter, where he informs us:

"It is the purpose of *The Stoker Story* to clear up the rumors, the many false impressions that have permeated the police mess involving me and to show, in behalf of public welfare, how a police-gangster setup, where the policemen are gangsters and the gangsters are policemen, operated in Los Angeles, in contrast to other big cities where coppers are coppers and mobsters are mobsters."

Enjoy the ride!

Steve Hodel
Los Angeles
January 1, 2011

THE LOW COMEDIAN

This is an episode you should read not once – but twice; if you can't read, you should have it read aloud to you – with the lights on!

How rotten can the body politic of a great city become, and still survive the virus of sin? What waste, graft and kick-backs in unknown millions of taxpayer's money might be uncovered if the men and women in City Government with knowledge of existing conditions had the courage to reveal them as forthrightly as the author draws the curtain from the vice picture, here?

This chapter is not intended as a factual indictment of a city. Its purpose is rather the exposure of a cunning politico whose deceits have kept him in office as Mayor of Los Angeles for more than a decade – a dark decade, indeed! Time and again, as much to the amazement of himself as to the people at large, the voters have returned this contradictory paragon to office by the narrowest of margins.

Universally disliked as an individual, with sanguinary indifference, Fletcher E. Bowron, a man who has gained his sustenance at the political trough virtually all of his adult life, has taxed his people to the brink of economic suicide, squandered their money and permitted their city to become the crime center of the world.

What is his charm, then? It lies not in his personality, for in that he is as flat as stale beer; not in his ability, for he is notorious for official ineptness and stupidity; not in his good looks, for one glance at him turns one away feeling a little the worse. What, then? The answer lies in the clever perversion of the phrase, "Yes, but he is honest."

In a community of 2,000,000 people an illusion has been created that Mayor Bowron is the only honest man. And this miracle has been wrought by a venal press together with a tax paid publicity budget for the Mayor's use in excess of half a million dollars.

This book, it is hoped, will convince even the most naive citizen that the aforementioned pious, petulant little man can no longer claim a monopoly on truth, honesty and veracity in violation of the natural and moral laws against sanctimonious trusts. The stench is too virulent, the slime too adhesive for any Angeleno, much less the Chief Executive responsible for the mess, to claim absolutism in Los Angeles' Good Government.

The thoughtful reader will pause over these startling revelations to ask:

"How and why did this shame come to Los Angeles?"

In arriving at a logical answer, it must be taken into consideration that the question is not so much how Fletcher Bowron became Mayor as *why* ... and why he continues in office.

Against a backdrop of municipal corruption, much of which was over-exaggerated, Bowron first ran for Mayor under the auspices of the lowest elements of the local underworld and the highest class of civic virtue. The first group was set in motion by the system or Syndicate; and the latter went along for the joyous, successful ride in delirious brotherhood with the strangest combination of Communists (they endorsed Bowron and took credit for it in their annual year book), fanatical do-gooders, and righteously indignant citizens ever to climb aboard a political bandwagon.

The Syndicate, which, incidentally, has not lost complete control of Los Angeles politics for the past twenty-five years, bought the gas and greased the wheels.

When Bowron was elected Mayor in 1938, the Syndicate was headed by Kent Kane Parrot, a clever political lawyer;

Guy McAfee, a canny ex-vice squad officer turned gambler, and Robert J. Gans, a conniving slot-machine mogul. They worked their will through various henchmen, not the least important of whom were three very real but vaporous underworld characters, James Francis Utley, Anne (Black Widow) Forrester and Anthony Stralla, quondam whiskey smuggler during prohibition, gambler and ex-convict affectionately known as Tony Cornero.

Utley was a dope peddler. Anne was the town's bawdy house entrepreneur. Tony ran luxurious gambling boats just off the Pacific's moonlit shores. You'll not consider these *nice people*, unless, of course, your physical hungers or weak instincts need their specialties. Yet, these three were guardian angels —a dope runner, a prostitute-panderess and a racketeer-gambler (and former bootlegger) who were assigned by the omnipotent Syndicate to guide the Honorable Fletcher E. Bowron into the Mayor's office. It is a matter of record that Racketeer Cornero financed much of the 1938 mayoralty campaign, and that Jimmy Utley provided Clifford Clinton, Bowron's political mentor, with smear material and support from the underworld.

Anne Forrester, branded "The Black Widow" by underworld associates with an eye for realities, was so-called because of her deadly potentialities as a procuress of young girls. She was given absolution by the good Mayor himself in a brazen, recorded display of public-be-damned expansiveness.

Operating several houses of prostitution in Los Angeles under Bowron's regime, "The Black Widow" had been arrested for procuring, and was convicted by the sheriff's office. She was either to be granted probation or be sent to Tehachapi prison for women.

Then Mayor Bowron, in a letter to Superior Judge Clarence Kincaid, urged the jurist to give this bedizened harlot probation in return for services rendered in his behalf.

This consort of panderers and pimps who had been given free rein to seduce and recruit young girls for bawdy houses was even then teaching her eventual successor, Brenda Allen, the tricks of the trade, the modus operandi of working with and making payments to a city's political machine. Brenda, at the time of Anne's downfall in 1939, was working for the latter as one of the girls in a prostitution ménage.

Thus it was that the middleman was eliminated from the business of sin and that a full partnership was set up directly with the vice squad on a more liquid and profitable basis.

Superior Judge Kincaid in his dealing with "The Black Widow" exhibited a similar aversion to the Bowron retainer as a Federal judge had displayed in refusing clemency to her male counterpart, Jimmy Utley, the underworld representative of Clifford Clinton, the man who had claimed chief credit for the election of Bowron as mayor, when he sentenced him to serve a two-year term on McNeil Island Federal penitentiary for selling morphine to a twenty-year-old Los Angeles girl.

Had it not been for the courage of the author of this book that extension of a political pay-off through Brenda Allen, who had learned all the artifices of the prostitution-graft game from "The Black Widow," might still be in good standing as an obligation of Bowron's vice squad.

Mr. Utley — twelve short years ago a craven dope peddler standing before the bar of justice — has become a millionaire under the benign sufferance of a City Administration whose influence could not save him from jail but could reward him in monetary ways not usually accorded ex-convicts. His rewards were not insignificant ones. He has been part owner of the city's $50,000 a day Bingo racket; unmolested owner of a swank Hollywood restaurant on Melrose Avenue, the rendezvous of vicious mobsters who have the keys to the city, and the California Crime Commission recognizes his importance as "The Eel" of politics and leader of the "Big Five," wielding great power in local police affairs, according to a recent Crime Commission report.

Guy McAfee still shares with Bob Gans joint overlord control over a city, the mayor of which in making it "pure" has also made it sterile. Was it through Guy's arrangements that the mayor rode a jackass to publicize the $90,000,000 a year gambling dens of Las Vegas, Nevada, at the very height of his last mayoralty campaign? It could well have been, since to gambler and politician the hand is quicker than the eye. McAfee boasts of pouring large sums of money into Los Angeles campaigns as insurance against the possible defeat of his greatest economic asset, a "closed town" Mayor.

Gans, on the other hand, still operates at home base, sharing alike the confidence of those who make their living from games of skill and chance, the mobsters' mouthpieces and the "civic leaders" who are, in the main, political lawyers like his former associate, Parrott. These men of local distinction are much too elegant to be referred to by the vulgar term "fixers"; but they trade on the reputation of being such, and their great influence in municipal affairs indicates that they are.

The cast of office-holders has changed, but the melodrama is much the same as it has been for the past twenty-five years. Terrifying and lustful sex crimes with violence and death done to innocent women and children, smut and smog have been added with heavy overtones.

In center stage sits a pudgy comedian to whom the voters of Los Angeles have unwittingly entrusted the decency, honesty and safety of over 2,000,000 people.

This book is only one of a dozen which could be written on the great shame of Los Angeles. It is a daring attack upon the hypocrisy of those who pretend to be desirous of improving conditions while secretly preferring the status quo.

While this is essentially the story of one idealistic man pitted against a powerful political machine, it may be the barb which goads God-fearing people to action, for we are at the apogee of Bowron misrule, resulting in every conceivable sort of crime.

Of this expose, it may be said:

"All the darkness of the world cannot dim the flicker of the feeblest candle light, and the deeper the night the brighter the flame!"

HISTORICAL BACKGROUND

Los Angeles is a city about which almost anything may be said in praise or in derogation; and about which a case can be made out either way.

Millions of words have been written about Los Angeles, the great and amorphous metropolis of Southern California — El Pueblo Nuestra Senora La Reina de Los Angeles — sentimental stories have been related about its early Indian culture, the forty-niners and the military, and about the impact they had on the territory; but for the purposes of this story, the modern history of Los Angeles had its beginning in the year 1921, when an obscure attorney on the make, Kent Kane Parrott, surprised the usually somnolent citizens by electing an almost equally obscure attorney, George Cryer, mayor.

George Cryer was undoubtedly as surprised as was his political mentor, Kent Kane Parrott, when he unseated Meredith (Pinky) Snyder, so-called because of the pink whiskers which offset his features in a flamingo aura. Mr. Snyder had been elected mayor of Los Angeles and was maintained as such principally through the support of the powerful Los Angeles Times and its publisher, Harry Chandler, a down East Yankee, whose commercial, real estate and financial interests were more potent politically than his newspaper was editorially.

George Cryer was not given a Chinaman's chance to defeat Meredith Snyder in the 1921 mayoralty election. In that campaign, Parrott, a graduate of the University of Southern California and a member of the college varsity football team during his scholastic days, was to display for the first time the amazing political sagacity which later was to stamp him as one of the outstanding political managers of his era.

Although the citizens of Los Angeles had heard little if anything about Kent Parrott prior to 1921, after that time and until the year 1938, Parrott managed the politicos of Los Angeles City and County with a cleverness and a shrewdness that left him virtually unidentified in the electoral consciousness.

During that period of eighteen years it was not at all surprising to the initiate to see the churches lined up behind candidates for the important public offices of mayor, sheriff and district attorney—candidates who had the whole-hearted support of the underworld forces. These office-seekers were led by Gambler Guy McAfee; slot machine king Robert Gans; underworld First Lieutenant Charlie (The Grey Wolf) Crawford; Zeke Caress, hetman of the bookmaking gentry; and Marco Albori, alias Albert Marco, caliph of the prostitution industry.

The fact that church elements were frequently unaware that they had unwittingly become political bedfellows of the forces of darkness led by the underworld cabal and masterminded by political genius Parrott, was only an academic point over which political neophytes could haggle. For the purposes of practicality, however, the combination was effective at the polls where it counted most, and where it enhanced Parrott's reputation for astuteness. Parrott evidently found it easier to handle the politicians representing the churches than those of the underworld.

Parrott's direction of the frequently daffy and always heterogeneous political elements that made up Los Angeles between 1921 and 1938 — whose offspring threaten to make Los Angeles still daffier between 1950 and 1975 — and his instinctive ability to weld such elements together into a homogenous whole for his own purposes, stamped him as a master political maneuverer of the highest calibre.

Parrott's eighteen-year-long mastery of the political scene in Los Angeles was subtle, ingenious and brilliant from the managerial standpoint. His influence was even more effective over the electorate because, had one asked a thousand voters who Parrott was, nine hundred and ninety-nine could not have furnished even a remote answer. Parrott's definition of politics was "People In Motion" and his criterion of political success was to achieve the possible. In diagnosing a Los Angeles political situation and bringing it to successful fruition from his point of view, Parrott was seldom caught outside the ambit of the possible.

Parrott's personal habits were beyond reproach. He didn't get drunk; and he had no liking for persons who did. He was married and a family man; and throughout all the years he had figured as head man in the Los Angeles political arena, his name was never coupled amorously with that of any "cutie." If Parrott, in love's illicit back alley ways, was ever indiscreet, no one ever heard about it.

Publicly and socially, Parrott was seen only with the best people — giants of industry, of finance and of the social register. He never appeared publicly with any of the illy-assorted mob that composed the framework of his political entourage. These he conferred with from time to time in a twelfth floor suite in Los Angeles' best downtown hotel. He shunned publicity as if it were a plague, and it is noteworthy that publishers of the Los Angeles newspapers gave him but little of it, either in praise or in condemnation. In fact the massive editorial silence accorded Parrott and most of his myrmidons gave support to the view that the publishers approved of Parrott and most, if not all of his works.

Frequently it happened that when two candidates would run for important offices such as those of district attorney, sheriff, or mayor, it didn't make a great deal of difference to Parrott which was elected, for both were generally Parrott men. His direction of the political forces in Los Angeles City and County, although fantastic and incredible, was detailed and comprehensive, and proved all the more effective because the voters, for the most part, had never heard of him.

Parrott, as an urban political phenomenon, was living proof of the axiom that a "handful of people make politics" and under Parrott, the citizens of Los Angeles City and County, for eighteen long years, generally had the choice of two candidates for important public offices, but it might be re-phrased that the voters had two alternatives and that most of the time both were bad.

Los Angeles, prior and subsequent to Parrott, has never had what one can accurately call a political organization comparable to those in other American cities, such organizations as Tammany Hall in New York; the Philadelphia- Pennsylvania crew of Boies Penrose, the Kelly-Nash machine in Chicago; the Frank Hague gallants of New Jersey, or Pendergast's artful dodgers of Kansas City.

Perhaps the composition of the population of Los Angeles, ethnic, racial and geographical, prevented the creation of a tightly knit political organization characteristic of the older cities on the Atlantic seaboard and in the Middle West.

But despite the political disparities, the abrasiveness and the dissidence of Los Angeles' political elements, Parrott ran the city and was its boss for good or evil during the eighteen years in which he held the reins. Parrott gave to Los Angeles its modern political style and political techniques.

Parrott's political range was extended in scope after he had solidified himself as the political master of Los Angeles City and County, because, as Southern California was most populous, he was listened to respectfully in matters having statewide importance.

After Parrott had master-minded George Cryer's election as mayor, he allowed no time to lapse. He was a rapid worker, and was adept at political compromises. He made his peace with the powerful Los Angeles Times and its publisher, Harry Chandler, but not until after 1925, when Chandler induced Federal Judge Ben Bledsoe to resign from the bench and joust with Mayor George Cryer who was seeking re-election.

Parrott won Cryer's re-election mainly by identifying Judge Bledsoe with Publisher Chandler in hundreds of billboards, which screamed: "Harry Calls Him, 'Ben'."

Chandler was chiefly interested in keeping Los Angeles an open shop, anti-union city and in putting down the radical and subversive elements, the anarchists and the "wobblies," out of whose ranks had come the men who had dynamited The Los Angeles Times building on October 1, 1910, killing some thirty odd employees of the newspaper as the climax of a bitter labor dispute. Accordingly, The Times and its publisher, Chandler, were mainly interested in seeing to it that the police authorities of the city shared their views in regard to organized labor and the suppression of radicalism.

After 1925, and during the years in which Parrott reigned as political boss, The Los Angeles Times named the chief of police whether it had supported the candidacy of the man elected mayor or had opposed him.

Parrott was a political realist. He evidently assumed that Los Angeles, like other great cities, was bound to have its underworld; and, being an Angeleno, no doubt he believed that the racketeering rights and privileges in the city, such as vice and gambling, should be reserved for local talent, first as they are and long have been in San Francisco.

At the time of Parrott's first political success, Charlie Crawford, another genius with a talent for rackets and their organization, was operating a combination saloon-bordello at Fifth Street and Maple Avenue, a short walk from the downtown district. Guy McAfee, a sharp and wily vice squad officer of the Los Angeles police department, with a predilection for gambling and the money to be derived therefrom, had been fired for involvement in a minor scandal. Robert Gans and his brother (the latter long since dead) owned a cigar and tobacco business, and had just learned how much money could be made from slot machines, or one-armed bandits, when Parrott came to power.

Parrott and Gans fought politically for a while, but inasmuch as they were all local people, perhaps it was only natural and inevitable that they should come together in a political-underworld coalition. Crawford became the No. 1 boss of the rackets, with McAfee handling the gambling house end, and Gans devoted exclusively to slot machines. Albert Marco, with Augustus Sasso, alias Chito, both of whom had worked with Charlie Crawford in Seattle, Washington, before Crawford had been chased out of that city and into Los Angeles, took over the prostitution industry, while Zeke Caress, a native son and a friend of McAfee, directed the bookmaking monopoly.

The Syndicate, as it became known in underworld and political purlieus, had few major or minor set-backs, political or penological, from 1921 until 1933. The first major trouble occurred in 1928 when Marco, who previously had branched out into bootlegging from his prostitute monopoly, shot Dominic Conterno during a drunken brawl at The Ship Cafe in Venice, a night life spot operated by an ex-prizefighter, Tommy Jacobs. Marco was convicted and sent to San Quentin prison. He was eventually deported to his native habitat in the Tyrol Mountains, bordering Italy and Austria.

The resultant "scandal," however, brought about the election of a "reform" candidate, Churchman John C. Porter, quondam county grand jury foreman, who took full credit for having convicted Marco. Porter had the solid backing of the church element, but his election, from the Syndicate's point of view was a minor happenstance, and the Syndicate took it in stride, the only noticeable practical result being a brief hiatus during which the rackets remained dormant.

In 1933, Frank L. Shaw, a former wholesale grocery salesman for the Haas-Baruch Company, was elected Mayor of Los Angeles. Previously, he had been elected to the Los Angeles City Council, and had then successfully run for election as a member of the powerful Los Angeles

County Board of Supervisors. Shaw ran against John C. Porter and defeated him handily, although there were many who wondered why The Syndicate had deserted the Porter banner and had supported Shaw.

The habit of dominating the Los Angeles City and County political scene and of operating the rackets therein had become fixed with The Syndicate. But with the election of Frank L. Shaw, its members were to learn that trouble was in the offing.

Frank had a brother, Joe Shaw, a "mustang" lieutenant in the United States Navy. That is, Joe Shaw was a naval officer who had come up the "hard way" without benefit of training at the Annapolis Naval Academy.

With Frank Shaw as mayor, Joe Shaw left his battleship and came ashore to assist his brother in politics. Whether this was an error in judgment on the part of the Shaws, only they can say. The Syndicate did not like Joe Shaw and Joe Shaw did not like The Syndicate. Joe Shaw was reputed to have told The Syndicate that his brother, Frank, was not going to be a rubber stamp for Syndicate purposes as some preceding mayors had been.

The Syndicate considered the attitude of Joe Shaw as significant of high treason as well as insubordination. The Syndicate, and the facts more or less supported its viewpoint, had come to look upon the four hundred and fifty-two square miles of Los Angeles City proper, as well as the other square miles in unincorporated Los Angeles County, as its private demesne and poaching grounds, much in the manner of a Norman baron in England in the year 1067.

Joe Shaw was branded an alien intruder and a threatened upsetter of the status quo, and with his entrance Los Angeles politics was destined never to be the same again. The first intimation of trouble to come was foreshadowed when an obscure cafeteria owner, Clifford E. Clinton, appeared on the 1937 county grand jury and by his pressure on the criminal complaints committee made of the jury what is known in underworld argot as "an outlaw" grand jury, one, that is, which is unreasonably and unwarrantedly intent upon investigating and indicting malefactors for crimes against the people.

Clinton's motives and sincerity were not questioned until it became known that he was associated in some manner with one James Francis Utley, a diminutive, sharp little racketeer, who appeared quite suddenly and inexplicably on the underworld front. Clinton's campaign against the status quo seemed to be getting nowhere until the morning of January 14, 1938, when Private Investigator Harry J. Raymond, a sleuth long accredited with being one of the sharpest operatives in Los Angeles, stepped on the starter of his automobile in the garage of his home at 755 South Orme Avenue. There followed a deafening explosion and Raymond was nearly blown to kingdom come!

Having suffered one-hundred and fifty wounds, Raymond was rushed to the Georgia Street receiving hospital, where it was at first believed that he would not live. But Raymond did live, and within three days Police Captain Earle E. Kynette, head of the notorious and infamous police intelligence squad which existed mainly to protect the racketeering interests of Los Angeles, was in jail charged with the crime.

Years later The Los Angeles Daily News about accurately sized up the situation when it said editorially in part:

"Captain Kynette headed the so-called 'police intelligence squad.'

"As far as can be ascertained at even this late date, the chief duties of Kynette and his squad seemed to be the harassment, arrest and suppression of any racketeers outside the ken of those who 'had' the town for gambling, slot machines and prostitution.

"Among the gentry who laid claim to and maintained a racket overlordship of Los Angeles during this era were such fabulous underworld characters as Guy McAfee, Tutor Scherer, Farmer and Stanley Page, Chuck Addison, now of Las Vegas, Nevada; Zeke Caress, bookmaking monopolist, and Bob Gans, slot machine mogul.

"It is a significant fact that Captain Kynette and his powerful police intelligence squad never arrested any of these men, and equally significant that they were extremely active in arresting and harassing other racketeers opposed to them. The taxpayers, therefore, were in the paradoxical position of paying the salaries of a large group of police officers who existed mainly to protect the racket hegemony of underworld personages — mugs who exerted power under the administration of Mayor Frank Shaw and presumably not outside the knowledge of his secretary, Brother Joe Shaw."

When Raymond was bombed, Angel City really started jumping.

The cracks and crevices in the City Hall yawned ominously, and the joists and uprights supporting the political regime of Mayor Frank L. Shaw sagged. Repercussions of the bombing were about equally rugged in the political purlieus of Los Angeles County. The ensuing scandal reached cataclysmic proportions.

District Attorney Buron Fitts, who had been playing political "footsie" with the Shaw administration, did a quick right-about-face, hoping to bolster his own shattered political fences before the racket tornado could blow them down. Fitts, however, was doomed to disappointment when, in 1940, he was defeated for re-election by Congressman John Dockweiler, son of the titular leader of the Democratic Party in Southern California.

Kynette was convicted and sent to San Quentin prison, where he served ten years, being liberated on parole in 1948 with a proviso that he not return to Los Angeles County until 1952.

Famous writer and noted American World I propagandist, George Creel, in an article titled "Unholy City," which ran in Collier's national magazine, September 2, 1939, wrote in part...

"Ranging the streets at night, not only did Clifford Clinton see roaring brothels, gambling houses and clip-joints with his own eyes, but out of the dark came nervous men with whispers of an all-powerful 'Syndicate' that ran vice and crime as an organized business. The Syndicate used part of its huge annual 'take' to corrupt officials and control the police department.

"Just to make his case airtight, Clinton named Guy McAfee and Bob Gans as directing heads of the Syndicate, with Kent Parrott as chief mouthpiece and strategist. Slim, saturnine McAfee, ironically enough, was once a member of the police department's 'purity squad' and Clinton, citing his ownership of a mansion and a yacht, charged that he had made millions out of wide open gambling. Gans, specializing in slot machines, was also put in the millionaire class.

"According to Clinton, the Syndicate carried efficiency to a point that made Chicago's gangsters look amateurish. Territorial rights were assigned and respected — or else — and an obliging police department kept out competitors. Eastern mobs were not allowed to enter Los Angeles, being met at the trains with curt orders to 'go back where you came from.'

"Now for the comparison between things as they were when the new mayor (Fletcher E. Bowron) took office and as they are today. Some 'houses of call' and 'escort bureaus' still persist, but there are no longer any wide-open brothels; all gambling establishments have been wiped out, likewise the slot-machine racket, and the Syndicate admits to liquidation. Mr. Gans has retired, pleading ill-health. Mr. Parrott is now 'just a plain lawyer,' and Mr. McAfee has transferred his 'investments' to Nevada.

"McAfee's Ninety-One Club near Las Vegas represents an initial expenditure of $500,000 and the Frontier Club another glittering gambling establishment hard by Boulder Dam, cost almost as much."

That was written eleven years ago. But did the Syndicate really lose? Remembering that Las Vegas, Nevada, has a population of thirty thousand; that it is three hundred miles due East of Los Angeles; that the latter city has a population of two million and that it furnishes most of the patrons for Las Vegas, it is questionable that the astute McAfee, now operating where gambling is legal, lost anything in particular when Fletcher Bowron became Mayor of Angel City.

The facts of the situation lend great support to the continuing and repeated rumor that McAfee and his Las Vegas gambling associates have consistently supported the re-election of Mayor Fletcher Bowron by spending huge sums of money in his behalf. Conceding that McAfee is no fool, the question is a natural: Why shouldn't they?

Such maneuvering, if true, would place Fletcher Bowron in an enviable political position. It would permit him to keep up his perennial political stance of "Fighting The Underworld," keeping Los

Angeles reasonably tight as far as wide-open gambling is concerned, while, at the same time, it would immeasurably benefit financially the expatriate overlord of Los Angeles gambling, Guy McAfee, who maintains an ornate residence in nearby Beverly Hills which he visits on week-ends.

Of such stuff is politics made.

But to return to the Raymond bombing. Clifford E. Clinton's campaign, politically speaking, was getting nowhere until the bomb went off. Then it picked up and gained impetus, setting the stage for the advent of Fletcher E. Bowron, then a Superior court judge of Los Angeles County.

But while Fletcher Bowron later was to chant the allegation that he was honest over the radio and in newspaper columns each week, while he was contending that he had *ridded* Los Angeles of organized rackets and had restored "Good, Honest and Efficient Government" to its citizens, unseen and unheralded a new underworld galaxy quietly moved into the picture.

This gang of crime worthies was led by Benjamin (Bugsy) Siegel, who was slated to be blasted to death in his Beverly Hills home on the night of June 20, 1947, by gunmen who used a rifle to fire through a front window and virtually obliterate his face. The murderers were never caught.

After Bowron became mayor of Los Angeles, "Big Greenie" Greenberg, a hoodlum who had served with Siegel in the ranks of Murder, Inc. , in Brooklyn and New York, was shot and killed on Yucca Street in Hollywood. The word was that he had threatened to talk unless given money. He got lead instead.

Siegel and several others, including Frank Carbo, reputed underworld controller of the nation's fight rackets, were tried for murder in a Los Angeles Superior court, but were acquitted.

The question of whether or not Siegel and his Easterners had a working agreement with McAfee and the Las Vegans was never satisfactorily answered, but there were grounds to suspect that such a coalition existed after Siegel built the ten million dollar Flamingo Hotel and gambling casino in Las Vegas, which act, it was believed, led to his murder when he encountered financial difficulties.

But a new racket meteor appeared on the Los Angeles scene in the person of Michael (Mickey) Cohen.

Cohen, now thirty-eight years of age, will be an integral part of this story as, since 1940, he has written many chapters of Los Angeles underworld and political history, including the slaying by him of Izzy Shannon on May 16, 1945, in a Beverly Boulevard bookmaking joint inside the city, casting doubt on Bowron's oft-repeated declamations that rackets no longer existed in Los Angeles.

Early in his Los Angeles career, Bowron had been a newspaperman. He had studied law, and had been admitted to the bar. Then suddenly and miraculously, he gained a position as secretary to Republican Governor Friend Richardson. Richardson, as his last official act in 1928, appointed Secretary Bowron to the Los Angeles Superior Court bench despite the fact that Bowron had had little, if any, practical experience in the law.

Of such stuff is politics made.

Bowron remained on the bench until September 16, 1938, when circumstances and the wand of political fortune beckoned. During his years on the bench, Bowron had kept up an intermittent warfare with District Attorney Buron Fitts who had made no record of disturbing the tranquillity and equilibrium of the Syndicate from the time he assumed office in 1928 until he was defeated by John Dockweiler in 1940.

The present district attorney of Los Angeles County, William E. Simpson, served as an assistant to Buron Fitts for some twelve years.

But to get on with our story. The Shaw freres were blamed for the Raymond bombing. A recall petition was circulated against Frank Shaw and the date of the election was set for September 16, 1938. Clifford Clinton, his previously moribund war on rackets galvanized by the bombing, took to the air and damned the Shaws and all their works.

At the same time Clinton stridently supported the candidacy of Fletcher E. Bowron whose public career he extolled in glowing terms.

When the votes were counted, Fletcher Bowron led Frank Shaw by 112,000.

Some savant once said, "The more things seem to change, the less they change."

McAfee, taking the remnants of the old Syndicate to Las Vegas, moved out. Parrott, getting along in years and weary, did likewise, settling down near the beautiful resort town of Monterey, California, in the northern part of the state, where, today he probably looks sardonically at the sea and ruminates about the follies and stupidities of men in politics and the never changing naiveté and nescience of the voters.

Bob Gans retired from the slot machine racket and ostensibly retired altogether, but it is whispered that he is still a potent force in city, county and state politics and there yet remains the suspicion abroad that in reality he is dug down behind Curly Robinson, currently the slot machine monopolist in the Southern California area.

The "home-grown" boys, outwardly at least, were "through in Los Angeles."

But with their exeunt from the stage, the city's gates were opened to hundreds of other racketeers who had written racket history in such cities as Chicago, New York, Brooklyn, Philadelphia and Boston. Evidently, racketdom, like Nature, abhors a vacuum.

Whether all of this was better or worse for the badly battered City of the Angels, or City of the Angles as some vulgarly term it, is a matter of opinion.

McAfee was content to have Los Angeles remain closed to wide-open gambling. He advertised his Las Vegas, Nevada, gaming places in Los Angeles newspapers, stressing the fact that one could do as one pleased in Las Vegas without fear of police molestation and hinting that if the visitor did not care for gambling, there were other pastimes for him to enjoy.

Mayor Bowron and Clifford Clinton quarreled.

Many persons said that Clinton was angry with himself because he had not run for mayor in 1938 and because he had supported Bowron's candidacy, since "anyone would have beaten Frank Shaw" as a result of the Raymond bombing and the ensuing scandal.

Neither Bowron nor Clinton gave any reason for the split in their long political love feast. However, many surmised that Clinton's "political" association with James Francis Utley, particularly after Utley had been convicted of having sold morphine to a twenty-year-old Los Angeles girl, had begun to prove embarrassing to Hizzoner, inasmuch as Utley was not bashful in letting people know he had great influence inside the Los Angeles police department.

Clinton made one last effort to regain his moribund political prestige when, in April, 1945, he was one of thirteen candidates who ran against Bowron. The latter won at the primary, with Clinton finishing a poor second. With that, Clinton went into a political eclipse and, politically speaking, little has been heard of him since.

And this is the historical background which furnishes the setting for —The Stoker Story.

The reader may ask how Mayor Bowron "drove" the old Syndicate out of Los Angeles. But did he? Be that as it may, Bowron opened the city's gates to James Francis Utley, Tony Cornero, Anne (The Black Widow) Forrester and Michael (Mickey) Cohen, as well as The Black Widow's former student in prostitution, Marie Mitchell, alias Brenda Allen, who will play the chief feminine lead in The Stoker Story.

If you believe the California Crime Commission report for 1950, Cohen and Utley are the top men in the Los Angeles underworld today.

Will the actions of our leading officials prove that the underworld-political program in the years from 1938 to 1950 was merely an attenuation of the same program which had its beginning in the year 1921?

Whatever the answer to that question: Let's have it.

THICKER'N THIEVES

No doubt some people will contend that I am merely a disgruntled and discredited copper. That is to be expected. But I am an angry copper, too, a copper who doesn't like what was done to him. And whether anyone disapproves my attitude, it doesn't particularly bother me.

However, I believe that it was not I who was discredited, but the Los Angeles police department.

When I first thought of writing my story for public edification and information, I visualized as a comparatively simple task the relation of a chronographic narrative dealing with my thirty-two years on earth and most importantly with my few years as a Los Angeles Police Department officer.

However, when it came time to lay my story on the line, I found that my mind was a bewildering maze of confusion as to data, details, circumstances and incidents. Not much of my material traveled in a straight line from here to there; it zigged and zagged and there was a plethora of switch backs and detours. Seemingly trivial incidents that had occurred when I first joined the vice squad tied in with other incidents of years later and two minor happenstances turned into matters of major significance.

So, when I sat down to write the story, I asked myself: "Where and how do I start?" Frankly, I didn't know. If the story seems to leap and jump, if it appears to have the wrong beginning and the right ending, or vice versa, or if it has neither, don't blame me.

I was continually leaping and jumping and in action as a police officer. Facts differ from truths. Truths are eternal, whereas facts are temporal and episodic. In this story I will try to relate the true facts as I saw them, as they unfolded before my eyes. Perhaps some of the truths and the facts in this story are incomplete, but this is to be expected on the premise of human fallibility and it must be remembered that the writer, Charles F. Stoker, is a microcosm appraising the macrocosm, the

City of Los Angeles, its underworld, police department and some of the political inter-relationship between the two.

While I was living this story, I picked up all sorts of information which became imbedded in my subconscious mind. Not all of it had to do with law enforcement. Much of it dealt with the connections between vice and gambling with politics, politicians, shadowy fixers, crooked lawyers, conniving bailbondsmen and makers of past Los Angeles underworld history. When you are a vice squad copper, you may hear startling and incredible stories about almost anyone.

For instance, when I first went on the vice squad, I heard that Mayor Fletcher E. Bowron was being paid $250,000 annually by Las Vegas, Nevada, gambling and business interests to keep the lid on vice and gambling in Los Angeles. I was told that although Mayor Bowron was elected on a reform platform to drive organized vice and gambling out of Los Angeles, the very individuals whom he drove out – namely Guy McAfee, Farmer Page and Tutor Scherer – erstwhile overlords of Angel City rackets, had erected a brand new empire in the Nevada city. I was also told that the gambling success of these gentry depended upon keeping Los Angeles closed to gambling in order that the "suckers" would be forced to journey to Las Vegas there to indulge their betting propensities and their penchant for prostitutes.

I was informed that the money paid to Bowron was handled by a member of a corporation with a suite of offices in the Union Bank & Trust Bldg., at Eighth and Hill Streets, and that Bowron's perennial political pose of "Fighting the Underworld" and his stentorian shouts that he was protecting Los Angeles from organized vice and gambling were, in reality, for the benefit and profit of the Las Vegas gambling interests who recognized in Bowron an airtight, bullet-proof political pawn who had kept, and could keep, the electorate of Los Angeles perpetually fooled.

Of course, it is difficult to believe, yet it is a fact that Las Vegas gamblers depend largely upon Los Angeles citizens for profit. If gambling operated openly in Los Angeles, what inducement would there be for an Angeleno to journey three hundred miles to the hot and cold Nevada city? I cite this as the kind of thing one hears as a vice squad officer.

It is a well-known fact that many, if not most, of the people have an aversion to thinking. Many insist that they do not believe what they read in the newspapers, yet only a paltry few analyze situations as they are reported. Most of those who are desirous of analyzing newspaper reports are powerless to do so because they haven't the facts upon which to predicate an intelligent conclusion.

To my untutored mind, the Los Angeles scene resembled a study in confusion. Lying awake nights, I used to reflect on it and try to connect this with that. Mentally I tried to line up cause and effect and to come up with answers that were logical and sensible.

Most of this tortuous mental travail was physically akin to chasing a dozen snakes under a field full of autumn leaves.

While standing on a street corner, engaged in trapping a prostitute or some other kind of law breaker, bookmaker or gambler, I would watch the commonplace crowd hurrying to and from work, scurrying about in the pursuit of pleasure and doing the thousand and one things that men and women do each day in a big city. I would think: "How remote they are from the police department. Many of them have spent a decade, half a lifetime, or a full lifetime in Los Angeles without the necessity of contacting a police officer for any purpose."

My position as onlooker gave me a lonely feeling. I felt like a man separate and apart, having no nexus with the people.

"But I am a public servant," I would remind myself, "an agent of these people who are traveling about the city's streets like so many ants. Some of the things they want done, they have assigned to me to do. They pay me to see that they are done. I have a direct responsibility to them. While they don't watch me, they trust me and at the proper time and place, they expect me to go into action and do my duty."

Still, I could not erase the thought that I had no kinship or understanding with them, no direct physical or mental connection. I have since learned that most police officers have experienced the feeling at times that they belong to no one; that they are utterly alone and that the anonymous crowd has a secret hostility for them and their kind. People seemingly hate the policeman until they actually, concretely, need him.

But, since my severance from the Los Angeles Police Department and the purported discrediting of Sergeant Charles F. Stoker, I have, with the passage of nine months, gained more perspective I believe and I have concluded, as I said before, that it was not I who was discredited, but rather the department.

Perhaps that conclusion is erroneous. There are, however, several thousands of letters and other kinds of communications I have received tending to support it. Since the denouement of the Brenda Allen and Mickey Cohen police scandals, I am certain that many share my opinion and these include dozens of police officers who privately have vouch-safed their opinions to me.

Much of the old bunk and coneroo went into the smearing and prosecution of Police Sergeant Charles F. Stoker and his eventual discharge from the police department for "conduct unbecoming an officer." Note that last — later, I shall go into that phrase, "conduct unbecoming an officer," very thoroughly for purposes of contrast and comparison, and let you judge whether my conduct as a police officer was so unbecoming as was the conduct of other police officers whose case histories I shall recite, in part at least.

It is the purpose of *The Stoker Story* to clear up the rumors, the many false impressions that have permeated the police mess involving me and to show, in behalf of public welfare, how a police-gangster setup, where the policemen are gangsters and the gangsters are policemen, operated in Los Angeles, in contrast to other big cities where coppers are coppers and mobsters are mobsters.

I think of the trite adage: "We live and learn." In my early days as a police officer, there was never any doubt in my mind about the integrity of the Los Angeles Police Department and most of its men. Instead there was only the conviction that the department was the finest in the United States and that the few who would make it less so were powerless to affect its elan and efficiency and basic honesty.

Then one night I received information that a racketeer from the East was in Los Angeles; that he was a dangerous man and carried a gun. I started out to track him down at the behest of Lieutenant John Stewart and track him down I did. But he didn't have a gun.

"Gonna book me?" he asked pleasantly.

"Mebbe," I replied

"Let's talk," he suggested.

"About what?"

"Los Angeles."

"What about Los Angeles?"

"I'm only here for a buggy ride," he said. "I plan to leave tomorrow if you don't get in my road."

"If you'll leave tomorrow, mebbe I won't get in your road," I said cautiously.

"Do you think I'd stay in this jerk burg?" he jeered.

"What's so jerky about it, Jerk?" I demanded, my Irish gorge rising.

"Cool off," he admonished. "Let's get a cup of coffee and if you promise not to get sore, I'll tell you."

I agreed.

We sat down. He asked me how old I was. I told him. He asked how long I had been on the department. I told him. Then he turned on me, a long, keen and appraising glance.

"You asked me what's so jerky about this city," he continued. "Now, if you'll agree to stay cool and forget that you are a copper for a moment and that I am, shall we say, kind of an outlaw, I'll tell you."

"Shoot. I got nothing to lose by listening," I green lighted.

"You got a cop setup in this town and that ain't no good, particularly for the cops," he opened. "It'll lead to trouble, bad trouble, inside the police department and that trouble isn't far off."

The month in which this pronouncement was made was April, 1946.

"I don't get it," I said.

"There'll always be a certain amount of stealing in all big city police departments," he said, "stealing from the rackets. This city isn't any exception. You got a cop setup here. There never was a cop setup anywhere that was any good, either for coppers or for thieves. Such setups always blow up. Look at Detroit in 1938! There they indicted over one hundred coppers in one pop.

"You gotta have a boss to handle police protection and the pay-offs. You gotta have a boss to tell everyone what they can and cannot do. That goes for coppers as well as for those in the rackets. When you've got a cop setup there is a scramble to get in on the graft and someone gets frozen out of the play, then there's jealousy and trouble. Then someone gets hurt because when the old snowball starts rollin' down hill, it picks up stones, twigs, leaves, boulders and plenty of manure and knocks a lot of people out.

"Cops are, in one respect, just like prostitutes. A prostitute without a man to tell her what to do and what not to do isn't any good; and a stealing copper without a political and racket boss isn't worth a damn to himself, to the police department or anyone else. And if he's going catch-as-catch can, he's a danger to himself and to the police department.

"The United States Steel Corporation hasn't got twenty-five presidents. Neither has the United States Government, or the United States Army got one hundred generals all with equal powers. Imagine what would happen if they did?

"When a copper gets out of line, the MAN, whoever he is, has to have the authority to pin his ears back and that without benefit of a police trial board.

"You've got nothing in this town but trouble. Nothing that I want. Remember what I tell you. It'll all blow higher than Heaven one of these bright nights and no one will know how it all started, nor will they know how it will all end. Every man admits that he is brilliant, but, bud, there are damned few men who are. A copper might be smart enough to arrest a prostitute or gambler, but that doesn't mean that he savveys the whole picture, or that he understands or can run the entire show.

"Your present Los Angeles cop setup is doomed. That's why, tomorrow when the Super-Chief pulls out, I'll be aboard. That is, with your kind permission. Under existing circumstances, you couldn't give me any part of this town. A guy in the racket here will wind up working and hustling for thieving coppers and the coppers will wind up in trouble and the racket guy along with them. I'm out here because I heard Los Angeles was this way, but I wanted to see it for myself. The idea that I have any evil designs on your fair city is ridiculous.

"Look at the setup here. You've got an administrative vice squad, a great big supervisory outfit supposed to keep a watchful eye out over the works. In addition, you've got divisional vice squads limited to their districts. Then you've got a gangster squad. Then you've got a vice squad working out of the chief's office and still another one working under the assistant chief. These various vice squads all watch each other, the chances are to see that one doesn't steal unless the others are in.

"In Los Angeles, you'd rather arrest a prostitute than a bank robber any day.

"Now, when you get all this scrambled together, and some of the boys start to steal, what do you think will happen? If you are an honest copper, and I'll concede for the purposes of the discussion that you are, when the jam comes, you'll be right in the middle of the switch with both legs caught in it."

He paused and musingly reflected. "That spells trouble with a capital 'T'."

"I ought to slug you and toss you into the bucket," I said finally. "Here you are, an egg, a highbinder, sitting here telling me, a copper, that police officers in this city are grafters, at least some of them."

"You said you wouldn't get sore," he reminded. "But if you are sore, let's drop it. Just remember what I told you. Remember to remember what I told you here tonight. Can I go now?"

"Blow," I ordered. "But you'd better be on that train tomorrow."

"Don't worry, I don't lie in this kind of spot," he tossed back over his shoulder. "I'll be on it. That you can bet on. Just remember and take care of yourself in the clinches. If you ever got a dead right steer, you got one tonight, kiddo. Whether you like me, I like you and if you ever come to New York, look me up. We'll see the town and you won't lose."

"The circus you are playing in has five rings, not three, and when they start looping into each other, it'll get rough and swift. So long and watch for the switches and triple crosses and don't forget to slide around those hot corners 'cause when you reach them, they'll be sizzling."

I looked after him and laughed out loud.

But a short time later, I thought of him and didn't laugh.

Time rolled along, and gradually my understanding developed as I added experience and knowledge.

I met Brenda Allen and many other prostitutes who were as different as snowflakes. In respect to police officers, I met many fine, courageous and idealistic badge-wearers. And I also met their antitypes — shoddy, thieving, slovenly, cowardly, lecherous and avaricious dogs. Speaking of the latter, I would hate to have a daughter or a son of mine fall into their hands for any purpose whatsoever, legal or otherwise.

A great deal of the hypocrisy that is part of the life we lead, came into focus. I began to see that there is a logic of words as opposed to a logic of facts, and that most of the time an unbridgeable abyss is between them. I learned that truth and words sometimes haven't anything to do with facts, but rather flow over, under and around them.

While I came to have a greater understanding of the racket mind, I also came to have a more profound insight into police mentality. I saw that there were many gradations in each category — that there were racketeers and racketeers — prostitutes and prostitutes — individuals as different as night and day and this applied to police officers as well.

I learned that one can't lump all the people in one category and come up with a homogenous whole.

However, before we get into the meat of the nut of this police, political and underworld saga, the reader has a right to some background material on Sergeant Charles F. Stoker, one of the chief protagonists of the drama.

Who is Stoker? And from whence did he come before he joined the Los Angeles Police Department and popped into newspaper headlines as the officer who had jailed Madam Brenda Allen, Queen Bee of the

Hollywood Hetaerae? Those are fair questions. They are deserving of answers. I will answer them here and now to the best of my ability, with as much objectivity and fact as I can muster and with a proper regard for egotism. In the matter of humility and pride, I shall try to strike a proper balance, if that is possible for anyone who is writing about himself, but in writing it, I think of that quotation from the third act of Othello, and this, indeed, delineates one of my major motives in writing this book.

> "Good name in man and woman, dear my Lord,
> Is the immediate jewel of their souls:
> Who steals my purse, steals trash; 'tis something, nothing;
> 'Twas mine, 'tis his, and has been slave to thousands,
> But he that filches from me my good name
> Robs me of that which not enriches him,
> And makes me poor indeed."

My background, viewed in retrospect, was average. Nothing particularly spectacular highlighted it. I can recall nothing specifically shameful. My years, prior to joining the police department, had ups and downs characteristic of the average man. More downs than ups, perhaps, but I am an average man. From the standpoint of reader interest, thousands of other men could tell comparable stories in point of time and achievement, as well as of failure, that would be more interesting than mine.

So, in relating this phase of my story, I shall try to boil down the facts and confine them to a minimum of space, without gilding them in any way.

I was born thirty-two years ago in a small Texas seacoast city, to a family composed of hard-headed Irish and proud Texans. Socially speaking, I was born of parents who were decidedly on the wrong side of the tracks.

When I was four years old, I distinctly remember that my mother took my father and me to the famous Mayo Clinic in Rochester,

Minnesota, in an effort to save my father's life. I remember the hardships of the undertaking and above all, my mother's determined Irish will, which, though penniless, she maintained. When we arrived in Rochester, the only people whom we knew were members of a small Negro family who had once lived in Texas.

My mother had to work in a factory to support us; and this colored family took me in to raise in order that my father could continue treatment in the sanitarium. Possibly, something of what I learned then has stuck with me because one of my best friends in the Los Angeles Police Department today is a Negro. I have never forgotten the kindnesses of that Negro family in Rochester, Minnesota.

When my father died, Mother and I returned to Texas where she remarried. My stepfather, who was a wonderful person, became a real father to me; and I even adopted his name. But he, too, was from the opposite side of the tracks. He was a business agent and an organizer for a dock worker's union. Things went well until he had his head caved in by a strike-breaker. Then the world of Charlie Stoker again came tumbling down.

I remember keeping one jump ahead of the truant officer while I gathered loose bananas from the wharf, and peddled them from door to door. I sold newspapers and magazines. Finally, my mother sent me to live with a maiden aunt, an old school teacher who was determined to make a gentleman of me. I do not know whether she succeeded.

Then the great depression began, and I was on my own at the age of fifteen. In the South where the depression was at its worst, I followed an uncle into the oil fields and there obtained a job as an apprentice in an oil well equipment supply house. I was paid the fabulous sum of twenty-five dollars a month for work which required evenings and weekends. I supplemented my income by racking pool balls in a billiard hall after finishing my warehouse duties.

I readily admit that I went to high school solely because attendance was the law. Those days were not too pleasant for a kid equipped only with Irish stubbornness, pride and a good physique. I recall how, during the school lunch periods, I frequently hid because I had no lunch, and I didn't want the other kids to see me. I would search the school grounds for small pencil stubs in the afternoons after classes.

While I was on the Los Angeles Police Department, I bore the distinction of being a well-dressed policeman. Possibly, this attention to dress can be traced back to my last year in high school, when I accidentally overheard one of the girls in the class ask if I was going to be invited to a party. The second girl replied that I wasn't because I wore my trousers too short and had holes in my shoes.

I recall that a young man came to town who was a widely known welterweight fighter. This man built a gymnasium and soon was conducting Saturday night prize fights.

He took an interest in me. I was then a gangling seventeen- year-old six-footer, and taught me some of the rudiments of the boxing game, enough that I could make a few dollars in the preliminary bouts on Saturday nights. I still have newspaper clippings telling of these fights and of my fighting the Army elimination bouts a few years later for the selection of amateurs to attend the 1936 Olympic games.

Times were tough when I finished high school in 1933, and no jobs were to be found, especially for untrained kids. I took a job with a wildcat oil well drilling crew in return for room and board and the guarantee of a percentage if we struck oil. I went with this crew into the swamps of Louisiana, where I contracted malaria. Ill and without funds, I then did what many a young man did in those parlous financial times. I enlisted in the United States Army. I received hospitalization in the Army and furthered my education by attending several Army training courses.

My boxing career came to a screeching halt in 1936. In an Army bout, overmatched and out-fought, I had my nose broken and two ribs fractured.

During the same year, I successfully passed an open competitive examination for a Federal police job, and was soon honorably discharged from the Army. I took the position and held it for two years, at which time I was furloughed out because of a reduction in forces.

Needing a job and having had past military experience, I was offered and accepted a rating in the United States Coast Guard in 1938. I served until I was honorably discharged in 1941, when I accepted an appointment as a United States Ranger in a national park. Later, I resigned to take a better paying position as a railroad officer, a job that led me to Los Angeles.

I took an open competitive examination for a policeman's job on the Los Angeles Police Department and was appointed in May, 1942. For six weeks, I attended the Police Academy in Elysian Park. After that I was assigned downtown as a beat patrolman working the field, that is, I worked as a relief man, filling in on all the jobs that a uniformed patrolman is given — some nights serving as booking officer, other nights walking a beat or working in a patrol car.

After a few months of this, I was told to report to the Commander of the Vice Division. This was a turning point in my career, an epochal event for me.

I knew nothing of vice law enforcement, but I was to learn plenty about it! Perhaps, to the dismay of many, I learned far too much and became entirely too capable in this line of police work. We shall see.

That, my friends, briefly is the background of Rookie Stoker to the moment when he became a Los Angeles vice squad officer — an officer destined to be the Nemesis of Harlot Brenda Allen and the center of a rocketing, bucketing police scandal.

MOBSTER COPPERS

Get thee glass eyes;
And like a scurvy politician, seem
To see the things thou does not.
King Lear, Act IV, Sc. 6 ... Shakespeare.

Do you know why we have so little racket trouble from genuine racketeers and true underworld characters in Los Angeles? The answer is elementary. The mobsters in Los Angeles are coppers. They wear badges, and use them to stifle any competition from dyed-in-the-wool mobsters like Frank Costello, the nation's No. 1 racketeer. The police in Los Angeles retain control of the rackets because they, themselves, are the mobsters. Judging by the constant reference to Costello, he may be the ideal local mobster whom police are striving to emulate.

The difference between the rackets in Los Angeles and those of other cities, if I make myself clear, is that the rackets in Angel City are operated and run by coppers and that the revenues derived from them, in large part, go into the pockets of coppers rather than gangsters. Therefore, it isn't the City of the Angels, it's the City of the Angles; and coppers hereabouts know how to play them. In this field they are as competent as Yehudi Menuhin on his violin.

It is difficult for the average citizen to form a conception, without developing schizophrenia, of a copper-mobster and a mobster-copper, but such anomalies exist in Los Angeles in connection with rackets and their control. Here, the copper and the mobster are one and the same person in the identical corporeal body.

Why does Mayor Fletcher E. Bowron continuously bleat about the threatened invasion of Eastern gangsters (the city has been loaded with them ever since he assumed his office) and the necessity of keeping them out of Los Angeles? The reason is this: If the Eastern gangsters invade Los Angeles in force, the copper-mobsters will have to go East. There won't be enough room in Los Angeles for both contingents.

The copper-mobsters know a good thing when they see it; and their hetman, Mayor Fletcher (Smoke Screen) Bowron, also known as "I'm Fighting the Underworld" Bowron, does an excellent job of keeping them virtually invisible like a squid throwing his ink in the water.

I defy the police department and Mayor Bowron to disprove this statement by adhering strictly to the facts and omitting the rhetoric. If you don't believe me when you have finished this book, then facts can have no impact on your intelligence.

At this point I wish to make it clear that I do not refer to honest police officers of whom there are many in the Los Angeles Police Department. However, the honest policemen will seldom if ever be referred to again in this story. If I do allude to one occasionally it will be out of necessity and because I can't help it, as an honest copper now and then is bound to intrude himself into the action of this drama. But honest coppers, from the basic aspects of this story, were ineffectives and from the standpoint of the great game of grand larceny inside the Los Angeles police department, they do not count.

This is no cry-baby narrative, however.

What happened to me may be of relative unimportance to many. It is, nevertheless, important to me and it should be of great significance to the public. I wouldn't be much of a man if I didn't react as I have for a man's reputation and record are his most precious assets.

Supreme Court Justice Robert Jackson, when he was United States Attorney-General, upon addressing a convention of Federal district attorneys, once said, "A man's reputation is a shadow which he casts before and behind him. A man's reputation is his most important possession. He's born with a good one, and it's up to him whether or not he keeps it. A sincere and honest man cannot afford to have his reputation sullied. He will protect it with everything at his command if he values it, for once he has lost it, he has lost himself."

Judge Jackson's words are mine.

If it is true that everyone has larceny in him, and I guess it is, there would be no point in failing to include myself. It would be untrue for me to state that I was never tempted. I was. On many occasions I had rolls of bills thrust under my nose when all I had to do was to walk down the street and forget that I was a copper.

But during the years in which I was a police officer, during the years I worked vice, I never took a button from a prostitute, a gambler or anyone else. While I say that and take credit for it, let me qualify the statement, in order that you may gain a truer insight into my mental processes.

Perhaps the thing that kept me technically honest, if not altogether intellectually honest, was fear. One way or another, society is ruled by fear. That is why we have police departments. In our lives, most of us have felt the omnipresent fear of the Eleventh Commandment —"Thou Shalt Not Get Found Out."

A police officer working vice has a great many individuals looking down his throat and breathing down his neck. From the major aspect, he is not of too much importance. He has his superiors, and there are many of them. They are experienced, smart old-timers for the most part. They've been through the mill, and they know all the holds and angles. A rookie cop who believes he can outsmart them has more egotism than I possess. The fundamental business of a police officer is to find out things and on a big police department quite a few officers are devoted solely to the business of finding out things about police department personnel.

If you were a sergeant as I was, working under a Lieutenant and Captain, and if it happened that the Lieutenant and Captain frowned on graft, you were a temerarious man if you grafted. You could easily wind up before a police trial board, and you might wind up in San Quentin penitentiary. These are braking factors on an officer's larcenous instincts. He never knows, if he is in action—"stealing"—when the roof might come crashing down on his head.

Then there is another factor, which, in my estimation, is all important for a police officer who is pondering the question —"Shall I steal, or shall I remain honest?"

This factor is that everyone talks, particularly in the rackets. If you are a police officer and you are accepting money from a prostitute or a gambler, the news will be all over the underworld in no time. And when it is all over the underworld, do not think it won't be all over the police department as well.

Police officers, and this includes all of them, are engaged in a perennial game of not only watching criminals and racketeers, but of watching each other.

There are many police officers who graft. These are like the climbers on the face of a crag — one misstep and it's all over.

And again, if you are a vice squad officer who accepts money from gamblers and prostitutes, do not believe that when they give it to you, they love you the more for taking it. Quite the contrary. If you are taking money from them, perhaps they do not talk to a police officer or public official about it, but they do discuss it among themselves. Talk about such things is part of the structure of their business. In order to continue to break the vice and gambling laws profitably, they have to know who is "all right"— i. e., who is dishonest and graft taking; and who is "all wrong"— honest and devoted to law enforcement.

Now, while I was neither the smartest man in the world nor the most brilliant vice squad officer, by the same token neither was I completely stupid. Primarily, by virtue of experience and what intelligence I have gained, I have no illusions about racket people and few illusions about police officers engaged in vice law enforcement. I know that racket people will do anything they have to do, anything they want to do, and anything they are big enough to do to make money. You cannot expect integrity and probity from those whose lives are dedicated to the purpose of making money illegally and dishonestly.

That, in the parlance of the gamblers, is like asking the dice to make thirteen. The dice won't do it. Twelve is the best they'll make.

So, when the hour of decision came to me — to remain honest or to graft — for the foregoing reasons; which I hope I have made clear, I elected to remain honest. That I did remain honest as a copper is of no particular credit to me- in the light of the exposition that police officers are supposed to be honest. Honesty is a theoretical requirement of the job.

But it is also one that is not observed by all police officers in fact. Now I hope I have given you a good look into my mind and motivations. If I have failed it isn't because I haven't tried.

Perhaps there were moments when I questioned my intelligence on the subject of grafting, when I momentarily thought it might be smart as well as profitable, and this means that for the nonce I was intellectually dishonest. That's about all it amounted to — a little self-doubt without any concurrent action other than that. I did not depart from my original resolve.

But, paradoxically, here am I, an honest John ex-copper, or "square apple" as the boys put it, daubed with mud, ousted from the department after doing my dead level best, while others who played fast and loose with their oath of office; who refused to enforce the law but rather used it in their own behalf and for their own selfish ends, came out of the police scandal virtually clean and with their jobs intact.

A lot of mud has been unjustifiably splattered on me. I do not intend to hold still and let it soak in. I feel that I was unjustly treated and it is my intention, insofar as it lies within my power, to clear up a few of the clouds hanging over my reputation, if not all of them. And it is my hope that the public and the police department will profit from this episode. To police officers who are honest, I say that if what was done to me can be done and gotten away with and dissipated without trace, it can happen to any one of you, or worse.

It is my conviction that the public should be informed of a great many things that have never come to light, if there is to be no repetition of the police scandal. Maybe that is too much to hope, since, judging from the past, there have always been police scandals.

An informed public is a wise public. If the public has the facts, the public knows what to do toward correction of abuses. It is my unshakeable opinion that the public has a fine and a profound sense of justice, a much better concept of justice than a great many public officials possess. The public, unlike its officials, is not subject to political pressures; it generates political pressures, either for good or evil.

Newspapers didn't, or perhaps they couldn't, tell all of the story. Therefore I intend to recapitulate the facts attendant upon my career as a police officer to buttress and support them with documents, names, dates and places, highlighting and detailing them with myriad incidents and circumstances.

After I have done this, the public should have a totally different conception of what went on in the police department regarding the administration of vice and gambling ordinances which culminated in my arrest of Brenda Allen, an arrest which set off a chain reaction of scandals that brought the Los Angeles Police Department under a dark cloud, the shadows of which have not been entirely dispelled to this day.

It must be kept in mind that the law is a theory which forms the basis for an action. If there is no action, the law remains an inactive, lifeless group of words. Action is what gives criminal laws validity and force. If that is true, and it is, one can envision what would happen if there were no enforcement of the laws against prostitution and gambling. In the realms of prostitution and gambling, you would have many Brenda Allens and Mickey Cohens — a condition that is possible with the help of grafting politicians, public officials and law enforcement agents. When prostitutes and gamblers operate with the collusion of police and law enforcement officials, the concomitant is corruption which always follows in their wake.

Prostitutes and gamblers do not operate with unlimited scope unless they have help from law enforcement agents, officials and politicians.

Since collusion between those in the rackets and law enforcement agents is necessary, if the former are to enjoy immunity from arrest and prosecution, which factors limit the scope of their operations as well as the financial profits from them, members of the underworld are engaged in a ceaseless campaign of bribery to ease up the pressures engendered by law enforcement; or, if that will not work, intimidation of law enforcement agents is employed.

The underworld refers to police officers as "the enemy." Its members allude to police protection as "juice." Monies paid for police protection they consider a part of the expense of operation just as a business firm considers advertising expenditures a necessary financial outlay.

Brenda Allen frequently had two dozen pretty young women working under her direction. At one time she employed one hundred and fourteen girls. These comely misses generally charged a customer twenty dollars a "trick" for their services. The cost was never less than that. If the man was loaded with money and indifferent to the cost of a good time, the servicing charge could be thirty, fifty or even one hundred dollars.

Now, if each of these girls turned five tricks a day, which was not at all uncommon, as some of them told me that they turned twenty on certain days, at the going rate of twenty dollars, that would be one hundred dollars, or a total of twenty-four hundred dollars a day with two dozen girls working. Brenda's split was half of that amount, or twelve hundred dollars a day. One can readily see that the gaudy and sordid Miss Allen had quite a bit of money to play around with. One can see that if she spent one-third of her income for help from the police department, it still left her a tidy sum for her old age, doctors and lawyers.

A dynamic, driving dame, Brenda was fashioned exclusively out of greed and a lust for underworld power. She was replete with ego, but in reality she was just a stupid, conniving, lecherous prostitute. Her ambition was to be Queen of the Madames and, for a while, she was. Her prototypes are many and soon enough one of them will make a bid for the top spot of honor, or dishonor, to assume the scarlet mantle which was long worn by Brenda before I put her in jail and convicted her.

The buck, or dollar, was the main interest in Brenda's life, and one must give her credit for, in the world of conniving towards that end, Brenda was better than a green hand. She made a lot of money, but it is a question how much of it she would end up with and how much of it she gave to bail-bondsmen and underworld lawyers.

If you like prostitutes, you would have liked Brenda, but as for me, anyone can have my share of her and of all her kind. This female slot machine gave me many a headache. Believe me, I wasn't a copper who particularly cared for the job of arresting the hetaerae that infest Los Angeles. On the contrary, I would much rather have been doing something else. But the police department is a semi-military organization in which a man is given a job, and he does it.

Under the best possible conditions, the job of a vice squad cop is a dirty one. If a man has been raised with fairly decent concepts, and if the extant shibboleths and conventions under which he lives have made their mark on his character and have influenced his thinking at all, contact with criminal and immoral scum is repugnant to him.

I do not wear a halo. I am not a perfect man. Nor have I always observed the moral code. In fact, I have breeched it at times. I admit that I have certain weaknesses. Temptation, on occasion, has been successful with me. But, while I was a police officer and before I became a police officer, I had no dealings with any prostitute sexually. If it had been necessary to satisfy the normal, biological urge in this manner, the situation might have been different, but I don't think so feeling the way I feel.

While I cannot be classified as a matinee idol, I am neither malformed nor physically ugly. I believe that I am not totally unattractive to the female sex, for, in the routine associations that accrue to most men in the romantic field, I have nothing to be ashamed of in the reception I have received. Many of the prostitutes I arrested tried their artifices on me, but there again, I have a loathing for gonorrhea and syphilis and a feeling of repugnance for prostitutes.

In my mind, there has always been a line of demarcation in the sexual field. To me prostitutes are dirty and filthy women. They may wear the most expensive perfume, fifty- dollar slippers and filmy underthings, but they are still prostitutes, women who will consort with almost any man if he has the price. I believe that every prostitute who has willingly entered the racket has a twist in her brain. Every prostitute whom I have ever met believed herself smart, yet how can a woman be so mistaken in her judgment as to commercialize and debauch the one thing that decent men and women hold most sacred? That to me is the key to a prostitute's mentality.

There have been moments when, in the abstract, I have felt a bit sorry for them. But that is something else again. I was encharged with arresting prostitutes; and that is just what I did. If there is any question on that score, I refer you to police records.

To intrude another thought into the business of being a vice squad copper, let me add that some individuals take a cynical, jaundiced view of the whole business. They conclude that there is, and that there has been resort to illicit sex from time immemorial. Of course, they are quite right. Police cynics know, too, that there are vast sums of money to be had from illegal sex and gambling. If you have the cynical viewpoint, and if you have larceny in you, you are but a short step from sharing in the revenues derived from sin and gambling.

Pope said: "First we look on vice with abhorrence; then with indifference and finally we embrace it." As for me, I still look on it with abhorrence and I cannot conceive of embracing it.

But as to graft, every police officer makes up his own mind, sooner or later. It has been said that larceny is in everyone. This is the theme of bunco men and confidence artists, who say: "You cannot beat an honest man!" They reason that, unless the victim, or chump, has larceny and cupidity within him, he will not buy a gold brick.

But despite the hazards that confront a grafting police officer, many disregard them lured by the promise of easy money.

I think, as you go along in this book and read the evidence and facts adduced herein, you will be convinced that there was at the time of the Brenda Allen and Mickey Cohen vice and gambling scandals, a cabal of dishonest and crooked police officers inside the department and, as my momentary racketeer acquaintance from New York whom I ran out of town put it, it compromised a larcenous, grafting cabal which extended police protection to law-breakers.

The fact that Sergeant Charles F. Stoker who herein proclaims his honesty, was the only casualty of the scandals is, in itself, significant in my opinion.

LAW - A DECEPTIVE WHORE

Anatole France said something to the effect that the law is magnificent in its equity; that it permits the rich as well as the poor to starve and sleep on park benches.

Professor Fred S. Rodell of Yale University, who tutored some of the country's brightest legal lights in the intricacies of the law, declared in his highly satirical book on things legal —"Woe Unto You, Lawyers!"— that the law is mumbo-jumbo and witchcraft. He implied that the law was like mental masturbation — that a person, or a judge "learned" in the law could come up with any kind of an answer for any sort of legal proposition.

This is all by way of a point germaine to this story.

But keep in mind something that was said earlier in this opus — "The law is a theory that forms the basis for an action."

It is my belief that not one layman in a thousand can give a delineation of the structural setup of law enforcement offices in California. Seemingly few men have any idea of the existing relationship between law enforcement agencies in California.

Do you know that, under the State Constitution, the Attorney-General is the top law enforcement agent; that theoretically each district attorney, each sheriff and each chief of police works and operates his office under the Attorney-General's supervisorial eye; and that if these officials fail or are remiss in their duties, the Attorney-General is empowered to step in and enforce the law?

Many persons believe that the Governor has the highest power among elected state officials. He hasn't. The highest power is that of the Attorney-General. Get a copy of the State Constitution and read what the Attorney-General can do if and when he wants to exercise his authority.

If he deems it necessary, the Attorney-General can step in and take over the office of a district attorney, sheriff, or chief of police. He can impanel a special grand jury at a moment's notice to look into anything he believes is wrong. He can hire investigators; and furthermore he can assume any or all of the powers and prerogatives of law enforcement officers anywhere in California. After him in the law enforcement hierarchy come the fifty-eight district attorneys of the various counties in the state. From a county-wide standpoint it is the district attorney who is top dog.

If there exists a "program" for the operation of vice or gambling; if there are pay-offs and corruption in law enforcement, the district attorney has to be "with them" in one way or another. He may be technically honest, i. e., he may decline to take underworld money. But if he holds still for protected vice and gambling, he is dishonest intellectually, politically, or both.

When an individual, or a group of individuals, plans to set up a vice and gambling program in one way or another, the district attorney must be included in their calculations. He must be "in" concretely, in which event either he or his agents will take cash to permit law violations, or he must be "in" intellectually, or politically.

Let us suppose that you are a vice or gambling operator in Los Angeles City or County. You may "have" the chief of police or the sheriff with you, but if the D. A. isn't batting on your team, you're a dead, stinking fish. A sheriff who wants to permit a protected vice or gambling program to operate must turn his eyes upward towards the D. A., and must also have a tacit or direct understanding with him if things in the realm of vice or gambling are to flourish unmolested in his jurisdiction.

An ancient political maxim with regard to protected vice and gambling in Los Angeles County, states that the district attorney and the sheriff must stand shoulder to shoulder to repel all "enemies" of the program, to emasculate and mitigate, to blow down and squelch any and all efforts anyone may make to interfere with the status quo.

So, we come to the lowest stratum in the law enforcement barricades — the chief of police. From the angle of ultimate authority — he brings up the rear. In the final showdown, when it comes hornlocking time, the chief of police is at the mercy of the district attorney and of the sheriff; particularly the latter. If the sheriff decides that the vice and gambling laws are not being properly enforced in Los Angeles City, he can wade right in and see to it that they are enforced.

There exists a perennial "gentlemen's agreement" in Los Angeles County between the sheriff and the chiefs of police of various cities within the county. City agents stay out of county territory; and the sheriff's agents stay out of the various cities unless they are purposely and directly called in by a chief of police for assistance, or until a vice and gambling situation within a city becomes so open and notorious that the sheriff feels he must act. Generally a word of warning is sufficient to correct the most malodorous situations of this nature.

For political purposes and in respect to gambling and vice and its protection, this makes for convenience. No one steps on anyone else's toes. In truth, such an arrangement does not work in behalf of the public welfare because it does not make for one hundred percent law enforcement. Nor is it the most efficient law enforcement in an all out drive to suppress and keep suppressed racketeers and their rackets. But it is of immense value to law enforcement officials and their agents, to corrupt politicians and to racketeers, any and all of whom may be engaged in the great game of grand larceny. And it is a game. Each second of every minute and each minute of every hour, thousands of individuals of diverse occupations and categories pursue the dishonest and illegal dollar that can be made from vice and gambling.

The word homogeneity, which means of a sameness, may be applied to the pattern of our vice and gambling law enforcement. Rackets, protected and unprotected, are always inextricably tied in with politics, the law, the religious element (against sin and racketeers), and the racketeers who want to subvert the law and to profit from its subversion.

An Olympian probably looks down on the Angel City and roars with laughter. An admixture of comedy and tragedy is in its parade of clashing and conflicting interests. There is great talk of honesty. Each public official is a staunch defender of the public weal and each public official affixes his own halo about his head. Each, to all intents, views the underworld myrmidons with alarm and threatens them with ruin should the resulting political rain fall on himself.

For decades, in American cities, public officials have been "fighting the underworld" orally, but the underworld seemingly is oblivious of these battle cries and goes right on.

The underworld, in respect to public officials who orally fight it for public deception, is like the bumble bee in regard to experts on aerodynamics. The latter have stated that the bumble bee cannot fly because the area of its wing space is too small to lift the weight of its body, but the bumble bee does not know this and flies anyway.

Mayor Bowron says that organized rackets do not exist in Los Angeles, but along comes a Black Widow, or a Brenda Allen, who directs the prostitute activities of dozens of young girls, and racketeers who slay one another in the city's streets due to quarrels over pelf and thus we see between Bowron's words and the facts there is a wide disparity. But despite these facts and their inexorable logic, no one apparently questions Bowron's oft repeated statement that he is giving Los Angeles "Good, Honest and Efficient Government."

And, more often than you may think, when the official is publicly threatening the underworld, he is secretly doing business with its members, or their representatives who sometimes are attorneys, or other individuals acting as center- fielders, or liaison agents, individuals who are, like Caesar's wife, above suspicion due to the fact that they own or direct legitimate businesses. This political or grafting technique is as old as the United States itself. Lincoln Steffens told of it in his newspaper muckraking series almost half a century ago. In regard to the public conscience, or public awareness, one is inclined to believe that rigor mortis has set in.

But to return to the theme of the public official: Perhaps he takes underworld cash, and perhaps he doesn't. If he permits racketeers the protection of his office, they are generally mindful of the favor on election day.

If the public official has been "nice" to them and has insured them the continuous operation of their rackets, they'll be nice to him on election day and will spend their money where it will do him the most good. Racketeers are extremely grateful to public officials who permit them to make fortunes by violating the law, and extremely hateful to public officials who prevent them from making money. And money talks in an election. It not only talks, it screams. Money is more powerful than words and ideas because it can buy words and ideas by the millions.

Some day, when you are driving down Wilshire Boulevard around election time, you may see the ugly, deteriorated, fat face of some slob politician, or office holder anxious to retain his office, peering down at you. Under the picture you may read the familiar words —"He's honest. He's fearless. He's Against the Underworld. He's For Good, Honest and Efficient Government. Elect him and Keep Out the Mobsters."

When that happens, let me remind you that the chances are as good as even that some prostitute like Brenda Allen paid for that billboard. If the billboard cost $500 at twenty dollars a "trick," you may be assured that a covey of prostitutes turned twenty-five of them to pay for that billboard, or rather that they turned fifty because the madame gets half. If you think this assertion is far-fetched, keep right on believing it. There are people who would rather face pistols than facts.

While you are looking at the billboard and reflecting on its message, the scarlet Madame who paid for it may be perched on a lounge in her bagnio, sitting in a brocaded robe, thinking of election day and praying with fervent hope —"I hope old Joe Slob makes it on election day. But the town has been awful hot and the suckers have been getting smart. But that dirty so-and-so running on the Church Ticket — I hope the heel drops dead."

Since I left the police department, I have been informed, and I believe reliably, that another reform mayor figured in Los Angeles' modern political history. Moreover, I have been told that the racketeers made more money under him than they made under his predecessor, whom he unseated and whose underworld connections were an open secret. Magicians demonstrate that the hand is quicker than the eye;

and in like manner politicians, through words, distort things until they become transfinite and have no relationship to realities.

So, you see again, it isn't the law that is important — it is the facts — but how many people have eyes that can see facts, or brains that can dissect and analyze them, even though they are obvious? There is a mechanics of politics; and the first prerequisite of successful politics is money. If you do not believe this statement try and elect someone to a public office without MONEY. Jesus Christ, with all his fineness of soul, in a modern day political campaign would be a lead pipe cinch to wind up dead last in a field of two if he were a candidate running for election without MONEY. He drove the money changers out of the Temple and signed his death warrant. In the 1950 years that have elapsed since the day He was crucified, MONEY, in the realm of politics and in the realm of facts, hasn't lost many decisions.

Every man in practical politics, every elected law enforcement official, who ipso facto is subject to the political process, knows these facts and is guided in action by them. Each politico, without money to spread the advocacy of his campaign for public office, knows that he is an ineffective political instrument.

Now, who do you think is desirous of furnishing a politician with the necessary financial sinews to get elected? Money needed to buy radio time; to pay for printing; to purchase newspaper advertising; to hire writers and speakers who will spread the word of his "worthiness" for public honor?

You guessed it. The purveyors of protected vice and gambling.

How many average citizens contribute a single dollar to a candidate for public office? What has the individual citizen to do with the selection of candidates for public office in a municipality, or in a county? Nothing at all. A handful of people, most of whom are never heard of, "make" politics behind the scenes and out of the public eye. Frequently, the office holders, or the law enforcement officers elected by the people are merely little men on pogo sticks; front men, marionettes for groups who don't give a damn about them personally. They are all right as long as they serve the purposes of the groups who support and maintain them; purposes which may be obvious or purposes which may be hidden from the public gaze. There are few great men in public office today. You can start with the dog catcher and go right on up. In politics, this is the age of mediocrity.

And it was the same in the last days of Rome, after Tiberius.

You do not believe for a second, do you, that the racketeering element is composed of high-minded, unselfish persons intent only upon electing a man to a law enforcement office who is mercilessly determined to enforce the vice and gambling laws as they exist on the statute books. If you do, you are an eighteen karat sucker.

Do you know why Michael (Mickey) Cohen has remained in Los Angeles as an underworld king for ten years? He's here because some official wants him around. If someone in authority hadn't wanted him here, it's a foregone conclusion that he would not be in our midst today. Mickey is a front man for someone.

J. Edgar Hoover, head of the famed F. B. I., once declared: "If you notice rackets flourishing in your community, rest assured that someone encharged with their suppression is taking money in order that they may operate."

That you can bet on! It can't come out any other way.

But honest law enforcement officials and heads of municipalities are constantly subjected to all kinds of pressures to slacken their enforcement of vice and gambling laws. These pressures are engendered by the so-called liberal element, liberal not in the major political sense, but liberal in that they want to consort with prostitutes and drink and gamble without police molestation. These liberals demand:

"What's wrong with it? If you don't like it, don't knock it."

You can call them misguided; you can call them ignorant and sinful; but you cannot escape the fact that there are thousands of them.

Inarticulate as individuals, they are nevertheless, political fodder for the articulate crooked politician, the thieving copper and his racketeering adherents, and for all of that element who hopes, directly or indirectly, to make a fast buck out of prostitution and gambling. Politically speaking, they constitute a formidable cavalcade, for among them are shrewd political intelligences. Many businessmen are included in this category — businessmen who want to "cut a few legal corners" which they do not consider too important from a law enforcement standpoint; yet which they think they should be able to cut without interference. Exemplifying this group is the businessman who thinks that a "wide open town" is the best kind of town "for business."

Such businessmen, merchants, bar owners and the like desire to see prostitutes and gamblers operating without restraint, because this element spends money as fast as it makes it.

So, we come down to the kernel of the nut. The public or law enforcement official, even though he may have taken office as an honest man, intellectually and concretely, is aware of the pressure of these forces. Perhaps, he had decided the day he was sworn in that he would arrest each and every law violator on sight, or when he got the deadwood on him. Still, he cannot help feeling the pressure, and it is a FACT that he wants to stay in office.

Some public officials, irrespective of the opinions they hold of themselves, are no better morally than Brenda Allen, Queen Bee of the Hollywood prostitute brigade. In my purview, the Brendas are finer in comparison. The Brendas have a commodity for sale; a commodity some, or many, men desire. They do not twist your arm to buy it. They set a price on it and if you agree to that price, they deliver.

The corrupt and intellectually dishonest office-holder is worse than a prostitute. He fornicates the entire public, whereas the prostitute is more limited in scope. Most of our political office-holders would starve to death if their noses weren't buried in a public trough. The following ancient gag about them is particularly apropos.

"What is the difference between a dope fiend and a politician?"

Answer: "You can cure the dope fiend."

Let us turn the spotlight on our hitherto Honest John, who has become mayor and who desires to stay mayor, as he reflects and analyzes the scene political and the stage of law enforcement.

So, here is Mayor Bowron, that self-acclaimed exemplar of "Good, Honest and Efficient Government." His stance has become a hardy political perennial. His eyes are continuously shaded by his hands in a faraway look at the horizon, while he conjures up the specter of a Frank Costello, a Costello loping in on a horse to take over the Los Angeles underworld.

And Bowron shouts in a voice loud and clear. "He's comin'! He's comin'! He's practically here! Either re-elect me or turn your city over to Frank Costello and his mobsters!"

And the eternally childish public, myopic as to situations, with a baby's naiveté and an aversion from facts, twitches its collective ears, stamps the name of Fletcher E. Bowron on a ballot and settles back somnolently, confident that Dragon Costello has been put in his place and will conclude that New York is far more comfortable for his purposes than Los Angeles.

Several months ago while Bowron was almost daily screaming the name Costello, a local newspaper reporter took a vacation and journeyed to New York where he has friends in the newspaper business. He informed his friends that Mayor Bowron was constantly exhorting the Los Angeles public to look out for Frank Costello and his minions. And when he expressed a desire to meet the great gangster, his friends arranged to have him meet Costello. The local photographer was pleasantly received, and being a loyal conscientious workman, and hoping to combine business with pleasure, he inquired of Costello: "If I'm not too much out of line, would you pose for a picture or two? There's been a lot of talk in my home city about your moving into it for control of its rackets. My office hasn't any good pictures of you and it would be a feather in my cap to return with several good likenesses. And remember no disrespect meant at all."

Costello, the photographer told the writer, grinned pleasantly and said: "I'm sorry, but I believe not. It wouldn't help me any. Besides, I have plenty of enemies and I'm not in the market for any publicity of any kind.

"But, so long as we're on the subject, you can tell that fat little Mayor back there that if he doesn't quit using me for a political whipping boy, or hobgoblin with which to frighten Los Angeles voters, I will move into his town either with him or against him. I hadn't given the idea of changing my residence to Los Angeles any thought, but his continual talk about me gives me ideas. Each time some nickel and dime hoodlum is shot in Los Angeles, the deal is accredited to me when the truth is, I've never even heard of the guy."

But let's take a look at the record and cogitate a little.

I recall a story that has been going the underworld and political rounds for years. It involves the late former President of the Los Angeles Police Commission, Raymond L. Haight, and Zeke Caress. The latter was known as King of the Bookmakers in the days of the old Syndicate composed of Guy McAfee, Charlie Crawford, Albert Marco and Bob Gans. Zeke had a monopoly on the bookmaking racket and made a fortune.

In 1938, when Fletcher E. Bowron was the successful recall candidate against Mayor Frank L. Shaw, who was accused of presiding over a rotten regime and a corrupt police department (I guess it was), Caress ceased operations.

He stayed in Los Angeles and retired. The rest of the old mob, Guy McAfee, Tutor Scherer and Farmer Page, together with a band of retired Los Angeles police officers, moved to Las Vegas. There they have made fabulous sums out of legal gambling and there they still hold forth.

Let us skip a few years. In 1941, Bowron had been mayor for three semesters. Haight, who was his police commission president, ran into Caress on the street one day. They knew each other well. Haight said: "Zeke, you were born and raised here. I've known you for years. You've always been a bookmaker, nothing else, and there isn't anything too bad about that. Bowron is no long hair. He has no objections to a little vice and gambling if it isn't too extensive and if no police officer takes graft out of it. If you can arrange a modest program with the view of liberalizing things a little bit, to the end that the boys can have a few fun houses, the city administration will have no objection to it."

Caress reputedly looked Haight in the eye and replied: "Look, Raymond, I appreciate your consideration of me. But if I can't deal out of the top drawer, I don't want to play at all. I'm sixty years old. I've made mine. If I accepted your offer, it would mean a one-way ticket to San Quentin prison for me. Do you really believe that any vice squad officer is going to protect anything without expecting pay for it in return?"

"Perhaps, you are right," replied Haight, according to the story. "I never thought of it in that light."

"You can't be a little bit pregnant," Caress reportedly added. "A woman is either pregnant or she isn't. It's the same way with a city; it's either open or it's closed. Bowron will have to make his own decisions and stick with them. You can't have bang, jam up law enforcement and even a modicum of protected vice and gambling. It's got to be one way or the other."

Apocryphal or not, the sense of what Caress reportedly said is true.

But let's go on apace and see what happened. It all bears on the Stoker Story. Remember, I told you that there was a homogeneity about all this which, though it seems incredible, indubitably must be wrought out in the crucible of fact.

I will now tell you where the Great Bowronic switch came in.

The key to all police departments — the factor that determines whether they are to be run dishonestly or honestly — whether they are to go in for graft or honest law enforcement — is the personnel division.

The personnel division is to the police department what the Bar Association and its investigators are to members of the legal profession. The bugbear that worries a dishonest attorney is not the client whom he trims — but the investigative staff of the Bar Association. If he transgresses the legal ethical code and is caught, the penalty is disbarment.

A crooked police officer always fears the personnel division if the personnel division is being operated honestly. If the personnel division is manned and directed by venal police executives, and the police officer knows it and also knows his way around, he doesn't worry too much. In that event he knows there is a way to "handle beefs."

But if the personnel division is honest, if it investigates complaints against coppers without fear or favor, then the crooked police officer has great grounds for worry. The least that can happen to him then is discharge, and the worst, prosecution and conviction and either a jail or prison sentence.

All of this has a bearing on the Great Bowronic Switch.

The Switch had its beginning on the day the Mayor permitted the making of Captain Joe Reed into an assistant Chief of Police. That promotion started a train of events which, although I didn't realize their importance at the time, were to mark a significant day in my life.

Joe Reed was jumped over the heads of deputy chiefs and inspectors who out-ranked him, all of which was contrary to the city charter and provisions of the Civil Service Act governing the police department. There was no such job as assistant chief of police, but after the Bowron *fait accompli*, in collusion with the Police Commission, the Los Angeles City Council created the position by fiat, or ordinance, it didn't matter which, the same being a maneuver to pick up Mayor Bowron's slack and put a pretty facade on the business.

Two deputy chiefs of police quit, retiring in disgust. They were Ervis Lester, who then took a position with the State of California, and Paul Harrison, who plainly retired. At present, they are in Japan re-organizing the Japanese police forces under General Douglas MacArthur, which seemingly is testamentary to the idea that they are competent men. While they were members of the Los Angeles Police Department, there was no question but what they were honest men.

Slightly less disturbed was President of the Police Commission, Van M. Griffith, a Bowron-For-Mayor man from taw. Griffith, who fought the battle for Bowron in the recall, had worked with Bowron when both were newspapermen. The son of the man who gave Griffith Park to the City of Los Angeles, a millionaire and a dead honest man, Griffith is a member of the Criminal Complaints Committee of the 1950 County Grand Jury. The jury succeeded the one that received such maltreatment at the hands of Mayor Bowron and District Attorney William E. Simpson when the Brenda Allen Hollywood prostitution scandal, of which I was the fulcrum, exploded over the Los Angeles political scene. It will be interesting to see what happens in Los Angeles County during 1950, as the three-year statute of limitations on felonious crimes has not expired with regard to the 1948-49 police mess and the people mixed up in it.

Griffith had warned Bowron that there would be great dissatisfaction in the police department at the spectacle of a captain jumping over the heads of several men who outranked him. But the chips were down and the die was cast. Bowron, for reasons of his own which were obviously political and contrived out of expediency, had let the curve ball ride hoping no one would knock it out of the police infield and Joe Reed became assistant to Chief of Police Clemence B. Horrall.

Horrall, a former cowboy, had been ailing for a long time; and he was eager and willing to let Joe Reed shoulder the major administrative duties of the Los Angeles Police Department.

Who was Joe Reed?

Reed was born in Boyle Heights, in a lower class Eastern suburb of Los Angeles. He was a man who wore an affable smile in front of a cunning, hard and Basilisk-like eye. True to his background, Reed was gifted with a lot of Irish con − they have it − the Irish − I'm Irish myself, and I know the Irish. A non-spectacular man during his years on the police department, Reed was a guy who always knew when he should be listening instead of talking.

Peering at a photograph of himself in his office one day during the high tide of the war in Europe when Winston Churchill was making English history − Reed had observed: "I was told today I look a lot like Winston Churchill."

Truth is, he did and he does. They could have been twins.

Naturally, he had a wide acquaintance in the police department and in the city. He was a home town boy and he had been around the town when the rackets were operated by Zeke Caress, Guy McAfee, Albert Marco, Bob Gans, Tutor Scherer and Farmer Page.

In those days, Kent Kane Parrott, the attorney and ex- football star of the University of Southern California, was political boss and the chief governor of all and sundry. Parrott had taken the political sceptre from the dying hands of Owen McAleer when that worthy dominated the city's politics at a time when Los Angeles was beginning its major ascent to metropolitan greatness.

Joe Reed knew all the holds and angle. He knew who was who and he also knew the political curves. Consequently, he became the de facto Chief of Police. The only thing he lacked was the title, and he didn't want that. Joe was satisfied to have the power and was willing to let Horrall keep the glory and the title.

Now that we have set the stage, let us walk onto it the other protagonists of the police-underworld drama who were to rock and shake the city government's foundation, and who were to make a scapegoat of Police Sergeant Charles Stoker whose chief claim to fame is that he had arrested a Hollywood Madame who controlled and purveyed illicit sex in the film capitol.

How are we doing thus far?

Hold onto your seat and your eye glasses, for, from this point on, we're really going to take off.

Aside from the persons about whom you've already read herein, who played their parts in the Stoker Story, there were, in addition:

Policewoman Audre Davis, 26-year-old four times married daughter of retired Deputy Chief of Police Homer Cross. The latter is now associated in the legal gambling field in Las Vegas, Nevada, where former Los Angeles gambling boss Guy McAfee holds forth.

Homer Cross reputedly still exerts a powerful influence in the Los Angeles police department.

Policewoman Audre Davis was assigned to work with the author in the investigation, arrest and prosecution of Brenda Allen on pandering charges. After the conviction of Miss Allen and her sentence to serve one year in the county jail for the felony, Miss Davis repudiated her testimony and told the district attorney that she had perjured herself at the trial of Miss Allen. She then said that she had accompanied the author while he burglarized an office building on Beverly Boulevard. As a result of her story, the author was charged with burglary and was prosecuted in Superior court on the charge by the district attorney's office.

The trial eventuated in a hung jury and the charge was dismissed after which the author was ousted from the police department on a charge of conduct unbecoming an officer. Miss Davis, however, despite her confession of perjury, was not prosecuted, but resigned from the department. Later she married Police Officer Marvin Stewart to whom she is still wed.

Next in importance on the agenda is Lieutenant Rudy Wellpott, quondam director of the powerful administrative police vice squad. Wellpott was the boss of Sergeant Elmer V. Jackson, second in importance in administrative vice to Wellpott. Both Wellpott and Jackson were indicted by the Los Angeles County 1949 grand jury on bribery and perjury growing out of accusations of Michael (Mickey) Cohen, Hollywood gambling boss, who charged that they tried to shake him down for $20,000 on the representation that the money would be used to re-elect Mayor Fletcher E. Bowron on May 31, 1949. The charges were dismissed.

Sergeant Jackson was Brenda Allen's police "connection" and although a quantity of evidence existed to tie him up and into the Hollywood prostitution ring operating under Brenda's aegis, the investigation was smothered.

Sergeant Jackson was part of a plot to frame the author because of his intercession through investigation into the workings of the protected vice ring.

Lieutenant John Jesse (then a sergeant), one of the many men involved in the romantic affairs of Policewoman Audre Davis, now right-hand aide to Deputy Chief Parker.

Sergeant Guy Rudolph, veteran vice squad officer who, for years, acted as an aide and counselor to Chief Horrall, particularly on matters involving vice and gambling law enforcement. Sergeant Rudolph was a vice squad big wheel in the days when Guy McAfee and Bob Gans "owned" the city.

Nate Bass, Main Street bar owner and director of a covey of B-Girls (girls who hang out in saloons to facilitate and expand the sale of drinks to lonely men), who was a close friend of Lieutenant Rudy Wellpott and Sergeant Elmer Jackson. Bass was a power in Main Street saloon politics as they affected the administration of vice laws.

Captain Cecil Wisdom, head of the potent police personnel squad, now a captain at Venice. It was Wisdom who signed the burglary complaint against the author and "arrested" him on the trumped up burglary charge and who directed the investigation into Sergeant Jackson's connection with Brenda Allen.

J. Arthur Vaus, ex-convict and electronics expert, who aided the author in tapping Brenda Allen's apartment telephone lines which revealed the scope of her Hollywood vice operations. Vaus later was hired by gambler Mickey Cohen and found that the police administrative vice squad, under Lieutenant Wellpott, had installed dictaphones in Cohen's elaborate Moreno Avenue mansion in West Los Angeles at the time the house was under construction.

Barney Ruditsky, former New York police detective, latterly the proprietor of the fancy nightclub on Sunset Boulevard in the famous Hollywood Strip where Cohen was wounded and Neddie Herbert, New York gangster, was slain when both were ambushed in the early morning of July 19, 1949. Ruditsky's office was used during the investigation of Sergeant Jackson's association with Brenda Allen as a "listening post" by means of a telephone tap.

Captain William H. Wingard, commander of the Hollywood police station, who insisted that Brenda Allen be driven out of his district and that her prostitution racket be ended.

Police Officers Jack Ruggles and Jimmy Parslow, members of the Hollywood vice squad, who aided the author in the Allen investigation. Because Parslow would take no guff from Inspector William Parker, he, too, was fired for conduct unbecoming an officer.

Assistant District Attorney Johnny Barnes, who "advised" the county grand jury on procedure in the Allen-Cohen investigations, which resulted in the indictment of Chief of Police Horrall; Assistant Chief Joe Reed, Captain Cecil Wisdom, Wellpott and Jackson, all of whom escaped unscathed.

These, then, are the main figures in The Stoker Story.

Now it unfolds.

MY FIRST ARREST

In 1942, after pounding a beat for a few weeks, I was transferred to the Central Vice Squad.

"Honest" John Stewart, my new commander and Chief of Central Vice, was an old hand at the business of arresting the racket gentry. And he was honest. Among police officers, Lieutenant Stewart was what is known as a "square apple," meaning that he didn't take graft, and that he didn't countenance the taking of graft by anyone who worked under him.

At the time when I first faced Lieutenant Stewart, the question of graft and who took it was as remote from my mind as is Jupiter from Orion. I was twenty-four years of age in 1942, and the war was on. I was just a young copper, overly anxious to make good. If my superiors wanted me to arrest prostitutes, okay, I'd do my best to arrest them.

Stewart looked me over carefully. Then he said: "I've got a tough assignment for you. I don't know whether you can carry it out or not. All I expect from you is your best."

"I'll give you my best, sir," I answered respectfully.

"There is the Hotel Blank downtown," he said, mentioning the name of one of the city's first class hostelries. "I've tried everyone working vice on this case, but none of them has been able to make it."

"There's a bell captain in this hotel," Stewart intoned, "who's an old hand at the girl racket. He's smarter than a sewer rat and he can smell a copper as far as Maxie Rosenbloom could smell a right hand punch. It seems that when a copper even gets near him, he breaks out in a rash which warns him off. He's allergic to coppers; and if one walks in the front door, bells ring in his head and whistles blow in his ears."

"What law has he broken?" I inquired, curiously.

"He sneaks prostitutes into this hotel, top flight gals from the Hollywood flesh mart, gals who won't lay the body down for less than fifty-dollars, and who generally get a hundred. When it comes to casing a sucker, and determining whether he's a copper or a sucker, this bellhop's uncanny.

"He's a clairvoyant, a mind reader, a palmist and an F. B. I. agent combined. He's so cute and smart, and I've been unsuccessfully matching wits with him for so long, I'm almost inclined to give him a pass out of sheer admiration and start looking for easier game. I've pitched every curve I've learned in years of vice law enforcement, but I can't drop the flag on him.

"I've thrown him high ones, low ones, sliders, curves and sinker balls, but he's got a deadly eye for my pitching and for every copper working under me on this detail.

"The War's on and the Army, Navy and Marine corps and all their brass say that we must, to cut down the incidence of venereal disease, go all out to stop paid for illicit sex in Los Angeles. But if there were a thousand procurers, or panderers, like this bellboy captain, the military could just throw in the sponge and lose the war to the Japs by default.

"I'm not going to tell you how to work," he added. "You dope it out yourself and if you come up with a prostitute and this bell captain egg, I'm on your ball team forevermore."

Stewart handed me a wad of secret service money, furnished vice squadders by the police department, and told me to go to work. I thought about it for a whole day. I'd never arrested a prostitute. In fact, you can believe it or not, my knowledge of prostitutes and their ways was virtually nil. When it came to the technique of arresting one of them, most of those working in Los Angeles at the time could have given me the ace, deuce and jack and have then stolen my watch.

The next day a friend of mine, a businessman of Fresno, telephoned and said that he was coming down to Los Angeles. As he talked over the long distance phone, an idea formed in my mind. I had already learned that the hotel had a bus which shuttled back and forth between the Union Station.

"I'll meet you at the depot when you arrive," I told him. "Do me a favor. Keep your ticket stub and be sure you have your baggage checks." He agreed.

I packed two suitcases with clothes, and met the train the following night. I had armed myself with phony credentials. When my friend got off, I gathered in his baggage checks, got his luggage, and told the baggage master that I needed a couple of checks. I showed him my police credentials, grabbed the checks, kept the ticket stub and boarded the hotel bus. I had a bottle of whiskey sticking out of an overcoat pocket.

When I arrived at the hotel, a bellboy carried in my luggage from which the baggage checks protruded prominently. Another bellboy carried my effects up to a room on the tenth floor. I pulled out the ticket stub and threw it on the floor in front of him, remarking that I wouldn't need it any longer.

Then I settled down, occasionally using the telephone to have the bellboys bring in whiskey and food. I tipped them lavishly.

And here was the touch that was to earn me the approbation of Lieutenant Stewart. I knew a pretty girl, and she agreed for a price to play a pre-arranged role. She came up to my room, disarranged her hair a little and stripped to her underskirt and brassiere, leaving a little bare skin exposed in places.

I telephoned for the bellboy, and my friend played drunk. I asked the bellboy to bring me another bottle of whiskey; and, in his presence, I told my friend to get out. She started putting on her clothes as the bellboy left for the whiskey. She left before he returned. I said to the bellboy:

"Say, how about getting me a hot number? That one I had was a cold tomato."

He said he'd see. He went away and a few minutes later returned with the wily bell captain, the old fox of the procuring racket. The man looked me over appraisingly. He knew that I had been in the hotel for three days. Evidently, he had cased my entrance and was aware that I had arrived by train and had come to the hotel in the hotel bus. Moreover, I had been ordering a considerable amount of liquor; that he knew, too.

The major production I had put on evidently had dispelled his suspicions. He sniffed the air suspiciously like a beagle and then said he would have a girl in the room within forty-five minutes, explaining that she had to come in from Hollywood.

"How much do you want to pay?" he inquired.

"Naturally," I said, "I don't want to spend a fortune for a one-night stand. I just want a matinee, but I don't want to be cheap about it, either."

"Well, you can settle that with the girl," he countered. "Just wait."

Forty minutes later, the bell captain came back and told me that the girl would be in my room in a few minutes. He left.

There was a knock on the door, and I opened it to see one of the most gorgeous females I have ever gazed upon. She smiled radiantly and walked in. I bade her be seated. She was expensively dressed, and her coiffure was right to a hair. I asked if she would like a drink. She said she didn't drink, but that she wouldn't mind if I did. So, intent on her beauty, I poured myself a drink and wondered how come such a beautiful girl could be in her business. But then I was a young rookie and I hadn't yet seen what I was destined to see in Hollywood.

But my visitor was all for action and evidently had other stops to make before dawn. We were talking pleasantly when suddenly, and without warning, she unzipped her dress and off it came. I stared and gaped, my lower jaw slackening off. Wouldn't you — if you were a young man of twenty-four and healthy? Under the dress all she had on was a pair of sheer black hose, each stocking rolled just above the knee. With the dress off, this and her suede pumps constituted her ensemble.

Then she plumped herself in my lap, blinked those mascaraed eyes furiously, smiled and said: "Don't you feel romantic tonight? Don't you want to get into bed with me?"

I gulped again and remembered that I was a police officer and had spent considerable of the taxpayer's funds to arrive at this moment. The girl, I quickly determined, was a shrewd psychologist. She was beautiful and she knew it — and she was naked in my lap.

"Yes," I stammered, "but how much is it going to cost?"

"Isn't it worth a hundred dollars?" she demanded in a manner which indicated that there could be little doubt about the value of her charms where a passionate man was concerned.

"Sister," I said gravely, "You will never know how painful this has been to me, but I'm a copper. You're under arrest for offering," and I fished out my police badge.

"Well, I'll be damned," she exploded. "A copper!"

"Exactly," I said, handcuffing her to the bed. Then I arrested the cute old bell captain for procuring, and took my prisoners to Central station and turned them over for booking. Stewart was there. I walked in and reported.

"I'm a son-of-a-gun," he said. "How'd you do it?"

I explained my method and he gaped. "Smart kid," he complimented me. "You'll go far as a vice squad copper. You've got brains. Nailed them the first time out and no one else could even get close. And you a rookie bull."

So I had made my first prostitute arrest and had established myself as a sharp operator in the mind of Lieutenant Stewart. I was on my way as an officer destined to arrest many prostitutes and to precipitate a major civic scandal because I was good at it.

Someone once said: "There is a destiny that shapes our ends." How many times have I reflected on the manner in which women's ends have shaped my destiny. But I'm not at all happy about it.

But then, don't women shape all men's destinies one way or another?"

I MEET RUDY WELLPOTT

Thus, I had entered a new phase in my career. I was now working under Lieutenant "Honest" John Stewart.

One day Stewart sat down with me and told me what he expected of me. He explained that above all, he wanted honesty and good police work. He said that, if I remained honest and did my work to the best of my ability, he would stand behind me no matter what happened. I learned later that this man spoke the truth. There was no double talk in him and he was typical of the thousands of honest, unobtrusive police officers in the United States, who work at the business of crime prevention and the arrest of malefactors without fanfare and without hope of reward other than that they receive in their pay checks.

This type of officer seldom makes newspaper headlines. He doesn't become involved in vice or graft scandals and he grinds along, getting a promotion now and then en route, working honestly and efficiently until the day of retirement arrives when he bids police work good-bye and disappears from the law enforcement scene.

Stewart then explained the vice setup as it existed in Los Angeles and the method of control which had been established by the Los Angeles police department. He said that, insofar as he knew, no houses of prostitution were operating under police protection in the city. He said that he felt, rather than knew, that there was some graft in the city. He said that he felt there always would be. He assured me that as a police officer working for him, I need not be afraid to make an arrest, regardless of whose toes I stepped on. He informed me that as long as I was right, I would have nothing to fear and that he would stand behind me.

But Fate is forever spinning her curious and intricate webs. As Fate would have it, Stewart assigned me to work with Officer Rudy Wellpott. At that time, Wellpott was both my senior in time and experience. He headed the detail which we were to work —the Skid Row district commencing at Main Street and extending to the Los Angeles River.

After working one night with Wellpott, I realized that he was indeed the man for the area to which he had been assigned. He fitted it and it fitted him like a glove.

At this juncture, I want to warn the reader about my present prejudice against Wellpott. While I am writing in retrospect, I realize that there is a possibility of my doing the man an injustice. But I want to make this story as objective as possible; and I will do my best to confine it to facts and to my own inevitable opinions. Every person who lives has prejudices. A man without prejudices is either an inmate of an insane asylum having no connection with reality, or he is too senile to think and feel.

While I worked with Wellpott, I cannot recall that he ever wore anything but a faded brown shirt which gave the appearance of never having seen a laundry. That was before the War.

Years later, after returning from the armed services and learning that Wellpott had been promoted by an examination to the category of sergeant, an examination which was held while the best men in the department were in service, I was somewhat surprised to find that Wellpott was in charge of a vice division working directly out of the city hall.

Imagine my astonishment when Wellpott and the powers that be gave news releases to the tabloids, as well as testimony before the county grand jury, designed to convince the public that Wellpott was virtually the sole repository of ability to keep the city pure and minus rackets and to keep gangsters out of Los Angeles. Wellpott, according to the publicity, had investigated everything from vice to murder. Actually, he had headed a vice squad and nothing more.

When I worked with Wellpott along Skid Row, he was known as a "ladies man" to all the cheap prostitutes and waitresses on Main Street and East Fifth Street. Unfortunately, I am not good at dissimulation if I do not like someone. Wellpott was soon to know that I didn't like him. The feeling was mutual.

Our first actual difficulty came on a night when I mentioned to Wellpott that I had received a letter from a labor union for which I once had been an organizer and member. The letter had inquired if it would be possible for me to obtain a leave of absence from the police department and return to Union headquarters to assist in the work of organizing.

At this point Wellpott informed me in a bragging manner that he had once been in charge of a strike-breaking detail. Then he gave me his elaborate opinion of labor unions in general, which was far from complimentary.

I resented this, particularly when I remembered that my beloved stepfather, a labor organizer, had had his head bashed in during a labor dispute. I resented it, too, because I was pro-union.

But the final break in the Stoker-Wellpott axis came one night when Wellpott told me that he had made dates for both of us with two girls whom we were to take to dinner. I have admitted that I don't wear a halo. But I wanted no part of that arrangement and tried to decline gracefully. I said that I was financially embarrassed. But Wellpott insisted that he would pay the check. So, there was no way out.

We met the two belles in New Chinatown. At first glance, I wondered why everything happened to me. Waiting for us were two of the best known street walkers in the Skid Row area. We met them and I found myself murmuring that I would have to make a telephone call and would join the party later in the restaurant. I waited until I was certain that the three had been seated. Then I strolled casually in. Who should be seated at the first table but a police academy classmate and his wife!

They immediately spotted me and called me to their table. They explained that they were celebrating the wife's appointment as a member of the Los Angeles Police Department, and insisted that I have dinner with them. I was making some sort of feeble excuse when my "lady love" of the evening ran up behind me, threw her arms around my waist, and yelled: "For Christ's sake, honey, where in hell have you been? We're waiting for you."

The following day, determined to make amends, I learned that my former classmate was assigned to a certain court. I sought him out and at the first recess, called him into the hall and explained that the two women who were with us the night before were Wellpott's friends. I asked him to be sure and explain that fact to his wife.

When I reported for duty that evening, Wellpott was surly. He informed me that a friend of his had overheard me telling an officer in the courthouse hall that he, Wellpott, ran around with prostitutes. He said it was obvious that I felt I was too good for him and his friends. Because of this, he said that he was going to have me transferred off vice.

I immediately went to Lieutenant Stewart and asked to be transferred.

Stewart wanted to know my reason. He said he had been pleased with my work. In specific and unmistakable language, I told him. He said that he would take care of the unpleasantness by assigning me to work west of Broadway. Further, he said that men of Wellpott's character and type were easy to find and that if anyone were to be transferred, it would be Wellpott - not I.

I continued to work vice until January, 1945, when I petitioned the draft board to permit me to change my exemption and allow me to enter the Armed Forces. During off hours, I had been taking Air Force training in preparation for Army flight training. On the first of February, 1944, I was inducted. In October, 1945, I was honorably discharged from the service due to demobilization.

When I returned to the department, I found that Wellpott had been promoted to the rank of sergeant during my absence, and was now in charge of the administrative vice division. The division worked directly out of the city hall, and directly under the supervision of Assistant Chief of Police Joe Reed. Now, there was a man for you! The de facto chief of police, Reed operated the department while the somnolent and drowsy Chief Clemence B. Horrall sat heavily in his leather upholstered chair and watched the passing police parade as if he were a spectator rather than the director of it.

Administrative vice division worked all types of vice investigations. It was not limited by the divisional areas, as were the vice divisions in each district which were limited by the district's boundaries whereas administrative vice worked in each and every district irrespective of the operations of the divisional squads. Central division, commanded by Lieutenant Stewart, embracing the downtown district, was where I labored in the vice vineyards.

Stewart, to the detriment of my ego, frequently expressed the opinion that I was one of the most competent men he had ever known. Because of his high regard for me, he gave me the authority to work as I pleased and to make whatever decisions I thought best and necessary.

He also gave me the authority to leave Central division and go into other divisions, if information led me there. And he empowered me to be in authority over other officers of Central vice with whom I worked, and to work my own hours.

When Stewart became ill and relinquished his command to Lieutenant Edwin Blair, the new commander let me continue to work as I had in the past.

Due to my proven performance, if I may say so without appearing unduly immodest, most of the important complaints were assigned to me. I was determined to find out if vice was organized in any capacity; if it was operating on a large scale. That, as events were to prove, was a fateful decision designed to affect the lives and fortunes of a great many people including many police officers.

I can also say in truth that those whom I arrested were always treated fairly, as long as their conduct permitted such treatment. If it didn't, *I took the necessary steps.*

ALONG COMES BRENDA

Perhaps the most fateful day in my career as a police officer was the day I met Brenda Allen, whose real name is Marie Mitchell.

If you were to call Brenda a "good kid, but a poor kid," you would be wrong on the first count because virtue is as remote from her as is South Africa from the North Pole — and you would be equally wrong on the second count because Brenda is by no means poor.

Brenda, to whom I gave the sobriquet, "The Angel City Express," was rootin', tootin' and gatherin' in the "scratch" (or money), at the apex of her career as Boss Madame of a regiment of Hollywood prostitutes when she was really steaming and rolling.

Now there was a gal for you! For you, *not me*. In her line, she believed in mass production with Rolls-Royce quality. No broken down bags worked for Brenda. She procured the best for her Hollywood and Beverly Hills carriage trade. There are hundreds of girls who come to Hollywood each year hoping that the lightning of film fame will strike. When it doesn't, and the percentage is strictly against them, some of them wind up working for dames like Brenda in the world's oldest business. But then, after watching Hollywood as long as I did, I concluded that it is indeed difficult sometimes to determine where the actress leaves off and the prostitute starts, or vice versa. A fantastic place, Hollywood, where the pitfalls are many.

But Brenda had a lot of beauty in her scarlet girl galaxy and the tariff, always high, was whatever she thought the customer would stand.

Brenda thought the world and all of men for one reason.
Men have money; that is, some of them, and Brenda had the oldest means in the world to separate them from it.

Prior to entering military service, I had frequently heard officers speak of a Marie Mitchell, a street walker who plied her trade on West Sixth Street between Union and Alvarado Streets. At that time, I knew her to be a street walker and arbitrarily assumed that she was just a little dumber than most prostitutes.

But, when I returned from the service, I quickly learned that Brenda was no longer pickin' 'em up and layin' 'em down on the West Sixth Street pavements, but that she had entered the big time.

And it was more than rumored that she owed her success to the smart business management of a vice squad copper. As I began to make more and more arrests out Hollywood way, the rumor began to take shape. I was given first-hand information that some of the girls I was arresting were in the employ of the former Marie Mitchell, who had assumed the name of Brenda Allen.

Peculiarly, these girls whom I arrested, although working for Brenda, expressed a hearty dislike for her; and with very little persuasion they started talking. I felt that one couldn't put too much faith in what they said; however, where there was so much smoke there likely was some fire. Still, it wasn't of too much concern to me.

I learned that Brenda worked in the following manner. She was a subscriber to a professional telephone exchange similar to those used by physicians, attorneys and some movie people. I knew that she had many girls on call, and that, in the early part of 1948 when I finally arrested her, she was working exactly one hundred and fourteen girls. Her method of operation was almost fool proof. I soon admitted this, and I also admitted that my original conception of her as a dumb street walker needed a little revising.

Brenda advertised quite openly. She gave the number of her telephone exchange (as her own), to cab drivers, movie people, bartenders, bellboys and satisfied customers and she even carried space in the Hollywood Actors' Directory.

Strangely enough, Brenda boasted to the girls who worked for her and to her customers that she was operating under police protection. And it was a known fact that the type of customer to whom Miss Allen catered, had to be reasonably certain that he wouldn't suffer the embarrassment of arrest.

Information I had was that a customer, or a prospective customer, would call the telephone exchange number and ask for Brenda. If he had been a customer, he would identify himself; or if he wasn't, he would tell Brenda the source of his reference. He would then describe the type of girl he desired, and a price was agreed upon which was never less than twenty dollars.

With the description in mind, Brenda would call a girl on the phone and dispatch her after giving her the pertinent information. It was said that no customer had Brenda's confidential home telephone number, and that she gave it to only a few friends and to those whom she trusted. When the assigned girl had completed her errand, she would call Brenda through the telephone exchange and in all probability would receive another assignment. Frequently, a girl who started her first assignment early in the evening would be traveling the major portion of the night – often until dawn.

Brenda had a simplified and satisfactory method of bookkeeping. She kept a card file listing the name, the address and a complete description of each girl. On this card she also kept a record of the girl's business transactions, naming persons, dates and the amounts of money received.

At the end of each week, Brenda would call the girl and arrange a meeting. She would then collect fifty percent of the amount the girl had taken in for the week's operations. I became aware of her method of operation; I also became aware of the rumor that a highly placed vice squad officer was supervising Brenda's operations, but of this I was not certain. You may hear anything when you are a vice squad copper, and you soon learn to depend upon facts and fight shy of rumors until they have a foundation in fact. I speculated that Brenda was using the police protection pitch merely to dispel the fear of her customers. Prostitutes frequently do that.

As Brenda's exchange number was common knowledge, I went to the exchange and spoke to the owner, identifying myself as a police officer. I requested his co-operation and asked him to give me Brenda's confidential number. I knew that once I had this number, I could check with the telephone company and get the address of the Madame. The owner of the telephone exchange laughed, however, and told me that the only way I could get him to divulge this information would be through a court order.

Despite the fact that, at the time, I thought I was a pretty good investigator, I did a stupid thing.

Thinking that I could readily obtain a court order, I went to the office of the District Attorney. There, I was politely but firmly given the brush-off. But I wouldn't give up. I tried another angle. One night, I waited outside the telephone exchange and followed one of the operators home. A few days later this operator had a new friend in Officer Stoker; and it was only a matter of a few more days until Officer Stoker had Brenda's home telephone number. It was a routine matter to check with the telephone company and learn that the number was listed to a Marie Mitchell, who had a large apartment in the vicinity of Ninth and Fedora Streets.

Shortly after I had located Brenda's lair, I was given a complaint to see the manager of an apartment house on Burns and Virgil Avenues. With two other officers, I went there. The manager introduced himself. This man, oddly enough, was destined to play a major role in the vice scandal that rocked Los Angeles.

And, incidentally, this man opened up a new phase of investigating technique for Officer Stoker. He was instrumental in teaching me wire-tapping and its possibilities. Many police officers, and I include myself, believe that wire-tapping should be legal when it is done by bona fide police officers for the purpose of ferreting out crime and arresting malefactors. I am aware, however, that a great many legitimate and honest citizens do not share this view. I believe that wire-tapping by a police officer for the purpose of arresting a law violator should be considered no more an offense than should a uniformed patrolman's running a traffic light in pursuit of a fleeing robber. I knew that several officers on the department were engaged in wire-tapping.

But to return to the story: The manager of the apartment house — who was to play an important role in my life — said that some of his tenants had complained that a prostitute was living in a second story apartment. He explained that she worked as a dime-a-dance hostess in the evenings, and frequently brought one or two customers home with her at night for purposes of assignation.

The manager said that the tenant was out at the moment. I suggested that he take me to the apartment so that I could see the layout.

One glance at the apartment, and I knew that the arrest was going to be difficult since laws governing the control of prostitution in Los Angeles state that defendants must be caught in the act of sexual intercourse. The apartment had a long hallway; and the rooms were so far from the outer door that it would be virtually impossible to detect incriminating conversation if the officer were standing outside and the prostitute had closed the inner bedroom door.

The apartment house manager said that he had a solution for the problem. He explained that he was an electronics engineer by profession and that if we desired it, he could place a small microphone in the girl's rooms, conceal it and run a line to his apartment. Then, when the girl arrived with her customer, we could hear their conversation and, at the opportune moment, with his passkey he would enter soundlessly and make the arrest. When this arrangement had been completed, I sat with the manager and waited. During our wait, the manager introduced himself as J. Arthur Vaus, Jr. He said he was a sound engineer and a college graduate, and had served during the war as an Army captain in charge of Army telephone communications in and near Los Angeles.

He further avowed that he was the son of a Los Angeles minister, that he was interested in good government and that he maintained a religious program on the radio. He played several religious transcriptions for me which, he explained, were part of his radio program.

After we had successfully concluded the investigation of the prostitute, Vaus inquired if he could go with us on some of our future forays into vice. We told him that we would be glad to have him as it was a departmental policy to let reputable citizens accompany officers on duty. I added that he might give us a telephone call at any time.

Several nights later when we reported for duty, Vaus was waiting. He said that he had been downtown; and that, since he had a free evening; he would like to accept our invitation and accompany us. We were glad to have him along. During the evening, we were in the vicinity of Brenda Allen's home at Ninth and Fedora Streets. We parked our police car and I instructed one of the other officers to enter Brenda's apartment house and observe her apartment. After thirty minutes the officer returned. He said he had watched Brenda's apartment from a vantage point but had seen no one enter it or leave it. He then went to the door and listened. He said that he could hear the telephone ring repeatedly; but could only hear the murmur of conversations.

Upon hearing the officer's story, Vaus remarked that he had some equipment which would permit us to listen to Brenda's telephone conversations. We were curious. He said he would bring the equipment the following night.

The next evening, Vaus appeared with a small box containing wiretapping equipment. We went to Brenda's, entered the basement through a rear door and in short order Vaus had tapped Brenda's line.

To say that I was amazed at what I heard would be an understatement. Calls were coming in so rapidly over Brenda's line that she was receiving them by priority and selection. There were more calls than she could possibly handle. As soon as she received one call and dispatched a girl, or girls, she would dial the telephone exchange number and contact the operator who would give her the names of waiting customers. Brenda would then decide whom she would favor or eliminate.

We listened for several nights. Occasionally, I would dispatch an officer to the address where Brenda had sent a girl, and he would arrive in time to make an arrest. The girls were being arrested night after night, and it was becoming difficult for me to convince officers handling the arrests that the information was through luck and coincidence. I knew that, eventually, Brenda would suspect that her wires were being tapped — particularly if the rumor were true that a policeman was running her business, or advising her on operations.

We never remained in the basement on the tap for more than ten or fifteen minutes at a time, for fear of being caught. We merely waited to hear the location where a girl had been sent and where we thought we could make an arrest. I told Vaus that Brenda was bound to become suspicious. I was eager to learn the addresses of the various girls who were working under Brenda's aegis so that we could stay away from her apartment house basement. It was in my mind to get the telephone numbers of all of Brenda's girls, so that we could "tail" them away from their residences when they left on call. Moreover, we could then tap the telephone lines of the various girls and take them out of the play, one by one.

"I can easily devise an instrument which will record the numbers dialed by Brenda," Vaus spoke up. "I'll bring it along tomorrow night."

The following night Vaus brought along a gadget which he called an *impulse indicator*. It was an instrument which would indicate each number as it was dialed — a very satisfactory piece of equipment. Within three hours' time the first night we had used it, I garnered twenty-nine telephone numbers that Brenda had dialed, most of them numbers of girls she had working for her.

The second night when we used the impulse indicator, Brenda dialed a number that rang a bell in my mind. *Then it struck me full force.* The number she had called was the CONFIDENTIAL NUMBER OF THE ADMINISTRATIVE VICE SQUAD.

"This is it," I breathed to myself and my ears twitched and my nostrils flared as I listened.

When someone answered Brenda's ring, she inquired if *Sergeant Jackson* was in. She was told that he was not in. She then left a message for him to be sure to call Mrs. Johnson. A short time later in came a telephone call, virtually the first we had heard that had not come from the telephone exchange. A man was talking.

His words were endearing. "Honey, I just came into the office and got your message. How's business?" He then inquired about a certain girl, giving her name. He said that he was going to be busy all the next day but that, on the following day, he would tell his wife he had to go to court. Instead, he would come and see Brenda, he said, and sleep with her all day. After arranging to be with her the morning of the second day, he hung up.

Brenda immediately made another out call to a number that we later traced. This time, she again talked to a man. Her conversation was littered with endearments. Among other things, she asked him why he hadn't called her. She told him how much she loved him and asked him if he were going to come over and see her that night. Then, in disgust, she informed the man that she had just had a call from Jackson. She said that Jackson had informed her that he would be over the next day to sleep with her all day.

"That son-of-a-bitch isn't satisfied to take my money — he wants to sleep with me, too!" fumed Brenda.

"As long as he is running things, you'll have to tolerate it," the man mollified her.

Until that time I had never heard of Sergeant Elmer V. Jackson, trusted aide and right arm of my old "friend," Lieutenant Rudy Wellpott, head of the police administrative vice division. Perhaps, I reflected, Jackson is just a foolish policeman who is infatuated with a prostitute who in turn is using, him as a tool for her own pecuniary advantage.

At that time I had high ideals concerning the Los Angeles police department. I was zealous of its good name; and when infrequently police officers had gotten into trouble, I had taken their trouble to heart and considered it a personal matter. All night long I thought about what I had heard. I was trying to figure out what to do. Finally, I decided. I determined that I would call Jackson the next day and tell him exactly what I had learned. In this way, I naively concluded, that I would be doing Jackson, a fellow officer, a favor as well as protecting the good name of the department.

The following day, I telephoned Jackson and told him the exact situation. I explained that I was acting out of a spirit of loyalty for a fellow officer. I advised Jackson that Brenda Allen was making a complete fool of him and that she had no regard for him whatsoever. I related the facts of her telephone conversation to the other man immediately after she had finished talking to him.

Now, I realized that this action constituted one of the most foolish things I ever did in my life. Jackson wasn't interested in my advice, but he showed a lively interest in what I told him. His major reaction seemed to be that of obvious jealousy. He wanted to know the name of the rival Brenda had called after she had finished talking to him. He did, however, promise me that he would have nothing further to do with Brenda.

Here is the payoff. If you believe that there is little honor among thieves, do not believe that there is much more among policemen if they are crooked. The following night we had been in the apartment house basement but a few minutes when Brenda walked in on us as brazen a whore as ever lived. She demanded that we go upstairs to her apartment. We did with Vaus accompanying us. Although she had never laid eyes on me, Brenda CALLED ME BY NAME.

"Stoker, you think you're just a wise son-of-a-bitch," she slurred.

I wanted to slap her right across her filthy mouth; but I deemed it wiser to listen to what she had to say inasmuch as I was now convinced that Jackson had told her everything.

"You're biting off more than you can chew," she continued. "I can either get you fired or transferred before the month is over."

You can well imagine how this declaration struck me — coming from a whore — the idea that my police career was at the mercy of a gaudy, bawdy strumpet madame. But, foolishly, I had under-estimated Brenda. At the time, my only answer was to laugh in her face.

Within a few months of that fateful night, I was convinced that graft in the Los Angeles police department was extensive and this despite "Good, Honest and Efficient Government" slogans as enunciated weekly over the radio by cherubic Mayor Fletcher E. Bowron.

I learned that graft existed in the police department under two individuals and in two chains. I learned that the retinues in both chains were quarreling over the spoils of prostitution, bookmaking and gambling.

My reaction to Brenda was one of aversion, disgust and controlled rage. I went to my superiors and asked to be transferred from vice squad duty. But unaware of the knowledge that I had gained, the vice commander, believing that I was a capable man in that field, recommended that my application for transfer be disapproved. I objected strenuously, but to no avail.

My having requested a transfer at that time should convince any unbiased person that I was not seeking the role in which I find myself today — that of a man who has concluded that he must tell what actually happened because what did happen caused him to be unjustifiably fired from the police department, with his reputation under a cloud.

SERGEANT ELMER V. JACKSON- HERO?

Several months after my meeting with Brenda, I picked up a newspaper and, to my astonishment, read that Sergeant Elmer V. Jackson was a *hero!*

It was reported that the previous night, while Jackson was sitting in an automobile with a lady friend identified as Marie Balanque, a bandit had stuck the nozzle of a machine gun through the open window of an automobile in which the couple was sitting and that brave Sergeant Jackson had slain the intruder. The article stated that another suspect in the robbery, or attempted robbery, an accomplice of the dead man, had been captured several hours later in a downtown hotel.

What the newspapers didn't know was that, before Sergeant Jackson made a statement to the newspapers, he had first conferred with his immediate superior, Lieutenant Rudy Wellpott.

Some months after this incident and after the county grand jury had begun a probe into police department vice operations, two newspapermen went to San Quentin penitentiary, where the dead bandit's youthful accomplice had been incarcerated, and there they interviewed him.

The imprisoned man told this story: He had been a transient in Los Angeles at the time of the attempted robbery of Sergeant Jackson and Marie Balanque — who in reality was Brenda Allen — and he was broke. He said that, a few days prior to the shooting, he had met the man who was shot and killed. The prisoner said that this man who appeared to have money, lent him small sums and took him to live at his hotel. Not long after that, the man had suggested that he accompany him on a robbery and he (the prisoner) had agreed. He said that his new found friend told him they would steal a car, commit a robbery and then make their getaway in the stolen automobile. They stole the car and, according to the prisoner, his companion ordered him to do the driving.

"Drive out towards Ninth and Fedora Streets," the bandit leader commanded him.

The leader of the duo, who was to die under Sergeant Jackson's gun, had told the youth that they would follow another car. When the car parked he would get out with his machine gun and perpetrate the holdup. Then they would flee.

The San Quentin prison inmate told reporters that he thought it strange that he and his companion should choose the Ninth and Fedora Streets area for the purpose, as it was decidedly middle class. He wondered why so many expensive automobiles passed them and why his companion did not direct him to follow one of them. He reasoned that the chances of loot would be much better. He said that he had voiced his wonderment, but his companion had mumbled, "Keep quiet and just wait. I'll tell you when."

It must be kept in mind that Brenda Allen's apartment was located at Ninth and Fedora Streets, and that the bandit leader had ordered the transient youth to wait at that spot.

Finally, a battered, inexpensive car, a sedan of several years' vintage, drove by, and the youth noticed that it was occupied by a man and a woman.

"Follow that car," his companion had ordered.

He did until the car stopped and had parked near the corner of Ninth and Fedora Streets. Then his companion got out with the machine gun and started for the parked car while he stayed double-parked with the motor running, prepared for the getaway. A few moments later, he heard a quick, bucketing shot and saw his companion fall. Without hesitating, the youth raced away. A few hours later he was arrested in the hotel room where he and his new found friend, now dead, had been staying.

Out of sheer curiosity, I had stepped into the coroner's room where the inquest into the dead bandit's death had been held and, as I had suspected, Marie Balanque was none other than Brenda Allen, Queen Bee of the Hollywood prostitutes.

I met her face-to-face. She followed me into the hall.

"Well, you son-of-a-bitch," she opened, "I see you're still snooping and you will see what it is going to get you!"

To everyone's surprise but mine, I was transferred immediately afterwards to the narcotic division of the detective bureau.

Nice bunch of kids, the higher police brass, excellent exemplars of the Bowronic brand of "Good, Honest and Efficient Government." But one must, I suppose, maintain his sense of humor, or at least a little of it.

They can tell anyone they want that dear little Brenda didn't get me transferred — they can tell everyone except one guy — me!

But, truthfully, I welcomed the transfer. My only resentment was that a dirty, slimy, foul prostitute, who had performed thousands of acts of sexual perversion on an army of men, had accomplished something that I couldn't accomplish when I had asked for a transfer. Apparently, her word was better than that of a guy who had spent thousands of hours in honest law enforcement.

But, transferred, I was determined to have nothing whatever to do with vice enforcement in any manner or form. I was determined to sever all connections with that type of investigation. I worked conscientiously as a member of the detective bureau assigned to the Newton Street division in the colored belt. And during that period I studied hard and passed the competitive examination for sergeant.

In January, 1948, I was near the top of the list for appointment as sergeant; and it was only a matter of time before I received the appointment. It was then the police department policy that when an officer was promoted to sergeant he would be transferred to another division to endure a six months' probationary period.

Imagine how flabbergasted I was upon being told to return to Central Vice Division. I was informed that, inasmuch as I was an experienced vice officer and as many of the vice officers working the Hollywood division were inexperienced, I was to be sent there on loan as a temporary assignment.

There I was again, right back in little Brenda's orbit, or playground. "I wonder if I'll meet the slut again?" I asked myself.

But I had no desire to meet Brenda. By this time I was fully cognizant of the fact that she had connections high in the police department and, after all, I was a policeman who wanted to be a sergeant.

However, I had no choice. I was given the assignment; and I realized that I had better do what I was told and do it to the best of my ability.

HOLLYWOOD VICE - I was being sent to the hottest spot in town. But with my sergeant's appointment in the offing, I was determined to take dead aim, keep my nose clean and HOPE for the best.

Before I went to Hollywood, I was told that Sergeant Howard Robinson, commander of the Hollywood vice squad, and Captain William H. Wingard, commander of Hollywood station, had called in the vice personnel and had informed them that a "hot shot" from downtown was coming out to Hollywood. Captain Wingard said that someone downtown was evidently dissatisfied with their work. He advised the men to co-operate with Stoker, but to offer him no information or assistance other than that which was absolutely necessary.

I was not acquainted with the officers working Hollywood vice at the time. I had never met Sergeant Robinson or Captain Wingard prior to my appointment to Hollywood vice. At the division, I introduced myself and Sergeant Robinson suggested that we go for a ride to talk things over. He said that he wanted to acquaint me with the area and with the operation of his division.

During the ride, Robinson pointed out various bars that were suspected of liquor law violations, other locations which were possible gambling joints and hotels that catered to or co-operated with prostitutes. I told Robinson that I hadn't worked vice for a year and consequently had lost all contact with the vice situation. Moreover, I told him the apparent reason behind my transfer from vice (not mentioning Brenda).

Then Robinson rattled off the names of a great number of prostitutes who were working Hollywood. He said that a notorious madame was operating a whore house full blast just over the city line in unincorporated county territory. He said that a number of complaints had come in from people who believed that the place was located in the city and was therefore under the jurisdiction of the Hollywood vice squad.

Robinson then drove by the house in question, an ornate place on Cory Avenue, one block off the famous Sunset Strip. He told me that the madame was working four or five girls in the joint, nightly and daily.

"The madame's name is Brenda Allen," he said. "Have you ever heard of her?"

"Holy mackerel," I breathed. "Here we go again!"

Prior to Robinson's statement, I had no idea where Brenda was operating. In fact, I didn't know whether she was working at all. I hoped she had left Los Angeles. Since my transfer from vice, I had heard Brenda's name mentioned only once. This was when Vaus contacted me and said that someone had gotten in touch with him and wanted to buy the recordings we had made in the basement of Brenda's apartment house. I told Vaus to lead on any would-be purchaser and let him believe that such recordings really existed.

When I told Robinson my story in regard to Brenda, he in turn was amazed. He said that, inasmuch as Brenda actually had four or five girls working in the house, he couldn't conceive that any intelligent police officer would associate himself with her in the venture. Robinson admitted that he had heard a rumor of the connection between Jackson and Brenda, but he had been disinclined to believe it.

"But I do distrust administrative vice," Robinson vouchsafed. "I believe it's working to discredit the Hollywood squad and that means me. I think someone wants the Hollywood vice squad discontinued," he added wryly, "and if they do, there must be a reason and that reason is someone wants to make money."

He then told me that he would like to see Brenda's place closed and raided by police officers. He felt that the many complaints which were coming in about her place tended to put the Hollywood vice squad under a cloud to the end that it helped administrative vice in its campaign to get Hollywood vice discontinued. Then he asked if I knew of any way in which we could get Brenda knocked over.

I suggested that we raid her house although it was in county territory. If anyone complained, I would say that I was new in Hollywood and unaware of the territorial boundary between the city and county, and that I had made a mistake.

Robinson thought it over and then told me to go ahead.

The next day I called an executive of a big Los Angeles firm and asked him if he would like to patronize a Hollywood call house at the city's expense. He said that he was agreeable if it would help me out. The young man followed directions.

He called an exchange telephone number which Sergeant Robinson furnished, left his business telephone number and name and asked the operator to have Brenda call him. Later Brenda called the number and the telephone operator of the business firm answered, giving the name of the company for which the young executive worked.

When Brenda asked for the man by name, she was transferred to his secretary; and by the time she was actually talking to him she had completely swallowed the bait and was convinced that she had another reputable businessman on her list of patrons.

He asked if he might come over, and she readily assented.

That evening with twenty dollars of city money in his pocket and in his big red convertible coupe, he pulled up in front of Brenda's flesh factory.

Later, he reported that Brenda trotted out four beautiful girls for his inspection and that he selected one of them. When he was leaving, as per his instructions, he asked Brenda if, at another time, he could bring some of his friends — some of the boys who worked in the office with him. He said he would like to do this on his next visit. Brenda readily assented.

When I told Robinson of my progress, he said he had two young new coppers who would accompany my friend to Brenda's. He then outlined my plan to Captain Wingard, who demurred. Wingard told me that, by making an arrest in county territory, we would be stepping on the sheriff's toes. He suggested that we first see Captain Pearson, head of the sheriff's vice squad. Then, he said that, if Captain Pearson didn't arrest Brenda, we could go ahead and arrest her ourselves.

Captain Wingard was explicit about the fact that he wanted to give the sheriff's office the chance to make the arrest before the Los Angeles police department stepped in.

THE CIRCLE CONSTRICTS

Following Captain Wingard's orders, I went to the sheriff's vice division and for the first time met Captain Carl Pearson, commander.

I explained my mission and told Pearson that, should he desire to raid Brenda's house, the police department could give him some cooperation and could loan him some men who were familiar with the setup.

Captain Pearson studied me intently. He paused to reflect. Then he admitted that he had known of Brenda's activities on Cory Avenue for some time. He said that he had been informed that a highly placed police officer was connected with Brenda in some fashion. He added that he wasn't quite certain whether her bagnio was in county or in city territory, but that it was his impression that it was just inside the city limits. I told him I was certain that it was in the county because Sergeant Robinson, commander of Hollywood vice, had so advised me. I pointed out that Robinson had worked the Hollywood detail for a number of years, and should know.

Captain Pearson suggested that, before he took any action, he would like to consult the confidential aide to the chief of police, Sergeant Guy Rudolph. He promptly telephoned Rudolph and introduced him to me over the telephone. Rudolph was an old time vice squad operator when the expatriate Syndicate "had" the city's rackets. Supposedly due to his specialized knowledge of vice and gambling rackets, Rudolph was a confidential aide to Chief of Police Clemence B. Horrall.

After Pearson had explained the situation to Rudolph in my presence, Rudolph confided that he had been working secretly on Brenda Allen. He asked Pearson and me to keep our conversation confidential. Captain Pearson, hanging up the phone, then asked if I knew that a police officer was involved with Brenda.

When I told him that I didn't know that, he informed me that the police officer involved with Brenda was Sergeant Elmer V. Jackson, right hand man to Lieutenant Rudy Wellpott, head of the police department's Administrative Vice Squad.

Later, I met Sergeant Rudolph at Pearson's office and he told me that he didn't want Brenda's place raided until he had gathered enough evidence to connect Sergeant Jackson with her. He said he had been handicapped in his investigation because he was afraid to mention the matter to Chief of Police Horrall, for if the Chief of Police knew of it he would immediately tell Assistant Chief Joe Reed. He said that once Reed was informed, he would tip off Sergeant Jackson. Rudolph remarked that, in his opinion, Reed, Wellpott and Jackson were working together. He added, however, that Chief Horrall had confidence in Joe Reed.

Captain Pearson, Sergeant Rudolph and I journeyed to a Santa Monica Boulevard shop. When we entered, I was surprised to find my old acquaintance, Vaus. He was now in business as an electronics engineer. I learned that Rudolph and Vaus were acquaintances of long standing and, from their conversation, I deduced that they had worked together before. While we were there, Vaus told me that he had marketed an improved model of the instrument he had used to record telephone numbers dialed by Brenda in her apartment on Fedora Street. He said he had sold some of them to the Los Angeles Police Department and that he had been negotiating with some bureaus of the Federal Government for the sale of electronics equipment he had devised.

I noticed that Rudolph was very secretive; and, inasmuch as he was a Big Wheel in the police department, having the ear of Chief of Police Horrall, I, a lowly sergeant, was in no position to ask him any questions.

Rudolph and Vaus then went into a huddle in an office. When they emerged, they loaded a quantity of equipment into Vaus's car and all four of us drove to an address on the Sunset Strip.

We entered the place, and Rudolph introduced me to a man named Barney Ruditsky, a former New York police detective who was reputed to have once thrashed the famous Broadway detective, Johnny Broderick, in a fist fight. Rudolph told me that Ruditsky was operating a private detective agency. However, I was introduced to Ruditsky under an assumed name. Rudolph told me later that he thought this best inasmuch as he didn't want anyone to know that Stoker was working on the case.

Rudolph left Vaus at Ruditsky's place and drove Captain Pearson and me back to Pearson's office. En route, Rudolph explained that Vaus had made an important connection in the telephone company's main office, and that this friend would make a mechanical adjustment so that a telephone in Ruditsky's office would become a party line to the telephone at Brenda's place. He said that for a few days he and Vaus would record all of the telephone calls received and made from Brenda's house of prostitution. Then when he deemed the time to be right, he would tell both Pearson and me, and the raid would be made.

Again, Rudolph warned me to tell no one of the day's activities. When I reminded him that I would have to report to Sergeant Robinson, he said to tell Robinson that Captain Pearson and his sheriff's squad would make the arrest and that the police department could forget it.

Returning to Hollywood station, I did as I had been told. I then started work on other vice investigations in the Hollywood district. At that time a rookie police officer, Jack D. Ruggles, was assigned to work with me as a partner.

A few days later, Sergeant Rudolph called me at my home and directed me to meet him at Ruditsky's place that evening. I had informed Ruggles of the Brenda investigation and how it stood at that moment. Ruggles accompanied me to Ruditsky's, where we found Rudolph and Vaus. There, an elaborate mechanical setup was in operation. It was later explained that this was the very latest thing in wire-recording devices, and that it had been made by Vaus. This device would automatically start the wire recording when Brenda lifted her telephone receiver off the hook. It would also stop the recorder as soon as she had finished talking and had hung up the receiver. It was quite a cute gadget, and I saw its possibilities as a bane to evil-doers.

Rudolph told Ruggles and me that he had some good recordings, and that he would play one for our edification. He turned it on.

The voice we heard was that of Sergeant Jackson. He was blasting Brenda for discharging one of her girls without first consulting him and receiving his consent.

In my mind that recording very definitely placed Sergeant Jackson, Lieutenant Rudy Wellpott's strong right arm, in the whore house business.

Seemingly, Sergeant Rudolph was perturbed because I had brought young Officer Ruggles along. He softened somewhat when I explained that Ruggles had been assigned to work with me, and that if I had tried to ditch him, it would have created suspicion. Rudolph then warned Ruggles to be careful and to mention to no one what he had seen or heard.

"We'll raid Brenda tomorrow night. You, Stoker, contact your friend and have him ready as a customer for Brenda and, Stoker, also see that Captain Pearson is ready to go," Rudolph ordered.

The next night I took my friend to the sheriff's office and introduced him to Captain Carl Pearson. The latter outlined a plan for the raid. My friend telephoned Brenda and told her that he would call at about eleven p.m., and would bring two friends with him.

Then Ruggles and I returned to Ruditsky's office. There, Rudolph played the recording of the conversation between Brenda and my friend, who was to be used as the "mule" or police agent, in the arrest of the Madame.

Rudolph then said that he and Vaus had made arrangements to "bug"— plant a dictaphone — in Brenda's home after she was taken to jail and had also made arrangements with Brenda's neighbors to use their garage, where the wiring and recorder could be stashed. He wanted me to assist Vaus in the "bugging" of the house; and he asked me to remain in the garage and record Brenda's conversations after she had returned from jail.

At the appointed time, Ruggles and I were waiting outside of Brenda's seraglio. I watched my friend and the two deputies enter. A short time later, we saw Brenda and three of her girls leave the place under arrest. We were presently joined by Vaus and two unknown men, whom Vaus explained were his assistants. We went to the back door and found it unlocked, as had been pre-arranged with one of the raiding deputy sheriffs. My friend returned and reported that Brenda was safely in jail.

Inside, we promptly went to work to wire the house for sound. We ran across Brenda's "business" book, containing the names of her clients and also another book which recorded names, telephone numbers and descriptions of the girls working for her, together with a record of their earnings on call dates. While I read this information, my friend copied it down. When this was done the books were left exactly where they had been found. I later counted the names of the girls and found that Brenda had one hundred and fourteen in her employ. Incidentally, these names were given to and are now the property of a reporter for a local newspaper.

Then Vaus and I went to the garage, where he gave me a short course of instructions in the operation of a wire recorder. I waited in the garage.

At about nine o'clock the next morning, from my hiding place, I saw Brenda and two of her girls arrive by taxi. A few minutes later, their voices came over the recorder clearly. They were arguing about my friend, questioning whether he had been a deputy sheriff, an informer or just a poor customer who had been caught in the raiding net. Brenda leaned toward the theory that he was merely an unfortunate customer. This, I suppose, because originally she had been induced to call him at his place of business where she first talked to a switchboard operator, then to his secretary and finally to him. Obviously, she couldn't believe that a reputable businessman would be operating as a police aide.

After Brenda's arrest and while the house was empty, the telephone had been ringing constantly. Now, with Brenda home again, the telephone rang and Brenda answered. The other party on the line was Jackson. Hanging up, Brenda told her girls that Jackson wanted them to meet him. They called a cab and left. Approximately an hour later, the trio returned and Brenda received another telephone call. I heard her tell one of the girls that the call was from her attorney, Max Solomon.

A few minutes later, the third girl returned. Brenda asked her why she was so late in arriving. The girl explained that she had had trouble with her bail bondsman.

Brenda then declared that, after she had left for jail, the deputy sheriffs had evidently taken the keys to the house and had come back to look around.

"How do you know?" asked one of the girls.

"Because I made a fresh pecan pie and some bastard ate some of the nuts off the top of it!" Brenda retorted hotly.

I remembered the pie, for it was I who had eaten the nuts off the top.

I then heard Brenda tell the third girl that they had been to see Sergeant Jackson. She said he had advised them to tell their attorney that some valuables had been stolen from the house, as it was against regulations for the sheriff's deputies to take keys or any of a prisoner's personal property after it had been booked at the booking office. In that way she could get the deputies fired.

This little incident has great significance, since it shows starkly and realistically, how law enforcement officers line up with racket people, and give aid and assistance to racketeers when they are grafting from them.

The girls agreed to follow Sergeant Jackson's advice; and one of them suggested that they say a fur coat was stolen.

A while later two officers entered the garage. I recognized them as men who had been working directly under Captain Cecil Wisdom, Commander of the Police Personnel. I gave them instructions regarding operation of the recorder; then, with the recordings I had made, Ruggles and I went to see Sergeant Rudolph at Ruditsky's. Rudolph played the actual telephone recordings between Jackson and Brenda Allen. As Sergeant Rudolph played them, we heard Sergeant Jackson ask Brenda "where in the hell she had been." She replied: "Where in the hell do you think I was?" He said he didn't know, and that he was in no mood to play guessing games.

"I've been in jail, God damn it!" Brenda spewed. "That's where I've been. In jail.In jail."

"Who took you in?" asked Jackson.

"The sheriff's office, the sons-of-bitches!" snapped the red- haired virago.

"I want to see you in a hurry," Jackson cut in. He gave her directions to meet him in the rear of a drive-in.

I inquired of Sergeant Rudolph why men from personnel division had relieved me of my duties on the wire recorder. I was under the impression that no one except Rudolph, Ruggles, Vaus, Pearson and I were to know of the investigation. Rudolph explained that a Lieutenant Bowman was in charge of the gangster detail, working for Assistant Chief Joe Reed. He said that Bowman had entered Ruditsky's office and had seen the recorders and that he, Rudolph, in turn had to explain the situation to Chief of Police Horrall. This was necessary, he said, since Horrall would order Lieutenant Bowman to say nothing about the matter to Joe Reed.

"I've already given all the information on this investigation to Chief Horrall," Rudolph said, "and he has promised not to inform Joe Reed. He thinks, however, that Captain Wisdom of personnel should have his investigators working on the case."

When I heard this, I went to Hollywood division and told Sergeant Robinson and Captain Wingard all that had happened. Captain Wingard telephoned Captain Wisdom.

At this juncture, I concluded that this was a job for police personnel, encharged with the responsibility of investigating police officers. From what I knew, from what I had seen and heard, I believed that this was a squabble in which I wanted no part. My intuition led me to believe that Sergeant Guy Rudolph had an ulterior motive in the affair — namely, to "get something on" Assistant Chief Reed, Lieutenant Rudy Wellpott and Sergeant Elmer Jackson, the whoremaster. I had a hunch that he wanted to cut himself in for a share of the profits, inasmuch as I knew that he had been a vice squad man in the days when the town ran wide open under members of the old Syndicate now happily and profitably engaged in Las Vegas, Nevada. I had heard many tales concerning Rudolph and none of them was good.

Ruggles, Robinson and I held a conference, and we were all of the same opinion. Robinson went to Captain Wingard and told him that we three wanted to have nothing further to do with the actual investigation of the conduct of a fellow officer. But Wingard replied that he had received orders from Captain Wisdom, that we were to cooperate with him and that we were to follow all of Wisdom's orders.

The people should begin to see about here that Sergeant Charles Stoker was caught in the web of a police net not of his making. When a man is a police officer, he doesn't have alternatives, he has orders. And he carries them out — or else.

Captain Wingard called young Officer Ruggles into his office.

"I hate to see you become involved in an investigation of this type," he began. "But I know Jackson to be a crook and a pimp. It is the duty of an honest police officer to see that he is put away."

Irrespective of and conceding Captain Wingard's sincerity, the situation is laughable when one realizes that Sergeant Elmer V. Jackson is still a police officer in good standing on the Los Angeles Police Department today. It would seem that the deus ex machina of being a police officer in good standing is to first become a Hollywood pimp and a protector of Hollywood's whore galaxy. Selah!

That evening I received a telephone call from Captain Pearson. He informed me that Brenda and her girls had appeared in the office of a county justice of the peace, had pleaded guilty and had been fined seventy-five dollars each — just a couple of hours' "work" on a good night. He added that, after the arrest, he had learned that Brenda's house was not located in county territory but was within the Los Angeles city limits and just inside Hollywood division. I was told by Wingard to keep an eye on Brenda's place and watch for her return. So several times each night, Ruggles and I drove by Brenda's joy house to see if any lights were burning.

For two weeks, we saw absolutely no sign of life. Then, one night the place was lit up like a Christmas tree. Ruggles and I sneaked up to the rear of the house. Through a window, we could see Brenda putting a fresh coat of dye on her hair.

Shortly after Brenda had been arrested and during the time she was away from home, one of the Hollywood officers had run a line from a telephone cable to a hidden place by the kitchen door near the basement. He had rigged up a telephone in the basement in such a manner that the wires leading to the phone were fastened to two pins such as are used as markings for locations on maps. To listen into Brenda's telephone conversations all one had to do was to push the two pins into the line. Knowing that Brenda was home, we went to the basement.

We found the telephone, took it to the line, connected it and waited for Brenda to receive a telephone call. After a short wait and after several calls from old customers who inquired when she was going to get into action again, Sergeant Jackson telephoned. He asked Brenda what she was doing and she replied that she was hennaing her hair. He asked if she had seen any real estate brokers about getting a new house. She said that she had, but that it appeared that she was going to have to get a location in the city.

"Guess what?" he ejaculated. "One of the head hunters (personnel investigators probing into a police officer's suspected misconduct) gave a lecture to a number of rookie policewomen at the police academy in Elysian Park, today. He says that personnel has enough evidence on a certain vice squad sergeant to send him to San Quentin penitentiary."

Brenda then asked Jackson how he knew this. Jackson replied that a policeman's wife, who was a friend of his wife's, was a rookie policewoman in the class.

"We'd better not talk too much over this phone," Brenda said. "I'll be seein' ya."

I went immediately to Hollywood division and told Captain Wingard what I had heard. In my presence, Wingard called Captain Wisdom at his home. Wingard asked Wisdom if some "damned fool from his office was giving lectures to policewomen at the academy, that day."

Wisdom replied that he did have a man lecturing that day. Wingard then told Wisdom what had happened. Wisdom promised to make an immediate investigation. Within an hour, Wisdom telephoned Wingard. He said he had questioned the sergeant who had made the speech, and that the "damned fool" had admitted his stupidity.

The next few nights no lights burned in Brenda's house.

Then one night, I took my flashlight, pointed it into the windows and saw that Brenda had moved. The Bitch Wolf was on the wing again.

Upon checking with various van and storage companies, Ruggles and I learned that Brenda had moved to a pretentious house in the exclusive hill section of Hollywood. The home was located on Miller Place north of the Sunset Strip. Brenda was the neighbor of a city judge.

I reported to Sergeant Robinson and Captain Wingard, and Wingard in turn reported to Captain Wisdom. I was ordered to watch Brenda's place that evening. When she went out, I was to notify Captain Wingard, who would notify Captain Wisdom. He had arranged with Crime Laboratory Technician Ray Pinker to "bug" this new place.

The following Sunday when I saw Brenda take off, I went into action, immediately calling Captain Wingard. I was joined by Pinker and several of his technicians, who thoroughly "bugged" Brenda's new ménage. The wires were run through the rear yards of the neighbors to a listening device and recording machine located in a house on another street.

At this address, recording machines were placed in Brenda's neighbor's garage. I asked a technician if Brenda's telephone were going to be tapped. He answered that the device we had formerly employed would be used again. He told me that the device at Ruditsky's had been used until Brenda had moved, and that he saw no reason why we should not use the same method of telephone wire tapping again that we had used before Brenda had moved to this address.

None of the recordings from the bugs placed in her house on Cory Street or the house on Miller Street was presented to the Los Angeles Grand Jury. Neither were the recordings of the telephone conversations at the Miller Street address ever brought forward, nor were any other recordings with the exception of some jumbled, incoherent recorded conversations on the telephone between Jackson and Brenda prior to the time she moved to Cory Street.

Soon after Brenda became settled in the Miller Place address, she began swinging again in full blast. Once more, prostitutes were sent scurrying through Hollywood's streets en route to points of assignation. I was told to let her operate until I was given the word to make an arrest. A month later, with Brenda's girls dynamiting the town with cash-and-carry sex, Captain Wingard called me in and told me to "go ahead and knock her over." I was directed to take two officers with me, besides Ruggles. They were to antagonize Brenda as much as possible.

Captain Wingard believed that, if Brenda were made extremely angry, she could be led to believe that Sergeant Elmer V. Jackson was double-crossing her. She could then be tricked into talking about him. Wingard did not want Brenda to see me. He instructed the officers to be careful not to mention that I was in Hollywood working vice.

The two officers were not aware that the house had been "bugged" or that all of their conversation with Brenda would be heard and recorded. I took the pair to the neighborhood, placed one officer in a hidden location in front of the house, and the other at the rear.

Officer James Parslow and I watched through a bedroom window until we observed a violation taking place in the house. Then Parslow signaled to Officer Roland Harris, who was in front, and both officers crashed in simultaneously. Officer Harris found Brenda and two of the girls in the living room; and Officer Parslow crashed into the bedroom where he found a naked girl and a naked customer in bed together.

Ruggles and I had snooped around Brenda's previously until we found a small basement room which had evidently been used by the gardener of some former tenant. In this room was an extension telephone. Ruggles and I would go into the basement occasionally and eavesdrop on Brenda's telephone calls.

When Harris and Parslow made the raid, I went immediately to this small apartment. I had been there only a few minutes when I heard the telephone ring. Brenda answered, and Sergeant Jackson replied.

The first thing Brenda said was:

"For Christ's sake, the cops are here!"

"What is it? A pinch?" asked Jackson.

"Yer damned right," fumed Brenda.

"Who are the coppers?" Jackson persisted.

"I don't know," said Brenda.

"Put one of them on the wire and I'll see what I can do," Jackson advised.

There followed a short pause.

"They won't talk on the phone," Brenda told Jackson.

After another pause, Jackson told Brenda to call him as soon as she bailed out. Officers Parslow and Harris then took Brenda and her two girls to jail. During their ride, Brenda asked the men who had sent them? As he had been instructed, Parslow told her that they had come from administrative vice, Jackson's detail.

"You're a damned liar," said Brenda. "You're not from administrative vice. Why, I'll bet you're working for that bastard, Stoker. I'll get rid of Stoker if it costs me $10,000," she threatened.

Brenda and her girls were out of jail in less than two hours; and the next night they were in business as usual. One thing about Brenda, she wasn't easily discouraged. But the huge revenue she was deriving from the sale of feminine charms was a terrific inducement to stay in business.

Under orders of Captain Wingard, Ruggles and I continued to watch Brenda's place. During our surveillance, we repeatedly went to the basement hideaway and listened to Brenda's business transactions. During a conversation, one of us made a noise which she heard, and we had only a moment in which to avoid discovery.

Brenda was entering the basement as I concealed myself in a small stall shower. Ruggles dived into a closet filled with empty wire clothes' hangers. He sounded like sleigh-bells at Christmas time, and was unable to conceal all of the six feet four inches of himself. I always thought that he was too big a man to be chasing whores.

No sooner had Brenda entered than I heard her exclaim:

"Your big ass is sticking out! Come out of there."

I emerged from my hiding place, and Brenda demanded:

"What in hell are you doing here?"

I told her that I had just been transferred to Hollywood vice.

"I thought I had you transferred *out of vice*," she countered. "What are you doing back?"

"Did you get me transferred that time?" I asked innocently.

"Certainly I got you transferred," she hotly replied. "I told you I would the day I caught you snooping around the inquest over that dead bandit who tried to hold up Jackson and me."

"Why don't you quit reading detective stories," she snapped. "Some times I think you're the most dim-witted louse I've ever met. But what are you doing here?"

"Browsing," I told her. "I read about your arrest and since this is my district, I thought it advisable to come out and look around."

"Come on upstairs," Brenda said in a voice which couldn't be called sweet, but was probably as saccharine as it ever got. "I want to talk to you."

Seated in the living room, she wanted to know why if I had been working Hollywood vice, I hadn't known of her arrest. "Hollywood officers made the arrest, didn't they?" she demanded.

We wanted to sow seeds of doubt in Brenda's mind. I told her that the officers who had arrested her weren't from Hollywood vice, but had come from administrative vice, instead.

"They weren't working for me; they were working for Sergeant Jackson," I blandly informed her. "Seeing that he was forced to arrest you, Jackson probably didn't want you to suspect that he'd played a part in the pinch." I told her I had heard that Jackson had purposely called her during the raid, to divert suspicion from himself.

"You know, I did get a telephone call from Jackson during that pinch and it did SEEM KIND OF PHONY," Brenda mused. "It could have been a little more than coincidental."

"Well, that's why it happened," I told her.

"I don't know," she continued doubtfully. "That's hard to believe. I don't see why he would do a thing like that." The Madame paused, then quickly changing the subject, asked: "What are *you* doing *here* in Hollywood?"

I told her that I had been loaned to Hollywood and that I was trying to help clean up the district. Brenda then made a significant statement in the presence of young and untutored Officer Ruggles.

"There's no use in your giving me a bad time out here, Stoker. You know, I never go to jail. Arrest just means driving down and paying a fine. Why make it hard on yourself? I'll tell you what we can do so that we'll both be in the clear and everyone will be happy.

"Why don't you call me once a month — I'll arrange to get some girl I don't like and some customer I don't give a damn about and then you can come out and make a pinch. I'll go down and pay the fine, and *everyone* will be happy. You'll be doing your job and we'll all be getting along. A little pinch once a month won't hurt me. *I've got the right connections.*"

I told Brenda that her suggestion sounded like a good idea. I wanted to string her along for purposes which should be obvious. Everyone would "be happy" and I wouldn't be sticking my neck out. Then I asked her if she could fix it up with Jackson.

"*Sure*," she said without hesitation. "*Jack will go for that. You don't have to worry about him.*"

"That will be okay," I assented.' "I'm about to make sergeant and I don't want anything to happen to me." I told Brenda that I had learned my lesson the last time when she had me transferred and that I realized there were bigger and more powerful people in the police department than relatively unimportant Charlie Stoker.

"That's fine," she laughed with a ring of satisfaction. "You should have learned your lesson a long time ago. Sometimes a copper has to almost have his brains beaten in before he tumbles things up. You listen to me and I won't give you a wrong steer. Hell, come by some night, you and Ruggles. We'll go down and I'll treat you to a dinner. We can be *friends*."

"We'll do it," I agreed as we left.

Ruggles and I went directly to the garage on Miller Drive and found Police Technician Ray Pinker making his recording. Pinker laughed about our getting caught, and said he had heard everything. He asked if we wanted to hear the recordings. He then played back all the conversation Ruggles and I had had with Brenda after she caught us in the basement.

A few days later, Captain Wingard called Ruggles and me into his office. He said he had heard that Brenda had rented a new place, an exclusive home that originally had been built for a well-known millionaire. It was in the Hollywood hills, not far from her Miller Place address.

Captain Wingard was getting tired of taking orders from Captain Wisdom. He felt that Wisdom had let too many different officers in on the investigation and that, in all probability, Jackson and Wellpott were aware of our activities. He told me to watch the new place with the full intention of making an arrest as soon as possible.

Furthermore, he said that if the next arrest didn't succeed in booting Brenda out of Hollywood, we should arrest her on every possible occasion.

"I want you to arrest and harass her until she gets out of Hollywood," Captain Wingard said hotly. "I don't want her in this division."

That same evening, I was instructed to meet Technician Ray Pinker at the new address, and to "bug" the house, just as we had "bugged" the house on Miller Place.

Brenda was in the process of moving in when we arrived. Pinker found that we would be unable to "bug" the place inasmuch as the house was built on the side of a hill and had a concrete floor; and wires running from it would necessarily have to be exposed.

Shortly after Brenda started operations in her new home, Captain Wingard called me into conference. He advised me that Captain Wisdom had decided to make an investigation of his own and had informed only Ray Pinker and several of his best investigators of his plan.

Not even Chief of Police Horrall or his chief aide, Sergeant Guy Rudolph, were to know about Wisdom's investigation since there was too much danger of its being disclosed. Wisdom had gone to great trouble and expense in arranging with the telephone company to tap all telephones leading into administrative vice headquarters, including even the pay booths in the hallways. I was told to take Ruggles with me and report to Ray Pinker at the crime laboratory, to assist the men from personnel in identifying the voices of Wellpott and Jackson.

We reported to Pinker, who secretively escorted us to a small room located in the attic of Central police station. There, an elaborate setup of wire recorders met our eyes. We were left with instructions to help in identifying voices; but we soon learned that our services weren't needed inasmuch as the men monitoring the calls had learned the identities of the various voices coming over the wires. Later, we were told that we wouldn't be needed. We were warned to forget what we had heard and seen.

We reported back to Hollywood division. Captain Wingard told us to stay away from Brenda's place until Captain Wisdom was ready to have us make an arrest. We were directed to go ahead and work vice throughout Hollywood, which we did.

Sergeant Robinson called me in. He said that he was particularly interested in having me concentrate my efforts on a large hotel, located near the downtown district. He told me that the owner of this hotel had at one time been a suspect in the Black Dahlia murder. It will be recalled that the victim in this case had been twenty-two year old Elizabeth Short, whose body was dissected and scattered onto a vacant lot at Thirty-Ninth Street and Norton Avenue by a sadistic sex fiend.

According to Robinson, the murdered girl had lived in the hotel for a few weeks. He said he had information that the hotel owner and others ran advertisements in newspapers in small southern cities offering girls employment as models in Hollywood.

Girls answering these advertisements, Robinson said, were ordered to report to the hotel in Hollywood, where efforts were made to induce them to enter a life of prostitution. It was a known fact that many prostitutes lived at the hotel. We discussed ways and means of furthering the investigation. I suggested that we borrow a policewoman who had worked with me on a previous case. This policewoman could register at the hotel, give the impression that she was a prostitute and glean much valuable information. With the knowledge thus gained, we could make a number of arrests, and possibly arrest the owner and abate the hotel under the red light abatement act.

Sergeant Robinson asked that this policewoman be assigned to Hollywood division, but was refused. Robinson then went to Captain Wingard, who made a formal request for the policewoman's transfer. This, Wingard did and I was informed that the policewoman would be transferred a few days later. In the meantime, however, Captain Wingard called and told me that the deal was off. The policewoman in question had not successfully passed her six months' probationary period, he explained; and he added that she was to be discharged from the department.

This news amazed me, as I had been given to understand that she was doing well with her police work. One of her superiors had told me that she was a very good policewoman, who undoubtedly would receive her permanent appointment at the end of her probationary period. The next day, I talked to her. To her surprise and to the amazement of all the officers who had been working with her, she had suddenly been terminated, although her superiors had given her every reason to believe that she had been doing excellent work.

Captain Wingard told me that I was to meet and instruct another policewoman who had been assigned in her stead. The policewoman in question was to refrain from going to Hollywood station, Wingard explained, as he wanted none of the officers there to be aware of her activities. She was to be known only to Robinson, Ruggles and myself. This was in April, 1948.

ANOTHER FEMME FATALE

Looking backward and considering that I was working a prostitute detail in a city of 2,000,000, I'm not at all surprised at the types of people I met — types including prostitutes, madames, coppers, fixers, underworld hangers-on and you name them.

Yet, from a purely personal point of view, only a few of these characters really made an impact on my life and mind. Among the more significant, of course, were Brenda Allen, and Sergeant Elmer V. Jackson who, although a fellow officer, appeared to my mind in the guise of a shadow, a ghost, a player who never personally strode onto my stage, but whose activities as an ally, a pimp, or a business partner of Brenda Allen, or collector of underworld revenue from her — whatever designation you care to give him — made him a very important person, indeed.

To believe that I hated Jackson, is wrong. I didn't. You have to know someone to hate him. I didn't know Jackson. True, I did not approve of what he was doing, nor would I have approved of his activities if some other officer had been in the role instead of Jackson.

Strangely enough, as I have told you, I did not want to be the chief protagonist in this drama of vice, which was to involve the police department, the sheriff's office, and the district attorney's office, and upon several occasions I had tried to transfer out of vice. This is a matter of record. Vice work was repellent to me. I wanted to work on another detail remote from vice, but my superiors prevented me from so doing. They wanted me to work vice. I took their orders and obeyed them. Insofar as I was concerned, Brenda's girls could conduct nightly Saturnalias in Hollywood; Jackson could share in her profits and give her aid and comfort within the police department; and the Big Brass could countenance it if they so desired, that is, just as long as it officially was no concern of mine; just as long as my assignment in police investigation did not involve vice. Not that I approved of laxity. Far from it. But there are times when the effluvia get up around a man's neck and he reaches a saturation point. I felt as if I were fighting a feather bed and frequently I would ask myself the question —"For what? Is this what I joined the police department for? To spend my days and nights in the entrapment and arrest of prostitutes?"

But Fate, I guess, plays a part in every man's life. Whether I liked it or not, irrespective of my personal feelings, I was to meet these people and become entangled in the intricate and vicious webs they spun.

Many years ago, I had promised myself that, where honesty and reputation are at stake, I would never back up — come what may. If I had failed to keep that promise to myself, you wouldn't be reading this story of my experiences with vice.

But to return to the people who played fateful and important roles in my life: Hollywood Vice needed a policewoman, and the one whom I had recommended, and for whom Sergeant Robinson had asked, had been suddenly terminated during her probationary period and had been discharged.

Captain Wingard told me that we were to get another in her place.

And by that turn of Fate, friends, it was decreed that Charlie Stoker was to throw craps once again.

The policewoman who was to assist me, proved to be Audre Davis, whose father, Homer Cross, had been a deputy chief of police under regimes which had written many ugly pages of Los Angeles' underworld history.

Homer Cross, I was to learn later, was engaged in the legal gambling business in Las Vegas, Nevada, where he evidently journeyed to join Guy McAfee, one-time police officer and boss of Los Angeles' city and county gambling prior to the advent of Mayor Fletcher Bowron, the man who, by his own admission, claims to have abolished rackets and gangsters in the City of the Angels.

Audre Davis, assigned to work with me in routine police fashion on vice, jeopardized my liberty by false allegations. She joined the conspirators in the police department who were seeking my destruction. She was to become a newspapermen's "project" with her construction of my asserted love for her and her love for me.

My "love" for Audre, and her "love" for me was an industry manufactured out of whole cloth. She had to have an ostensible reason for "turning" on me and what better reason could she have than unrequited love? Yes, Charlie Stoker was depicted as the wrecker of a poor innocent woman's heart, but while this phase of the story was being prominently displayed in the newspapers, they, at the same time, played down the fact that three husbands had had a crack at it before I arrived on the scene.

It was, of course, a good story and Audre and the newspapers made the most of it. Much was written about our "affair" and if you want to accept the word of Audre – she was in "love" with me. When I first heard that one, and then saw it in print, I couldn't believe my ears or eyes.

Before writing about Audre, I did a great deal of soul searching and reflecting. Should I ignore Audre and all her works, part of which were designed to send me to San Quentin prison on a "bum beef," or shouldn't I?

I concluded that I couldn't ignore Audre for she is an integral part of this story. If the facts I am about to write anent Audre, are hard on her, remember she projected herself willingly and intentionally into the act. I reasoned that if I failed to mention Audre in this narrative, the reader would have a legitimate right to inquire: "What about little Audre? Come on now, Stoker. What about her? Was she the *woman scorned*? Confess now, Stoker. Weren't you a gay blade, a Don Juan, a handsome cur who played fast and loose with the hearts of many women, including little Audre? Didn't you break her heart, causing her to retaliate in the only manner that she could? Come on now, Stoker. What about Audre?

Love is a word that takes a great beating and it is a word capable of many interpretations. So, no matter how I analyze it, no matter what my personal desires in the matter may be, whether or not I would like to be gallant, I can't shroud Miss Davis and her "love" for me with anonymity and silence. Accordingly, this part of the book is strictly for the birds, but everything I shall relate is dead on the level.

Anyone with an eye for the facts is aware that whenever a man tangles with a woman in any sort of trouble, he is, as the bookmakers say, eight to one against on the morning line. Men have more female trouble than women.

If, judging from newspaper accounts you may have read heretofore, you have sympathized with Audre and her plight, and with the treatment she allegedly received at my hands, let me explain that Audre, although only twenty-six years of age, had been married three times when I first met her. When she joined the police department, she reported only two of these marriages. Seemingly it worried her that she had failed to tell the police department about the third marriage. She talked to me about it. Audre's current marriage is her fourth, her husband being Police Officer Marvin Stewart.

So, if the romantics, the propagandists and the connivers would have it that I broke her heart, is it unfair to point out now that three other good men and true probably abraded it first? If I broke her heart, it doesn't speak very well for her first three husbands, particularly when you consider that I wasn't one of her husbands, or even her lover.

The legal theory is that when you are charged with a crime, you are innocent until proven guilty. However, if you are a man engaged in mortal, amorous, or any other kind of combat with a woman, the reverse is true. You are guilty until you have proven yourself innocent. I suppose thousands of persons will never be convinced that I was entirely "clean" in the "affair" Audre. So be it. I would be a greater optimist than I am if I expected full understanding.

I am aware that when I launch into this phase of the story, I am going to brand myself as ungallant, perhaps as a cad. I see no way out of that, either. But after much cogitation, I ask: Why shouldn't I be ungallant towards Audre? She had a motive, that's for sure. As to that, I can only surmise but I have an opinion as to just what her motive was. I can only tell you that it was not unrequited love for me.

I say this, and I say it with a bitterness well watered down, that Audre was a vicious little vixen and that what she attempted to do to me was indefensible. I never made a pass at her, and she knows it; nor did I give her any indication that I thought of her as anything other than a friend and working partner. As you read my story, after you have assayed the facts set forth herein, and have finished surveying them as a comprehensive whole, I want you to judge whether or not I am lying or telling the truth. I am willing to rest on that judgment after you've made it.

For my friendship and consideration of her — which included "cooling off" a minor executive of a large transportation corporation who was in love with her and who "blew his top" when he found that she had been unfaithful to him — Audre Davis repaid me in reverse. She was a very cute kid with a penchant for burying a knife in the back of anyone on the basis of self-serving expediency.

I saw Audre Davis for the first time when Officer Jack Ruggles and I were sent to meet her on her beat near the Biltmore Hotel at Fifth and Olive Streets in downtown Los Angeles. I told her that she was to report to Sergeant Robinson the next day, and that she would be assigned a case. That was the last I saw of Miss Davis for a week. In the interim, however, Sergeant Robinson informed me that Audre had registered at a Hollywood hotel where she was posing as a prostitute in search of a "connection." She was giving the impression that she was a recent arrival from Las Vegas, Nevada, and that her virtue was on the block for interested males.

A few nights later, Sergeant Robinson called me. Policewoman Davis had been approached by a man, whom she had every reason to believe was a procurer. This man had made a date to take Audre out that night. Sergeant Robinson told me that he wanted Ruggles and me to "tail" them both very closely to see that she wasn't harmed. Robinson said that she would report to us as soon as her "date" was over. We followed instructions.

Afterwards Audre told us that she believed the man would furnish information that would further our investigation. I didn't hear of Audre again until the evening of May 2, 1948, when she telephoned me at my apartment. I was then living in Hollywood with an officer who had worked with me in the detective bureau.

Audre said that she had called the office and had tried to contact Sergeant Robinson, but that he wasn't in. The officer on duty had given her my home telephone number. She then related how she had received a telephone call from an unknown woman, who had given the name Brenda Allen. The woman had explained that she understood that Miss Davis was a recent arrival in Hollywood and was looking for a job and that if this were so, she had a proposition to offer her.

If Audre were interested, she should take a taxi-cab to an address on Harold Way. Miss Davis then asked me if I had ever heard of a Brenda Allen. Reluctantly, I told her that I had.

I had never heard of Audre Davis prior to the time when Captain Wingard informed me that she would be assigned to Hollywood division to help Robinson and me in vice work. But during the two weeks in which she said she had been assigned to Hollywood, officers with whom she had previously been working and who were friends of mine, began to tell me about her.

Several of the officers warned me not to trust her too far. One man told me that Audre's father had been the protégé of Charlie Crawford, Los Angeles underworld boss of the 1920's, who was shot and killed by Deputy District Attorney David Clark on May 21, 1931, in Crawford's real estate office in the 6600 block on Sunset Boulevard. Herbert F. Spencer, former city editor of the defunct Los Angeles Evening Express, was shot and killed by Clark at the same time as the result of an underworld row involving Guy McAfee.

It was Crawford who had imported Albert Marco into Los Angeles from Seattle, Washington, to operate some sixty-five bordellos under police protection. Marco, during a drunken fight in the Ship Cafe at Venice, a bootlegging joint, had shot and critically wounded a citizen, one Dominic Conterno, for which crime he had been sent to San Quentin penitentiary, and subsequently had been deported to Italy.

This pair, Crawford and Marco, along with Gambler Guy McAfee, had ruled the Los Angeles underworld. My police friends informed me that, as a result of their power, Audre's father had rapidly gained a position of importance in the police department. I was further given to understand that he had gambling interests in Las Vegas, Nevada, where he was residing at that time, and that he still had many connections in the Los Angeles police department.

Qualifications for policewoman were very strict, yet Miss Davis had been appointed although she lacked several of the necessary requisites. Consequently, I thought it best to talk to Captain Wingard before we proceeded with the investigation of Brenda Allen. I told Audre that I would like to have her contact Brenda, but that she must have Wingard's okay. I said nothing to her regarding the Allen investigation then in progress. I thought it coincidental that Brenda had called Miss Davis.

Sergeant Robinson approved our plan to have Miss Davis make the contact with Brenda, but Captain Wingard was reluctant, principally in the fear that she might be harmed.

Wingard's fears were dissipated, however, when it was arranged that I would precede Miss Davis to Brenda's lair and would hide in the bushes surrounding a large estate directly across the street. Should Miss Davis become involved in any trouble, she would have only to raise her voice and I would go to her assistance, regardless of the investigation. Captain Wingard agreed.

Miss Davis took a taxi-cab. I preceded her, concealed myself and watched. I saw Audre meet Brenda in the front yard. They then went into the house. Audre remained there for about half an hour, during which time a man arrived. He stayed inside for a few minutes. Miss Davis then left by taxi-cab and I followed her in my police car to Sunset Boulevard, where I picked her up and drove her back to the vicinity of the hotel at which she was stopping.

In relating their conversation, Audre said that Brenda had suggested that she go to work for her. "You'll be a thirty-dollar girl," Brenda had assured Audre. Brenda explained that her girls worked from one o'clock in the afternoon until about three or four o'clock in the morning; that they were given their evening meals which she prepared herself and that the average girl's earnings were one hundred dollars or more a night, of which amount she, Brenda, received half and the girl half. Furthermore,

Brenda said, she didn't care what her girls did when they were away from the place, but while they were there, she expected them to conduct themselves as "ladies." When Miss Davis asked about the possibilities of arrest, Brenda assured her that she had police protection.

"There's always the possibility of an arrest," Miss Davis quoted Brenda as saying, "but there are only two vice squads around Hollywood. You don't have to worry about them because they are fixed. I haven't much to fear from Hollywood divisional vice officers because, with the exception of one man – a bastard by the name of "Stoker"– they aren't smart enough to make an arrest. He's strictly out to make a name for himself and you can expect the worst of it from him."

It was nice and comforting to know that while Brenda didn't love me, she did respect me.

Brenda boasted to Audre that she had been arrested eighteen times in Los Angeles and had never served a day in jail. While Audre was talking to Brenda, a customer came in and Brenda asked Audre to "take" him, but Audre escaped this dilemma by explaining that she was menstruating and couldn't. Audre left with the understanding that Brenda would make an appointment with the doctor for a required medical examination, after which she would call and tell her when to report for work. That was the extent of the conversation as reported back by Miss Davis.

I reported to Sergeant Robinson and Captain Wingard what Audre had told me. Things bounced along without any action for a few days; then Captain Wingard called me in. He couldn't understand why Captain Cecil Wisdom, the personnel chieftain, who was going to knock Brenda out of the box, hadn't taken any action.

Wingard said that, regardless of Wisdom or anyone else, as long as he was commander of Hollywood division, no prostitute was going to operate in the area if he knew it. He told me to go ahead and knock Brenda's joint over.

Brenda then telephoned Audre, who explained that she had been unable to make an appointment with her physician. She said, however, that if she got rid of a girl who was expected to leave that night, Miss

Davis could come and start work around eight p.m. She arranged to telephone Audre at about that time.

Miss Davis reported this to Sergeant Robinson and to me. For her protection, I took great pains to get a policeman into Brenda's as a customer at a time to coincide with Audre's arrival. It so happened that an acquaintance of mine was available. He was a very fine officer and had been a ship's master in the merchant marine. He still carried his master's license.

As a result of having previously listened on the basement extension telephone at the Miller Street address, I knew the identity of a good customer of Brenda's, who was employed in the studios. I also knew that the man was out of the city at the moment.

At about seven p.m., on the evening that Audre was to begin work in Brenda's brothel, I had my officer friend telephone Brenda. He gave her a line, explaining that he was a master in the merchant marine and that he was being employed as technical advisor on a sea picture that was being filmed at the studio. He told Brenda that she had been recommended by the movie man who was her customer, and that the man had given him her telephone number. He added that Brenda could call the man if she desired, but that he had sufficient papers with which to identify himself if she would take a chance.

Brenda said that she would be satisfied if he had the papers, and could identify himself. She asked if he knew her address. When he said that he didn't, she told him to drive to the Sunset Strip and, as soon as he reached there, to telephone her for further directions. She asked him when she should expect him; and he told her he would call at about eight p.m.

Audre was waiting for Brenda's telephone call, notifying her to come to work; and Sergeant Robinson and I were awaiting developments in Hollywood vice headquarters. Two other officers were with us.

When the officer reached the Sunset Strip, he telephoned Brenda. The switchboard operator at the exchange told him that she was not at home.

Shortly before eight p.m., Audre called. She had received no telephone call from Brenda. At eight o'clock, the officer again called Brenda. He was told that Brenda was not at home.

We waited until eight sharp. Each time the officer telephoned Brenda, the operator would ask his name and he would give it. I concluded that someone downtown had gotten wind of our plans and had tipped Brenda off, or had tipped off administrative vice, where her pal, Sergeant Jackson, held forth.

Ruggles, the two other officers and I drove to the vicinity of Brenda's place, parked our cars and went through the bushes into the yard of Brenda's Harold Way home. There, we could easily distinguish Brenda's voice and voices of the girls inside.

They seemed to be in a great hurry. We heard one of the girls ask where her shoes were. Brenda replied: "You'd better wear a pair of mine. We've got to leave before that stool pigeon gets here and all of our fannies land in jail!"

Beyond the shadow of a doubt, Brenda had been tipped off. I was aware that *only one man* downtown knew that the borrowed officer was working Hollywood vice that night. Later, after I had effected the arrests at the Harold Way spot, I talked to one of the girls present on this occasion, and she substantiated my suspicion. The Central Division police sergeant, whom I suspected, had telephoned Brenda and tipped her off to the fact that I had borrowed the man from him. No doubt, he had put two and two together and had figured that I was borrowing the officer to aid in knocking over Brenda's spot.

This should convince the reader that some of these officers are nice kids, who are deserving of all the trust and confidence one can place in them. The taxpayers pay them while they tip off prostitutes and various and sundry criminals who are about to be arrested by fellow officers.

Captain Wingard was angry and upset at our failure. Weary of the run-around he had been getting from Captain Wisdom, he ordered me to arrest Brenda without further delay, and to get her out of Hollywood if I had to use the entire vice squad to accomplish the trick. To hell with secrecy!

To insure more than a small fine, I took a gang of newspaper reporters with me when I made the arrests.

Brenda who could talk a blue streak, didn't do herself any good on this — the occasion of her nineteenth arrest. In front of the reporters she warned that she'd get my job (and she did), she called me a peanut in a big barrel and said that I was tampering with something a lot bigger than myself.

The reporters duly noted Brenda's warning, and recorded her boast that she'd been arrested many times, but had never done a day in jail.

The Great Whore of Hollywood, Brenda wasn't a smart one. Smart criminals and racketeers may have certain police officers assisting them in their illegalities just as Sergeant Elmer V. Jackson assisted Brenda, but if they have any sense, they don't tell police officers they'll get them fired.

Truly, I had become Brenda's Nemesis. Because I had prevented her from accumulating a huge fortune from her flesh-peddling activities in the Hollywood film capital; because she couldn't stop me no matter how she tried, and because I had given her a sense of frustration, Brenda's red hair sizzled and she went into a towering rage. Brenda now saw in me a determined law enforcement enemy who wouldn't quit. Her estimate was correct. But Brenda was a fighter whatever else might be said about her.

Captain Wingard had ordered me to drive Brenda out of Hollywood, and in a manner that would convince her that she couldn't operate in the district as long as he commanded the division. I intended to follow orders to the letter.

"I'll get you, Stoker, if it's the last thing I ever do," she screamed in her best fish-wife, or whore, manner. "You son-of-a-bitch, you think you're so damned smart, don't you? I'll show you. Wait until administrative vice hears about this!"

So great was the Madame's fury that she cast all discretion to the winds.

I laughed in her face and said: "Throw a glass of water over yourself, and shut up. I kept laughing at her and this shot her temperature up ten degrees and really caused her to blow her top. I've heard dock workers, soldiers and all kinds of men use profanity and obscenities in my time, but you should have heard Brenda. She threw all the dirty little four letters at me along with the profane ones and she tossed several that I hadn't heard. In filth and profanity, Brenda added to my knowledge that night.

But Brenda hadn't seen anything yet. Brenda, whose prostitute and scarlet managerial activities in Los Angeles and Hollywood, had never cost her a single day in jail, was destined to spend quite a few days in that Monastery of Despair known as the county jail atop the Hall of Justice in downtown Los Angeles. I felt pretty good about that — but my pleasure was short-lived. As a result of my tangling with the red-headed buzzsaw, I was to receipt for a number of headaches and to get kicked off the Los Angeles police department.

In ancient times, the community would procure a goat, saddle him symbolically with the inhabitants' sins and drive him off into the wilderness. This strange procedure was supposed to purge the people of their sins. Hence the Biblical term — scapegoat.

We Americans have another term synonymous with scapegoat — fall guy. That phrase describes me. As a reward for enforcing the law, taking dead aim on evil-doers, and working to the best of my ability, I was to get it "in the neck." The technicality on which I was discharged was "conduct unbecoming an officer." This because, when I had good reason to believe that I would be framed, I had the temerity to go before the Los Angeles county grand jury.

Now the grand jury is composed of a group of respectable citizens chosen by the Los Angeles county Superior court bench. The purpose of a grand jury upon its impanelment each year is to investigate the conduct of public officials and their administration of the people's affairs for the purpose of seeing that everything is in order. Theoretically if a man, any man, appears before the county grand jury and produces valid evidence of evil in a community, he is doing something commendatory because he is acting in the public interest.

But, and remember this, when a police officer appears before the county grand jury to give the jurors evidence of police protection of vice, gambling and rackets, he has committed a heinous offense in the eyes of the district attorney's office, in the eyes of the police executives of the Los Angeles police department and in the eyes of the Mayor of Los Angeles.

Now do not think for a moment that any of these individuals will admit the accuracy and truth of that pronouncement. They won't. They'll give lip service to "Good, Honest and Efficient Government," truth, justice and law enforcement, but watch them in action.

Forget their slobbering drivel and the pious looks they wear on their faces and just watch them in action.

I speak from experience. Despite any adulation my readers may have for District Attorney William E. Simpson and Mayor Fletcher E. Bowron, they may be assured of one fact, that a dead rotten law enforcement setup rules in this county and city with an iron hand.

FINALE FOR BRENDA

Throughout this narrative, I have attempted to show the culpability of Sergeant Elmer V. Jackson and, indirectly, of his superior, Lieutenant Rudy Wellpott, in the affair Brenda, as well as the complete smothering of the extensive investigation made of Jackson by higher police executives. When a police officer is in the fix in which Jackson found himself, while under investigation by the big departmental brass, he invariably resorts to one or two techniques to escape the onus of his acts. He either says that the underworld is "attempting to frame him," or he explains his association with underworld personages on the premise that he "was trying to get information which would lead to magnificent arrests of prime underworld characters." Those are the "outs" for a corrupt police officer.

It has been my intention and purpose to give the reader such a mass of detail and circumstance, together with names, dates and places, that he can judge for himself who were the real culprits in the late police scandal. I am writing in the knowledge that a man can tell one lie and get away with it; but that he cannot tell a thousand lies and detail and buttress those lies unless he is a genius, which I distinctly am not.

But let us return to the thread of the story. Shortly after Brenda's arrest, I talked to Captain Wingard and Sergeant Robinson. We discussed what we had obtained thus far in the way of evidence against her. Through the contact which Miss Davis had made with Brenda, we decided that we had sufficient evidence to obtain an attempted pandering complaint from the district attorney's office.

Providing that we could secure this complaint, we would have two arrests — the one I had made and an arrest to be based on the attempted pandering charge.

To secure a felony complaint, I went to the district attorney's office and was assigned a deputy. I gave him the evidence exactly as I have related it here.

I told what had occurred when Audre first contacted Brenda. I described their meeting, and related Brenda's attempt to persuade Audre to work for her as a prostitute. I informed the deputy that a prospective customer had attempted to prevail upon Audre to submit to him sexually when she first visited Brenda's house. I saw the deputy district attorney on a Friday. He seemed to be impressed, but, nevertheless he told me to come back the following Monday.

I considered this extremely odd, inasmuch as I had been to the district attorney's office many times before with all types of complaints, and I had never been told to return. Usually, the deputies listened to what evidence I had to offer and immediately wrote the complaints. The customary procedure was to wait until the complaint had been typed and signed, and the warrant of arrest obtained. However, on this occasion, I was told to return the following Monday.

On Monday, I appeared as scheduled. To my amazement, the deputy district attorney informed me that we had insufficient evidence on which to warrant the issuance of a complaint. I asked him to explain exactly what I lacked in the way of necessary evidence and I added that I had perhaps neglected to state something that would be pertinent to the case. Oddly enough, he refused to discuss the matter at greater length, and virtually threw me out of his office in his haste to end the discussion abruptly. He dismissed me, saying that he was very busy, and repeating, that I hadn't sufficient evidence to justify a complaint. That was all. I left.

Later, I talked the case over with several police officers who had handled similar cases. All of us felt that we had sufficient evidence, and the following day, probably with more determination than good sense, I returned to the district attorney's office and asked to see another deputy. I did not state my reason for wanting to see him. I explained the case to the second deputy, taking care not to mention that I had already talked to another deputy or that I had been refused a complaint on the same evidence.

After I had finished, the deputy told me that the evidence constituted one of the best cases of attempted pandering he had ever heard. He was more than willing to issue the complaint. He left the office to secure the necessary papers.

Within a few minutes he returned. "Weren't you here last Friday?" he asked.

"Yes," I replied.

"You were refused a complaint, weren't you?"

"That is correct."

"Well, Stoker, to tell you the truth, I can't go over anyone's head. You were refused Friday. There's nothing I can do about it. That's final."

I think by this time that you will have judged that when Brenda said that she had plenty going for her; that she had the "connections," she wasn't just talking to hear her head rattle. Here we have a Madame directing the activities of one hundred odd whores in Hollywood, and police officers who have the deadwood on her, yet the district attorney's office refuses to issue a complaint against her. Keep this in mind. It may have a further bearing on what I will relate.

So I left again, realizing that the district attorney's office, despite the fiery pronouncements issued from time to time by the D. A., and his aides, was a joke—hot air—and nothing more. I concluded that, in some manner, the district attorney's office was an important spoke in the wheel of vice and corruption. What else could I conclude?

Believing that malefactors cannot escape the penalties of the law — if law enforcement agents are properly assiduous and are willing to exhaust all avenues, I then went to the newspapers. I explained what had happened to a close friend of mine on The Los Angeles Daily News. He told me to go to the Press Room at the City Hall and tell the press reporters exactly what I had told him. I did. The press reporters put their heads together. In the company of a reporter, I went back to the district attorney's office. We were admitted to the office of the deputy whom I had first seen. The newspaper reporter virtually sat in my lap. Again, I demanded to know why I couldn't obtain a complaint. Needless to say, *I made no friends and I gained little popularity in the district attorney's office*. I was told to return the following day with Audre Davis.

The next day, Audre and I saw Chief Deputy District Attorney Ernest Roll. Miss Davis related to Roll exactly what she had told me and others; and a transcript was made of her conversation with Mr. Roll. At Brenda's trial, some months later, Audre testified verbatim to this transcript. (Remember this).

Although the district attorney's office was reluctant, having shown every indication of a desire to protect Prostitute Boss Brenda, I then received what proved to be a satisfactory complaint, inasmuch as Brenda was convicted on it and her conviction was upheld by the courts and the Supreme Court of California.

As was stated in the forepart of this book, the law is a theory forming the basis for an action. If there is no action, the law remains a jumble of words on the statute books. Yet, it must be recorded that, throughout the Brenda Allen case, the D. A.'s office favored inaction. Remember this particularly when you think of District Attorney William E. Simpson and when the question of the integrity of his office arises in your mind.

After Brenda's arrest, she returned to her Harold Way address for a short period. During the time she had been in jail and pending issuance of her bail bond, officers from Hollywood vice division had tapped her telephone line. At frequent intervals, Ruggles and I listened over the tapped wire. Now that the arrest had been made, it was no secret where Brenda was living. Ruggles, another officer and I were listening over the line one night. The other officer was unaware that an investigation was being made concerning Jackson and Wellpott. We believed that the police action against Brenda merely involved another Hollywood prostitute.

I watched the officer's face as he listened, and saw an expression of amazement creep over his countenance when he heard Brenda call administrative vice headquarters. This officer was even more dumbfounded when he heard Brenda tell Jackson: "I'm going to have Stoker killed."

"That would be foolish," was Jackson's reply. "Just wait. Wellpott and I will take care of Stoker in our own way."

"Well, you'd better take care of him," Brenda warned. *"If you don't, I will and I don't care what the cost will be."*

Project this, if you can, against a backdrop of the sonorous intonations of Mayor Fletcher Bowron, the exponent of "Good, Honest and Efficient Government, and the Best Police Department in the World."

If you have any illusions about the integrity of the Los Angeles police department at that time, let me remind you that Rudy Wellpott enjoyed the confidence of Assistant Chief of Police Joe Reed, who, in turn, enjoyed the confidence of Chief of Police Clemence B. Horrall whom Mayor Fletcher E. Bowron had described as the "best chief of police in the United States."

The links in the chain are all there for anyone to see — Brenda Allen to Sergeant Elmer V. Jackson, to Lieutenant Rudy Wellpott, to Assistant Chief of Police Joe Reed to Chief of Police Clemence B. Horrall to Mayor Fletcher E. Bowron. Who's kiddin' who?

Shortly after we had listened to the Jackson-Allen telephone conversation, Ruggles and I entered a bar, owned by a man who was suspected of handling police graft for Skid Row joints. This graft reportedly went to the administrative vice unit under Lieutenant Rudy Wellpott.

After inviting us to be seated, the owner sat down with us. Very casually he asked where I had been keeping myself.

I replied that I had been assigned to Hollywood. Then, by strange coincidence, Sergeant Elmer V. Jackson walked in — the man who, a few days before, had told Brenda Allen, mistress of the Hollywood fallen ladies, to let me live a while longer.

When Jackson saw Ruggles and me, he immediately turned on his heel and strode out. At this juncture, the bar owner turned to me.

"You know, there goes a very fine fellow," he said.

"Is that right?" I queried.

"None better." Then he added: "There's nothing between Jackson and you, is there?"

"No. Not that I know of. Why?"

"Well, I thought maybe there was," he mused. "You didn't look too friendly at each other."

"Well, there's nothing between us as far as I know," I said. "I scarcely know Jackson. He never did anything to me that I knew about," I concluded dissimulatingly.

Ruggles and I then got up and walked out. We had a hunch. We raced to Central police station and made our way to the little room which we had been told to avoid – the listening post set up by Captain Cecil Wisdom, head of the personnel division encharged with investigating police officers. Happily, we noted that the gadget was still in operation. We made ourselves at home much to the chagrin of the man operating the equipment.

A few minutes passed. Then administrative vice received a telephone call; and we heard the following conversation between the bar owner, whose place we had just left, and Lieutenant Rudy Wellpott, Jackson's superior.

"Hello Rudy," the bar owner began. "Is your boy, Jack, there?"

"Yeah," Wellpott replied. "He just got here."

"Did he tell you what happened?" the caller inquired.

"Yeah, that was sure something, wasn't it?" Wellpott ejaculated.

"Yeah. Let me talk to Jackson." The bar owner's request seemed urgent.

Jackson came on the line and asked: "What did you find out?"

"Oh, I was just beginning to pump him when you walked in," the man replied.

"Oh, then you didn't find out anything?"

Jackson was disappointed.

"No, I didn't, but give them enough rope and they'll hang themselves," was the rejoinder.

"Give them enough rope and they might hang us," Jackson quipped. "Never mind. We're going to hang them without any rope. We've got ways and means."

Jackson and the bar owner then agreed to meet at a place on West Sixth Street. A few days later Brenda disappeared. Captain Wingard told me that he had information that Jackson and Brenda were living together as man and wife in a small hotel in Hollywood. He said that they were registered as Mr. and Mrs. Johnson. Wingard was of the belief that Jackson was spending part of his time with another prostitute who lived in an apartment house near downtown Los Angeles.

Captain Wingard gave me both addresses but warned me to stay away from the hotel as I might be seen and recognized. He told me to tap the prostitute's telephone at the apartment house, if possible, and listen.

Captain Wisdom had informed Wingard that Jackson's wife was aware of his activities and that she was being paid as a partner. As instructed, we half-heartedly watched Jackson's house for a few days. Jackson was never around. We also watched the apartment where he was supposed to be living with the prostitute. We didn't see Jackson there, either.

One day, we decided to have a policewoman call Jackson's house and ask for him. Mrs. Jackson answered the call. The policewoman asked if Jackson were home.

Mrs. Jackson replied that he wasn't, but that she was expecting him. She asked if there was any way in which Jackson could return the call. The policewoman said that there wasn't, since she had just arrived in Los Angeles. Upon hearing this, Mrs. Jackson remarked, "Perhaps, I can help you. Don't be afraid to talk to me. I know *everything* and you can talk."

"Well, I just got into Los Angeles and I was told that Jackson could find a place for me to work," the policewoman said.

"Well, Jack isn't here now," Mrs. Jackson hesitated. "But his daughter is ill and the doctor is coming this morning so he's sure to be here."

"Well, I don't know. I've got to find a spot," the policewoman told her.

"Do you know Brenda Allen?" Mrs. Jackson rejoined.

The policewoman said that she didn't know Brenda.

"Well, I'll tell you what I can do," was the reply. "I'll give you Brenda's telephone number. You can tell her I asked you to call."

Then she gave the policewoman Brenda's number, which tallied with the number of the hotel where Brenda was reportedly living with Jackson.

As this maneuver had been successful, we decided to try it again. This time we called the prostitute with whom Jackson was supposed to live infrequently, near the downtown area.

The policewoman called her number. When a woman answered, she again asked if she could talk to Jackson. The woman replied that she didn't know anyone by that name. The policewoman then explained that she had been given the number to call. However, the woman insisted that she knew of no one named Jackson.

Ruggles and I hastened to the listening post in Central station. We had been there but a short time when Sergeant Jackson received a call at administrative vice. We heard the voice of the second woman whom the policewoman had called.

"Honey, you received a telephone call here from a woman who said she'd been given this number. She wanted to get in touch with you," the woman explained to Jackson.

"Did she leave her name?"

"No, I told her that I'd never heard of you," replied the prostitute. "Well, that's the smart thing to do," Jackson approved.

I reported this information to Captain Wingard; who, in turn, immediately reported to Captain Cecil Wisdom. Shortly thereafter, I was transferred from Hollywood vice to Central division.

No sooner had I arrived at Central than I was told that I was to be transferred into uniform. No reason was given. When the newspapers heard of my transfer, reporters immediately went to the Chief of Police. As a result, the transfer order was rescinded, and I remained in Central vice division as a sergeant.

When I left Hollywood, I was told nothing further about the investigation into Jackson's connection with Brenda, nor was I told later. I was merely warned that I was to forget it.

As far as I was concerned, no investigation of Jackson had been made.

Several months later, I was summoned to Captain Wisdom's office. An investigation was in progress regarding an incident that had occurred in the Gali-Gali cocktail bar, during my stay in Hollywood. It appeared that some arrested persons had complained of being beaten by police officers. James Parslow was accused; and one of the victims had identified me (by picture) as having also beaten him.

I remembered the incident. I gave the following statement: Officer Ruggles and I had driven into the police court yard, located between the Hollywood police station and the Hollywood emergency hospital. At that time the officers had seen a badly beaten man being carried into the receiving hospital. Officer Ruggles had remarked to me that the beaten man resembled a new officer who had been assigned to vice.

I went into the receiving hospital with Ruggles. There, we saw this man in a semi-conscious condition on the operating table. Ruggles positively identified him. We then went to the police station, where an officer told us that the beaten man was Officer Marvin Stewart (Stewart later married Policewoman Audre Davis after the police scandal generated by the arrest of Brenda Allen had blown high, wide and handsome and after Audre had resigned from the police department following her "confession" that she had perjured herself at Brenda's trial on attempted pandering and following her story that she had accompanied me on the night I was supposed to have committed a burglary.)

We learned that Stewart, along with Officers Jimmy Parslow and Roland Harris, had been making an investigation of the Gali-Gali bar on information that prostitutes were taking customers from the bar to an adjoining hotel. We were told that, while Parslow and Harris were out of the bar, a number of persons had beaten Officer Marvin Stewart.

I attempted to find Officers Parslow and Harris, but was unable to do so. I did see several men in the custody of a number of uniformed officers. I told the investigating officer that I had had absolutely nothing to do with the case other than to call Sergeant Robinson. Later,

Robinson told me that one of the persons who had been engaged in the beating of the officer was missing. I then went to look for him.

Unable to find the missing suspect, I returned to the station and reported to Robinson. I also informed the investigating officer that I had given a businessman who was interested in police activities, permission to accompany me on that particular night. Ruggles and this man had been with me at all times during my duties on the evening in question, and both were willing to give statements to that effect.

Some months later, I received a telephone call at my home. The caller identified himself as Inspector William Parker.

Parker asked if I could meet him. He had some matter he wanted to discuss. We agreed on a location for the meeting.

Then, for the first time, I met Inspector William Parker, a highly ambitious man, who is now trying with might and main to become chief of police.

Parker told me that he and two other officers had been appointed to investigate the activities of the Hollywood vice division. He said he wanted me to relate to him exactly what had happened the night of the Gali-Gali fracas. I did this to the best of my recollection. When I had finished, Parker told me that he knew for a fact that Officer Marvin Stewart, who had been badly beaten, was intoxicated on the night of the raid and that his beating had come as a result of his drunken behavior.

"You were aware that Stewart was drunk when you called Sergeant Robinson. You remarked that fact in the presence of a sergeant when you telephoned Robinson," Parker reminded me.

I told Inspector Parker that, when I had made my original report to personnel, I had made it solely in my own interest. It wasn't my desire to involve other officers, particularly when they were not working with or under me. Further, I told Parker that I wasn't positive that Stewart had been drunk; that it was only my opinion. When I first saw him being wheeled into the receiving hospital, he had been badly beaten and, for all I knew, was semi-conscious and probably rum dumb from sluggings about the head.

Parker asked me many questions about the operations of the Hollywood vice squad.

I told him exactly what I knew about Hollywood vice and its operations.

"I know that both Robinson and Wingard are crooks," he said. "After vice officers make an arrest in Hollywood, these men go to the arrested persons and offer to fix the charges if the arrested people will pay. I know that they are especially active in shaking down bars, and in trying to run certain bars out of business so that a syndicate can purchase them. I also know that Robinson is padding expense accounts and playing the proceeds on the races. I intend to see that the entire Hollywood vice squad is abolished and a new squad formed."

Parker was under the impression that I knew Parslow had beaten some of the persons in the Gali-Gali cocktail lounge. He explained that if I would assist him in abolishing the Hollywood vice squad, he would see to it that I was placed in Sergeant Robinson's position in the new squad. He stated that I could help him when I was called upon to testify by stating that I knew of Stewart's drunkenness and of Parslow's brutality.

I told Inspector Parker that, even though I would like to be in charge of Hollywood vice, I would not testify to anything about which I was not positive.

Truly, I had an extreme dislike for Captain Wingard. I felt that he was incompetent and, above all, that he wouldn't stand behind a policeman. I thought that he was only looking out for Captain Wingard, and that anyone working for him had to protect himself at all times as best he could without depending upon him for any support if the going got rough. Nor had I any reason to like Jimmy Parslow. He had been Ruggles' partner prior to my assignment to Hollywood and had tried to prevent Ruggles from becoming my partner.

However, despite my dislike for Parslow and Captain Wingard, I told Parker that I didn't believe that either of them was dishonest, nor did I distrust Robinson. The story of their dishonesty seemed fantastic and ridiculous if one studied the facts. Parker told me to think it over.

The next day I was taken before a board of officers, of which Parker was a member. At that time, I refused to testify other than as I had at the first hearing.

I continued to work with Ruggles in Central division. Although I had been on the department only six years, two of which had been spent in the Army, I had been made a permanent sergeant. I was in charge of Central vice during morning hours, where I was given the privilege of choosing and working whatever hours I thought were necessary to complete an investigation.

After a lull lasting nearly six months, I was beginning to believe that the threats that Brenda Allen, Wellpott and Jackson had made against me were merely wishful thinking. Then a prostitute, whom I had arrested many times, brought me word that she had been approached by Sergeant Jackson, the police department's eager beaver pimp and procurer. According to the woman's story, Jackson had told her that, if she would go with him to Captain Cecil Wisdom and tell him that she was paying me for protection, he and Rudy Wellpott would see that a narcotics charge against her was dismissed.

She admitted having at first agreed to play her part in this frame-up. Later, she had discussed it with her attorney, who had directed her to have nothing to do with such a scheme. She said, however, that Jackson had actually taken her to Captain Wisdom, but that once she had confronted him, she had refused to talk or to co-operate.

Perhaps, the reader can imagine my train of thought. I had broken up a police-prostitute combination that had netted hundreds, if not thousands, of dollars daily. I had cut off the revenue of several persons, some of whom were powerfully placed. As a result, I had incurred their undying animosity. I knew that Jackson and Wellpott were vicious, unscrupulous men — police officers though they were — men who would stop at nothing in the erasure of an enemy who was in their way. I also knew that both men, and Wellpott in particular, had connections high up in the police department. I had seen how abortive was any investigation into Jackson's activities with Brenda and her whore houses despite a plethora of evidence indisputably connecting Jackson with the flaming haired Madame. Nothing had happened. Failure of the police big brass to act against Jackson led to the logical deduction that his connection with Brenda had, if not their outward approval, their tacit consent.

If the big brass of the police department knew that Jackson was accepting graft from Brenda (and there was no question in my mind but that he was) the logical deduction was that others in the department beside Jackson were participating in that graft. Perhaps, that explained why, from a prosecutorial standpoint, Jackson was a "POLICE UNTOUCHABLE." There could be no other answer.

In tapped telephone conversations with Sergeant Jackson, I had heard Brenda threaten my life, and I had heard Jackson reply that he and his superior, Wellpott, would take care of me *in their own way*. Knowing the calibre of the pair and being aware of their unscrupulousness, I had no illusions whatever regarding their ability to *take care of me* and I also had the somewhat disquieting thought that neither would hesitate at murder to achieve this end.

Hence I determined to protect myself with every legitimate means at my command. It is necessary that the reader understand my state of mind at that time inasmuch as it had an important bearing on what was to follow.

Shortly after the prostitute had told me of Jackson's scheme to undermine me, I was given an assignment in the Wilshire district. This complaint came from Harry Lorenson, commander of the police commission's investigative staff. Lorenson, incidentally, was to be indicted later on a conspiracy charge growing out of an assault on Alfred Marsden Pearson by several of Mickey Cohen's henchmen.

In view of the fact that Lorenson had a bevy of investigators at his beck and call, I considered it strange that I should be assigned to investigate a bar that featured lewd entertainment. But I was in no position to refuse the assignment.

Ruggles and I went to the bar which was located in the Wilshire district. We arrested the owner and a singer for conducting a lewd show. We also arrested a bartender for violation of the alcoholic beverage control act when we saw him serve liquor to two intoxicated persons, a misdemeanor. Ruggles and I transported these five persons to Wilshire station, and there attempted to book them. We met with nothing but opposition. Several detectives and uniformed officers attempted to persuade us to release the prisoners.

They delayed the booking as long as they could by finding other duties for the booking officers. Ruggles and I were told that the owner of the bar was a friend of Jack Swan, detective captain of Wilshire — who was later to become a defendant in the conspiracy involving Lorenson, Michael Cohen and his hoodlums, Jimmy Rist, Dave Ogul and Eli Lubin.

When I at last cornered a booking officer, he found that the prisoners were in a huddle with some "well meaning" officers who were trying to get them turned loose. Finally, I had two of the prisoners booked. However, I was told by the watch commander that I could not book the remaining three prisoners as there was a regulation against the booking of four or more prisoners at that station. I knew that such a regulation did not exist. It was a fact that, only a few weeks prior to this occasion, I had booked an equal number of prisoners whom I had arrested in a gambling raid, and had met with no opposition. Becoming angry, I then loaded the remaining three prisoners into my car, drove across the city five miles, and booked them at Lincoln Heights jail.

The next day, a complaint supposedly written by the watch commander, stated that I had allowed one of the prisoners to call a bail bondsman from Wilshire station after the arrests in a violation of police regulations. What this watch commander didn't know was that I had been suspicious of the complaint from the beginning. Nor did he know that I had taken a civilian building contractor along on the investigation as a witness. This man had been with me every second since I had warned him that something fishy was afoot.

I made a check and found that the bail bondsman who had been called by the prisoners, lived in Glendale and maintained offices in that city, some twelve miles from Wilshire station. With that in mind, I demanded that a check of the telephones in the Wilshire station be made. That spiked the charge. I heard nothing further on that venomous pitch.

Several days passed. Then Arthur Vaus telephoned me at home and told me that he wanted to meet me. Vaus indicated that he had something important to discuss. We met. Vaus said that he had been employed by Mickey Cohen and a prominent Latin-American band leader to install electronics equipment in their respective homes. He explained that, while he was working for Mickey Cohen he had discovered that Cohen's home had been "bugged." He seemed confident that Jackson and Wellpott had been recording all of the conversations there. It was his belief, he said, that they intended shaking Cohen down, but he added that that wasn't why he wanted to see me.

Vaus said that he had spoken to a big motion picture executive concerning the "bugging" of various offices and departments at the studio and the possible tapping of telephones of some of the studio personnel. He said that this famous man felt that certain screen writers were selling ideas and materials to other studios, and that he wanted a complete *spying* system. Vaus suggested that I resign from the police department, obtain a private detective's license and work with him. He asked what amount I would consider as salary on a ten-year contract basis. I wasn't interested. When I suggested that he could obtain the necessary detective license, Vaus for the first time told me that he had a felony record, having served time in a Federal prison.

In a self-satisfied, boastful manner, Vaus confided that he had twice been arrested, first as a youngster charged with impersonating a police officer, and later for armed robbery. After the second offense, he had been convicted and sentenced to San Quentin prison for three years, but his father had gotten his sentence reduced to one year in the county jail.

Later, in the Army, Vaus had been put in the guardhouse for selling priorities, he said. However, he was released and given his commission as an army officer. The army had assigned him as the officer in charge of all telephone communications in the Los Angeles area. During this period, he had sold some scarce government materials and equipment.

Investigators for the telephone company, learning of the sales, had reported Vaus to Army Intelligence.

As a result, he had been given a court martial, and had been sentenced to McNeil Island Federal Penitentiary off the coast of the State of Washington, to serve a term of five years.

I asked him how he had managed to receive an honorable discharge and Vaus laughingly explained that his father had at one time wanted him to become a minister. Vaus admitted that he had received a great deal of religious training, and that once he was in prison, it wasn't hard for him to talk the chaplain into giving him a job as assistant. According to Vaus, he soon became so religious that he convinced the chaplain that he was really saved and wanted to lead a Christian life. The chaplain, assured of his sincerity, aided him in being sent to an army rehabilitation center at Leavenworth, Kansas.

At Leavenworth, Vaus actually took over the chaplain's duties. His act was so convincing, he said, that he was restored to duty in the army, was given a non-commissioned officer's rating as sergeant and was sent to other rehabilitation centers throughout the country as a shining example for erring soldiers.

After hearing Vaus's story, I wasn't interested in entering into partnership with him. From that day to this, I have never laid eyes on Arthur Vaus.

In more ways than one, Vaus was wrapped up in the mess. Later, when the vice scandal broke he attempted to ride it in all directions; but inasmuch as a man can proceed in only one direction at a time, Vaus was feeling many gravitational strains and stresses. He decided that it was time to "get religion" again. He got it.

A nationally known evangelist was conducting a revival meeting at Washington Boulevard and Grand Avenue. To the tune of much newspaper publicity, Vaus got himself a new coat of celestial varnish. He said that he was tired of being a sinner and wanted to return to God. He had told me before how he had wriggled off the law's hooks by *getting religion* so it wasn't surprising to find him once again in this Protean role.

Hot from the revival tent, J. Arthur Vaus trotted down to the courtroom prepared to testify for Sergeant Jackson and Lieutenant Wellpott. He had completed the circuit. He had worked for me, for Sergeant Guy Rudolph and for Mickey Cohen. Now he was intent upon *helping* Jackson and Wellpott.

When I voiced skepticism at Vaus's purported reformation, someone said that I should be charitable and give him the benefit of the doubt.

"He's already had the benefit of too many doubts, and it is highly doubtful in my mind that Vaus will ever be anything other than a confirmed criminal, or a dealer in chicanery," I replied.

It is an accepted belief that newspapermen's lives must be fascinating because they meet so many interesting people. What do you think of the life of a police officer?

Do you find fascination in the galaxy of bums I have trotted out for your scrutiny?

ANGEL CITY ABORTION RING

Although I wanted no part of Vaus's "business" scheme, I was thoroughly convinced that Vaus had been telling the truth.

A week prior to my meeting with Vaus, Officer Ruggles and I had located a beautiful party girl whom we knew to be a friend of Mickey Cohen's henchman, Harry "Happy" Meltzer.

We had found the girl's love bazaar in the swank Hollywood district only a hop, skip and jump from the exclusive Wilshire Country Club, had tapped her telephone wire and had listened to Mickey's henchman, who used her home as a meeting place to discuss business and to throw wild parties.

The phone was in constant use by gangsters. I occasionally heard Cohen himself in conversation with these men. While I was listening one night, Meltzer told an unidentified person that Cohen had been sold some recordings for which he had paid twenty thousand dollars. Not satisfied, the salesmen were trying to sell him an additional copy for thirty thousand and Mickey was in a tough spot as a result.

At the time, I wasn't aware of the nature of the recordings.

I maintained this listening post until I was discovered by the erstwhile gangster squad, directed by Lieutenant Willie Burns. Immediately after my discovery, the prostitute and her friends changed their abode.

I could draw only one conclusion. Lieutenant Burns had tipped off the gangsters.

A short time later, I further engendered the animosity of the police department by learning of the operations of an abortion setup within the City of Los Angeles.

One day I received a telephone call from a retired police lieutenant, who had a temporary appointment as medical inspector with the California State Medical Board. The man said that he would like to see me. Although I wasn't acquainted with him at the time, I had been informed of his honesty and good reputation while he was a member of the police department. I had heard that because of these qualities, he had been shelved until retirement. He wouldn't connive, play ball or cut corners. I agreed to see him.

A regular inspector of the State Medical Board accompanied him on the occasion of our meeting. Quite frankly, he told me that he had heard of my work and ability, and that he admired my courage. He then explained that he had come to ask a favor.

An organized abortion ring was operating within the City of Los Angeles, headed by a Dr. Audrain, he said. This inspector and others intuitively felt that its doctors were being protected by a very unique method. Actually any person outside the ring was directly shaken down by homicide detectives of the police department, working through a setup that was maintained for that particular purpose.

He detailed the Medical Board's method of operation. Upon receipt of a complaint or information that abortions were being performed by doctors, chiropractors, midwives or others, the Board would make an investigation. Although it had powers to make arrests, the Board's policy was to furnish information to the homicide bureau of the Los Angeles Police Department, or to the district attorney's office and to allow those two law enforcement agencies to effect the arrests. After conviction of the abortionist, the Medical Board would go to the state with the information and the supporting results of the conviction and would then take action against the implicated physicians or other persons licensed by the state who were involved.

To this inspector and to others it appeared that when positive and conclusive information or evidence were conveyed to their immediate superior, even if an arrest were made it was smothered and no action was taken. Too, it appeared that when they themselves were working on the case, the guilty doctors were invariably tipped off if they were members of the protected abortion ring. However, when information was obtained on some doctor outside the clique, or on someone who was without funds, in almost every instance a prosecution and a conviction would result.

Their purpose in meeting me was to enlist my aid at that particular time. Inasmuch as their superior was on his vacation, they felt that anything they could accomplish while he was away would keep them from having to go through the police homicide squad. They wanted me to function secretly in place of the homicide squad.

I knew that I would be sticking my neck out by entering this protected phase of police work. I went to Lieutenant Ed Blair, in charge of vice, and told him that the state inspectors wanted me to help them. I informed Blair quite frankly that they suspected homicide officers of taking pay-offs to protect the abortion ring.

Blair advised me to go ahead, but reminded me to take it easy. He didn't want to become involved. A smart officer!

The medical board men then told me that they knew the identity of a woman who had gone to the suspected Doctor Audrain, who, incidentally, was the purported head man in the ring. They suggested that I obtain the services of a policewoman, who could go to the doctor, pose as a pregnant woman, and give the name of their informant as a reference for the purpose of having Dr. Audrain perform an abortion on her.

I told Policewoman Audre Davis none of the particulars of this case other than to state exactly what I wanted her to do. We arranged the details and she went to the doctor's office. The nurse gave her a casual examination. Perhaps I should make it clear that any woman who goes to an abortionist, whether or not she is pregnant, will be told that she is pregnant and that an "abortion" should be performed.

Policewoman Davis was given an appointment for the latter part of the following week. She was directed to bring two hundred and fifty dollars with her and to come early. The appointment hour was seven thirty a.m. We knew that doctors performing abortions usually handled them in their offices between the hours of midnight and nine a.m.

At the appointed hour, Officer Ruggles, the policewoman and I met the two inspectors from the State Medical Board. The inspectors were down in the mouth.

"Sergeant, the deal is all shot to hell," one of them exclaimed. He added that their boss had returned from his vacation the day before and that they wouldn't dare proceed without first telling him. The other remarked that, although he had been told to go ahead, he well knew that the doctor was probably in Old Mexico by now.

Being unacquainted with all the facts, I was consequently unconvinced. "What the hell," I retorted. "Let's take a chance. What have we got to lose?"

I ordered Policewoman Davis to keep the appointment. We planned to allow her thirty minutes in the office at Sixth and St. Paul Streets. Miss Davis left. A few minutes later, the three officers and I followed her into the building. We found the doors of the medical offices tightly locked. With the exception of two nervous customers waiting in the hall, the place was deserted. Then I was convinced that the Medical inspectors were right. The planned raid had been tipped off.

To satisfy my own curiosity, I checked throughout the following week, and to my knowledge the good doctor never returned. The incident seemed to be closed; and I erased the abortion racket from my mind, since it was outside of my duties.

Later, however, I received another visit from the inspector on the State Medical Board. He said that he again wanted my aid. He and his partners were purportedly disgusted with the setup as it was; and the ex-police lieutenant told me that he was leaving the job in the near future. He said that it would do his heart good to put at least one sharp bastard in jail before he left.

He advised that a woman doctor had been performing periodical abortions for well recommended customers, and that she was operating in expensive offices in the movie colony district in Sherman Oaks on Ventura Boulevard.

Again, he assured me that he had received information and that we could have the co-operation of a satisfied customer who would permit us to use her name as reference. He made only one request, that I pretend to have received the information from my own sources. In so doing, the medical board men would not be on the spot with the state board. Having effected the arrest, I was to call them and they would carry the ball to home plate. In that manner homicide could be bypassed.

I was to assume the role of a hard-working officer who had found a law breaker and had done his job in blissful ignorance of the protection ring, which hitherto had permitted the abortionists to operate on scores and hundreds of pregnant women with immunity.

Having little choice, Ruggles and I again obtained the services of Policewoman Audre Davis who, incidentally, was one of the two women assigned to the Los Angeles vice division. The other policewoman so assigned was an aged stenographer at Administrative Vice.

With the inspectors and Policewoman Davis, Ruggles and I went to the vicinity of the woman doctor's offices. Miss Davis, whom we had briefed in her role, went in. She remained inside for several minutes. Upon her return, she explained that she had seen the woman doctor. According to her story, the woman had told her that she wasn't performing operations inasmuch as she had no dependable assistant. However, since she was convinced that Miss Davis was *all right*, she wouldn't hesitate to recommend her to a doctor friend. She said that she would even call and make an appointment. In Miss Davis's presence, the woman dialed a number. She was told that the doctor was out and wouldn't be in until the following morning.

Miss Davis was advised to call her the following morning. In the meantime, she would contact her doctor friend.

When Miss Davis telephoned, the woman told her that she had spoken to the doctor and that he was expecting Miss Davis to call him. She added that everything was "okay."

Then the woman doctor named the abortionist, a Dr. Eric Kirk, and gave Audre his telephone number. I immediately called the State Medical examiner, who told me that Dr. Kirk was a suspect. He remarked that, insofar as he knew, Kirk wasn't working in the ring. He was a chiropractor, and only M. D.'s were permitted as working members of the protected ring. He told me to go ahead and see if I could make an arrest.

I had Audre telephone Doctor Kirk. He advised her to go to his offices for an examination. She went. After the examination, an appointment was made for three p.m., the following Saturday. The price of the abortion was to be two hundred and fifty dollars.

With this amount in marked money, Audre drove to the doctor's offices on Riverside Drive to keep the appointment. Ruggles and I parked a block away and kept her under observation. We saw her go to the doctor's office door and try it. We noted that the door was locked.

Audre stood at the door for a few minutes, during which time, a big car drove up and double-parked. A woman got out of the car, spoke to Miss Davis, then unlocked the doctor's offices and entered. We then saw Miss Davis enter the waiting car and drive away in it. By the time Officer Ruggles and I were able to return to our police car, Miss Davis and the car's other occupant had disappeared.

We made a fruitless search of the vicinity, but were unable to find a car that even remotely resembled the one we had seen at a distance.

It is a cardinal rule of the police department that the security of a policewoman is paramount to any investigation. Ruggles and I immediately went to the doctor's offices. Inside, we found the woman who had climbed out of the vanished car. We presumed that she was the doctor's nurse or secretary.

I inquired where the doctor was. The woman said that she didn't know, he hadn't been in all day and she didn't expect him. I then identified myself as a police officer and told her to cut out the bunk unless she wanted me to throw her in jail post haste.

I told the woman that her doctor employer was in the company of a policewoman, and that I wanted to know where the doctor had gone. She broke into tears.

"I knew it, I knew it! He's done it again!"

She confided that Kirk had been arrested a few days before on an abortion charge and that he had promised her he would never perform another illegal operation. She began to upbraid the doctor, calling him a disgrace to her daughters and herself.

"I hope you catch the son-of-a-bitch and send him to jail for life," she wailed. "If I knew where to find him, I'd surer than hell help you."

We then knew that the woman was Dr. Kirk's wife.

I telephoned Central Vice Division, told the officer on duty what had happened, gave him the telephone number of the doctor's office, and asked him to call me immediately if he heard from Miss Davis. I added that I would get the license number of the doctor's automobile and have it broadcast over the police radio.

I had scarcely finished making my report when Miss Davis walked in with Dr. Kirk. She told the following story:

She had climbed into the doctor's car whereupon he explained that they would have to get out of the neighborhood as quickly as possible because he "was as hot as a pistol." He then told her that a few days after she had first visited his offices, he had been arrested. He declared that, under the circumstances, he wouldn't dare perform an abortion. He felt certain that he was being watched. However, he assured Audre that he had a friend who would do the job. He promised to contact his friend and make an appointment.

Dr. Kirk then returned Audre to his own offices, where he learned that she was a policewoman. When I asked him to identify the officers who had arrested him, he named two homicide detectives. For the purposes of this story, we'll call them Joe Small and Bill Ball, which are not their names. I didn't know Small but I knew that Ball at one time had worked for Lieutenant Rudy Wellpott.

Inasmuch as we had been found out and caught off base and since we did not have enough evidence to make an arrest, I telephoned homicide headquarters and asked to speak to the detectives. I felt that, although our evidence wasn't sufficient for an arrest, it most assuredly would bolster their case.

When I talked to the detectives and told them what had happened, they were very perturbed. They immediately wanted to know why I was making abortion investigations. When I repeated what had occurred, the detectives warned me to get the hell out of there. Furthermore, they commanded me to shut up and attend to my vice work.

I then informed them that, from what I had heard, they were a pair of God damned phonies and that they weren't kidding me.

I summoned my two officers and left. During my conversations with Small and Ball, Officer Ruggles tried to secure the name of the doctor whom Dr. Kirk had promised to obtain for Miss Davis. Ruggles indicated to Dr. Kirk that his co-operation in supplying him the name would in all probability go a long way toward helping him out of the jam he was in with the medical examiners.

Reluctantly, he agreed to secure the name and address of the doctor and if possible to make an appointment for Audre. To my knowledge, Miss Davis knew nothing of the abortion setup at this time other than the details she had been given in the performance of her work.

The following day, Audre called Doctor Kirk to ask if he had made the appointment with the other doctor. Kirk replied that he had been unable to contact the other doctor.

In the early part of 1949, I again stuck my neck out. I was still determined to throw a monkey wrench into crooked police cliques, when inspectors of the medical board again paid me a visit – this time with what they described as a hell of a fine case. They mentioned a nurse who made arrangements for girls to have abortions at a cost of five hundred dollars an abortion.

One girl who had learned that she wasn't pregnant, was indignant at the thought that she was about to be fleeced and butchered at the same time. She was eager to accompany medical board inspectors if she could aid them in making an arrest. There was only one drawback, however. If the inspectors went to their boss and asked for five hundred dollars, they would tip off the play, because this doctor definitely was in the circle of the chosen few receiving police protection at a price. They asked me if I could raise the necessary money.

I went to Lieutenant Blair, who told me that he'd try and get the money for me providing I would not get him involved. I signed for the five hundred dollars. We were ready to go, and everybody was happy.

I arranged to meet the medical board inspectors and their informant at nine a.m., the next morning. My telephone rang at eight a.m., the following morning. Joe Small, one of the two homicide detectives working abortions, asked me what the hell I was up to. He reminded me that I had been told once before to mind my own business. He added that someone was coming out to pick up the five hundred dollars.

A police officer whom I had not seen before called to pick up the money. He gave me a receipt for the five hundred dollars. That was my last foray into the Los Angeles abortion ring investigation. Yet, strangely enough, it was to have an aftermath.

Doctor Eric Kirk, the chiropractor, was tried and sent to San Quentin prison. Neither Davis, Officer Ruggles nor I were subpoenaed to testify at his trial. As a matter-of-fact, we were unaware that there had been a trial until later. When the story of my testimony broke at the grand jury investigation into the abortion ring, Kirk was an inmate of San Quentin penitentiary. Later, Kirk was brought back from San Quentin before Superior Judge Charles W. Fricke in his attorney's attempt to secure a new trial.

Kirk, unaware that I had been sent by the State Medical Board, and having no knowledge of my telephone conversations with homicide Detectives Small and Ball, was of the opinion that I was working with those officers.

According to his written statement submitted to the court, he had been told by three different attorneys that some politicians, or the police department, were out to get him, but that they could not identify the interested parties or give their reasons for wanting him out of the way. A Mr. Tulley, who was his co-defendant when he was tried, had told him that another doctor named Grossman had learned the identity of the pay-off man. To "square the beef," he would have to pay twenty-five hundred dollars by the Monday following his arrest. The money was to be taken to the offices of Dan Bechtel, 71-year-old "public relations" man with offices at Third and Spring Streets.

Doctor Kirk maintained that, after considerable telephoning, he arranged to borrow one thousand dollars from a Doctor Pixler, and a like amount from a Doctor Pollom, who later became his co-defendants. Since he could raise no more money, he explained that he had delayed his appointment with Mr. Bechtel and went to the bank with his wife to arrange a car loan of another thousand dollars. He then went to Mr. Bechtel's offices, where Mr. Tulley was waiting for him. There, they both gave Bechtel twenty-five hundred dollars with the understanding that, if he could not quash the charges, the money would be returned.

Kirk stated that they had heard Bechtel give instructions to his secretary to get a New York bank draft for three thousand dollars. Bechtel later explained that he was preparing the weekly revenue for the pay-offs. He mentioned no names. Bechtel was aware that Doctor Kirk had been visited by Officers Stoker, Ruggles and Davis and he asked what reason they had for calling at his offices. After Kirk had explained, Bechtel picked up the telephone and dialed a number. After some discussion, during which the name "Joe" was frequently mentioned, he hung up. He then explained that the charges were dropped, having been quashed by "Joe."

Here's where the possible answer to Policewoman Audre Davis's whirling, elusive and contradictory maneuvering in connection with her work with me may be found.

Bechtel explained that "Joe" personally had had Audre Davis and other young women appointed to various details and I learned that prior to Audre Davis's having been assigned to work vice, she had worked with the homicide officers on abortion cases. Doctor Kirk informed me that Bechtel had related several stories about Audre Davis. According to Bechtel's account as related to Doctor Kirk, Audre had carried quite a chip on her shoulder. Bechtel took credit for having knocked the chip off Audre's shoulder and with cutting her down to size in the police department. Bechtel inferred to Doctor Kirk that Audre was a pretty loose woman who would do anything.

Doctor Kirk said that at the time he left Bechtel, they shook hands.

Several days later he was informed by Mr. Tulley to return to Bechtel's office and pick up his twenty-five hundred dollars. Tulley explained that the deal could not go through as too many people were involved.

Doctor Kirk went to see Bechtel and found Doctor Grossman waiting. Bechtel called Kirk into his offices and returned the money in an envelope. Kirk counted the money in Bechtel's presence. Bechtel expressed regret that he could do nothing at least while "the heat was on."

He then called Doctor Grossman into the office. Grossman told Kirk that he knew of a man who could help him. This help would cost Kirk thirty-five hundred dollars. Grossman said that the man had previously helped him out of the same kind of mess. He had withdrawn that amount from the bank to make a pay-off, after which Detectives Small and Ball came to Doctor Grossman's office, returned his instruments and files and released his nurse from similar charges.

Mr. Tulley, who knew this man only as "Cap," made an appointment for Doctor Kirk. He and Tulley went to the St. Paul Hotel on West Sixth Street two days later. "Cap" admitted them, Kirk said, and discussed the matter in detail. According to his story, Kirk would need at least six thousand dollars, but since "Cap" had already talked to Tulley and had learned that Kirk could not pay that amount, he agreed to take one thousand dollars and spread it out to the "right" people in the City Hall. "Cap" specifically mentioned the homicide division and said that Kirk could be assured that the money would reach the topnotchers. He mentioned that he personally knew Detective Ball, who, among other officers, had to "make a living." He explained that the captain who commanded homicide at the time was the head of the detail, but that the brass went still higher.

A former police officer himself, "Cap" was now secretary in a local union. Kirk, Tulley and Doctor Pollom paid "Cap" one thousand dollars then left "Cap's" room.

A few days later, Tulley contacted Kirk and announced that he had again talked to Bechtel. Bechtel had told him that the boys were now willing to quash the charges for sixteen thousand dollars. Kirk replied that he could not afford that kind of money, nor could he raise his share of the sum.

Later, Kirk was told that a Mr. Becker, with offices at Fourth and Spring Streets, could arrange a fix. An appointment was made for him; and together with Pollom and his wife, he went to see Becker. Becker telephoned the City Hall, asked for someone and received the desired information.

Becker said that he also knew Detective Small well. He said Small was trying to "make a lot out of your case."

"He's very cagey, though," Becker confided, "when he takes a pay-off. Small is no dummy."

Kirk stated that he and his wife returned to see Becker the following day. He gave Becker five hundred dollars down. More was to be paid if sufficient evidence was not obtained.

Despite his attempts to free himself from San Quentin penitentiary, and his relation of the facts set down here, Kirk was unsuccessful. He remains in the penitentiary today.

The above portion of Doctor Kirk's story is a matter of court record.

IT'S FRAME-UP TIME

After my appearance before the Los Angeles County Grand Jury on May 5, 1949, speculation was rife as to the motive, or motives, which had caused me to testify before the inquisitors.

Self-proclaimed experts, wiseacres who declared they knew everything, sped the rumors around Los Angeles' police and political circles, that I had made a deal with City Engineer Lloyd Aldrich, candidate for Mayor of Los Angeles, who was opposing Mayor Fletcher E. Bowron in the May 31, 1949, election.

According to these rumor mongers, I had appeared before the grand jury to "tell all" about police department corruption in the expectation and belief that Lloyd Aldrich would defeat Bowron and become Mayor, and that I would profit from the change in city administration through promotion by Aldrich when he assumed Bowron's office.

In short, I was accused of having a political, selfish and monetary interest in the outcome of the May 31, election. I was charged with having the intent of "crawling over the prostrate bodies" of my numerous police colleagues who, in one way or another, were involved in the graft ring concerning vice and gambling.

These groundless accusations were a complete fabrication. My motives in appearing before the grand jury were not political. They were not monetary. They were not designed to promote my standing in the police department.

My principal object in appearing before the grand jury was the desire for self-preservation.

I had every reason to believe that the vicious and unscrupulous men in the police department, whose graft and corruption trails I had crossed, were out to get me in one way or another. I knew that they were intent upon discrediting me in any manner they could. They were seeking to destroy my reputation and question my honesty as a police officer. I felt that they might resort to murdering me, for racketeers, whether they are police officers or gangsters, play rough when their aims are thwarted.

In her tapped telephone conversations with Sergeant Jackson (Lieutenant Rudy Wellpott's man), I had heard Brenda Allen tell Jackson that she was going to have me "rubbed out." Do not believe that this whore would not resort to murder if she felt that she had a better than even chance to get away with it. Under orders I had given Brenda and her "business manager," Jackson, sufficient grief to have furnished them with enough motive to want to get rid of me.

I knew that Jackson had approached a prostitute whom I had arrested on numerous occasions, in an effort to frame me. In exchange for her false statement that I had accepted pay-offs, he had promised this woman that he would quash a narcotic rap in which her husband was involved at the time. I reasoned that if Jackson, a vice squad man, could square a narcotic rap inside the police department, he could do a lot of reaching in that department. I concluded that the personnel investigation of Jackson by Captain Cecil Wisdom was dropped because higher police brass didn't dare jam Jackson, and if they didn't dare jam Jackson, that meant they were in on the graft, too.

After due consideration, early in February, 1949, I consulted a Mr. Edward E. Mix, president of the Bronson Fan Manufacturing Company, and told him my story, much as I have related it here.

Mr. Mix had his stenographer type the material so that, in the event I was murdered, he would be able to take it to the proper authorities. After the story had been written, Mr. Mix advised me to go to the grand jury.

I then sought the advice of a retired police captain and a retired police lieutenant, both of whom were of the opinion that I should go to the grand jury. Yet, I was still reluctant to take this course.

During this time of personal perplexity, I was building a house at 2107 Apex Avenue, Los Angeles. My partner, Officer Jack D. Ruggles, who was financially interested, was assisting me with the work, a portion of which we had to place under sub-contract. We had obtained an FHA loan from the Bank of America. However, before the loan was granted, we found that it was compulsory to place our money in the hands of an agency that would distribute the cash as it was needed.

The City of Los Angeles had two such agencies. The bank lending the money used the services of an agency known as The Builders' Control. The lending officer, Mr. Keith Krug, arranged an appointment with this agency, and I talked with its representatives, who explained the agency's services. It required that an appraisal of the cost estimate be made according to plans. After completion of the estimate, the builder would place the estimated amount in the hands of the agency and pay it a percentage of the complete cost. The agency in turn would distribute the money as the work progressed.

Members of the firm informed me that they would be in my employ; that they would answer to me, and that their services included not only payment of my bills as the work progressed, but periodical inspections by inspectors who would either make criticisms, offer suggestions or aid in any way possible.

The representatives, however, felt that the amount of money loaned by the FHA commitment was too low. They were fearful of accepting the job unless I could raise a larger amount. I returned to the bank. There the lending officer told me of another organization in Los Angeles, namely Joint Control. He stated that the bank was reluctant to use the services of this organization as it was considered a haphazard outfit but that, as a personal favor, he would allow us to use its services if I wished.

I went to Joint Control. Its policies were supposedly identical with those of Builders' Control. Its representatives made it very plain that they were eager to get the business from that particular branch of the Bank of America, and were more than willing to take on the responsibility. This willingness was strange since, to my knowledge, Joint Control hadn't seen a copy of the plans of the building I was constructing, or the property on which the building was to be constructed. As a matter of fact, representatives of Joint Control did not see the property until after the actual building was in progress.

The bank ruled that the money would be paid to my partner and me in five progressive payments which would call for five inspections. The fifth payment was to be made after completion. The cost estimate of the building was $10,500, $7,600 of which was loaned by the FHA.

Ruggles and I were to pay the difference between the cost and the amount of the loan. We borrowed the money individually. I borrowed two thousand dollars from the police credit union, and Ruggles borrowed the remainder from his mother.

We placed an additional sum of approximately twelve hundred dollars with The Builders' Control, so that we would be on the safe side. This money was to be paid as the last disbursement upon completion of the job. However, if it were not needed it was to be returned to Ruggles and me.

We neared completion of the house and were well within the estimates made by the FHA. Yet, when we started construction on the garage, which was at the base of a steep hill FHA inspectors told us that it was compulsory that the garage be made of reinforced concrete and steel to earthquake proof specifications. To do this work, the lowest bid we could obtain from a contractor was $3,200, or virtually half of the amount loaned by the FHA in the original commitment. When FHA had made its original estimate of a frame garage, the cost was to be in the neighborhood of four hundred dollars. Both city and FHA inspectors told us that it was the obligation of The Joint Control corporation to check and advise us inasmuch as they were acquainted with city and FHA rules and regulations.

Before we could receive our next progress payment, the terms called for completion of the garage. Ruggles and I were determined to finish the job, and we decided to pour the concrete for the garage. We had obtained the services of two carpenters, who were to build the framework and the forms for concrete. These men had set cabinets for a cabinet maker, who, they said, was fairly reasonable. Soon afterwards, the cabinet maker appeared on the scene. He gave us a cost estimate on the cabinet work for the building. The major portion of the cabinet work that Ruggles and I had originally wanted was disregarded, and a minimum number of cabinets was considered.

We had only one cost estimate for the original number of cabinets and it totaled eight hundred dollars. When the cabinet maker returned, we told him that we were compelled to cut our cabinet work to a minimum. We intended to wait until completion of the building before installing the cabinets so that if need be, we could use the money that we had deposited with Joint Control.

We explained to the cabinet maker that we were hard pressed for cash at the time, due to the unforeseen cost of the garage, which we had to complete before we could proceed to the next building phase. He indicated that he would be more than willing to wait until we had finished, if we would allow him to place the cabinets in the building, and that he would welcome our co-operation. He explained that he used non-union cabinet makers, who as a general rule were transients, so that he had a hard time keeping help. As a further inducement, he explained that he had materials on hand at that time and was idle. Half-heartedly, we agreed.

The new cost estimate was made. Meanwhile, installation of the cabinet work was begun. With the aid of friends, Ruggles and I poured a total of forty-three tons of concrete into our garage.

The cabinet maker had our carpenters install the cabinets. No sooner were the cabinets installed than he came to me and told me that he wanted money as it was necessary for him to meet a payroll. He said he was compelled to pay the men for the cabinet installations. I reminded him that my agreement with him was that he would wait until my completion of the work before receiving payment. He retorted that he well remembered the agreement; but that, under the circumstances, it would be to my benefit to have him make the payroll. Otherwise, my job would be tied up under a mechanic's lien.

Being unfamiliar with building and legal technicalities, I told him that I couldn't understand why I should be held responsible, since he had contracted for the work. He informed me that, regardless of my opinion, the law stated that in buildings where the work has been performed, a mechanic's lien was the controlling factor.

I explained to him that Joint Control had set aside a certain amount to be paid for the cabinet work, and that at the moment that would be the only money I would be allowed. It would have been impossible for me to draw a portion of the amount, because I would have had to draw the full amount. Consequently, I told him that if I paid him the full amount I would run short of money in my construction and would be unable to proceed with the next phase of the work.

He said that all he desired was the amount necessary to meet his payroll which was approximately one hundred and fifty dollars. He told me that the complete job would cost in the vicinity of four hundred and fifty dollars. I assured him that there was a probability that Ruggles and I could raise the money to meet his payroll, but that we would have to be paid back as it was money that came from our pockets and that we needed to meet our personal obligations.

I suggested that if he would give me a statement covering all the work, I would draw the full amount for the cabinets from Joint Control. I would take one hundred and fifty dollars, repay Ruggles and myself and deposit the remainder in the bank to be used in construction. To this, he agreed.

I paid him the sum with which to meet his payroll and he in turn gave me a statement for the full amount of the cabinet work. I took the statement to Joint Control and obtained a check to the amount of four hundred and fifty dollars. The check was made out to the cabinet maker's company. I gave him the check and he returned it to me endorsed. I then took the check to my bank, deposited it to my account, repaid Ruggles and myself and subsequently used the remainder in the construction of the building. We heard nothing further from the cabinet maker until approximately three months later.

In the interim, I was told by the carpenters who had made the installations that *they had not* been pressing the contractor for wages. They said that he had asked them to add one hundred and fifty dollars to their wages for other work that they had done for me. He had warned that, if I became aware of this padding, they could claim that the work was for the installation of cabinets. They stated that they had refused; and at that time they asked if they could see the written agreement of contract between the contractor and myself.

When I informed them that I had no written agreement, they chided me for my stupidity and told me that, without a contract, any contractor could say that I owed any amount and in all probability could make it stick. They hoped for my sake that this wouldn't happen.

In the early part of April, 1949, I received a telephone call from the cabinet maker, who told me that he expected the remainder of his money. I reminded him of his verbal agreement. He replied that he knew of no such agreement and that he wanted his money, then and there.

I found myself in a spot which reminded me of the story about God's and Satan's agreement to build a concrete highway between Heaven and Hell, to replace an outmoded thoroughfare which was in a ruinous condition. God broached Satan on the deal and suggested that they share the expense fifty-fifty, to which Satan agreed. When the work was finished, however, Satan refused to pay his share of the costs. God reminded him of their oral agreement. Satan retorted that he had made no oral agreement, and, added that if he had, it wasn't any good. God threatened to sue Satan.

"Where are you going to get your lawyers?" archly inquired the Evil One.

In this conflict with the cabinet maker, I realized that it was *his* word against *mine*, but that, legally speaking, he had the best of the argument because he had finished the work.

I then asked the amount of the entire bill. He said that he wanted eight hundred and seventeen dollars. I told him that the FHA inspector and the Joint Control inspector had estimated the cost of the cabinet work, and that both estimates were for less than four hundred and fifty dollars. I told him that his own employees had expressed willingness to duplicate the work in any other building for three hundred and fifty dollars. Regardless of that, he wanted his money and he warned that if I didn't give it to him he would cause trouble. When I asked him how, he sneeringly informed me that the check I had deposited to my account had not been signed by him.

"Who in hell did sign it?" I demanded.

"Well, I didn't," was the answer. "It's not my signature."

"You old son-of-a-bitch! You'll not get a damned cent from me," I blasted him. "I'll go to the district attorney's office and obtain an extortion complaint against you. We'll see who is going to give whom trouble, you dirty, lying rat!" Then I hung up.

He called me back and told me not to be too hasty, we could talk it over.

I told him that I was going to the district attorney's office regardless.

The next day I went to a deputy district attorney whom I believed to be honest, and explained the situation to him. He suggested that I go to Joint Control and ask to look at the check and the statement the cabinet maker had given me. As the check and the statement had been written at a time when I had no reason to doubt the integrity of the cabinet maker, that portion of my dealings with him were a trifle hazy.

The deputy district attorney also suggested that I take an investigator with me, which I did. A young deputy accompanied me to the offices of Joint Control. There, we viewed the check. I talked to one of the executives of Joint Control. He was very antagonistic, which did not surprise me inasmuch as during my dealings with this organization, I had received nothing but trouble through their services, or lack of them. Each time I had obtained any service from them, I had been compelled to go to the bank, and have the banker call and give them a rousting to force them to comply with the terms of their agreement.

I left the Joint Control offices with the intention of obtaining a complaint against the cabinet maker.

I then went into the deputy district attorney's offices, to see two investigators, who had made a preliminary investigation of the cabinet maker prior to my arrival.

Much to my surprise, I found that Aldo Corsini was one of the investigators. The other was Chester Sharp. Although I had met neither of these men, I had heard of Corsini directly and indirectly, ever since I had been a member of the police department's vice squad.

I knew that Aldo Corsini, prior to his retirement from the police department, was accredited with being a "sharp apple."

Seldom had I arrested an old time Italian bookmaker, ex-bootlegger or gambler that the name of Corsini hadn't arisen in the conversation. Veteran police officers often recall the days during the Frank L. Shaw administration when Corsini kept the Italian element in line for ballotting purposes.

I had nothing but contempt for the majority of the investigating staff of the district attorney's office. One of them who assertedly had changed his name, is rumored to have worked with, or to have been associated with, two notorious gamblers, Bob and George Goldie, when they operated a gambling joint at Eighth and Spring Streets in downtown Los Angeles. Purportedly he had been tied in with S. C. Lewis and Jack Berman, two swindlers who promoted the Julian Petroleum Corporation and mulcted millions from its investors. This man, a former Burns detective, and another retired Burns detective, who had married the widow of the one-time owner of a big league baseball club, had worked with Gaston B. Means. It will be recalled that Means made international headlines as the aide of Attorney-General Daugherty of the notorious Warren G. Harding administration's Teapot Dome scandal.

As a result of this knowledge, I had little confidence or respect for the investigative staff of the district attorney's office. I felt that all a man could expect from its members would be the "worst of it."

Previously, I had been approached by one of the D. A.'s investigators, to assist him in the shakedown of Pierre Martel, who ran a modeling agency in Hollywood. When I told him that I would have nothing to do with the affair, I was advised to forget what he had said.

Soon afterwards, however, I noticed that Martel had been convicted and sentenced.

Gamblers whom I had arrested said that it was the duty of some investigators on the district attorney's staff to make collections from bookmakers operating within the incorporated towns in the County of Los Angeles. They explained that the bookmaking collection setup was split three ways. Collections from the city's bookmakers were made by the Los Angeles police administrative vice squad; from the county at large by the sheriff's office's underworld agents, and from the incorporated towns by the district attorney's investigators.

However, let us return to Corsini and Sharp, whose investigation of the cabinet maker had uncovered the facts that the man was in debt, owed his employees and had given some bad checks. In their opinion, they said, he was strictly a phony. They expressed willingness to investigate him and help with the extortion complaint. They said they would begin work as soon as I gave them the green light. They had already questioned the investigator who had accompanied me to the offices of Joint Control and who seemed to be convinced that the man at Joint Control was exceptionally unfriendly towards me.

In the midst of our discussion, a sergeant from Central vice division entered the office and told me that he wanted to talk to me. We went outside at his suggestion. The sergeant explained that the Joint Control officer had made a complaint to the police department that its offices had been burglarized the night before, and that the check involved in my dispute, had disappeared.

The sergeant said that I was wanted in Captain Cecil Wisdom's office, Wisdom being chief of the personnel division.

I returned to the D. A.'s investigators' office and explained what had happened. They told me that they weren't a bit surprised. In all probability, the cabinet maker had gone back to the offices, entered and taken the check. There was also a possibility that the man in Joint Control had destroyed the check and reported a burglary to give me a bad time in return for the trouble I had caused the agency with the Bank of America. Or maybe he was just a guy who didn't like cops. I can't say that I blamed him too much, if he didn't.

I went to Captain Wisdom's office, where I found a smirking group, including Wisdom and a police captain for whom I had worked as a rookie when I first walked a beat. At one time this "apple stealing"

Captain had made me a proposition. He had asked me to make a certain amount of money by catering to and acting as a bouncer for bars while I was on duty. He had offered to set up the deal himself, so that we could split the revenue fifty-fifty. Some officers were actually engaged in this petty graft. Furthermore, this captain maintained an employment agency for a chosen few, where he arranged off-hours jobs for officers, such as guards at social functions, in return for which he received a percentage. I also knew that officers on chosen beats supplied him with groceries and vegetables they had obtained from the merchants.

I was thoroughly questioned about my relations with the cabinet maker and specifically about my actions the previous night. Needless to say, I was wary of these individuals. I recalled certain threats that had been made and I knew that if possible they were going to try and book me for the alleged burglary, regardless of my innocence.

Racing through my mind were newspaper headlines: "Brenda's Nemesis Booked For Burglary."

But I knew exactly what I had done on the previous night and knowing that I could prove my actions, I felt easier. The inquisition over, I determined to see every person whom I had seen the night before as quickly as possible, so that all would remember times and places should their testimony become necessary. I knew that, if I didn't get to these people as soon as possible their recollections would become hazy, and they would be unable to present accurate testimony.

I then re-visited the persons whom I had seen the night before and established my time from minute to minute, especially the time during which the burglary was supposed to have occurred. This time was absolutely and positively corroborated by substantial persons. I knew that I had no cause to worry concerning the burglary. My only fear was that I would be framed. In a position of this kind, one's imagination begins to run riot. I remembered a book from the public library—"Convicting The Innocent" —that I had read and which had convinced me that many people have gone to prison for crimes they didn't commit, and that many others have gone there after being framed. These recollections didn't make me feel too happy.

I contacted a friend of mine in the crime laboratory, who promised to keep an eye on the examination and see that I got a fair shake. He also assured me that the lieutenant in charge of the crime lab would countenance no frame-up. I felt that I had no reason to worry after receiving these assurances.

This occurred on April 6, 1949.

Although political and underworld forces were at work against me, I knew that I could rely upon my many friends in the police department. They were men who thought as I did about the police administration under Mayor Fletcher E. Bowron; his chosen favorite, Chief of Police C. B. Horrall, and his aide and assistant, Joseph Reed. These friends ranked from lowly rookies to deputy chiefs.

A few days later, I was notified by my friend in the crime laboratory that my clothes which were worn on the night of the burglary were absolutely and positively clean; and that the burglar, if there had been a burglar, had pried the ventilating vanes from a vent on the sheer side of the Joint Control Building, fourteen feet above ground.

The burglar had crawled through a small opening, he said. He added that the ventilator which was twelve by seventeen inches in diameter had been installed at the time the building had been constructed. He explained that it was littered with grime, dirt and deteriorated calcomine paint. The burglar had entered through this hole into an attic that had gathered dust over a period of years. The head space in this attic was less than three feet, my friend stated, and a hole had been broken from the attic through the ceiling plaster and plaster board. It was clear that the intruder had gone through this hole in a shower of debris to the floor ten feet below. He had then crawled back up, and had left in the same way he had entered.

The crime lab expert said that, had I been the intruder, my clothing would have been saturated, especially when one considers my size. I am six feet two inches tall, weigh 217 pounds, have a forty-four inch chest measurement and a diameter of eighteen inches across the shoulders, stripped.

The suit I wore on the night in question was a wool gabardine, particularly susceptible to dirt. Yet, the suit was exceptionally clean.

Again I was fortunate. I had another friend working directly under Captain Wisdom. The information he was able to supply proved invaluable to me and to my attorney in the days prior to and during my trial on the trumped up burglary charge, designed either to convict me of a felonious crime, or to discredit me in the public eye because I had become a menace to police graft and because my threatened disclosures promised to rock the City Hall.

This officer informed me that, even though corrupt officials were trying their best to hang the burglary charge on me, they would find it impossible to do so. All of the investigations either pointed to the guilt of the cabinet maker, or to connivance between members of the Joint Control organization and police officers out to nail me on a bum rap. He was of the opinion that they actually suspected that some small burglar (possibly a kid), might have entered the place, looked around, seen the check, and pocketed it, believing it to be of value, even though it had been cancelled. It was more than likely, however, that the place had been broken into, and that nothing had been taken. An opportunity would thus have presented itself for someone in Joint Control to clout the check, knowing that, in all probability, I would be accused of the crime.

The man under Captain Wisdom told me that the investigation was never turned over to the burglary detail of the Los Angeles police department for probing, according to the general routine when a burglary has been committed. He said that all of the probing had been done by untrained officers, working in personnel under direct supervision of Captain Wisdom.

Furthermore, he was certain that my enemies feared to turn the investigation over to skilled investigators of the burglary division, for by so doing, the real burglar would doubtless be apprehended. My enemies didn't want to see that happen, inasmuch as I was in the bind. My friend told us that the modus operandi files of the police department had not been consulted.

My clothing was returned to me and I was told to forget the sordid affair.

This was early in April. I was to hear nothing more about the burglary allegedly committed by me, until the latter part of July.

GRAND JURY PREVIEW

Despite the fact that I was loaded with bona fide information on the relationship of underworld figures with law enforcement officers, my first appearance before the Los Angeles County Grand Jury on May 5,1949, was not of my own volition. *I was subpoenaed.*

While the political-underworld-police pot was boiling with all sorts of rumors, Gang Leader Michael (Mickey) Cohen, who had been bled white by persons who represented that they could do something for him, rebelled at the constant tapping of his money.

Cohen had been repeatedly sold wire tapping records that had been taken in his own home; but when Sergeant Elmer V. Jackson, Brenda's friend, made a "plant" of a gun on one of his henchmen and demanded twenty thousand dollars to squash the beef, Cohen finally decided to do something about it. Cohen refused the demand.

According to Cohen, the price was later reduced to five thousand dollars.

Lieutenant Rudy Wellpott and Jackson were of the opinion that Vaus and I had also made recordings in the basement of Brenda Allen's apartment building, prior to Jackson's shooting of Peewee Lewis, the bandit. Knowing that Vaus was in Cohen's employ, these officers thought that Cohen could obtain the recordings. At this juncture, Vaus sold the racketeer a bill of goods. He told Cohen that if he would negotiate with Jackson, he – Vaus – would be able to reverse the play and make recordings of the attempted shakedown. Cohen went along with Vaus and a meeting was arranged. Vaus was supposed to have made the recordings, and in turn, Harry Meltzer, who had been charged with possession of a gun, pleaded not guilty to the Concealed Weapons Act.

Cohen, believing Vaus to have the evidence, let one and all at the Meltzer trial know that he was going to play the recordings and expose the plot to extort money from him. He went so far as to describe his meeting with Jackson at the time of the attempted shakedown.

Jackson quickly denied the shakedown meeting, but his denial was refuted by the statement of a deputy sheriff who had chanced to see the meeting on the night in question. Cohen stated in open court that over a period of years he had wined and dined Sergeant Jackson, Lieutenant Wellpott and several of their friends in the more luxurious Beverly Hills and Hollywood night spots.

This too, was denied by both Jackson and Wellpott, but when a procession of waiters, waitresses and others testified at Meltzer's trial, both Wellpott and Jackson were forced to admit on the witness stand that they had not only been Mickey's guests in various Hollywood restaurants, but that a girl friend of Wellpott's had accepted an expensive gift from Cohen in their presence.

Both Wellpott and Jackson used the usual police "out" to take the onus off themselves, declaring that their meetings with Cohen were in the "line of duty" and in the "course of investigation" of Cohen.

I may be wrong, but in so far as I know, this is the first time in the history of police investigation that officers who were investigating a leading mobster actually broke bread with him and accepted presents from him. A very strange method to use in investigative work, I should say, and one of which J. Edgar Hoover would heartily disapprove, if it were used by his agents.

Realizing that all hell would break loose if recordings of the attempted shakedown were played, Mayor Fletcher E.Bowron and his cohorts began to bring pressure on the courts in an attempt to have the case continued until after the impending election, which was scheduled for May 31, 1949.

Accordingly, there were more "stalls" in the Meltzer trial than there are at Santa Anita and Hollywood Park race tracks.

The case was finally continued. However, at this point the county grand jury decided to latch onto the scandal. It demanded that the recordings be played for the jurors' illumination. Then the defense attorneys, employed by Mickey Cohen to defend Meltzer, his ally, declared that they would be only too *happy* to give the recordings to the grand jurors.

Knowing that if Vaus brought the recordings before the grand jury, I would automatically become involved, I decided to take the advice I had been given — and testify before the grand jury. But *before I could act* on this resolve, I was served with a subpoena by the Criminal Complaints Committee of the grand jury.

I appeared before the Criminal Complaints Committee on May 5, 1949, and answered each of its questions, truthfully and to the best of my ability. I told of the Brenda Allen investigations and explained in great detail exactly how they had occurred.

I was warned to say nothing regarding the fact that I had been before the grand jury.

When I appeared before the Criminal Complaints Committee, I was questioned by several of its members and by Deputy District Attorney Arthur Veitch, assigned as an advisor to the jury. I was informed that I would be called again at a future date.

About a week after my appearance before the committee, I received a telephone call from Inspector William Parker. He asked me to meet him at the same place where we had met on the occasion when he had wanted me to put Officer Jimmy Parslow of Hollywood vice in the middle. I kept the date, and Parker gave me a preliminary build-up to the effect that he and I were of the same faith, and that it was directly due to his hard work that the Catholic boys on the Los Angeles police department were getting an even break. He reminded me that we were both veterans of World War II.

After these pleasantries, Parker asked what I knew about the Brenda Allen investigation in Hollywood. When I related the story as I had told it to the grand jury, he indicated that it was as he had suspected, since he knew positively that there were two sources of corruption in the police administration.

According to Parker, one source was controlled by Chief of Police Clemence B. Horrall. Aligned with him as a lieutenant was Sergeant Guy Rudolph, his confidential aide. He then related this story concerning Rudolph, which I have never verified.

For years, while Bowron was in office, Rudolph had controlled the vice pay-offs in Los Angeles, and when Horrall held the chief's job, Rudolph was under his wing. At one time, Rudolph had kicked a colored prostitute to death on Central Avenue; and during the investigation of that incident, he and his partner had gone to a local downtown hotel where they engaged in a drunken brawl with two women. Then, while Rudolph was out of the room buying a bottle of whiskey, one of the prostitutes had been killed.

He asked me if I had heard the story. When I replied that I hadn't, Parker told me that he could prove what he had related to me. He added that Rudolph also controlled the lottery and numbers rackets operated by Chinese and Negroes, and that he had a Chinese as a partner, and maintained a business office on San Pedro Street.

According to Parker, Horrall's other lieutenant was a Captain Tucker, who was commander of the metropolitan squad, which numbers over one hundred men. He said that the metropolitan squad furnished Los Angeles police officers to act as strike-breakers in studios for so much a head. The taxpayers paid the policemen's salaries, while Horrall and Tucker collected the revenue, Parker declared.

Parker explained that this money was split with members of the city council, and that Tucker maintained a metropolitan vice division, whose only duty was to see that Chinese, gamblers and prostitutes were kept in line.

He also related this story, which I later verified. One of the officers on this squad used solely for collection purposes, had built a $100,000 motel in the City of Los Angeles, although he was drawing only a police officer's salary. This officer, having become greedy, was doing a little collecting on the side without coming up with the money. He had registered at a hotel owned by the powerful Consolidated Hotel Chain in Los Angeles, had called a bellboy to his room after whiskey-selling hours and had asked the bellboy for a bottle of whiskey.

The bellboy, Parker said, accommodated him. When the officer received the bottle, he tried to put the "shake" on him by giving him a choice of either paying off or of going to jail. The bellboy had told the officer that his money was in his street clothing, and that he would go and get it. The bellboy disappeared.

Then, determined that he wouldn't be outsmarted by a mere bellboy, the officer had gone to a man whom he believed to be the night watchman, or night maintenance man, and had passed the word that the bellboy had better come up with the money — or else.

What the vice officer didn't know was that the man to whom he had spoken was a poor but honest, retired police officer, who was trying to augment his pension by working at the hotel. Together with the bellboy, the retired officer went to the management of the hotel and then went directly to the City Hall.

When Chief Horrall could do nothing to quash the complaint, a summary investigation was made and the two officers were temporarily assigned to traffic.

I, myself, had a slight brush with this powerful police officer when I arrested the night manager in his motel on a charge of renting rooms for prostitution. To my knowledge, this case *never came up* in the courts of Los Angeles.

The impetuous alacrity with which the police and city and county prosecutorial officers prosecute some malefactors and their terrific disinclination to prosecute others is a law enforcement paradox which, if generally understood and widely known by the public, would completely erase any confidence remaining in elected officials.

Parker went on to say that the other sources of corruption within the police department directly were controlled by Assistant Chief of Police Joe Reed. He explained that Joe Reed's chief aide was Lieutenant Rudy Wellpott, head of the powerful administrative vice squad, who in turn had as his assistant, Sergeant Elmer V. Jackson. Parker related that Jackson had been exempted from military duty with the police department's help and had stayed out of the war. The department's main source of revenue during this period was the "shaking down" of bar owners on Main and East Fifth Streets to allow B-Girls, a polite name for prostitutes, who are proscribed by law, to operate.

This activity constituted a million dollar source of revenue, according to Parker; and although the average cost of a liquor license was in the vicinity of five hundred dollars, a license in those areas sold for not less than ten thousand dollars during the war.

Parker said that Nate Bass, a bar owner, was middle man between the police and bar owners.

I was well acquainted with Mr. Bass and was aware of the powers that he wielded. Bass was known as Mr. Main Street among the officers.

When I returned from service in the Army, I was contacted by a war veteran who had attended the infantry officers' candidate school with me. This man was looking for a civilian job.

I knew him to be a man of high calibre, who had received nearly every decoration with the exception of the Congressional Medal of Honor, and who had been "top man" both physically and scholastically in the officers' candidate school. Consequently, I felt that he would make a fine police officer. During that period officers were being hired directly by the department and given temporary appointments to fill existing vacancies, prior to the time of civil service examination.

This man was Allan Ostervik. Ostervik obtained the job and I requested that he be assigned to work with me.

I was then making periodic investigations of prostitution in the Main Street area; and on several occasions, Ostervik and I entered the bar owned by Nate Bass. While there, we noticed that the B-Girls were operating quite openly.

When Ostervik suggested that we arrest some of them, I agreed. But I added that, inasmuch as we weren't working B-Girls and since certain officers were assigned to that specific job, we should consult the officers whose duty and assignment it was to control such activities.

When we consulted these officers, Ostervik and I were informed that we had better lay off for our own good. Several days later, Ostervik took the civil service examination for appointment to the police department and became one of the top men on the eligibility list. He attended the Los Angeles Police Academy and was first in his class.

When he was graduated from the Academy he was again assigned to work with me.

Ostervik's work was superior, but he had one "fault." He couldn't get over the fact that flagrant violations of the law were being committed and that he had been told to "lay off" making arrests. One day Ostervik told me that he had checked the record of the bar operated by Nate Bass and had found that only a few arrests had been made there over a period of years. Compared with the arrests which had been made in other bars, arrests in Bass's bar had been negligible. Having gone to the other bars, Ostervik remarked that he hadn't seen the violations that he had noted in Bass's bar.

"God damn it," he exclaimed, "I'm going to Bass's bar and the first chance I get, throw some B-Girl's 'can' into jail!"

I told Ostervik to include me out, that it wasn't my detail.

True to his word, the next day he informed me that he had gone down on his own time, and had thrown a B-Girl into jail, after having arrested her in Bass's bar.

I wondered what was going to happen. However, I didn't wonder long — for on my next tour of duty, I found that I had a new partner and that Ostervik was working uniform. A few days later, I saw Ostervik. He told me that he had fully intended to go back to the bar at the first opportunity, and that if he saw another violation, he would make more arrests.

"For Christ's sake, take it easy," I warned, trying to reason with him. I told him that he should at least wait until his probationary period was up, inasmuch as he could be fired for the slightest cause. He replied that he was a veteran, that he had fought hard for his country, and that he had a wife and child. However, he stated that if the police job was as it appeared to be, he didn't care for it. As you may see he was a man of conviction and determination and it is obvious that he didn't see eye to eye with Mayor Bowron's concept of Good, Honest and Efficient Government and the finest police department in the world.

Ostervik insisted that he would rather work as a day laborer than be told whom to arrest and whom not to arrest, particularly when the law violations were occurring in front of his eyes. After all, he said, he had a conscience to live with and he considered it wrong to arrest one person for an offense, and to refuse to arrest another for the same offense.

"If that's the type of man wanted on the Los Angeles police department, they don't want me because I will not be that kind of an officer," Ostervik blurted heatedly.

That day, Ostervik went off duty, donned his civilian clothes, and entered the bar where a B-Girl made the mistake of flaunting a violation in his presence. To jail she went. A few days later, Ostervik was dismissed from the Los Angeles police department.

The above instance shows how much substance there is, or was, to Mayor Bowron's claim that Los Angeles has "Good, Honest and Efficient Government" and the "finest police department in the United States." It was efficient only in the manner that a Main Street dive owner could get an honest copper fired. This was an illustration of how an honest officer could get fired for enforcing the law against rackets and racketeers — his sworn duty.

The reason given for Ostervik's dismissal was that he was *temperamentally unsuited for police work*. This was obviously untrue. Ostervik's Army officer's commission and decorations were proof that he had been temperamentally suited to fight the Japanese in the Pacific. Ostervik's temperamental unsuitability consisted of the fact that he was intent on enforcing the law and unsympathetic with the aim of a Main Street bar owner with political connections to break it. The last I heard of him, he was playing in a symphony orchestra in a big Eastern city.

But let us return to Inspector Bill Parker, who had described the two police cabals which controlled graft under what he termed a "cop setup." By this he meant that no true underworld boss ran the rackets in Los Angeles and that racketeers were controlled and plucked by department members of the two police outfits who, in reality, were themselves racketeers as averred in the forepart of this book.

Parker stated that Administrative Vice controlled all book-making pay-offs and that Mayor Bowron was a "God damned stupid ass, who had no idea what was going on." That statement I questioned then, and

I still question it now. Parker concluded that the politicians were keeping Bowron in office on a "sweet and pure" program and that the police department under the two setups was just about as corrupt as was any department in the United States. The department's principal reason for keeping the gangsters out of Los Angeles was *not* one of civic purity, according to Parker. It was done in order that those operating together with their police allies, would have no competition.

Bowron presented Mickey Cohen to the public as the "ghost in the woodpile" so that, if anything were to go wrong, Mickey could be used as a "whipping boy." Fingers would then be pointed at the Mick and exclamations would be piously made: "He did it! He did it!"

Parker explained that he was telling me these things because he wanted to make a fair and square proposition. If I *would go* to the grand jury and relate what he had told me, together with what I knew about the Brenda Allen investigation in its entirety, due to the pending election Bowron would be forced to rid the department of both Horrall and Reed. Parker reminded me that the police department was out to "get me" in one way or another, and he suggested that, if I would "play ball" with him, he would see to it that I was made his assistant for he knew "damned good and well" that he was the logical man to step into Horrall's shoes.

Throughout his conversation, it was obvious that Parker did not know that I *had already been* to the grand jury. I asked him if my going to the grand jury at that time wouldn't insure Bowron's defeat?

"Hell, no," he replied. "If anything, it will insure his success. I've been Bowron's legal advisor. You know, I am a lawyer in my own right. I'm sure that if Bowron would expel these people, he'd go into office with an overwhelming majority."

I could not agree with Parker. Still, I told him to go ahead. I told him that if he could arrange to get me subpoenaed before the grand jury, I would tell everything I knew, and answer any questions that were asked of me. When I left Parker, it was with the understanding that he would arrange to have me called before the grand jury. Of course, we agreed that our meeting was to be a top drawer secret.

At this writing, newspaper headlines proclaim that Harold (Happy) Meltzer will be re-tried on the gun charge. It was on May 14, 1949, that the first jury had disagreed regarding Meltzer's guilt, having claimed that the police department had planted the gun in the car in which he was riding with Cohen. The news report follows. Quote:

"That sensational first trial produced charges by the defense that vice squad officers, Rudy Wellpott and E. V. Jackson, tried to shake Cohen and Meltzer down.

'The thing bounced around from there through a grand jury investigation, a full blown police scandal, retirement of Chief of Police C. B. Horrall, shake-up of the force, a handful of indictments against assorted policemen, then some dismissals and some trials where the police were found not guilty.

"Yes, and since the day when Cohen blew the lid off things by saying he had wire recordings to back up his shake-down charges things have changed Meltzer and his boss, Cohen. In fact, there's a $17,000 civil suit pending against Meltzer, filed by Mickey Cohen himself.

"So there was considerable speculation today whether Cohen would take the stand in "Happy's" defense again, although both were in the same boat at the moment as defendants in another trial involving conspiracy to beat up one radio repairman, Alfred M. Pearson." (Subsequently Cohen, members of his mob and two police officers were acquitted of the conspiracy charge for the Pearson beating.)

"Investigator Tom Slack of the district attorney's office notified Meltzer's attorney, Vernon Ferguson, that attempts will be made within the next thirty days to reset the illegal gun case.

"Meltzer, being an ex-convict, can't carry guns without violating the law. And this he did on January 15, 1949, the D. A. charges." Unquote:

Personally, I believe Meltzer was framed.

VICE AND POLITICS

*All, all look up with reverential awe,
At crimes that 'scape, or triumph o'er the law.*
(Epilogue to Satire, Dialogue 1.-A. Pope.)

Mayor Bowron and his spokesmen had done a pretty thorough job of convincing the voters that, unless they reelected him, gangsters would take over Los Angeles and the gutters would run curb-high with blood. He had stressed what he claimed to be a fact that Los Angeles "had the most honest, most efficient and smartest police department in the United States; that the city was particularly free of graft and corruption and that no pay-offs or organized graft were tolerated within its boundaries.

Bowron, like an old time bunco man, tells the tale beautifully. That what he declaims frequently, if not all the time, is unrelated to the facts, should not be held against him. He wants to retain his office, doesn't he?

He fancied himself as an "Horatio at the Bridge" holding back the tide of evil-doers who were intent upon capturing Los Angeles for the rackets. In his speeches, he became "the indispensable mayor." If there was any good deed for which he could take credit, he latched onto it. He became a first class "lens louse." If a newspaper photographer was in hailing distance, Bowron's ears twitched, his nostrils flared and he pawed the earth like a plunging stallion who had just seen a trim filly.

In 1938, Bowron had been elected on a recall platform whose avowed purpose it was to "destroy the underworld" and to free Los Angeles from the tentacles of police graft and corruption. During his 1949 campaign for re-election, he spoke as if these purposes had been accomplished facts.

Before Bowron, pay-offs, racketeers and corruption; after Bowron, purity, civic cleanliness and municipal decency. Whereas coppers had sprouted horns in the administration preceding Bowron's; coppers under Bowron wore halos.

It is passing strange how the average citizen swallows political propaganda whole without digesting it. Bowron had declared the city to be free of gangsters, despite the fact that members of various gangs had been killing one another on the city's streets. If the reader believes that I am writing from a purely prejudicial standpoint, let him examine the record.

The police department's gangster squad was in charge of one Lieutenant Willie Burns. At this late date, I defy anyone to go back over the record and show me a single instance in which Lieutenant Willie Burns arrested one important gangster and in which the gangster in question was convicted. I ask anyone to show me the factual results of his arrests of unimportant gangsters. None was imprisoned for any length of time.

It was well-known that police officers serving under Lieutenant Burns were frequenters of Mickey Cohen's cocktail bar on Santa Monica Boulevard, where they sat hour after hour in a rear room drinking Cohen's whiskey. Much to their embarrassment, a Los Angeles Times' police reporter surprised a gang of them there one night drinking Cohen's whiskey and eating his food.

Yet, here was Bowron tilting at gangster windmills while Los Angeles was chock-full of gangsters — gangsters who had been here during all the years he had served as mayor of Los Angeles.

To an insider, Bowron's speeches were amusing. Through the knowledge I had gained in investigations, I knew exactly how rotten his police administration had become. It was a cop setup in which police thieves were taking all routes to make a fast dollar. Whereas some control of the thievery existed at the top of the ladder, middle and lower rungs, coppers were taking their best aim in sniping at dishonest dollars.

Bowron's police administration reminded me of a beautiful building, its facade shining in the sunlight, immaculately clean as to exterior, but with its foundation nearly eaten through by police and underworld termites.

Oddly enough the "important" institutions of the city, the banks, the insurance companies, the advertisers and the newspapers — along with a group of ministers, wanted to perpetuate Bowron in office. All of these elements got together to paint glowing pictures of the fearless, fiery mayor keeping closed the gates of the city to gangster Frankie Costello and his eastern hoodlums.

On the other hand, Bowron's opponent, a mild mannered man with the introspective mien of an engineer, Lloyd Aldrich, was depicted as the repository of everything evil. By innuendo, he was linked to the underworld. There must have been two of them for Bowron's administration was linked to one. Aldrich, to hear Bowron's word hirelings tell it, was supported by sinister men. Compared to Bowron, Aldrich appeared to have had little money to spend on his campaign.

The eventual resignation of Chief of Police Clemence B. Horrall as a result of the Cohen-Allen police scandals, and the interim appointment of Marine General William A. Worton, did not change the basic picture in the Los Angeles police department. The rats merely holed in to await the end of the storm.

Worton's appointment by Bowron was a desperate measure on the part of the latter to retrieve lost prestige. Political through and through, it was akin to plastering fresh icing on a stale cake. Bowron, reading the returns from the May 31, 1949, election, had been around political purlieus too long not to be able to read their significance. They said that the jig was nearly up.

Despite the fact that Mayor Bowron had everything in his favor in the way of money, newspaper support and most other media of propaganda, he had a narrow squeak at the polls, having won the election by a mere thirty-one thousand votes, which meant that, had there been a difference of sixteen thousand votes, Aldrich would have been mayor and Bowron an EX.

Significantly, Bowron's pluralities down through the years since 1938, when he first became mayor, have narrowed. Facts have a way of finally impinging on the public mentality, and they have an erosive ability to dispel the windy fogs of propaganda and half-truths.

I do not contend that Lloyd Aldrich would have made a better mayor than Fletcher E. Bowron. That is something about which I know nothing. However, I am certain that he couldn't possibly have made a worse mayor — regardless of how hard he tried.

I do not know Lloyd Aldrich, nor have I ever met the personages who sponsored his campaign and tried to root him home as mayor, despite the fact that my motive for appearing before the Los Angeles county grand jury was linked with his candidacy. In all truth and sincerity, I can state that I have never sponsored anyone's candidacy for public office. The only person whom I sponsor is Charles Stoker who got a dirty deal at the hands of conniving politicians, slimy racketeers and crooked police officers.

The appointment of Marine General Worton as chief of police by Mayor Bowron after Horrall's enforced resignation was designed to restore Bowron's prestige and confuse the issues by stirring up the muddy waters of the police mess to shield the ugly facts.

General Worton's sole contribution, as far as I can see, to the rehabilitation of the police department in the public eye, was to make innumerable batches of transfers. Inasmuch as he was a total stranger to Los Angeles and to the police department, he could not possibly know what he was doing, whether or not it was for the best or for the worst when he made the transfers.

After a few months of Worton, the newspapers supporting the city administration, wrote editorials stating that "Worton had restored public confidence in the police department."

Who says so? The newspapers, Worton, Bowron, or the public?

Whatever excuse may be offered in mitigation, to my knowledge the police administration of Mayor Fletcher E. Bowron is rotten to the core. If it's any better now than it was, it is because Bowron HAD to deodorize it. Bowron may divert blame from himself by fancy political maneuvering; those who would continue him in office may create a smoke screen by attacking his enemies and critics; but in the final analysis the blame will rest with him and with no one else.

Bowron knew what he was doing when he jumped Captain Joe Reed over the heads of inspectors and deputy chiefs of police and made Reed the factual head of the police department as assistant chief of police. Joe Reed by his administrative linkage with Rudy Wellpott also knew what he was doing.

Let those who wish continue to believe his two-faced perorations, predicated on "Good, Honest and Efficient Government." As for myself, I have no illusions about Mr. Bowron.

Although Mayor Bowron insisted that Candidate Aldrich was in league with the underworld, Mr. Aldrich incessantly demanded proof of these charges. He offered to meet the mayor in a public forum and to answer any and all questions that Bowron might choose to ask. Bowron refused to meet Aldrich. Why? Was it because Aldrich knew the facts attendant upon Bowron's administration of the police department? Or, was Bowron fearful that Aldrich would propound questions that he could not answer? Was Bowron afraid that Aldrich had the uptown lowdown?

Be that as it may, Aldrich appeared eager to lay his record alongside that of the Mayor and to let the voters judge them on character, honesty, probity and background, but Bowron wanted no part of it.

Bowron must have found little comfort in his "Victory" on the morning of June 1, 1949. Scanning the election returns, he knew that he had been in a major battle and that, with everything in his favor, there were many signs that Los Angeles voters were catching up with the bunk. His theme song, "I'm fighting the underworld, I'm protecting you from gangsters," was, politically speaking, becoming threadbare and inefficacious as an instrument of political propaganda certain to ensnare the unwary voter into a "Yes" vote for Hizzoner. Politically, Bowron emerged from the campaign badly clawed and scratched.

His previously tightly calked political barrel was beginning to drip slime, scandal and dirty mud. Its staves were becoming loosened by the pressure of facts.

Bowron's whipping boy, Michael (Mickey) Cohen, was becoming aware that the thousands of dollars he had been ladling out to a locust swarm of police chiselers, newspapermen and other self-important figures on the underworld- political fringe, were doing him no good in the realm of practicality. He was enraged at the predicament in which he found himself when Sergeant Elmer V. Jackson arrested his aide, Harold Meltzer, on the concealed weapon charge. Mickey, who had to foot the bill for the trial, was determined that he wouldn't "lose" brother Meltzer to San Quentin prison. He served notice of his intention to prove in open court that the motivation behind Meltzer's arrest, which he characterized as a frame-up, was attributable to the fact that he wouldn't part with several thousand dollars to satisfy the insatiable appetites of grafting police officers.

Whether Mickey lied, or whether the police officers lied, is something for you to determine. In my opinion, the best index is the verbatim transcript of the Harold Meltzer trial which resulted in a hung jury. Obviously some of the jurors believed Mickey. But before we go into that, here is the gist of Mickey's testimony at Meltzer's trial:

According to Mickey, Meltzer had been arrested by Lieutenant Rudy Wellpott and Sergeant Elmer V. Jackson in county territory. This meant that technically these officers had stepped out of their jurisdiction to make the pinch.

On the witness stand, Cohen declared flatly that the gun had been "planted" on Meltzer; that he hadn't a gun in his possession and that he had not been carrying a gun. Cohen said that Wellpott and Jackson were impelled by revenge because he, Cohen, had refused to submit to a twenty thousand dollar shakedown. Furthermore, he pointed out that he had wire recordings of telephone conversations to prove his statements. He also had wire recordings of conversations between Sergeant Jackson and Prostitute Brenda Allen. On a technicality the presiding judge refused to admit these recordings as evidence, ruling that they were not legal evidence. This ruling brought relief to Sergeant Jackson and Lieutenant Wellpott.

The grand jurors' collective ears began to twitch. Remember, this was a grand jury that wasn't fixed and couldn't be fixed. The grand jury summoned numerous police officials all of whose stories were "pat." The grand jury learned nothing.

Attorney Vernon Ferguson, defending Meltzer on the gun charge, dropped the first hint of what was to develop when he said: "If we show you that Lieutenant Rudy Wellpott and Sergeant E. V. Jackson tried to extort five thousand dollars from Mickey Cohen, would it affect your decision in this case?"

"This is the most cold-blooded frame-up ever perpetrated—and a dirty shame!" commented Cohen.

Attorney Ferguson said that, although none of the mayoralty candidates knew anything about the attempted extortion of Cohen, he would show that attempts at minor extortion of Cohen by Wellpott and Jackson had taken place two years previous to the Meltzer arrest. Defense Attorney Samuel Rummel said at the opening of the trial: "We will prove by testimony of witnesses from the stand that for a period of one and a half years before Meltzer's arrest, Lieutenant Rudy Wellpott and Sergeant Elmer V. Jackson kept up a constant extortion of Mickey Cohen.

"They (the police officers) would take their women to high-priced restaurants — The House of Murphy, The Brown Derby, Dave's Blue Room, Slapsie Maxie's and other places—would wine and dine them lavishly and when it came time to pay the check, would say, 'Send it to Mickey Cohen.'

"We will have witnesses from these places to prove that these shakedowns occurred. We will prove that this entire case is a frame-up because Cohen refused to contribute ten to twenty thousand dollars to what Wellpott and Jackson said was the campaign fund of Mayor Fletcher E. Bowron."

Bowron's campaign manager, Martin Pollard, a wealthy north Hollywood automobile distributor, testified that no one save members of the campaign committee, had been authorized to accept money on behalf of Mayor Bowron, or to seek money for his campaign.

"When Cohen refused to give them the money, we will show that they reduced the price to five thousand dollars," Rummel shouted.

"About three months before Meltzer was arrested by Wellpott and Jackson, Jackson telephoned Mickey and suggested that they meet. Jackson had called him a number of times, using the name 'Jake.'" "'I told you Wellpott is a treacherous guy,' Jackson told Cohen, 'But you can get in good with him and won't get rousted any more. Get together with Rudy. We've got you down on the list for a ten to twenty thousand dollar contribution to Mayor Bowron's campaign.'

"Cohen refused. 'I don't give a damn who is mayor,' he told Jackson. 'I'm from thirty to forty thousand dollars in debt now. I'm in a legitimate business and I haven't got that kind of money. You guys know if you had anything on me you'd get me. I just run a haberdashery store.'

"About two months before the Meltzer arrest," Rummel continued, "Jackson called Cohen again, and said: 'I've got the man with me, now. Meet us in the usual place.'

"Several times before, they had met in the 9000 block on Sunset Boulevard in county territory. Mickey's driver drew up and parked behind the police car on a dark street. Jackson came back to Cohen's car, and demanded: 'Get that car the hell out of here, and come with us!'

"So, Mickey got in the police car with Jackson and Wellpott, and they started to go toward the beach through Beverly Hills. The car was riding sort of erratic, and a Beverly Hills police car started after it.

"There was a wild ride all through Beverly Hills until they finally eluded the police car. Then they began to talk. 'Why don't you be reasonable?' Jackson asked. 'You know what Rudy has done down on Main Street? Everything down there is going good with the boys. The B-Girls are working and everything is all right.'

"Then they suggested a ten thousand dollar contribution; and Cohen told them he was in a legitimate business. He said he didn't see why he should pay anybody. Wellpott and Jackson were sore. They drove back and let Mickey out at his haberdashery.

"But they weren't through. A few days before they arrested Meltzer in Cohen's automobile, Jackson made another telephone call to Mickey.

'You mishandled things very badly with Rudy,' he said. 'I'm telling you he's treacherous. Now, Mickey, how are the boys? You'd better keep them clean, or Wellpott is going to get you.'

"Several days later Meltzer was arrested by Wellpott and Jackson on the gun charge. Jackson again came to Cohen and they drove off in his automobile. 'You didn't use your head,' Jackson told him. 'Wellpott's going to get you. He'll keep rousting and arresting you until a jury finds you guilty of something. We'll square away the Meltzer charge for five thousand,' he promised, then volunteered, 'I'll tell you something — they're going to smash Meltzer's automobile.'

"They returned to Cohen's haberdashery, and Cohen left Jackson's automobile. Deputy sheriffs, who were watching near-by, saw that there was no license plates on the police car; and they went over and shook down Jackson and the automobile.

"The sheriff's deputies made a report of this, and we will introduce it as evidence that Cohen has at all times refused to comply with their (Wellpott's and Jackson's) request, knowing that it was a cold, deliberate shakedown," Rummel concluded.

On May 7, 1949, Rummel electrified the courtroom when he announced that Sound Engineer, J. Arthur Vaus, would help establish a direct link between Sergeant Elmer V. Jackson and Hollywood prostitute, Brenda Allen. He also stated that he would introduce certain recorded conversations between Jackson and Cohen, to substantiate the shakedown charges.

Still on the witness stand, Jackson was asked by Rummel if, in a telephone conversation with Cohen, he hadn't said that he was in hot water with the police department because he was sitting in an automobile with Brenda Allen on the night he had killed Highwayman Roy "Peewee" Lewis. Jackson, caught by surprise, looked beseechingly at his attorney for help; but before that worthy could intercede, Rummel asked Jackson: "Would you like to hear the conversations?" As he said this, Rummel moved towards the sound recorder. But the court barred the highly interesting and damning evidence. Whatever the court's move, one thing was certain — Jackson was sitting in an automobile with Brenda Allen on the night he killed the "Peewee."

Deputy District Attorney William Russell, in his closing argument, said that he saw nothing wrong in Wellpott's and Jackson's eating with Cohen, since they were police officers interested in keeping Cohen under observation, and since Mickey was a racketeer and accordingly anxious to win their friendship.

Harold "Happy" Meltzer stuck to his story that he had no gun. However, the public gaze by now had shifted to the county grand jury which was determined to get at the bottom of the mess. After a long wait, the Meltzer jury reported that it was hopelessly deadlocked and was unable to reach a verdict in the case.

Said one juror: "We couldn't decide who were lying — Mickey Cohen and Meltzer or Lieutenant Wellpott and Sergeant Jackson."

The court reset the Meltzer gun charge for re-trial. Meltzer went free and the question of whether he actually had a gun on the night in question, or whether Wellpott and Jackson with their cohort, Police Officer G. A. James, had planted a gun on him, still remains moot.

Jackson testified that he had been a police officer for nine years. He admitted that Cohen had, on occasion, picked up checks for meals he had eaten at restaurants in Hollywood; but he vehemently denied having attempted to shake Cohen down.

Here is a verbatim account of Jackson's testimony:

Attorney Rummel:	Did you ever dine with Mickey Cohen?
Jackson:	Oh, no, I have never eaten at the same table with him.
Rummel:	When you and Wellpott ate at Dave's Blue Room with your friends, did you pay the check?
Jackson:	I didn't pay the check. I don't know who did.
Rummel:	Ever eat at the Piccadilly?
Jackson:	Yes, I have eaten there with others.
Rummel:	Did you pick up the check?

Vice and Politics

Jackson:	No. I don't know who did.
Rummel:	Now, how about the House of Murphy?
Jackson:	Well, uh, — yes. I was there with another officer and a lady friend. Cohen and a party were at another table.
Rummel:	Did you pay the bill?
Jackson:	When I asked for the bill, I was told Cohen had paid it.
Rummel:	Ah, you didn't say to the people at the House of Murphy, 'I don't want this character, Cohen, paying my bills — I want to pay them myself!' Did you say that?
Jackson:	No?

On the stand, Lieutenant Rudy Wellpott denied that he ever had been in an automobile with Mickey Cohen. However, he admitted that he had been Cohen's guest at several expensive dinners and at the grand opening of Mickey Cohen's swank haberdashery, where a lady friend who was with him had received a handbag as a gift.

The grand jury screamed for the wire recording mentioned in the Meltzer trial, whereupon attorneys for Cohen pointed to Sound Engineer J. Arthur Vaus, and said: "He's got 'em."

Vaus then put the switch on the deal, declaring that the wire recordings had been stolen from the rear of his truck which he had parked on the main street of suburban Baldwin Park. When it was pointed out that Vaus and his recordings were supposed to be under guard by the district attorney's office, Vaus changed his story. He said that the recordings hadn't been stolen after all. He then came up with the six coils of wire recordings.

It was my turn to be flabbergasted. The public was greatly confused and with reason; but looking back on what had occurred, I see no reason why I should have been confused. I was then placed in the same boat with Harold (Happy) Meltzer even though he was a racketeer and I was an honest police officer. However, certain aforementioned individuals had reasons to nail both of us although their reasons and the motives for them weren't the same. Remember what I wrote regarding homogeneity?

As a result of false testimony and fabrication, I was suspended from the police department and charged with burglary. And who do you think was responsible for my plight? The deduction is elementary, Watson. I was led to the slaughter by none other than my erstwhile charming little co-worker, Policewoman Audre Davis.

Intent upon casting me to perdition on a burglary charge, Audre made things even murkier by declaring that her testimony against Brenda Allen for attempted pandering had been perjured.

While people were all at sea regarding her motive in this right-about-face, Audre startled them again by declaring: "I am, or was, in love with Police Sergeant Charles Stoker!"

I want you to remember this amazing declaration, inasmuch as it has important bearing on what is to follow. If, at the end of this account, you believe that Audre Davis ever was, or had been in love with me, then, in my opinion you will believe anything and you will be very welcome the next time a carnival comes to your town with a three card monte man operating its shell game.

But in the great political-underworld-police game of punching and countering a punch, it was my turn to speak. I testified as follows:

"So much has been said about connections between policeman and underworld figures, about telephone-line tappings and strange wire recordings, that I'd like to tell you my own story from the beginning.

"I can tell you how Brenda Allen operated and I can tell you about some of those tapped telephone lines. No one could be more surprised than I at the weird picture of things which came out of it all.

"It's an ugly mess.

"Policemen always like to think of their fellow officers as straight shooters. If one gets off the straight and narrow, we want to see that he gets back on it again. But we don't like to cause him any trouble if we can help it.

"After I came back from the Army in 1945, I was returned to my old job on the vice squad, doing the usual routine that goes with such work.

Then one night, I met J. Arthur Vaus in the course of an investigation. He was a minister's son and a former choir boy with a yen for things electronic."

I then related the details of this meeting and explained how Vaus had started to assist me and how the investigation of Brenda Allen had its beginning. I told of the night when we heard Brenda dial the number of the administrative vice squad, and leave word for Sergeant Jackson to telephone her after she had been told that he was not in.

I testified as to the events of the following night when we heard Sergeant Jackson telephone Brenda and tell her that he would be over to see her; of how she had "honeyed" him over the telephone; and of how Brenda had then called another man, explaining that she couldn't see him the next day because she had to see Sergeant Jackson. I related that what I had first considered a "romance" between the pair had proven more than that. Their unholy alliance was for purposes of business, dirty business involving underworld money and police graft.

That was the gist of my statement. But before we launch into Audre Davis's expressed love for me, a highly important phase of The Stoker Story, I must first tell you of the plot which (unknown to me) was under way to discredit anything that I might say, and also to discredit anything that I had accomplished in honest police endeavor.

This plot, in my opinion, began with a personal call paid me by Chief Investigator H. Leo Stanley of the District Attorney's office.

Through no act of my own, I knew that I was in a tough spot. My intuition, or sixth sense, told me that. Too, there had been straws in the wind of a factual nature, indicating that the individuals whose wrath I had incurred were not idle.

When a police-protected playhouse starts to come tumbling down, and its inmates suddenly drop some of the graft balls they've been secretly juggling, fear and tension pervade police purlieus and those with guilty consciences quickly begin to consider how they're going to pick up the slack and evade unpleasant consequences.

I was an "unpleasant consequence" personified; and I judged correctly that the forces of darkness were at work in a plot designed to discredit my work in uncovering sin and corruption.

I reviewed all of my past actions on the police department and concluded that if anything were done to me, it wouldn't be done on the level. But that was small consolation. I reflected that a man is just as dead from a bullet whether or not it is fired by accident or on purpose. I knew that participants in the racket have many elusive and shadowy conspirators who come to their aid in times of jeopardy, and one never knows until the play is made just who they are.

Under the circumstances, I had a right to suspect everyone's motives and I did. Consequently, I determined that, no matter what kind of a curve ball would be pitched, I would not be caught with my bat on my shoulder and I wouldn't be surprised by the pitch. However, we live and learn and I must admit that I was surprised.

CONSPIRATORIAL LADY

I realize that this book is replete with the sexual element, albeit sordid and vile, but this is through no choice of mine. Brenda and her retinue are germane to my story, and if the narrative of my personal experiences as a Los Angeles police officer is to be thoroughly aired in the public weal, and for the purpose of refurbishing my reputation, Brenda and her sisterhood cannot be ignored.

But there is more to the spindle, or feminine side, of the story than is exemplified by Brenda and her doings. There remains Audre Davis, the policewoman, who said that she had perjured herself in the Brenda Allen pandering trial. Audre, who tried to send me to the penitentiary on a trumped up burglary charge.

Whether Audre Davis told the truth at Brenda's trial — and I think she did — or whether she told the truth when she said that she had perjured herself, is obscure. With little Audre, the truth is an elusive thing.

But the fact remains that she had the gall, gall which I believe to have been inspired by someone else, to tell the new chief of police — Willam A. Worton — the fantastic story that I had burglarized the offices of Joint Control at the intersection of Beverly Boulevard and Alvarado Street. She stated that I had confessed to having climbed through a hole in the ceiling, a semi-circular hole made for a ventilator, sixteen inches wide and twelve inches high.

The purpose of my purportedly felonious entrance, she said, was to retrieve a cancelled check, attendant upon the construction of the aforementioned duplex I was building.

Presumably a hitherto loyal co-worker and a "friend" of mine, Audre was questioned as to her motive in making the accusation against me.

Her motive, she said, *was love, unrequited love*. Yes, she had been in love with me. She implied that she had given me her "all" and that I, vile man that I was, had cast her aside without qualm or reason. According to her testimony, she wanted to clear her conscience — an ambitious job I would say. To quote Audre: "I couldn't stand aside and see fine men on the police department suffer at another officer's hands."

If you view me through Audre's eyes, I am truly a monster. Regardless of the fact that her story was a fabrication, Audre's testimony placed me in a tough position. Anything I said would be suspect. A denial would only heighten the suspicion of those ready to believe that what she had said was true. I was in a comparable position to that of a man wrongly accused of being a homosexual. If he denies it, people ask: "What did you expect him to do?"

The majority of people, and particularly is this true of men, is inclined to accept a woman's word rather than a man's despite the fact that history is filled with examples of woman's treachery, unfathomable duplicity and congenital and emotional inability to tell the truth. Legal text books have been written on the shaky veracity of women as witnesses.

But let us once and for all time demolish the myth that Audre Davis was in love with me at the time she made her accusation against me, or before she made it, or that my relations with her were ever other than those of a police coworker and friend.

I regret that it is incumbent upon me now to emblazon Miss Davis's name in the white and glaring light of truth and fact; a light that is uncomplimentary to her. But I have no other alternative. I would be less than honest if I were to say that I feel sorry for Miss Davis. Basically and intellectually, I have no sympathy for a liar — or for anyone who will deliberately attempt to lie a man into a penitentiary.

Audre Davis, for reasons of her own, or for motives of others which she adopted as her own, elected to place herself in the position in which she now finds herself.

It is my hope that a factual and detailed account of my relations with Miss Davis will correct the false impressions which have already been widely disseminated in local newspapers. After you read the following pages, you may judge who was lying — Miss Davis or I.

As I have related, Miss Davis arrived in Hollywood at the time when the Brenda Allen investigation was nearing conclusion. She had been sent here, primarily to work with the divisional vice squad on another investigation which was in no way connected with Brenda. However, she did become a party to the Brenda Allen probe within a few days of its conclusion.

After the Brenda investigation, I remained in Hollywood for several months, working vice. In the interim, Miss Davis *periodically* worked with Officer Jack Ruggles and me.

During this period, Miss Davis frequently evinced a more than professional interest in Officer Ruggles, rather than an interest in Charles Stoker. This is understandable. Officer Ruggles is a young, handsome, clean cut, six-foot-four inch giant. When I first noticed her interest in Jack Ruggles and thought that it was amatory, I warned Ruggles that I had my suspicions of Miss Davis. I pointed out to him that we had originally requested the services of a far more competent policewoman and that this policewoman had been dismissed from the department at the end of her probationary period, apparently without cause. I reminded Ruggles that, when we had asked for other policewomen to come to Hollywood, their commander had refused to honor our requests. I told Ruggles that this, on the face of it, was peculiar and that it was more peculiar than ever when Miss Davis was aced into the Hollywood vice division, which was hot and steaming because of the Brenda Allen investigation.

But, in justice to Miss Davis, Ruggles and I had come to respect her ability as a policewoman. We felt that it was largely attributable to the fact that she had been raised in Hollywood, had an exceptional knowledge of bars and bartenders, and in addition was the daughter of a police officer who by fair means or foul had attained high rank in the department — as deputy chief of police.

In working with Policewoman Davis, my suspicions faded somewhat because of her excellent performance as a policewoman.

During the Brenda Allen trial, Officer Ruggles, Miss Davis, two newspaperwomen and I decided to go to Chinatown to have dinner.

One of the newspaperwomen sat in the back of the car with Ruggles, while the other newspaperwoman occupied the front seat with Miss Davis and me. I was driving. The woman sitting with Ruggles began to shower him with attention, displaying considerable affection for him. This, I may say, was done in a joking, frivolous manner, perhaps superinduced by a few drinks she had previously consumed. However, I noticed that Miss Davis was obviously showing resentment. It was apparent that the newspaperwoman was trying to irritate Audre and was having fun at her expense. Finally, Miss Davis could stand it no longer.

"You must be desperate for a man!" she flared.

"You just wish you were back here — that's your trouble," the reporter quipped, proving that one woman can see through another at a glance, while a man can't, even though he has an X-Ray machine trained on a gal.

We arrived in Chinatown, parked our car and entered the cafe. I went to the rear, and Ruggles and the newspaperwoman began to dance. For several minutes, Miss Davis sat on a bar stool glaring at the couple. Then, before anyone could halt her, she walked to the middle of the floor, pulled the dancers apart and belted the newspaperwoman in the eye.

Before the excitement had died down, I beckoned to Ruggles, who seemingly was enjoying the fact that two dames were rowing over him, or that one dame was giving it to the other because of him.

"We'd better get the hell out of here!" I warned. We marched out and drove off, leaving an irate Audre Davis in command.

This incident in itself was proof that Miss Davis was not in love with me, or if she was, her actions that night tended to becloud that fact. She didn't slug the newspaperwoman over the affections of Charles Stoker; she slugged her because she was jealous of her attentions to handsome Officer Ruggles.

The following day, I talked to the other newspaperwoman. "Charley, what the hell's wrong with Davis?" she asked. "She's been coming to my house on the beach virtually every day and always talks about her boy friend — Sergeant Jesse — in Hollywood. What's this business between her and Ruggles?"

"Hell, I don't know anything about her affairs," I answered.

Later, I took Miss Davis aside and read her the riot act. I told her that her personal affairs and her love life were of no concern to me as long as they didn't involve me or my job.

"I want a promise out of you that this will not occur again," I informed her. "Or in lieu of that promise, I'll ask that you be transferred."

"It won't happen again, Charlie," she said. "The only reason it happened last night was that I had been drinking."

I then warned her to leave Officer Ruggles alone.

"I don't care anything about Ruggles," she replied. "He's too young for me, anyway. Besides, I have a steady boy friend."

She then confided that her "boy friend" was Sergeant John Jesse. The newspaperwoman had been right.

This occurred after the Brenda Allen trial and conviction. Yet, Miss Davis was to testify later that she had *perjured* herself in the Brenda Allen trial in compliance with my wishes *because of her love for me*. Now, add that up any way you can.

After the slugging incident, things went along smoothly for a while. Miss Davis worked with Officer Ruggles and me, performing efficiently and giving no reason for criticism. We made several spectacular arrests which were newsworthy and in which Miss Davis played leading roles. As a result, she received considerable publicity and was fast building a reputation as a better than competent policewoman.

We three worked hard together. We had been successful and we became quite friendly. There was no longer any suspicion in my mind regarding Miss Davis, despite the fact that other officers had warned me against her when she had first appeared in our midst.

Six months after the Brenda trial, Miss Davis approached me one day. I could see that she was worried. She said she would like to talk to me alone, and she suggested that we go to her apartment. I assented.

"Charlie," she began, "I know what a hell of a temper you have. Because of that, I want you to listen to me until I'm through. And, for Christ's sake, don't jump to conclusions!

"I need your help. I'm going to tell you a few things you should know and I want you to believe me. You're the finest guy I ever knew and the smartest police officer I've ever worked with — including my father." She paused briefly, then said: "It probably will surprise you to hear that I was sent to Hollywood to become friendly with either you or Ruggles, and to find out what you were doing."

"Who sent you?" I demanded.

"Hell, I don't know who sent me," was the reply.

"What were you supposed to find out?"

"It's funny," she answered. "Just before my probation ended, I was called into personnel and Captain Cecil Wisdom talked to me. He said that in making my application to come into the police department, I had sworn that I'd been married twice. Captain Wisdom told me the department had found that I'd been married *three* times. He said that it had checked with the courts and couldn't find a record of a divorce from my first husband.

"Wisdom questioned me about the divorce. I told him that my first husband had sued me for divorce but that I had fought the suit. Later, my father told me that he had obtained an annulment. Captain Wisdom said that the department was going to discharge me anyway for having made a false application. I called my father and he came to Los Angeles from Las Vegas, Nevada. After he came, my father told me that everything had been fixed and that I was to be transferred to Hollywood vice. He told me to find out everything I could about your activities and in turn to report BACK TO HIM.

"Later, he gave me hell for having gotten mixed up in the Brenda Allen case as I'd also been told to report to him and get his advice on everything I did. I thought you should know all of this, Charlie," Audre told me in a burst of confidence and in a half-whisper as if she were about to cry. If one believes Audre's story, evidently the long arm of Las

Vegas gamblers and racketeers still reached into the Los Angeles police department.

Audre confided that she was in desperate need of my help, concerning an affair that she couldn't discuss with her own father. She feared that, if the police department got word of it, inasmuch as its members were unhappy about her role in the Brenda Allen business, they might fire her.

"I've been going with a married man," she confessed, "a special officer downtown. I broke off relations with the guy when I started to go with Sergeant John Jesse. Now, he's jealous and is spreading stories among police officers he knows. He's been bothering me constantly. He can't seem to understand that I don't want anything further to do with him. And as if that isn't enough, his wife has threatened to go to the police department."

I asked Audre what stories the man had been telling.

She replied that he boasted of having a key to her apartment – that he had entered unexpectedly and had caught her en flagrante delicto with a police officer.

"Why doesn't your boy friend, Sergeant Jesse, take care of him?" I inquired. "Can't he speak to the character?"

"I dare not ask Jesse to do that," Audre exclaimed. "If I did, he'd find out about the other police officer."

"If the story is untrue, what difference does it make?" I persisted.

"But the story is true," she confessed. "I was in bed with the other officer." She then named her bedfellow.

I then suggested that she go to the police officer who was responsible for her plight, but she replied that it would only make matters worse, inasmuch as the officer was of Mexican descent and had a terrible temper. Furthermore, he didn't like the special officer who had been circulating the stories. If he learned that the special officer had been talking, he'd go downtown, start one hell of a fight with him and get them all into trouble.

I promised that I'd see what I could do.

I then called upon the special officer and told him that I'd heard he was spreading stories about Miss Davis. I suggested that he had better desist — unless he was eager for trouble.

"What I said about Miss Davis was no lie," he assured me. "Furthermore, I know a few other things about Miss Davis that I'm not telling." He implied that I obviously had an interest in her, and hinted that in all probability, I was sleeping with her, myself.

I repeat that I have never worn a halo in so far as women are concerned; I've had my share of them and have had to rape none; but this man was placing me in the category of one of the boys in Miss Davis's stud stable. I had, and I still have an aversion to being classified in such a manner.

I was incensed. I told him that, if he chose to link my name with the sordid affair, I certainly would put a stop to his story telling. He asked me what I meant to do.

"I may be compelled to come down and slap you around a little on my off duty time," I said. To emphasize my point, I proceeded to persuade him that I meant business. I regret this exceedingly now. Under the circumstances, I feel that I owe the man an apology. He was right about Audre; and I was wrong. Perhaps there is no better place than this to extend an apology. So, I apologize.

The next day I told Audre what had happened. I assured her that the man had promised that he would never again mention her name. Then, she asked if I would check the records regarding her divorce. She said that she was still worried, having obtained no word about the action other than a statement from her father that he had "fixed" it.

Audre accompanied me to the Hall of Records, on Broadway. Refreshing my memory from notes made at that time, I found that she had given her age as sixteen when she married twenty-four-year-old August Ottiger, who had been born in Germany. They were married July 16, 1937.

The records revealed that on August 23, 1939, two years later, Ottiger had filed suit for divorce, charging extreme cruelty. He alleged that Audre had an ungovernable temper, called him vile names, repeatedly went out with other men, drank excessively, had three times attempted to commit suicide, had at one time choked him, had cut her wrists with a bread knife, had drunk iodine, and had attempted to jump off a high porch on several occasions.

The record revealed that Audre had contested the complaint and that on September 28, 1939, a dismissal of the action had been made.

Diligently, I tried to find some record of a divorce or an annulment, without success. Miss Davis and I both questioned the clerk at the time, and were assured that there had been no divorce and no annulment.

I learned that, on January 4, 1940, Audre had married Raymond Russell Ruth, aged twenty-four, who gave his occupation as an artist; and that she had stated on their marriage application that she *had not* been previously married.

On January 10, 1941, Ruth sued Audre for divorce, charging great and extreme cruelty. He said that she had humiliated and embarrassed him. Audre again came up fighting. She filed a cross-complaint. The divorce was granted by default in 1941.

The record revealed that on August 4, 1943, Audre married Victor R. Davis, a musician. On August 30, 1944, reversing the procedure, Audre sued for divorce, charging Davis with cruelty.

After perusing the record, I suggested that she pin her father down and find out just what had been done concerning her first divorce. She said that she would. I further suggested that she see an attorney and have a thorough search made of the records. She replied that she dreaded publicity since she had told no one of her first marriage. She seemed especially interested in keeping the knowledge from her current boy friend.

Audre informed me that Sergeant John Jesse intended to obtain a divorce and that when he did, they would marry. She explained that Jesse was on the eligible list for lieutenant and couldn't afford to have anything go wrong. For that reason, they would wait until he received his appointment.

Soon after this incident, I was re-transferred to Central division.

However, since Miss Davis lived in a small bungalow court directly opposite the house that Officer Ruggles and I were building, I still saw her quite frequently. Knowledge of Miss Davis and her love life, gained as the result of her voluntary disclosures and her yells for assistance when her affairs in the amatory field grew involved, led me to believe that she was not immoral, that she was *amoral*. I was still of the opinion that she was a "good head" and I accepted her as a friend, despite her emotional irregularities with men. The fact that she confessed she had been sent to Hollywood to spy on me, convinced me that her friendship for me was an honest friendship at least.

I had occasional disputes with her, just as I had with other officers with whom I worked. That is a common occurrence in police work. Officers frequently hold different opinions on procedures.

After I had appeared before the county grand jury, I had an argument with Miss Davis. She and other officers, not assigned to my detail, had been working on a bar in Hollywood which was purportedly the scene of bookmaking operations. Miss Davis had entered the bar and had made an arrest. The bar owner protested, loud and long, that he was "being framed."

A few days later, Ruggles came to me: "Charlie," he began, "a friend of mine went to a cocktail lounge with Audre a few nights ago, as guests of the bar owner. The woman tells me that Audre danced with the bar owner and that their conduct on the floor was reprehensible. She says that Audre was wearing an 'off shoulder' gown and that the bar owner was taking advantage of what was to be seen.

"My informant," continued Ruggles, "forgot the name of the bar and its location, but she described the place in such detail that I'm convinced it's the very spot where Audre made the bookmaking arrest."

I immediately contacted Miss Davis. I told her exactly what I had been told, and asked her if it was true. I reminded her of the complaint of frame up at the time of the arrest, and informed her that her actions would cause suspicion. Frankly, I told her that I was also suspicious.

At first, Audre denied that she had been in the bar since the arrest she had made there. However, when I confronted her with the story I had heard, and offered to take her to the girl and give her a chance to deny it, she admitted that she had been to the bar. Still, she denied that she had been friendly with the owner, or that she had engaged with him in any unseemly conduct on the dance floor.

"That's your God damned trouble, Stoker," Audre blurted. "You're always ready to believe the worst about me. I'm all mixed up. I don't know what in hell's wrong with me. I can't understand myself. I've got a nice boy friend. He's in love with me. I don't know why I get off my trolley. At one time, I thought I was stuck on you, but then you're too God damned stuck on yourself. I just don't know."

"Don't give me that shot, Audre," I said. "Your broken marriages, your numerous affairs, are proof that you don't know the meaning of the word *love*."

"I guess you couldn't feel any other way knowing what you do about me and the other men," she replied.

I told her that that was her business, *not mine*.

"Forget about what happened. I won't do anything like that again," she said, ending the incident.

Inasmuch as she had raised the question of romance, or sex — to soften my wrath over her conduct in the bar — I told her that it would be best if we did not work together any longer. She agreed that that was the wisest course. I told her that I had enough troubles of my own without becoming involved in her romantic tangles with other men, and that I was totally disinterested in her personal affairs. She said that I was right, and we agreed that we would see less of each other although our relationship had been predicated entirely upon friendship.

A few days later, Miss Davis was transferred to the city jail where I had occasion to see her. She told me that she didn't mind her new job, inasmuch as Sergeant Jesse had also been transferred and was working at the jail with her. Again, she explained that she was sorry about the flare-up and that she was "all straightened out," now. She said she guessed she was wrong to feel as she did about me and she attributed her behavior to propinquity.

"Let's be friends just as we were before," she suggested.

"Why not?" I answered. But today I'm still trying to pull her knife out of my back.

Weeks passed, during which Ruggles and I worked on the duplex we were building. It was nearing completion, when we rented one side of the building to a police officer and his wife. I went to Miss Davis's apartment and asked if I might use her telephone. While I was there, I noticed a key lying on a table near the telephone. I recognized it as the key to the apartment in which the police officer and his wife were living. I intended to ask Miss Davis about the key before I left, but after making the telephone call, the matter slipped my mind.

A few days before Ruggles and I had rented the adjacent side of the duplex to a man and his wife, who had just moved in. I had been told by a neighbor that our other tenants, the policeman and his wife, had gone to Northern California.

His wife was to judge a dog show.

I remembered having seen the key to the policeman's apartment in Miss Davis's house, and thought it possible that the key had been left with her for some purpose. The following morning I stopped by the duplex on my way to work to meet a city building inspector who was to inspect the construction of our garage. To my surprise, I noticed that Sergeant Jesse's car was parked directly in front of my duplex.

Playing a hunch, I went around to the rear of the building and looked into the back door. I saw a coffee pot on the stove, and smelled burning coffee. The fire was smoking the pot. With my passkey, I entered the apartment. I walked into the bedroom.

Knowing Audre, I shouldn't have been astonished at what I saw. She and Sergeant Jesse lay abed, stark naked. Their clothes were strewn all over the place; whiskey glasses littered the floor; and they were sound asleep.

"Get your damned clothes on and get the hell out of here!" I shouted.

I reminded them that new tenants had moved in next door and that I was not at all desirous of having them think I was leasing the premises as a police assignation parlor.

LAPD officers, Lt. Rudy Wellpott and Sgt. Elmer Jackson also under felony indictments, put on their best faces for the press

Sgt. Guy Rudolph (left) making 1940s Hollywood nightclub vice arrest

Mayor Fletcher Bowron (left) with former Mayor Frank Shaw

Mayor Bowron, DDA Johnny Barnes with newly appointed LAPD BIA (Bureau of Internal Affairs) Insp. Bill Parker 1949

Interim LAPD Chief General William Worton 1950

1951- (1) Sgt. E.V. Jackson, (2) Capt James Hamilton, (3) Dep. Chief Thad Brown, (4) Mayor Fletcher Bowron, (5) Capt. Jack Donahoe, (6) Chief William Parker, (7) Lt. Grover Armstrong (8) Lt. Rudy Wellpott

Sgt. Charles Stoker working plainclothes Vice Detail and in uniform 1949

LAPD Policewoman Audre Davis

Audre, age 26, after extensive "grilling" by LAPD then claimed she gave perjured "Pandering" testimony against Madame Brenda Allen. In trade for a promise of "no prosecution," she then testified that she "waited in the car while her vice partner, Sgt. Stoker committed a business burglary." Most of the jury believed Audre was lying and the case against Stoker was dismissed. Photo above right shows Audre and Stoker seen in court. Stoker whispered to her, "They are only using you to get to me." Audre responded, "I don't know what to do, Charlie."

At the time these photos were taken, Audre, the daughter of retired LAPD Deputy Chief, Homer Cross, is about to marry her fourth husband, LAPD officer Marvin Stewart. Just prior to her wedding she was booked by LAPD for DUI (driving under the influence) and shortly after her marriage Audre was arrested by LAPD for "bookmaking" in Hollywood. Audre's DNA was also reportedly linked to Los Angeles' most powerful vice boss, Charlie "Gray Wolf" Crawford.

I quote from author Gerald Wood's authoritative and highly respected book, *The Police in Los Angeles: Reform and Professionalization*. (Garland Publishing Inc., New York, 1993) where he has this to say about Audre Davis on page 212:

"The policewoman was the daughter of Deputy Chief Homer Cross and the granddaughter of vice boss Charlie Crawford, which could explain Cross's rise from patrolman to deputy chief in seven years."

Since there is no reference to this in Sgt. Stoker's book, I can only assume that he was unaware of his partner's "family connection." Too bad, he would have loved it.

Steve Hodel

Audre waiting to testify in Superior Court

HOLLYWOOD MADAME BRENDA ALLEN- "THE QUEEN OF HEARTS"

Brenda Allen, aka Marie Mitchell, aka Marie Balanque
Sgt. Stoker personally tagged her: "The Los Angeles Express"

Brenda's "calling card" reminiscent of one of my old informants, a 1960s Hollywood streetwalker who used to help us on some of our prostitute related homicide investigations. She would hand out her personalized cards to her *trusted customers*, which read:

> "It's been a business doing pleasure with you."
>
> Dorothy Love
> 485-xxxx

Steve Hodel

Michael "Mickey" Cohen
1948-1949

Los Angeles gangster Mickey Cohen's Brentwood home (upper right) was bugged by LAPD. After obtaining the "Cohen Tapes" LAPD detectives attempted to extort and sell back the recordings to Cohen for an alleged $20,000. Once the scandal was exposed by Stoker the tapes "disappeared" then resurfaced, with possible editing. Cohen's haberdashery store on the Sunset Strip (lower left) was just outside LAPD "city limits" in the sheriff's jurisdiction.

In July, 1949,Cohen was rumored to be planning on testifying before the Grand Jury about police corruption. However, on July 20, 1949 he was persuaded to rethink his position about testifying. As he and his entourage were exiting Sherry's cocktail lounge several suspects, lying in wait across the street, fired shotgun blasts into the crowd. Cohen's number one man, Neddie Herbert was slain. Also, wounded in what became known as "The Battle of Sunset Blvd." were: Attorney General Investigator Harry Cooper, newspaper columnist Florabel Muir and actress Dee David. Cohen (upper middle) is shown in his hospital bed with his henchmen, Frank Niccolli and Eli Lubin (standing) Bottom right Cohen is seen with wife, LaVonne.

Steve Hodel

Ex-NYPD, Barney Ruditsky 1947- P.I. and part-owner of Sherry's nightclub where the July, 1949 "Battle of Sunset Blvd" shooting occurred. Shots fired from south-side of Sunset Blvd into Cohen's entourage as they left the club.

Arthur J. Vaus Jr.
Wiretapper finds "Higher Calling"

Vaus displaying his electronic equipment. After admitting to perjury regarding some "missing Cohen tapes" the repentant wire-tapper informed the press that he, "Had found religion in an Evangelical tent, and was walking the "Sawdust Trail" in search of salvation."

J. Arthur Vaus's Electronics Consultancy in same building on Sunset Strip as Mickey Cohen's Haberdashery store. Vaus was an equal opportunity employee. He simultaneously wiretapped for LAPD while employed to install equipment and "sweep for bugs" for gangster Mickey Cohen

Elizabeth "Black Dahlia" Short

Elizabeth Short's January 15, 1947 murder is mentioned in Stoker's chapter, "The Circle Constricts" where he references her movements and temporary residences in hotels in both Hollywood and downtown Los Angeles

The Stoker Story – 1948-1949
Some Headlines

What was Stoker's reward for his service and sacrifice?

When the dust settled, it was like an ending to a Hollywood noir film. LAPD's real bad guys were either pensioned off and allowed to retire, or promoted and praised.

Stoker's reward? The Stoker Story was relegated to a short obituary on the back pages of a local Los Angeles newspaper with one sentence casually mentioning he played a "key role in exposing corruption."

Stoker, became a brakeman for the Southern Pacific railroad yards in Los Angeles, and died in 1975, at the relatively young age of 57. In the end he was alone and forgotten.

A sad finale to a remarkable street cop, who twenty-five years earlier had stood alone and singlehandedly was responsible for exposing the graft and corruption that ruled 1940s LAPD and City Hall.

> *Los Angeles Herald Express*
>
> March 10, 1975
>
> **Stoker, Ex-Officer, Dies at 57**
>
> Former Los Angeles Police Sgt. Charles Stoker, who was a central figure in a 1949 department scandal, has died of an apparent heart attack.
>
> Stoker, 57, died yesterday morning in Glendale Memorial Hospital, where he was taken after suffering chest pains, while working in the Southern Pacific railroad yards. He was employed as a brakeman.
>
> Stoker played a key role in exposing corruption in the LAPD vice squad, but was later accused of a burglary, which led to his dismissal from the force. Stoker contended that he was framed on the burglary charge.

In Chapter 3, "Mobster Coppers" page 32, Sgt. Stoker provides us with an excerpt from an address that former Supreme Court Justice, Robert H. Jackson gave before a convention of Federal District Attorneys. Stoker tells us that, "Judge Jackson's words are mine." :

A man's reputation is a shadow which he casts before and behind him. A man's reputation is his most important possession. He's born with a good one, and it's up to him whether or not he keeps it. A sincere and honest man cannot afford to have his reputation sullied. He will protect it with everything at his command if he values it, for once he has lost it, he has lost himself.

Robert H. Jackson
U.S. Supreme Court Justice

(Justice Jackson was the real life jurist and presiding judge portrayed by Spencer Tracy in Stanley Kramer's 1961 film classic, *Judgment at Nuremberg*.)

SKH

GRAND JURY

I, Charles Stoker, was now facing the grand jury proper! Having already appeared before the Criminal Complaints Committee in the preliminary to the main event, I now girded my loins because, better than anyone, I knew that double- trouble and a load of red-hot soup were riding on the next pitch.

When I had talked to Inspector William Parker, I knew that he was unaware of the fact that I had already appeared before the Criminal Complaints Committee of the grand jury. I deduced this by his conversation and by his exhortation to have me appear before that body.

After digesting Parker's statements regarding various police officers, most of whom were in the higher brackets, there wasn't the shadow of a doubt in my mind that I had become deeply involved in a major vice and gambling investigation and that, willingly or unwillingly, I was deeply enmeshed in the city's and county's political skeins.

I didn't relish the role. I knew that I was possessed of very little political acuity and that in the game of matching wits with politicians, I was out of my depth, or element. I had never been interested in politics. I was a copper — the kind of a copper of whom men say: "He's all copper!" It wasn't my nature to "tin can" it; yet here I was facing the grand jury, as ready as I'd ever be for action.

In my purview, laws had been made which were meant to be enforced; and I viewed myself as an instrument of their enforcement. Perhaps that was a naive or juvenile outlook in this cynical, Godless age. But I held to the conviction that police officers, of all people, shouldn't break the law.

If the public in general holds a low opinion of politicians, police officers and law enforcement officials, it is for the reason that recurring vice and gambling scandals have caused doubt as to the probity of these officials.

I have now had enough experience to know the definition of politics. Fundamentally, politics (the science of government) means people in motion. Every stratum of life, in one form or another, is dominated by politics. If twenty men are digging a ditch, politics of a fashion, however lowly, is an ever present factor. I realized that politics could be my undoing and I dreaded the lies that I felt certain would confront me. A man facing death in the electric chair does not relish the position in which he finds himself, yet he can do nothing to improve it. By the very nature of the case, he must deal with the situation as he finds it, on the basis of the testimony which frequently writes the decision against his will and desires.

Parker's conversation had led me to one inescapable conclusion. He was a man of overweening ambition – a man whose one desire was his objective – the office of Chief of Police. He had expressed himself freely as to what he thought of the personages involved in the mess in which, willy-nilly, I found myself playing an important role.

I had already formed an uncomplimentary opinion of Inspector Parker, when he had attempted to persuade me to put Hollywood vice squad officer Jimmy Parslow on the spot. Although I held no brief for Parslow, or his methods of operating, or his personality, I was satisfied in my own mind that Parslow was an honest copper. I believed this because of my experiences, working Hollywood vice. In short, I felt fairly certain that Parslow was not "on the take."

I am fully aware that Inspector William Parker was a man compounded out of sheer ruthlessness, a man who would ride rough shod over anyone who got in the way of his becoming Chief of Police. I felt that he would use any police officer, guilty or innocent, as ammunition in his campaign for the top police spot.

But, out of justice to Parker, I must say that much of what he had told me about the vice, gambling and pay-off picture in Los Angeles was true. I knew this because of my own experiences. I am willing to credit him with knowing the score, and with having plenty of savvy in the matters of police politics.

As to his previously announced aim of changing the Hollywood vice squad for the good of the department, Parker may have been correct if what he told me was fact.

Be that as it may, I left Parker with the understanding that I would appear before the county grand jury, speak my piece and tell the truth. Secretly, I hoped that he would not learn that I had already been before the criminal complaints committee of the grand jury. I wanted none of Parker's promises and I wanted no reward for my grand jury testimony. I believed then and I still believe that I was acting primarily in behalf of the public welfare and in the cause and hope of a better police department.

If the public insists upon saddling me with another motive, I have already explained that motive. I had every reason to believe that I would be framed and murdered. Certain types of criminals become desperate men when their crimes are made known, whether or not they wear badges. I had no illusions about the calibre of the men with whom I had been sparring.

Prior to this appearance, I had never thought much about grand juries. They were, in my mind, something remote. I have since learned a great deal about grand juries. I have also learned a great deal about the history of Los Angeles county grand juries. I have learned how they are selected.

Each of sixty-five Superior court judges selects two prospective veniremen. The original list of one hundred and thirty is then winnowed down until thirty names remain. These names are placed in a wheel. Nineteen names are then withdrawn from the wheel. These nineteen comprise the individuals who are selected to serve for one year as grand jurors.

The presiding judge of the Superior Court selects a grand jury foreman. Each juror receives two dollars a day, plus fifteen cents a mile one way from his home. The jury must meet at least twice a week.

In my opinion, the weakness of the grand jury system lies in the fact that jurors, under the law, are dependent upon legal advice from the district attorney's office, and that its investigative work is dependent upon the district attorney's investigators.

If the district attorney, his deputies or his investigators are corrupt, or are intellectually or politically dishonest through the fact of underworld alliances, it can readily be seen that virtually all of the work done by the grand jury investigation of racketeers and police officers who take their money, can easily be stultified and made ineffective.

I maintain that a blue ribbon grand jury with its own investigating staff and special prosecutor, both totally removed from any liaison with, or obligation to, the district attorney's office, or the mayor's office, would uncover appalling evidences of crime, graft and racketeering in Los Angeles City and County. Such a setup would bring about the prosecution of hundreds of malefactors in the city and county, who, thus far have successfully subverted the law.

In a radio broadcast, Mayor Bowron made the snide remark that the 1949 Los Angeles County Grand Jury's investigation into the Los Angeles police department was *prompted by underworld interests,* insinuating that the grand jury had underworld ties. That was the most bald-faced political lie I have ever heard made by a shabby politician, who found himself caught in a tight corner of his own making with waning political prestige as a result of the evils flourishing under his regime.

The men and women of the 1949 grand jury were above censure. They had been thoroughly investigated by the district attorney's office prior to their induction into service. Bowron's insinuations that the underworld was using the grand jurors as pawns in a political game, had no basis in fact and was an indefensible slur against the characters of the men and women who comprised the jury.

In the final analysis, Mayor Bowron is just another sleazy politician who, when he is caught in a mess of his own making, tries to saddle the ignominy of it upon the "underworld," upon the grand jury and upon his so-called "political enemies."

That is what this ruckus is all about — the underworld — and that segment that figures in this story was inside his own police department and under his own aegis.

The district attorney's investigators had examined the 1949 grand jurors prior to their induction into office, and had found nothing wrong with them, morally, reputationally or otherwise. Proof that the 1949 grand jury was looking down the necks of evil-doers without fear or favor, lies in the fact that the jury was highly critical of the manner in which the district attorney's office conducted its end of the probe into police graft and maladministration. As a matter-of-fact, the grand jurors let the district attorney's office know that it believed efforts were being made to obstruct justice.

Let Mayor Bowron and District Attorney William E. Simpson — who are political pals — explain that anomaly if they can. One thing is certain. Neither of them will explain it satisfactorily to any member of the 1949 grand jury.

But, to continue the story, the most important unit of the grand jury is the criminal complaints committee. It listens to evidence presented on felonious crimes. If the committee deems that sufficient evidence exists to warrant the indictment of an individual, the evidence is then placed before the entire grand jury and if twelve or more jurors signify affirmatively, an indictment, or indictments are voted.

From time to time, certain stuffed shirt, or professional politicians will declare that the grand jury system should be done away with — that it is an archaic, out-moded relic of the horse-and-buggy days. You may be assured of an ulterior motive, or motives, in these assertions. You can bet that every corrupt or political dishonest public official who, in one way or another is operating in behalf of the underworld and organized rackets, would dearly love to see the abandonment of the grand jury system.

It cannot be stated too emphatically that the county grand jury is the greatest weapon in the hands of the people for the correction of evil criminal, political and racketeering conditions in a community. It is the legal instrument that each and every thief and grafter, whether in public office or out, most fears.

Far from being abandoned, the hand of the grand jury should be strengthened. This, if the voters saw fit, could easily be done. The county grand jury should be divorced from any dependence upon the district attorney's office, either for legal advice or investigation. It should have its own legal advisors and its own investigators, each of whom should be carefully investigated prior to being chosen, to ascertain that they have no political alliances, friendships, or sympathies with any public office holder, be he district attorney, mayor, sheriff, chief of police, or the head of any political commission or bureau under these individuals, or under any other individual in public office.

The weakness of grand jury dependence upon the district attorney's office lies in the fact that a district attorney who has ulterior motives which are not visible to the naked eye, may make alliances, political or otherwise, with the underworld, and may operate against rather than in behalf of public welfare. Consequently, if the D. A. is not leveling against racketeers and criminals, but is acting in league with them, the deputy district attorneys and investigators he assigns to the grand jury for legal advice and probing, will be fully aware of the direction in which their boss wants the grand jury to "go."

So when the "hot" ones come along for investigation by the grand jury, if the district attorney is "interested" in "blowing down the beef rather than in bringing malefactors to justice, his deputy will follow the boss's line. He will advise the grand jury against indictments in certain "spot" cases — even if the jurors have all the evidence in the world upon which to base an indictment and to bring about conviction of a criminal or racketeer. After a grand jury indicts, the D. A. still prosecutes; and there is many a turn on the road between these two points.

In the argot of crooked politicians and corrupt office holders, a grand jury which takes the bit in its teeth and refuses to follow the advice of the assigned district attorney is branded as "an outlaw grand jury."

This so-called "outlaw grand jury," far from living up to its name, acts in the public weal. It is a sincere grand jury, determined and anxious to bring wrongdoers to justice. A district attorney does not like an "outlaw" grand jury a little bit. He desires a jury he can steer and channel. Through his assigned deputy, he prefers to "control" the grand jury in its actions. He wants a jury that will take advice from him and suggestions from him and his aides.

During the trial in which I was involved, the district attorney's office proved intellectually dishonest, if not worse. After the scandal had begun to die down, I questioned numerous persons who were familiar with the Angel City's politics and grand jury action over a period of years. I was informed that in 1938, when Mayor Bowron was elected to the office he now holds after a recall campaign, a scandal broke out in regard to the selection of grand jurors. This was to the effect that Bob Gans, quondam slot machine czar of Los Angeles city and county, through friendly and political connections with certain judges, had selected the names of prospective veniremen.

According to my informant, it was charged and never refuted that Bob Gans would hand friendly judges a list of names of individuals he wanted on the grand jury. These judges would then place the names in the jury wheel. It was a percentage cinch that enough of Gans's selections were in the wheel that he was certain of representation on the grand jury and it was a dead mortal cinch that jurors chosen in this manner would protect his interests and the interests of other underworld personages with whom he was in alliance.

No better proof of this public scandal was needed, I was told, than the fact that Abe Chapman, a relative of Gans by marriage and himself engaged in the slot machine business, served on one grand jury. The story of how Gans built and maintained his highly secretive liaison with Superior court judges revealed that he financed many political campaigns in behalf of the candidates of certain judges. Their method of repaying him for this "political" aid was to permit him to select the names they would place in the jury wheel.

Reportedly, Gans is no longer interested in the slot machine racket; nevertheless he still exerts a powerful political influence although his fine Italian hand is never publicly visible.

The nescient public is wont to assume that, because the district attorney is prosecuting a man for a crime, he is acting in behalf of law and order and against crime. This may or may not be true. We might well ask: "Is the district attorney leveling?" There are prosecutions and "prosecutions," meaning that upon occasion the district attorney merely "punches the bag" for public edification, having no intention of convicting the criminal before the bar of justice. Lawyers know that this is not a difficult feat and in the parlance of questionable legal maneuvering it is known as a "tank job," or a "boat ride." There are several methods of waylaying justice. One is to assign a youthful and inexperienced prosecutor to oppose a veteran and astute criminal attorney. Another is to assign a prosecutor, who is aware that the district attorney does not want a conviction.

The prosecutor may have sufficient evidence, if correctly presented, to convict the person charged with the crime beyond the possibility of a doubt. But if he isn't "leveling," he merely fails to present all the evidence. Or he hesitates to bear down in the interrogation and examination of witnesses for the state, and neglects to elicit all the details and information they may possess about the crime. It is an artful maneuver, and usually not one layman in a thousand is aware of what is happening even though he sits in the courtroom and sees it all unfold before his eyes.

It should be remembered that the prosecution of a criminal case is theatrical through and through. Frequently, it is a burlesque on that abstraction called "justice." Possibly you are unaware of the motives that propel and impel the actors on the stage. Far more frequently than you think, the public in general hasn't the faintest conception of what the play is all about.

Each man and woman will admit that he or she is brilliant whether or not there exists any justification for the belief. In truth, brilliance is the exception rather than the rule and this applies to jurors in criminal cases. A common trick used by criminal attorneys, and many lawyers are criminals in fact and at heart, is to flatter a juror's ego. Because of this and other factors, many a dip, switch and turn are made between the time a man is arrested and is convicted for a crime. There are numerous imponderables. Particularly does this apply to criminal cases involving important racketeers and to criminal cases having political connotations. Most racketeering prosecutions are both criminal and political for the inexorable reason that the racketeer who has political connections is able to break the law, or laws, with impunity, whereas the law bears down upon the racketeer who is sans political influence.

To most people this situation seems very complex and confusing, but to the initiate, to most police officers, honest or dishonest, it is as simple as ABC. In a racket infested community such as Los Angeles, the following applies: "As long as the top public officials hang together, no harm will befall the thieves."

These were my thoughts as I presented myself to the grand jury as a whole.

Having been sworn in, I testified to the Brenda Allen story just as I have related it here. During the course of my entire testimony, the district attorney made no effort to conceal the fact that his office was intent upon defending the Los Angeles police department. When I told of having gone to the district attorney's office to obtain a felony complaint, charging Brenda Allen with procuring, Johnny Barnes, the assistant district attorney, impatiently tried to brush the facts aside, stating that they were irrelevant to the grand jury probe.

"Answer the question. Answer the question," he barked. But I persisted.

AND, DUE TO MY PERSISTENCE, THE LOS ANGELES COUNTY GRAND JURY OF 1949, THEN BECAME AN "OUTLAW" GRAND JURY NO LONGER UNDER THE CONTROL OF DISTRICT ATTORNEY WILLIAM E. SIMPSON'S OFFICE.

When I realized that Barnes was trying to forestall my testimony, I asked the grand jury as a whole if I could address its members without the presence of Deputy District Attorney Johnny Barnes. At this point, Barnes "blew his top." He immediately called in two other deputies — Fred Henderson and Adolph Alexander — who stated that *they would not allow* such a course of action.

The grand jury members then rebelled. They told the embattled trio of deputy district attorneys that they saw no reason why Barnes and the deputies should not be excluded from the jury room while I told my story. They added that, if the deputies had the interests of justice at heart, they would permit me to testify as I pleased.

The grand jury then decided to appeal to Presiding Judge Robert Scott for his opinion and decision as to whether or not the district attorney's representatives should be barred from the jury room during my testimony.

But Judge Scott favored the district attorney's office. He ruled that the deputies should and would remain in the jury room.

In their presence, I then told the grand jurors how Johnny Barnes, Chief Deputy District Attorney, and H. Leo Stanley, chief Investigator for the District Attorney, had come to my home and had attempted to persuade me to "blow down" my testimony involving police officers Lieutenant Rudy Wellpott and Sergeant Elmer V. Jackson.

Barnes and Stanley did not deny my accusation before the jury, nor have they ever denied it in so far as I have been able to ascertain.

I quoted Barnes and Stanley as follows:

"We think the police department had its reasons for doing what it did in this Brenda Allen deal. Just take it easy when you're called back before the grand jury. Don't volunteer any information. We've been around a lot longer than you have and we've seen grand juries come and go."

I explained to the grand jury that, at the time Barnes and Stanley so advised me, I had failed to agree with them. I warned the grand jury that they would get nowhere in the police mess as long as they had to depend upon the district attorney's office for investigation. I added that a special prosecutor should be called in and that they (the jurors) should not rely upon the district attorney's office.

I informed the jury that I was personally acquainted with the investigator assigned to the grand jury and that, in my opinion, he couldn't find a base drum in a telephone booth and that if he could, he wouldn't.

I stated that I wanted to debunk certain situations involving the police department, the sheriff's office and the district attorney's office. In particular, I said that I wanted to make known the facts about the abortion and bail bond rackets in Los Angeles, pay-offs by sex degenerates, and the squelching of complaints by the combined co-operation of the police department and the district attorney's office.

Assistant District Attorney Johnny Barnes then interpolated that the grand jury "wasn't interested in these matters at the present time," although the grand jurors had indicated otherwise. Barnes then avowed that those phases of the crime and racket picture *would be taken up later* and that, when they were, I would be called.

If you read the newspapers at the time, you will recall that these probes were side-tracked, not temporarily but permanently.

I reminded the grand jury that there were many criminal cases which, if action were not soon taken, would be outlawed by the statute of limitations, a statute which runs out within three years on every crime but murder, embezzlement of public funds and the alteration of public records.

The district attorney's office is well aware of THE STATUTE OF LIMITATIONS. This office frequently aids in keeping the statute of limitations in force rather than stopping it by prosecutorial action.

When a grand juror asked my opinion as to the honesty of the Los Angeles police department as a whole, I answered that the preponderance of police officers were honest men. Another juror asked me about gambling in Chinatown, about which a great deal had been written in the newspapers. I told him that gambling and Chinese lotteries operated in the section. He then asked me if I thought they were protected by police.

"Gambling joints cannot operate unless they are protected by police," I replied.

During the course of my testimony, the grand jury met twice a week, on Tuesdays and Thursdays. I testified on a Thursday. After the session, I met H. Leo Stanley, the district attorney's chief investigator in the hallway outside the jury room. He approached me in friendly fashion.

"Stoker, I want you to do me a favor," he said. "Will you see J. Arthur Vaus and ask him for the wire recordings he made on Mickey Cohen and the Wellpott-Jackson shakedown attempts? I know Vaus will give them to you because he trusts you."

I considered this a strange request, indeed. I knew that at the Meltzer gun trial, Attorney Sam Rummel had shouted out in the courtroom that he had the recordings and was anxious to give them to the grand jury. I was suspicious of Stanley and his motives. I told him that I hadn't seen or heard of Vaus in months and that I didn't know where he lived. This, incidentally, was the truth. I hadn't seen Vaus and I had no desire to see him — after he had told me that he was in the service of Michael (Mickey) Cohen.

Stanley insisted upon giving me Vaus's address. The next day newspaper headlines screamed that someone had broken into Vaus's automobile in Baldwin Park, and that certain wire recordings had been stolen. When they were apprised of this, Johnny Barnes and H. Leo Stanley issued a joint statement to the effect that they knew the identity of the person who had stolen the highly important wire recordings and that they were about to make an arrest and expose the guilty party.

The district attorney and his aides will be unhappy to learn that I had a friend in the district attorney's office, who perforce shall remain anonymous. This friend telephoned me.

"Charley, have you read the newspapers?" he asked.

I told him that I had.

"Well, when Barnes and Stanley stated that they knew the identity of the man who stole Vaus's wire recordings and were about to arrest him, do you know who they had in mind?"

"How in hell would I know?" I answered.

"Kiddo, they meant you. You'd better get busy and ascertain definitely where you were last night and you'd better be able to come up with an airtight alibi."

"You're joking," I said.

"I was never more serious in my life," he declared. "Just look out."

There was only one difficulty with this plot, if it was a plot. I had an airtight alibi. I knew where I had been every second of the night the records were stolen, if they had been stolen. Moreover, I could prove it if I had to.

Newspapermen got wind of the angle and telephoned me. They asked if I had an alibi. I assured them that I had one and that it was bullet proof. They informed the district attorney's myrmidons of my reply to their question. Then the switch went in fast, just like that, when the ineffable J. Arthur Vaus, who had used religion to cloak his skullduggery, came out with the story that the records hadn't been stolen after all, that he had buried them in his backyard.

The next edition of the news stated that the district attorney's investigators were about to dig up the recordings. This they did surrounded by a full panoply of reporters and news cameramen. But when the records were examined, what do you think they discovered?

THE RECORDS WERE BLANK. MICKEY COHEN HAD ALSO BEEN GIVEN THE DOUBLE CROSS.

Although testimony before the grand jury is supposed to be secret, my testimony was kept as shady as the December 7th bombing of Pearl Harbor. In great detail it was splattered over the front pages of the Los Angeles newspapers. If any details were missed, I cannot now recall what they were.

But since officials had to preserve the "dignity of the law," J. Arthur Vaus was tossed into jail. No charge was lodged against him, however, and after spending a few days in the cooler, he was escorted out onto the street and turned loose.

There were times when the flame of battle burned low within Charles Stoker; there were times, and this was one of them, when

Charles Stoker doubted the existence of anything decent, honorable or worthy.

When the story broke, the police department was indeed startled. So was our effete mayor, Fletcher (I'm Fighting the Underworld) Bowron. By this time it was becoming difficult for me to reconcile the Bowronic pose with the facts. If Hizzoner was fighting crime, where was he fighting it? Over the radio? In the Stoker mind, the battle lines between Bowron and the underworld were hazy and obscure. Indeed it was a very fluid front, to the point of collision between Bowron and the underworld. He wasn't fighting the underworld on the sector where I was engaged. He wasn't rooting and tooting for the grand jury to get to the bottom of the police mess with stentorian shouts to do it and let the chips fall where they may.

When it suits his purposes, Bowron knows all about the underworld and its legions, who are forever bent upon unhorsing him so that the racketeering tide can inundate Los Angeles. But at this time, it didn't suit his purposes to play the role of "underworld expert." The facts were jumping dangerously close to his official posterior. Upon being informed of the story, he maintained that he had never heard of the Brenda Allen investigation and that he knew nothing about any wire recordings. In short, Hizzoner expressed amazement.

America's leading metropolitan mayoral underworld expert said he was a complete blank about the scandal that had broken on his own doorstep and under his nose.

Of course the sordid tale was not in keeping with the mayor's oft-spoken lines that there was no underworld in Los Angeles; that this city was free of organized rackets and that it had the best police department in the United States.

But Hizzoner's declaration of nescience in connection with the Brenda Allen probe did not square with the facts. The grand jury, *having unearthed an investigator* who had worked for Hizzoner, was informed that Mayor *Bowron knew every phase of the affair Brenda Allen* and its attendant investigation.

Chief of Police C. B. Horrall was equally startled. Like Mayor Bowron, he had been riding on Cloud No. Nine when it all happened. In a statement to the press, Chief Horrall said that he had never heard of the Brenda Allen investigation, or of the wire recordings, and that if he had, he would have acted immediately. This, despite the fact that Horrall's personnel chief, Captain Cecil Wisdom, as I have related, was involved up to his neck in the investigation.

On May 14, 1948, Jerry Ramlow, a reporter for The Los Angeles Daily News had dropped the "business" in the lap of that wily and cunning individual, Assistant Chief of Police Joe Reed. Ramlow, who had carried the mail to Reed, assumed that what he had done would remain a top drawer secret in so far as he and his newspaper were concerned. After all, The Daily News was an administration paper, having stridently and consistently supported Mayor Bowron and his administration of the city's affairs.

Imagine Reporter Ramlow's astonishment when his confreres, the other reporters on the police beat, informed him that Assistant Chief Reed had told them all about his visit with the damning and potentially inflammable information. It had been The Daily News and one of its reporters, Meta (Chubby) Trent, who had originally broken the Brenda Allen story, when I raided her place on Harold Way.

It is remarkable how dumb some people can be when stupidity suits their purposes and how intelligent they can become when brilliance suits them instead! As you can readily see, genius depends upon circumstances.

But like sheep following their leader in jumping a fence, in this case a highly difficult fence, Captain Cecil Wisdom, who had talked to me frequently about the Allen investigation as well as to Hollywood Captain William Wingard, now *denied all knowledge* of the unsavory mess. So did Joe Reed, the assistant chief of police, whom Inspector William Parker had identified as the palsy-walsy of Lieutenant Rudy Wellpott and Sergeant Elmer V. Jackson.

But, dishonest as they were in denying knowledge of the situation, Sergeant Guy Rudolph, the confidential aide to Chief Horrall and the

"Big Wheel" in the vice-gambling administration setup, went them all one better. Speaking as though he were talking about something in the far distant past, Sergeant Rudolph told reporters that *he vaguely remembered* something about an investigation of Brenda Allen and something about wire recordings. Then he recalled very indistinctly that I had taken him to an office on Sunset Boulevard, where I had played some recordings I had made.

An amazing statement that, when you remember that it was Sergeant Guy Rudolph who had taken me to the office of former New York copper, Barney Ruditsky, operator of Sherry's swank cocktail lounge on the Sunset Strip.

Anent the grand jury investigation, The Los Angeles Daily Mirror ran a column of the dramatis personnae titled: "*In the Know*" which went as follows:

BRENDA ALLEN – Hollywood "madam" now serving a county jail sentence for attempted pandering.

MICKEY COHEN - Kingpin of L. A. gamblers now under indictment for conspiracy in the A. M. Pearson beating.

E. V. JACKSON – Vice squad sergeant accused, during the Happy Meltzer trial, of trying to shake down Mickey.

CAPTAIN CARL PEARSON - of the sheriff's department. Pearson was present at the raid on Brenda's call house and has admitted hearing at least part of the wire recordings of a conversation between Brenda and a member of the vice squad.

SERGEANT GUY RUDOLPH - Confidential aide to Police Chief C. B. Horrall. Rudolph also heard the recordings and identified the voices as Brenda's and Sergeant Jackson's.

BARNEY RUDITSKY - Ex-New York cop and former private dick at whose office the wire recordings were made.

SERGEANT CHARLES STOKER - Vice squad officer who made the first raid on Brenda's house. He testified to the grand jury's criminal complaints division about tie-ups between Brenda and the vice squad.

J. ARTHUR VAUS - Sound engineer who made the famous records. Last week he claimed they had been stolen.

LIEUTENANT RUDY WELLPOTT - Administrative head of the vice squad. Also accused of trying to shake Mickey down

AUDRE DAVIS — Beauteous policewoman who trapped Brenda into offering her a job in her brothel and thus brought about Brenda's downfall.

J. D. RUGGLES - Police officer who testified with Stoker before the criminal complaints committee of the grand jury. Ruggles is Stoker's partner on the vice squad.

JOE SHAW - Brother of former Mayor Frank L. Shaw and himself a mayoralty candidate in this year's primary. Shaw was subpoenaed yesterday and will appear before the grand jury today.

The Daily Mirror's run-down was absolutely correct. I know. Moreover, they didn't get the information from me on which their grand jury "score card" was based.

But Mr. Rudolph didn't tell that story to the grand jury when he was called to testify. He gave Chief Horrall the lie, informing the jurors that *he had confided* in his superior, Chief of Police Horrall, and that that worthy had known about the investigation from beginning to end. Rudolph explained that the same thing went for Reed and Wisdom; they, too, had known all about the deal.

Midnight oil was burning in the city hall. Horrall, Reed, Wisdom, Rudolph, Jackson and Wellpott, whether they liked one another or not, were in a mess together.

Significantly, if not surprisingly, I was at no time questioned by any of these dignified gentlemen who had operated the Los Angeles police department and who were supposed to *know* what was going on — and did — but who, by their own admissions, or let us say declarations, *didn't know* what was going on.

The vice squad officers who had worked with me on the Allen case and who were privy to some, if not all, of the details appertaining to it, *were not called.*

In any situation of this nature, in which the whited sepulchres are endangered, there arises the necessity of creating a "Devil." Now, who do you suppose was the "Devil" in this case? You are right. He was Sergeant Charles Stoker, the man who had asked to be transferred off the prostitution detail not once, but several times, only to be refused by those who were empowered to transfer him, most of whom were now caught up in a police scandal.

A college professor, Hooton by name, once wrote a book on the stupidities of historically great figures, generals, statesmen and the like. These broad-assed coppers were not great men, that's for sure; but there remained no doubt in my mind but that they were stupid men to earn a place in my book, including Bowron, who took the attitude that they were severely put upon, and that they were the victims of a deep, double-dyed plot to discredit them.

Yet, when news reporter, Jerry Ramlow, laid the dynamite in their collective laps on May 14, 1948, they could have avoided the consequences of a full-fledged investigation by transferring Lieutenant Rudy Wellpott and Sergeant Elmer V. Jackson to uniform.

Had these transfers been made at the propitious moment – that is, when Jerry Ramlow laid evidence of the pair's culpability in the lap of Joe Reed, there would have been no Brenda Allen scandal.

The determined Captain William Wingard could then have chased Brenda out of Hollywood; other police officers like myself would have made her hotter than a dime store pistol and that would have been the end of it. But, although they had been forewarned of the incipient scandal, these two self-acclaimed police geniuses – Horrall and Reed – directors of the "finest police department in the United States" according to Mayor Bowron, chose to ally themselves with two officers, who had been proven beyond a doubt to have been out of line. There must have been a reason and you can figure it out just as easily as I. Small wonder then that the ensuing scandal blew up with a loud report in their faces! Yet, they wanted to blame someone else for their predicament. Above all, they wanted to and did blame Charles Stoker.

When one considers that Chief Horrall and Assistant Chief Reed kept Wellpott and Jackson on the administrative vice squad despite incontrovertible knowledge of their activities, the question automatically arises: "Why?"

I have been required to defend myself in a situation wherein I should have been given every assistance. Instead of the hostility of the aforementioned individuals, I should have gained their whole-hearted co-operation – if our laws have any meaning.

Well, let them defend themselves now. The road may be long but it has to bend sometime, somewhere. Certain persons—not I—received the graft—so, let them take the lumps.

Horrall, Reed and Wisdom, when called before the grand jury, had denied all knowledge of the Brenda Allen business.

Sergeant Guy Rudolph, however, had pulled the switch when he spilled. Perhaps, he had been thinking of perjury and didn't want to wind up a rather spotty police career with an indictment on his neck. In any event, he told all.

Deputy Chief Richard Simon looked sideways, backwards and forwards and probably told himself that he was in no position to play games with the grand jurors. That somebody was lying was self-evident. With the district attorney's office trying to "blow the thing down" and with the top brass in the police department telling conflicting stories, the grand jurors were in the position of bloodhounds baying on a fresh trail.

Doubtless, police executives were inwardly howling: "Stoker! that son-of-a-bitch, Stoker!" To them I was no longer the honest police officer who had earned the praises of various superiors for *work well done*. I was old Mephistopheles, himself, with horned head and forked tail.

What to do? What to do? Imagine their dilemma!

Then, someone had a brilliant thought. Ah, wire-tapping.

Get a Federal complaint against Stoker for having tapped telephone wires. Wire-tapping is illegal by virtue of a Federal law. Sergeant Guy Rudolph immediately contacted the United States district attorney's office. Fortunately, for the department, he failed to get a complaint against me. I say "fortunately" because I would have had a lot of company. That charge would have been dumped right back in their laps.

I was getting worried, none the less. There are moments when the bravest of men feels his confidence shaken. I telephoned Inspector William Parker, who suggested that I go to the Los Angeles Daily News, lay my story on the line and tell everything. It was The Daily News that had first broken the Brenda Allen story.

I telephoned and asked for Phil Garrison, the managing editor. I was told that he was in San Quentin prison interviewing the crime partner of Bandit "Peewee" Reese, who had been shot and killed by Sergeant Jackson on the night when he and Brenda Allen were parked in front of her apartment at Ninth and Fedora Streets.

When Garrison returned, a meeting was arranged. I told the whole story which The Daily News ran, after having contacted Officers Jack Ruggles, Jimmy Parslow and Roland Harris for confirmation. Officer Harris of Hollywood vice, was in Georgia on a leave of absence. He was serving as an Army captain, so his interview was handled over the long distance telephone.

At this point, Chief Horrall and Assistant Chief Reed came up with what they no doubt considered an astute strategical maneuver. Wellpott, Jackson and I were suddenly transferred. Undoubtedly, they hoped that through this move some of the effluvia attaching to Wellpott and Jackson would rub off on me inasmuch as we were transferred together. It would have been a smart move, as I said before, had it happened several months before. It might have discomforted Wellpott and Jackson, who wanted to work vice, but it would have made me happy indeed because I didn't.

But although we were transferred together, an important difference in our transfers should be noted. Wellpott and Jackson were transferred to "soft" police berths. And where was your friend, Charley Stoker, sent? You guessed it again. Into uniform and into traffic and street intersection control. Horrall and Reed were still taking care of their pals, Wellpott and Jackson, and still giving Charley Stoker the old Stacy & Adams treatment, or boots. Chief Horrall and Reed were sweet, sweet kids to the very end. It must also be reported that Wellpott and Jackson were given approximately two months' paid vacation before reporting to duty. Do I have to tell you what Stoker received from them, or can you guess?

On the other hand, although I had one hundred and twenty-five days of accumulated vacation and overtime coming, I was ordered to report immediately for duty.

But if the going was getting rough for little Charley Stoker, it was also tough traveling for Horrall, Reed and Rudolph. All three retired on pension.

"I've given the best years of my life to the Los Angeles Police Department," Rudolph whimpered. "I'm a broken man. I've been sold out."

Chief Horrall retired on pension at approximately six hundred dollars a month, as did Assistant Chief Joe Reed, who likewise received half his salary in pension.

Needless to say, these personal tragedies — if that's what they were — presented a political opportunity to Mayor Fletcher E. Bowron. With tears in his eyes, and a throb in his throat, he publicly praised Chief Horrall and told of what a fine chief he had been. This, after secretly slitting Horrall's throat and forcing him to resign. En route to the mayor's office one afternoon as the fury of the police mess mounted, Horrall had told newspapermen that he would not resign.
When he came back from the interview with Bowron, he had changed his mind. Why? What were Bowron's orders?

But Bowron, ever the politician, with his "Good, Honest and Efficient Government" throne foundation tottering and shaking in the muck of a dirty police mess, proved that he was still the master shover of the old coneroo. He took to the radio and yowled and howled that the gangsters were coming, ta-ra, and that Good, Honest and Efficient Government — my God — in Los Angeles was again being assailed by his, Bowron's, mortal enemies.

When one is in a storm, he'll grab anything to hold on to. Bowron was about to be immersed. His police department had been rent asunder by internal bickering and by two factions quarreling over the loot from underworld rackets. He needed a life-saver. With self-preservation in mind — of course he decried that it was for the public welfare — Bowron dug up a retired Marine General, William A. Worton, the idea being that the "Marines Have Landed. The Situation Is In Hand."

With no disrespect to the General, Worton's police administration, despite windy and praiseworthy editorials in the local press, has consisted mostly of ceaselessly transferring great coveys of police officers — no one seems to know why — under that marvelous euphemism —"For The Good of the Service."

With a fresh hand on deck, the police department's opportunists eagerly began to curry the favor of the dictatorial Worton. Plenty of chivs, or knives, were shoved into countless backs and the front runners kept in Worton's good graces for a while. But the pace was killing, and many dropped beside the road.

At the current writing, two fair-haired boys are vying for the benign glances of the Marine General and Mayor Bowron. They are Inspector (now deputy police chief) William H. Parker and Deputy Chief of Police Thad Brown. It was Parker who told me what dirty stinkers Horrall, Reed, Wellpott and Jackson were. He may have been right, but then, with Stoker under fire from the police department for "conduct unbecoming an officer," Parker considered it the part of wisdom, to go down another street.

THE ENEMY GLOATS

Lieutenant Rudy Wellpott made a point of being at work that evening after his extended vacation, and it was reported that he joyfully introduced himself at roll call as Lieutenant Wellpott. He said with eloquence: "Today, the bubble has bursted" Wellpott proceeded to acquaint the assembled officers with the facts that Audre Davis had that day gone to the chief of police and told him that I was a burglar. Indeed, the bubble had burst, but not in the manner in which Wellpott thought. I had suspected that an attempt would be made to discredit me.

Officer Jimmy Parslow had testified before the grand jury, substantiating my testimony. He had even gone further when he testified that vice and corruption flourished in Hollywood and in the unincorporated territory in Los Angeles County. He testified and gave evidence to prove that protection of rackets existed in both these localities, and that the D. A.'s office was apprised of it. Later, Parslow was taken before the police trial board and on a trumped up charge was dismissed from the Los Angeles Police Department.

Now, when I read the newspaper headlines and the stories of Audre's accusations against me anent burglary, I telephoned my friend in the personnel division and asked what it was all about. He told me that Sergeant Jesse had taken Audre into Inspector Parker's office that day. He said that for several days prior to the false accusation, Inspector Parker and a personnel investigator named Smith had had their heads together. With the breaking of the news story, he judged that their discussions had involved me. He said that Audre had worked at the jail from midnight until 7:30 a.m., and that Jesse had then met her and had taken her to Parker's office.

He added that they had then repaired to the Mayfair Hotel on West Seventh Street where a suite of rooms had been engaged. I knew that Inspector Parker had been appointed head of Worton's newly created

Bureau of Internal Affairs. Among police officers, this bureau is now commonly known as "The Gestapo" of the department.

You will see that my "devoted friend," Inspector Bill Parker, was now obviously intent upon finding Sergeant Charles Stoker's head when he reached the end of the thoroughfare, a lovely fellow — Parker. A few days later I was suspended.

As you already know, Audre had stated that she perjured herself in the Brenda Allen trial, which in itself, was a lie. I am certain that when she testified against Brenda, Audre told the truth from the witness stand, and that she lied to the grand jury when she declared that she had not told the truth. With Audre, however, lies and truths were interchangeable. I have, however, my own opinion as to her motives for repudiating the story she told at Brenda's trial. I believe that her motives were double-barreled, that first she wanted to mitigate and smear any and all work I had done as a police officer, particularly my work involving Brenda Allen — for it must be recalled that Brenda interlocked with important members of the police department and Audre's father's intercession with Captain Cecil Wisdom, chief of personnel, when, by her own admission, she was about to be fired, may have added significance.

I cannot say that Audre was given money for reversing her testimonial field, for I do not know. However, I will say that the circumstances placed her under the gravest suspicion.

But Audre resigned and I was fired from the police department, despite the fact that we occupied contrary positions in regard to the police scandal. Audre, however, found herself unable to quit thinking. She found that she still had to live with Audre. Evidence that she was thinking most seriously, and that her conscience was beginning to bother her, came suddenly and surprisingly out of a clear sky.

But when I say that Audre's next move was prompted by "conscience," perhaps I am wrong again in crediting her with a conscience. Although she had escaped the penalty of her self-confessed perjury, she had doubtless heard rumors to the effect that I intended to seek and obtain action against her as a result of her confession. Thus, fear rather than conscience, was her motivating factor.

Just before my trial on the phony burglary charge was to begin, I came home approximately at one a.m. The telephone rang. I raised the receiver and a male voice which I had never heard before, asked: "Is this Charley?" When I replied that it was, the man said: "Someone here wants to talk to you."

"Charley," Audre's voice then came over the wire. "I'd like to talk to you for a few minutes."

"Start talking," I advised.

Audre informed me that she was calling from a service station and had the attendant make the call. "I have to talk to you in person," she insisted. "Can you meet me at Wilshire and Sepulveda Boulevards in about thirty minutes?"

I told her that I couldn't. It would take me at least an hour. She then agreed to see me in an hour. She warned that, if I brought anyone with me, she wouldn't talk.

The newspapers had been carrying stories of how the district attorney's office, fearful of an underworld plot against Audre's life, had been protecting her. Her sanctuary was a top drawer secret. It was known, however, that she had made a trip to the Del Mar race track near San Diego, flanked by official bodyguards, and that she had been stopping at highpriced hotels. This at great expense to the taxpayers.

I was startled at her daring. There she was, the target of an underworld plot and of my "revenge," telephoning me at one a.m., and asking me to meet her alone at an outlying intersection.

I immediately telephoned an officer whom I could trust. I told him what had happened and asked him if he would hide in the trunk compartment of my car and go with me to keep the rendezvous with Audre.

In typical manner, he assented: "Hell, yes, I'll be right over!"

We drove to within a few blocks of Sepulveda and Wilshire Boulevards, which is a short distance from the Veterans' Hospital in

Sawtelle. I stopped and the officer climbed into the rear compartment of my automobile, taking my fully loaded .45 automatic with him.

I drove to the darkened corner, where I saw a sedan which I recognized as the one owned by Police Officer Marvin Stewart. You will recall that Stewart was the officer who was accused of having been drunk in the Gali-Gali cocktail lounge in Hollywood. Stewart had precipitated the terrific fight, which resulted in Inspector Bill Parker's accusations that I had shielded his drunkenness and Parslow's brutality. After my transfer to Central Station, Stewart had worked with Audre in Hollywood vice operations. (Audre later married Officer Stewart.)

I pulled alongside of Stewart's car. Audre was at the wheel.

"Here I am," I announced. "What do you want?"

"Come, get in my car," she said.

"Hell, no," I rejoined. "If you want to talk to me, we'll go in my car."

"Follow me," she directed. "We'll drive somewhere else and then talk. I don't want any cops driving by and seeing us."

She then led the way, driving to a lighted corner, several blocks distant. She got out of her car and climbed into mine.

"Well, Charlie, I just want to say a few things to you," she began. "I know you think I'm a dirty bitch, and I guess nothing I can say will change your opinion. But, I suppose that's the way it has to be.

"I've heard," she continued, "that you are going to a justice of the peace to swear out a complaint against me for perjury. I don't want to threaten you, but if you do that, I'll do everything in the world to see that you are convicted. You know damned well that you'll beat the case. They haven't a chance in the world of convicting you. You've got a perfect alibi."

"You mean, then, that you admit your story that you accompanied me on the night that you say I burglarized the offices of Joint Control is false?" I asked her softly, realizing that here, indeed, was a spot.

"Of course I lied," she admitted glibly, almost flippantly. "I had to. I can't tell you why. There was a lot of pressure put on me. But that doesn't make any difference. You'll beat the rap. They know they haven't got a case against you."

"Why are you trying to do this thing to me?" I demanded. "I have never done anything but befriend you. I can't see why you're trying to pay me back this way."

"That burglary accusation is just to smear you up and destroy the weight of your grand jury testimony against other police officers," she explained. "That and to confuse the issues so that the public will forget the vice, graft scandal and concentrate its attention on you, as you are the chief person they have to worry about. No one will believe me because I've already confessed I perjured myself at Brenda's trial."

I have had many surprises in my life, but that cold-blooded admission of Audre's that she had fabricated a story out of whole cloth for motives she hinted were furnished by someone else, struck me in the face like a hammer blow. I think if I had had a pistol, I'd have killed her then and there, but, upon reviewing it in perspective, that would indeed have played into the hands of those who were seeking my undoing. Under the circumstances, a murder, no matter how justified, could never have been explained. Had I killed her, and I was tempted, people would have said the deed was done to destroy her as chief prosecution witness against me.

But while we were sitting there talking, I thought of the police officer in the rear trunk compartment, I wondered if he had heard Audre's admission.

Audre then asked me if I remembered an anonymous telephone call I had received, wherein an individual reminded me to see certain women to whom I had talked on the night of the supposed burglary.

When I replied that I did remember, Audre explained that it was she who was responsible for the call. She said she had wanted to make certain I wouldn't forget.

"What the hell is the score?" I demanded, with a feeling that I was sitting beside a cobra.

"The whole thing is this, Charlie," she answered. "You found Sergeant Jesse in bed with me. He's afraid that you'll tell people about it and ruin his chance of becoming a lieutenant. He confided in a friend of his who works in personnel, and they got their heads together. Inspector Parker had promised to make Sergeant Jesse his assistant if he (Parker) succeeds in becoming chief of police when Chief Worton leaves the office.

"They promised that I'd be protected and kept on the job although I've been suspended," Audre confessed. "It wasn't my intention to say that I was in love with you. The only thing I intended to say was that you told me about the burglary.

"Inspector Parker assured me that you wouldn't be convicted, or lose your job, but that you'd be discredited to such an extent that the grand jury would have to back off and everything would cool down. So I decided to go along with them. But, Charlie," she said almost tearfully, "I've been double-crossed. If you'll just take it easy," she begged, "you'll still wind up on top."

Then she explained that Sergeant Jesse, the man who had tossed in the hay with her in my duplex, had thrown her over; and now that he was an assistant to Inspector Parker, even refused to see or talk to her. Furthermore, she said that she was going to marry Officer Marvin Stewart, whose car she was driving that night.

If this appears to be slightly confusing to you, you can well imagine how confusing it was to me — facing a burglary charge predicated on the false allegation of a policewoman who, publicly at least, had hitherto enjoyed a good reputation.

I expressed my amazement at this revelation. I had no idea that Audre was romantically interested in Stewart, or that she even liked him. Audre explained that she and Stewart had arrested some bookmakers in Hollywood, and that the attorney for one of them had virtually accused them of shaking down his client. Well, if they did shake the bookmakers, I'll hazard a guess that it wasn't the first time in Los Angeles police history under Mayor Bowron that a bookmaker had been shaken by police officers.

Audre continued to say that someone had informed Stewart and her that the attorney would in all likelihood go before the grand jury in connection with the asserted shakedown. If worse came to worst and they were accused of a shakedown, they would be protected inasmuch as a husband cannot be forced to testify against his wife, nor a wife against her husband under the law.

"The other night after we had done some drinking, Stewart and I went to the home of a girl friend and went to bed. My girl friend came home with a newspaper photographer from The Los Angeles Examiner, and I think the son-of-a-bitch took some pictures of us."

Thus did Audre explain her unexpected plan to marry Officer Stewart to me.

Audre then warned that, if I ever mentioned anything about her planned marriage, she would deny it and would deny that she had seen me.

While I was talking to her, I could see that she had been drinking. She began to feel sorry for herself and started to weep. I was getting bored with the act and told her I would see her in court. She climbed out of the car. I drove a few blocks and then let the officer out of the compartment.

I asked my friend if he had heard the conversation.

"You ought to have beaten hell out of her, right there," he said. "What a bitch."

At the beginning of my trial, a newspaperwoman still in Los Angeles heard Audre whisper: "Good luck, Charlie!" Later, Audre told the reporter that if she printed what she had heard her say, she'd deny it.

Thirty minutes after I left Audre at Wilshire and Sepulveda, she had gotten herself into another jam and was arrested for drunk driving. She wrapped her new police sweetheart's automobile around a telephone pole. Wonder has been expressed as to what she was doing in the West Los Angeles police division alone that night with Officer Stewart's car.

I have thought a great deal about Audre since the great police scandal. I have often wondered what made her tick as she ticked. Her contradictions were and still are a puzzle, but I can say in all honesty that I never slept with her, nor was she my sweetheart at any time during our association as officers.

The evidence of her amorous interludes, as I saw them unfold and as she told them to me, would indicate that she wasn't in love with me. Obviously, Audre changed her affections as she changed her addresses. She had married three times, and the so-called mysteries of sex as they appertained to her were no longer a mystery.

It would be difficult for anyone possessing the slightest skepticism to reconcile Audre's "broken heart," or "unrequited love" for me, with anything that had happened while I worked with her. There were many men in her life and she wasn't hesitant in letting 'em know she liked 'em if she did as witness her play for Officer Jack Ruggles.

Personally, I have concluded that Audre Davis was a badly spoiled, emotionally unsound and over-sexed dame, but I cannot bear factual witness to the latter part of my opinion.

THE SMEAR TECHNIQUE

Many persons who should have been acquitted have been hanged, or sent to prison; and many who have been hanged should have been acquitted.

Most police officers will agree that this is true; that the guilty frequently go free and that the innocent are just as frequently punished. Some time ago, a national magazine ran an article entitled, *"Convicting the Innocent,"* relating in detail dozens of instances in which innocent persons were convicted of crime.

One may ask, "Where does this leave justice?"

Justice is an abstraction, a word. Although one may be innocent of the commission of a crime, he can be convicted. However, if an innocent man is charged with a crime and succeeds in freeing himself, in many minds the suspicion remains that some guilt must have attached to him, otherwise he would not have been so charged.

The public is not aware of the fact that innocent parties may be charged with, or accused of crimes, because those responsible for the accusations are prompted by political motives. Smearing of persons has become a modern political technique. Once a man has been "smeared," his testimony against others becomes far less potent.

One may walk through the curtain of fire a free man; yet, nevertheless, a certain odium adheres to him and to his reputation, once he had been subjected to the flames.

Many people had many motives for having me charged with a burglary. The efficacy of my grand jury testimony had to be weakened, since the liberty and the reputations of top brass officials in the police department were at stake. My record as a police officer and as a person was clean. It offered the "enemy" nothing upon which to capitalize. Hence, a "smear" became mandatory to lessen the gravity of the implications involving police officers in the vice and graft ring.

Before you ponder what I've written here too profoundly, I want to stress the necessity of your understanding police psychology anent the graft, vice, gambling scandal and my relative position within the department.

A police sergeant is a relatively unimportant man in the Los Angeles police department. He's one grade above a police officer. When you understand this, you can properly view the attitude of a lieutenant, a captain, an inspector, etc., towards a sergeant. In my mind's eye I can hear the higher brass snorting:

"Who the hell does that punk Stoker think he is? A sergeant and a lousy one at that. We'll show him what it means for a punk like him to get out of line?"

This attitude, you may rest assured, is held by high police brass towards any sergeant, and you may also believe that this police attitude is communicated in just that fashion to a district attorney who may be involved in prosecuting members of a police cabal, and if the district attorney happens to be friendly to the police brass, the sergeant who finds himself in the bind that I was in can protect himself the best way he can because he'll get little help from any other source.

Inspector William Parker, the chameleonic copper who proved that he could follow the Biblical admonition and be "all things to all men," reversed his story. You will recall that he damned Chief of Police Clemence B. Horrall, Assistant Chief Joe Reed, Lieutenant Rudy Wellpott, Sergeant Elmer V. Jackson and many other high police officials, as men who composed the personnel of a two-ply graft ring within the police department.

You will also recall that Inspector Parker asked me to go before the grand jury and tell my story. However, he now deemed it best for his own interests to travel down the other street and to become an anti-Stoker man. Although he had expressed himself vehemently and critically regarding Lieutenant Rudy Wellpott, he was now moved to write a polemic defending Wellpott and Jackson. This literary gem, according to newspapermen, appeared in The Los Angeles Times. Truly, Inspector Parker, like Rover, had rolled clear over.

Where previously Sergeant Charles Stoker had been a saint fighting the police dragon of graft and corruption, Sergeant Charles Stoker was now a devil that must be destroyed at all costs.

In the Parker purview, Chief Horrall and Assistant Chief Reed, erstwhile authors and instigators of evil, now became whited sepulchres; badly put upon and misunderstood men who had tried valiantly to do their duty and who, as a result, had become the targets of a Machiavellian underworld.

In his professional, propagandized leap from pole to pole, Inspector Parker never hesitated a moment at the equator. There was no personal profit there. We find him running almost perfect interference for newly promoted Lieutenant John Jesse, and proving himself a fast man on the draw when retired Marine General William A. Worton was handed the reins of the Los Angeles police department.

Worton had come to Los Angeles knowing nothing about the background of the police mess and knowing little, if anything, about the department personnel and the leading protagonists in the vice-graft drama. He was in absolute darkness concerning local politics.

We find ambitious Inspector Parker bobbing up beside Worton and feverishly capturing both ears of the doughty Marine. Instead of criticizing Horrall and Reed, Parker became their chief defender. Parker expressed himself in glowing terms regarding Sergeant John Jesse, quickly made Sergeant Jesse his trusted and confidential aide, and promoted him from sergeant to the grade of lieutenant.

This was the situation on July 10, 1949, when Captain Cecil Wisdom, chief of the personnel division (the man who had tapped administrative vice headquarter's telephone wires and who had listened to many incriminating conversations between Lieutenant Wellpott and Sergeant Jackson), on the statement of Audre Davis signed a complaint charging me with burglary.

While many people in the department had sufficient reasons to want to discredit me, Captain Cecil Wisdom probably had the greatest motive. He had purposely suppressed and diverted my deleterious official action against Wellpott and Jackson, yet both were now in grave jeopardy. I had brought about this jeopardy, as Captain Wisdom well knew. Moreover, Wisdom could not plead innocence regarding the Brenda Allen conspiracy. He couldn't since he had heard many of the details on the wire recordings. In addition, too many police officers knew all the details, including the part he and his office had played in the probe. Yes, indeed, Captain Wisdom had every reason to undo Sergeant Stoker and it is police history that he did his best.

Captain Wisdom's moves against me were with the knowledge and approval of his superior, Inspector Bill Parker, the man who had expected to use me along the road to promotion and higher pay.

On July 10, 1949, the battle lines were clearly drawn and everyone involved in the police scandal knew exactly where he stood.

I was astonished — although I shouldn't have been — to find that I stood alone with no support, ill-equipped to do battle with a corrupt police department and district attorney's office. And, to add to my misfortunes, I was broke. This statement is no bid for sympathy. I merely wish to impress upon my readers the facts of the situation. If you want to know how I felt, put yourself in my place.

Although you may be charged with a crime of which you are innocent, if you know that powerful persons and interests are intent upon your destruction, you have a queasy feeling. No matter what concepts you had previously held regarding justice, it is almost certain that you will believe justice to be blind.

When the powers that be are intent upon destroying a man, they overlook no bets that will harass, worry and intimidate him. In the realm of pettiness, they are comparable to little girls quarreling over a doll. The theme of their attitude is to leave nothing undone that will disconcert and worry their victim. The circulation of infamous stories about one's sex life and honesty are automatic; and these conniving, heartless personages know the power of whispering campaigns. They hint darkly about ulterior motives and associate one, politically and otherwise, with persons whom he never knew, declaring him to be a pawn of these individuals who are using him for purposes that cannot stand public scrutiny.

Against this type of lying aggression, one has no way of defending himself. Such conspirators know that the general public is eager and willing to believe the worst about anyone, and that such propaganda, while it may not be one hundred percent effective, in some measure will stick in the public mentality.

The technique is as old as civilized man. It is employed by the wily criminal attorney who has a guilty client, and who seeks to focus the attention elsewhere. He tries the judge, the jury, the public and his client's accusers, but never his client. It is an effective measure, as has often been proved, because it is human nature to want to believe the worst about people.

The transition of my reputation from good to bad, from light to dark, was rapid. Persons who had been my friends now viewed me with suspicion. The full impact of the assault, hit me with the force of a typhoon. Here was I, a police officer and a man who had always held up his head proudly, on the defensive, falsely charged with a crime which I had not committed.

The thieves, the grafters, the intellectually dishonest police officials were no longer in the spotlight. It was I who was on trial. The "spot" had been turned off the malefactors and focused on me. Dozens of persons played their allotted parts in the conspiracy to discredit my accusations against members of the police department.

The district attorney and his office led the vanguard. The bloodhounds at my back were in full cry. The switch had been pulled, and the investigational train was traveling down another track. The boys do it so artfully, and the newspapers? — well, it's just another "good" story to them.

When Audre Davis's tale of my asserted burglary came to the attention of members of the grand jury, they went to the district attorney and asked for a record of her report, for the purpose of reviewing and probing it, in order to decide whether a complaint should be issued against me.

The district attorney's office *flatly refused*, stating that this investigation was not a part of its duties. The jurors then informed the office that the vice-graft investigation was the most important case on the agenda, and that, inasmuch as the asserted burglary had been committed four months previously and nothing had been done about it, the probe into protected vice and graft should be given priority! They expressed the opinion that any criminal action against me should be held in abeyance until the more important probe had been concluded.

This, I think you will agree, was reasonable.

But proof of the fact that the D. A.'s office had a part in the conspiracy to abort and minimize the graft-vice probe came quickly, when that office disagreed with the grand jurors and pushed action against me. It was becoming increasingly urgent that the district attorney's office divert the attention from vice and graft to me, and it acted with alacrity, much to the grand jurors' disgust and despite their protests and criticism.

When the conspirators went into action, they moved with rapidity. A sergeant in Captain Cecil Wisdom's office telephoned me that Wisdom was going to seek a complaint against me. He said that Wisdom had already contacted the district attorney's office. However, due to the nature of the situation, the district attorney had evinced a desire to be absent from the city when the complaint was issued.

My informant in personnel said that it was planned to arrest me in full uniform – I was on a street traffic detail at the time – to the end that my arrest would receive the widest possible publicity and would completely discredit me in the public mind.

I contacted Attorney S. S. Hahn and explained my dilemma. When I informed him that I had but little money, he explained that he was a very busy man, and that he was beleaguered by the necessity of handling many cases already in his office. However, he offered to appear for me at my preliminary hearing, after which I could retain other counsel to represent me during trial of the charges.

Hahn took me into Superior court and surrendered me. I want to say that he treated me fairly and unselfishly. He didn't charge me for his services.

By surrendering in Superior court, I had circumvented Captain Wisdom's plan. He was enraged. Wisdom contacted me in the courtroom, where he informed me that Chief of Police William A. Worton had ordered me to report immediately to the district attorney's office for questioning.

Need I remind you that this demand that I submit to questioning without benefit of counsel was in violation of my Constitutional rights?

I do not know that Chief Worton had given this order. I believe that he had, however. Our Constitution and the rights which it insures citizens, mean little to some military men. The fact is that the Constitution of the United States and the rights it provides have been relegated to use as a subject for neophyte lawyers. The Constitution today consists of shadow, not substance.

To see to it that I went immediately before the district attorney's representatives in this auto-da-fe, or Spanish Inquisition, Captain Wisdom, stalwart pillar of police department "integrity," accompanied me with his aides.

The scene that greeted my eyes could have been appreciated only by those who were privy to what was at stake.

Present were *five deputy district attorneys*, three of whom were assigned to the grand jury, namely, Chief Deputy District Attorney Johnny Barnes, Fred Henderson, and Adolph Alexander. That man of great probity, Johnny Barnes, with Chief Investigator H. Leo Stanley, had advised me to "be careful" what I told the grand jury anent police department vice-graft and corruption. "Grand juries come and go," they had said.

But if Barnes had once been reluctant about probing into police corruption, he wasn't at all reluctant in his valorous attempt to saddle ignominy upon Sergeant Charles Stoker. To the contrary, he was avid and eager to destroy this upstart police sergeant who had participated in an honest effort to reveal a slimy cancer in local law enforcement.

And what of that other noble exemplar of honest law enforcement, H. Leo Stanley, the district attorney's chief aide? It must be noted that

Stanley was present to lend aid and moral support in fixing up Sergeant Stoker, as were Investigators Aldo Corsini and Chester Sharpe.

From an honest police officer working in behalf of the public weal, I had become a heinous offender, a felonious breaker of the burglary law and these individuals were determined to aid the newspapermen in giving the story of my "downfall" the widest publicity possible.

While every incident involved in the Brenda Allen mess had been exceedingly hush-hush, no one was reticent regarding Sergeant Charles Stoker. Despite the fact that I was given the full treatment, I refused to answer questions. I doubt if the infamous Los Angeles child killer Fred Stroble drew more attention than I did that day.

When Attorney Hahn had surrendered me, I had been admitted to bail. In the courtroom, I was in full uniform with my police pistol strapped to my side in a holster. Hahn asked the judge if he wanted me to surrender my pistol, inasmuch as I had been charged with a felony.

"No," replied the judge, "I don't look upon the defendant as a vicious character."

The newspapers once spoke of Captain Wisdom's name as a misnomer; the implication being that he was a stupid man. I agree with that estimate of him. In the courtroom, Wisdom had warned that he was going to arrest me, despite the fact that I had been admitted to bail.

"What for?" I asked.

"For carrying a gun," was his rejoinder.

At that point the bailiff stepped up and told Wisdom that he was the law enforcement representative in that court and that if anything were to be done in the way of an arrest, he would do it; *not Wisdom*.

When I was taken to the county jail, Wisdom tagged along. I was fingerprinted and mugged in full uniform, and my gun was booked as my personal property. Later, when I was released on bail, I retrieved my gun. Downstairs in the lobby of the Hall of Justice, two deputy sheriffs whom I knew were waiting for me.

"Charley, two of Captain Wisdom's men are waiting outside in the parking lot to arrest you for carrying a gun," one informed me. "We'll take you home."

I told them that, inasmuch as Chief Worton had ordered me to report immediately, I would have to go to the City Hall and to Wisdom's office or be in violation of orders. The deputy sheriffs then told me they would take my gun home for me. I gave it to them. Outside in the parking lot, two of Wisdom's myrmidons pounced on me as if I were a John Dillinger.

"You're under arrest," they hissed, in their best opera bouffe manner.

"What for?" I demanded.

"You're carrying a concealed weapon," they retorted.

"Listen, you bastards," I belched, "Do you think that I'm that stupid? Go, tell your Captain Wisdom that he can _ _ _."

I went directly to Captain Wisdom's office. There, he again told me that I was *suspended for conduct unbecoming an officer*.

"Do you think Chief Horrall is a crook?" Wisdom demanded.

"Yes, I certainly do," was my reply, "and so are you."

"Do you consider Chief Worton dishonest?" he continued.

"If he is a friend or a collaborator *of yours*, I am sure that he is," I said.

This incident calls to mind a story I heard in the Army. A private had been court-martialed for having called an officer a bastard. He asked the tribunal if a soldier could be tried for thinking. "No," was the reply. "I still think that officer is a bastard," ejaculated the private.

I now found myself in a very uncomfortable spot. Many persons were eager to seal my lips; and virtually all of them were police officers. I had no illusions about the calibre of my enemies. I knew that if murder were the only means by which they could save themselves, they would not hesitate to resort to murder.

Meanwhile, in San Francisco, the story broke that Mickey Cohen's house had been planted with recording devices by the Los Angeles police department. It was reported that numerous recordings had been made of conversations between Mickey and persons who had conferred with him. Mickey had bought back one set of these recordings, when Attorney-General Fred N. Howser had assigned an investigator, Harry

Cooper, to act as bodyguard for Mickey Cohen while his office conducted an investigation into the affair.

I knew that on the morning of July 19, 1949, a nearly successful attempt had been made to rub Mickey out. This ambush had occurred in front of Sherry's cocktail lounge on the Sunset Strip. Cooper was severely wounded as was Dee Davis, an actress and motion picture bit player; and gangster, Neddie Herbert, Cohen's chief aide, was perforated and died of his wounds. Cohen was shot in the shoulder.

The gunmen had hidden across the street behind a dark retaining wall. When the Cohen entourage was leaving Sherry's at 3 a.m., to go home, their assailants had let fly with shotguns loaded with Double 00 buckshot. This is the type of buckshot used in shotguns employed by the police department.

I was then and I am now convinced that the murderous attack had been made by members of the Los Angeles police department, whose motive it was to seal Cohen's lips. Police officers, who found themselves in jeopardy on the graft front, had reason to fear what the attorney-general's office might do in connection with the Cohen recordings and with other angles which had become, or threatened to become, public knowledge.

I reasoned that, if certain members of the Los Angeles Police Department were in jeopardy on the vice and graft front, by virtue of Cohen's knowledge of their activities, I was in even greater jeopardy because I had concrete, incontrovertible proof of graft activities and malfeasance in office.

Even the proper authority to carry a pistol would not have been ironclad insurance against assassination by determined men. But in the spot in which I found myself, a pistol is better than a toothpick and much more comforting. While I didn't want to die under an assassin's bullets, I felt that I could die much more amiably if I had a gun and could go down trying.

Consequently, I appealed to the sheriff's office for permission to carry a gun. I was told that, inasmuch as I was at liberty on bail, charged with a felony, that office could not issue me a permit.

Several deputy sheriffs, aware of the gravity of my position, talked the matter over among themselves and decided that I was in danger. They came to me with the suggestion that they serve as my bodyguards. They offered to take turns in protecting me during their off-duty hours and to so arrange their time that I would not be alone in the event of trouble.

I am grateful to them. Today, that offer still stands. These deputies, honest officers all, stand ready at a moment's notice to give me every protection within their power. At that time, however, I declined the proffered aid. This offer was heartwarming, and it will forever be appreciated by me, but I didn't want to put them on the spot and had I accepted their offer, that's where they would have been — *on the spot*.

Perhaps, what I am about to tell you will more clearly delineate the character of Inspector William Parker than anything I have written thus far. It will show you the kind of man he was and is.

Policewoman, Alice Houghton, who is in the Los Angeles Police Department, has remained a friend of mine throughout every misfortune which has assailed me. I met her in the Army, when I served as an intelligence investigator, and she as an Army WAC sergeant. She is a fine, intelligent young woman. Alice, her Army boy friend, and I, became good friends.

When the war was over and I had returned to Los Angeles and the police department, I received a letter from Alice stating that she was about to be discharged from the Army in California.

She was desirous of obtaining employment and, as a result of her experience, wrote that she felt qualified to become a policewoman on the Los Angeles department. She was not well off financially, and was badly in need of employment.

I tutored her for an examination which was coming up for policewomen. She took that examination, and another for deputy sheriff. She also took the examination for investigator for the State Board of Equalization. She bears the distinction of being the only woman who has ever passed the examination for the latter position.

As a result, she was offered employment as deputy sheriff, investigator for the State Board of Equalization and policewoman. She chose the latter position. When my difficulties arose, Alice was aware of them. I met her one day and we discussed the charges against me. I mentioned the fact that I could not carry a gun.

"Charley, you have befriended me in the past," she said. "I know you are not guilty, and I believe efforts are being made to ruin you because of your disclosures I think that it is apropos that I return a favor. I have an automobile that you can use. I'll leave my gun in the glove compartment. In the event you are stopped and searched by police, you'll have an alibi, inasmuch as you will be driving my car. You merely can say that I left the gun in the glove compartment."

While I now realize that agreement was an error in judgment on my part, at the time I didn't envision Miss Houghton getting into trouble as the result of trying to help me, whom she considered a friend.

Incidentally, Miss Houghton was one of the policewomen whose assistance I had requested during the Brenda-Allen investigation. The request had not been granted; they gave me Audre Davis instead for reasons which, by this time, should be apparent. However, on her own time, Miss Houghton had aided me in small ways in the Brenda Allen investigation. She was with me on the night that I listened in on Brenda's conversation with Sergeant Elmer V. Jackson, during which Brenda discussed the idea of having me killed for ten thousand dollars which she said she would pay. *Miss Houghton had heard that conversation.*

I took Miss Houghton's car, in which her gun was concealed.

At about this time, Brenda Allen went before the grand jury and stated that I had taken graft from her. She said that she had paid me one hundred dollars a week per prostitute with the agreement that I would not molest her or her scarlet personnel.

I didn't take long to find out how District Attorney William E. Simpson stood in the matter, or which side he favored in the police controversy. To the tune of a screaming newspaper headline, he commented: "The little girl (Brenda Allen) is going right down the line in her grand jury disclosures and she will let the chips fall where they may."

Brenda Allen had been temporarily freed on a writ granted by the state Supreme Court, after Audre Davis had recanted her trial testimony and declared that she had perjured herself to convict Brenda of the attempted pandering charge.

Newspapers stated that reporters had been trying to locate Brenda following her liberation from jail; but that her attorney had informed them that she was out of the city; that she had gone to visit relatives.

On the night when this story appeared in the newspapers, a woman companion and I had gone to the Warner's Wiltern Theatre at Wilshire Boulevard and Western Avenue to see a movie. When I drove into the parking lot, I saw Brenda Allen get into a car with a man, preparatory to leaving. I judged that she and her companion had attended the show.

Three hours later, I left the theatre and drove my woman companion home. I double-parked across the street from the woman's apartment and waited for her to get out and enter her abode. When she got out, she glanced down the street.

"Charley," she said. "I think someone is following us."

I directed her to get back into the car. I made a quick "U" turn in the street and drove head-on toward the shadowing car, so that the driver could not escape. As I had suspected, the driver of the car was the man whom I had seen three hours earlier with Brenda Allen. I jumped out of the car, strode over to him and told him to get out, that I was going to slug hell out of him.

"For Christ's sake, Stoker, wait a minute!" he pleaded. "I just want to talk to you. I was waiting until you got rid of your girl friend."

"All right, talk," I ordered.

"I think you're a swell guy and an honest copper," he began, "and I want to thank you for having left my name out of the newspapers. If I'd been dragged into this mess, it would have killed my folks."

I thought the guy was going to cry. He seemed so sincere that I almost felt sorry for him. I did feel sorry for him, but then, I should have known better. He was a sweetheart of Brenda's.

"I'm no pimp," he sobbed. "I was in the Navy during the war, stationed at San Diego. Came to Los Angeles on leave.
Then, at the Ambassador Hotel one night, I met Brenda. Had no idea she was a whore. Every time I came to town after that, I'd look her up and go out with her. I thought she was a swell fellow. Still do."

He paused, waiting for me to speak. I said nothing and he continued while the eyes of the young woman I was with widened in astonishment.

"Brenda's out on this writ, and she has a chance of staying out if you don't throw a monkey wrench into the machinery. I know you hate her because she testified she paid you for protection. But she had no choice. Those people told her to do it.

"She isn't a bad sort, and she isn't rich. A lot of her relatives have been sick and she's been sending them to clinics all over the country. That costs money. Brenda's just a country girl who thinks she's smart, but isn't. I've tried to get her out of the racket, but there's things I don't understand about the mess — like her living with Jackson as man and wife. She never explained that to me and I didn't ask her.

"I don't blame Brenda too much. I blame the guy who turned her out in the racket when she was a kid — and I blame guys like Jackson who kept her in it to enrich themselves. That's why I'm asking this favor. Don't do anything to put her back in jail."

The man seemed to be wound up. When the first opportunity presented itself, I demanded to know if Brenda had sent him to me.

"For Christ's sake, no," he retorted. "She'd give me hell if she knew about it."

I recalled Kipling's lines —"A fool there was and he made his prayer to a rag and a bone and a hank of hair, even as you and I."

"Here's a fool who's stuck on a prostitute," I reflected, and I felt a twinge of pity for the guy because I couldn't agree with his estimate of his beloved Brenda.

The following evening, Policewoman Alice Houghton was dressing in her apartment, getting ready to go on duty. At 5:30 p.m., she heard a knock at the door. She opened the door, and was confronted by two of

Captain Cecil Wisdom's head-hunters. They informed her that she was wanted immediately at the police personnel offices. She thought the order peculiar, inasmuch as it was after office hours.

She accompanied the officers to personnel and to her surprise, found herself face to face with Inspector William Parker, that charming and intellectually constant police inspector, and Lieutenant John Jesse (the quondam sweetheart of Policewoman Davis) whom I had routed out of my house when I found him in bed with the delectable Audre.

Lieutenant Jesse took Miss Houghton into a private room to question her. He said he had information and proof that she had been seen with me the night before. Alice denied it, properly and truthfully. She said that she could definitely account for her movements on the previous night, and that she had not seen me on that night. It had been her night off and she explained that she had spent it with a woman friend in the latter's apartment. This friend was a registered nurse at a local hospital, and she suggested that if Jesse wanted proof, he could check, then and there.

"Regardless of that, Lieutenant Jesse," Alice continued, "Being seen with Charles Stoker doesn't constitute a crime."

"Do you know the license number of your automobile?" asked Jesse.

Miss Houghton gave the number verbally.

"Stoker was driving your car last night and he was up to something," Jesse declared. "What was it?"

"I loaned Stoker my car," Alice replied, "but I don't know where he was or what he was doing, last night." Miss Houghton informed Jesse that she would loan her car to anyone she saw fit and that she wouldn't account to the Los Angeles Police Department for such actions.

Then Jesse went off on the age old tangent. Assuming that Miss Houghton was in love with me, he tried to make her jealous.

"You know, Stoker's been making a fool of you," said the sagacious Jesse. "He's been going with Audre Davis."

"Oh?" she inquired. "Tell me more."

"I'll let you in on a secret — Audre Davis had an abortion and Stoker paid for it."

Alice laughed in Jesse's face.

"Who's kiddin' who?" she demanded. "For your information, I've worked with Audre Davis — and from what I've heard, I'd believe that of you, not Stoker."

Jesse, aghast, hit the ceiling but came right back down again.

"Oh, it was probably you who telephoned my wife," he mumbled in a thoughtless admission of guilt.

"I never cared enough about you to take the trouble to telephone your wife," Policewoman Houghton told Jesse.

At this point, Inspector William Parker stuck his head in at the door; and Jesse told him he couldn't get any information from Miss Houghton. Jesse remarked that she apparently believed that the police department was persecuting Stoker.

Upon hearing this remark, Alice told him that she had not expressed such a sentiment or opinion. Then Parker asked if she believed that I was right.

"I know nothing about the merits of the case," she replied. "However, whether Stoker is right or wrong, I still value him as a friend."

It infuriated Parker to be confronted by a woman whom he could not bulldoze.

"We know that you worked with Stoker on some cases in Hollywood," Parker said with a slurring inflection.

"Yes, I helped Stoker on cases in Hollywood at various times," was her rejoinder.

"What were the cases?" Parker demanded.

Miss Houghton then gave the details of several cases she had been assigned. Parker told her that he wasn't interested in those cases, but that he was concerned about other investigations upon which she had worked with me.

"To what cases are you alluding?" asked Alice.

"You know what I am talking about," smirked Parker.

"Oh!" her inquisitive inflection angered Parker.

Finally coming to the point, he asked: "What do you know about Brenda Allen?"

"Not a thing," was the reply.

"You're lying," accused Parker. "We have a file on you and we can discharge you from the police department."

"I've done my work on the police department to the best of my ability," countered Miss Houghton. "I have no idea what kind of a file you have on me. However, I do know the truth can't be uncomplimentary," she said, and added: "*I believe you are a liar.*"

Her refusal to show fear was more than these two police stalwarts could stand.

Police personnel, when interrogated by them, were wont to shake with fright. When Parker had recovered his usual aplomb, he chided: "I want you to know that as long as I have been on the police department, I've never had an officer so insubordinate and so disrespectful. I'll tell you, right now, that this department isn't big enough for the two of us!"

Lieutenant John Jesse took the cue. This individual, who had tossed so gladly in the hay with Policewoman Audre Davis in my bungalow, now grabbed a flashlight, flashed the beam into Policewoman Houghton's eyes, and blurted dramatically:

"Inspector, I think she is under the influence of narcotics."

"Get this woman out of here," Parker commanded.

Miss Houghton was taken home. A few minutes later she heard another knock, the second of the evening. She was confronted by a police sergeant and a policewoman when she opened the door. They told her that they had orders to take her to the Georgia Street Emergency Hospital for a physical examination.

Miss Houghton tearfully accompanied them to the hospital, where she was forced to submit to a thorough physical examination to determine whether or not she used narcotics. Much to the embarrassment of the policewoman, she had been herded into the hospital like a common street walker. She felt a futile sense of outrage at being examined in the presence of a number of officers and other persons.

When the doctor had completed the examination, he expressed indignation at the investigative farce: "What the hell is this, a joke?" he demanded. "This woman is not a user of narcotics. She probably doesn't even know their effects."

The doctor patted Policewoman Houghton on the back. "You can go to work," he assured her. "I don't know what these people are trying to do to you, but they're not going to get any help from me," he said, scowling at the assemblage.

Miss Houghton returned to her apartment. She found that it had been entered, probably by someone with a passkey and had been crudely and thoroughly searched. All of her personal mail, her diary and papers had been inspected by someone.

Today, I consider Miss Houghton was fortunate, knowing the calibre of the police officials with whom she was dealing. It is a wonder that either morphine or cocaine was not planted in her apartment. I consider her fortunate in that no attempt had been made to frame her with narcotics.

Today, when I hear guileless persons speak of constitutional rights, I want to vomit...

Newspaper readers are continuously regaled with stories depicting the horrors perpetrated by the M. V. D. Russian Secret Police, and by the German Gestapo, which received considerable publicity, or notoriety, during World War II. It is not comforting to know that we have men on the Los Angeles police department, who, if they dared, would employ the most horrible and infamous tactics of totalitarian police organizations.

Lieutenant Jesse and Inspector Parker were fully cognizant of the fact that a narcotic rap is the roughest of them all. These official rattlesnakes, in their attempt to incriminate an honest, fearless policewoman, who had the courage to remain steadfast to a friend she had known in the Army – who had the temerity to believe in his innocence because she knew him well – gave concrete evidence of how low police officials can stoop.

I am relating this story in detail for the reason that I want the general public to know what type of men direct the administrative affairs of the Los Angeles police department.

I have already stated that I did not care for Hollywood vice squad Officer Jimmy Parslow. I didn't like his personality or his method of operating.

You will recall that Parslow was dismissed from the police department, essentially for his participation in the Brenda Allen investigation. Although the reason given for his dismissal was "conduct unbecoming an officer," the truth was that Parslow had run contrariwise to the wishes of his police superiors, as I had.

But, whatever criticism may be leveled at Jimmy Parslow, it must be said in his defense that he is a fighting demon.

LIEUTENANT JOHN JESSE AND INSPECTOR WILLIAM PARKER, BOTH OF WHOM HAD DISPLAYED UNLIMITED COURAGE IN THEIR DEALINGS WITH POLICEWOMAN ALICE HOUGHTON, LEARNED THEY WERE DEALING WITH A DIFFERENT SEX AND A TOUGHER BREED OF CAT WHEN THEY GRABBED HOLD OF PARSLOW'S TAIL.

A few days after Miss Houghton's ordeal, Officer Parslow and his brother arrived at Jimmy's home early one night. As they drove up, their trained eyes saw a dark sedan lurking on the street. Parslow's brother, a California State Highway Patrolman, loosened his revolver in its holster. "Get ready, kid," he told Jimmy. "This looks like it."

Instead of stopping, the car slowly passed by and parked. Two men got out and identified themselves as Los Angeles police officers. "Someone downtown wants to see you," an officer advised Parslow. "Don't ask any questions — just come with us."

When William A. Worton had assumed the office of police chief, he had made various statements to the effect that any citizen could talk to him. However, when Parslow sought to take advantage of this offer by going to Worton's office, Worton was "too busy to see him" and said that he would call Parslow at a later date. Parslow assumed that the order to go downtown had come from the chief, but he had never been with two more non-committal officers than the pair who had approached him in front of his home.

When he attempted to question the pair, they replied, "Parslow, we don't know what the hell this is all about. We're following orders – we don't think so much of this kind of crap!"

"Where are you taking me?" Parslow inquired.

"We don't know," was the reply. "We'll have to make a telephone call."

The telephone call was made. Then Parslow was driven to the Mayfair Hotel on West Seventh Street, where he was escorted to a suite of rooms in which he found the ubiquitous Inspector Parker and Lieutenant John Jesse waiting for him.

He was told to be seated, after which an interrogation began.

Parslow was asked about various bars and vice activities in Hollywood. Then Parker and Jesse got around to the Brenda Allen affair. "Why are you protecting Sergeant Stoker?" they demanded. "And what side are you going to be on – the police department's side, or Stoker's side?"

Parslow was subtly reminded that he had a family and a job.

"I'm not on any side," retorted Parslow. "I don't see that there are any sides. All I can see, insofar as it involves me, is that *I tell the truth!*"

"We've got a file on you," Parker interjected threateningly.

"We can get you fired."

"Parker," began Parslow, "I think you have an ulterior motive in attempting to get rid of the Hollywood vice squad. I'm pretty sure I know what this is all about. If you want to find the dirty linen closet in the police department, look in the administrative vice squad's offices, not in Hollywood. You know and I know that the Hollywood vice squad is clean and you know and I know that the administrative vice squad is filthy!"

Parker got red in the face. "You've been listening to Stoker," he bellowed. "And Stoker's God damned friend, Harry Lawson, the foreman of the county grand jury."

"Are you calling me a liar?" Parslow demanded, his gorge rising. He got to his feet and stood facing Jesse and. Parker.

"If either or both of you have the guts," said Parslow, "Get on your feet and call me a liar. If you do, I'll bat the brains out of both of you simultaneously and throw you out that window. I'm going to leave here and if you know what is best for you, you won't get in my road!"

Parker and Jesse didn't get in Parslow's road. They weren't dealing with Alice.

Without interference, Parslow strode out of the hotel.

Soon afterwards, he was brought before the police trial board and was dismissed for "conduct unbecoming an officer." Parslow had lost his job, but he had retained his self-respect and, on the Los Angeles police department, self- respect is the one thing you may not retain if you would fare well with those individuals who run it.

No, on the contrary, you must be a lap dog, but even then, they won't like you.

I am certain that there was no hesitation in Parslow's choice. He's that kind of a guy and despite the fact that he and I weren't buddies, I have to hand it to him because he was a fine police officer and he had what it takes deep down inside -guts.

As Parslow, shorn of his police badge, was leaving the personnel office, a lieutenant gloatingly commented: "If you hadn't stuck by Charles Stoker, this wouldn't be happening to you."

Parslow looked at the lieutenant witheringly, with contempt: "Some people like you have no regard for honesty, but I have," and he walked out.

A few days later, Officer Jack Ruggles was summoned to the offices of Inspector Parker, who apparently had learned the lesson that rough tactics weren't paying off — and that they might be physically dangerous unless he was bulldozing a policewoman — for he tried something new — honey and oil. Parker and Jesse buddy-buddied Ruggles, dusted off a chair and greeted him like a long lost brother.

Picture the position of officer Jack Ruggles. An Army Air Force Veteran, Ruggles had had forty-seven combat missions over Germany as a B-17 pilot. He had twice been shot down. Upon returning to America, elated with victory, he had decided to join the Los Angeles police department and make it his life's work. Despite his Army service, Ruggles was still young and somewhat naive in the ways of the police department.

When called in before Parker and Jesse, his sole "crime" consisted of the fact that he had been assigned to work Hollywood vice with Sergeant Charles Stoker.

That remarkably brave man, Lieutenant John Jesse, whose best tactics were employed in browbeating policewomen and accusing them of being narcotics users, was a man who had taken full advantage of an "understanding draft board" when his country had been at war.

Immediately, Jesse started nicknaming Ruggles "Jake" and began patting him on the back. In Jack's twenty-four years, no one had ever called him "Jake" before. It was ultra friendly.

"We're your friends," Jesse assured him. "We want to look after your best interests. Stoker is out to ruin you. We know that he isn't smart enough to do what he has done to the police department without having some powerful and conniving politicians behind his actions.

"And 'Jake,' we know that he's doing things behind your back —got you transferred off the Hollywood vice detail. *He's using you.* Now, we want you to tell us here and now whose side you are going to be on — Stoker's or the police department's?"

"Are there sides?" asked Ruggles. "All I know is that I've been doing what I'm supposed to do. I don't care whether I work vice, or not."

"He's out to ruin you," insisted Parker and Jesse.

"If you can prove that to me," said Ruggles, "I'll be willing to listen to you and believe you."

The pair then became mysterious. They said they couldn't divulge proof at that time; Ruggles would "just have to take their word for it."

But, despite his tender years, Ruggles, like Parslow, wasn't as gullible as Parker and Jesse evidently believed him to be.

He said that he didn't know what they were driving at; but that if they would explain one thing to him, he would be inclined to believe that what they said regarding me might be true.

"Why certainly, 'Jake,' just tell us what it is."

"Why were Lieutenant Rudy Wellpott and Sergeant Elmer V. Jackson kept on the administrative vice squad — after everything they'd been doing was made known to high officials of the police department?" was the question propounded by the rookie to the two smart police officers who were interested, not in Wellpott and Jackson, oh no, but in Sergeant Charles Stoker.

"No man is indispensable to the police department," continued Ruggles. "Any man's place can be filled by another officer."

Ruggles reminded Parker and Jesse of a remark made by one of their own investigators to a class at the police academy. The investigator had stated that personnel "had enough evidence on a certain police sergeant working vice to send him to San Quentin penitentiary."

To this, Inspector Parker and Lieutenant Jesse had no answer. Ruggles was admonished that he "should believe in them."

Knowing what he knew, Ruggles thought this request rather unreasonable. He knew that there were answers and he wanted answers.

"We're just looking out for your own good," repeated Parker and Jesse. "Just keep us informed of anything you think we should know about Stoker. We'll all work together."

Good old "Jake" was soon transferred to the "sticks" in uniform. When I think about him out there inhaling the fog, I wonder how he feels about his "pals"— Inspector Parker and Lieutenant Jesse. Recently, Ruggles took an examination for motorcycle officer possibly in the belief, that if he remained a patrolman, he would spend the rest of his days walking a beat far out in the dreary and lonely police belt.

Ruggles passed in the top bracket of the eligibility list for motorcycle officer. Days later, he learned that those officers chosen for the motorcycle detail had been selected. All but Ruggles; he had not been called. He wondered why. When he telephoned the personnel bureau, a snippy chit of a girl clerk answered the phone. Ruggles asked her why he had not been selected.

"Why, just because of your personnel record," she said, implying that it was "very, very bad" and that he had done something terrible.

Imagine that! A fine, courageous young officer who was always dead on the level, Ruggles had worked vice with me because he had been so assigned. In actuality, he had no stomach for that detail and hadn't chosen it. But because he had refused to join forces with the police conspirators who were out to wreck me; because he had refused to lie and to distort the truth and because as an honorable man he was "not to be trusted" by the scummy lice in police executive positions, he is today paying an unjustified penalty.

Thus, Ruggles, too, became subject to the "roust" by police executives, solely because he was the working partner of a police sergeant who had incurred the enmity of the "powers that be," by exposing graft and maladministration in the police department.

When I review the fate of young Ruggles vs. the State, I am reminded of the line: "Some of the greatest scoundrels hide in the folds of the flag."

It is ironical to think that a group of phony, hypocritical, scandal blowing-down police executives is in a position to give an honest officer a "bad personnel record."

Well aware that the executives in question won't and can't answer the question, I demand to know why Officer Jack Ruggles's police personnel record is bad. Is it because he is an honorable man? Is it because he refused to lie about the Brenda Allen investigation? The public has a right to know what is taking place in its city government; and it has the duty to remind police executives and officers and their political masters, such as Mayor Fletcher E. Bowron, that they are merely public servants, if not very good ones.

Now, I can look upon my fate and the termination of my police career philosophically and with equanimity. What has happened to me, in the larger aspect of the situation, doesn't particularly matter. But what has happened to Officer Ruggles, whose sole guilt consisted in "telling the truth" about what he knew, does matter very greatly. It not only matters to Officer Ruggles; it should be a source of grave public concern.

IF AN HONEST POLICE OFFICER CAN BE VICTIMIZED BY POLICE BRASS FOR DOING HIS DUTY AND TELLING THE TRUTH, WHAT INCENTIVE HAVE POLICE OFFICERS TO REMAIN HONEST AND DO THEIR DUTY? TODAY, INCENTIVE AND REWARD ARE RESERVED FOR THOSE WHO LIE, CHEAT AND STEAL.

The police department now has on its roster thousands of young and highly impressionable officers. They talk to one another and are aware of what takes place in the police department. They know what happened to several police officers who honestly did their duty but who had the misfortune to get mixed up, in one way or another, in the late police scandal.

When young police officers see what happens to such youngsters as Jack Ruggles, through no fault of their own, they reflect and think things over. The conclusions they reach are the result of inevitable logic. There is a penalty for honesty and forthrightness, and a reward for dishonesty and the ability to follow the line laid down by crooked and intellectually dishonest superiors. This idea is summed up in the police phrase which one recurrently hears if he is a police officer: "I'm not sticking my neck out."

Ruggles "stuck his neck out" by telling the truth and by refusing to be a party to dishonesty. For that, he is paying the penalty, today. There will be additional police scandals in the future as there have been in the past. Other officers will be mixed up in underworld graft and skullduggery. Today's young officers have learned from our ordeal; and when the next scandal appears on the horizon, many of them will tin can it and will refuse to do their duty honorably and according to their oaths because of the fear of executive reprisals.

AND THAT, READERS, IS A MATTER OF GREAT PUBLIC CONCERN.

In that connection I believe that I am rendering the public a service by shedding as much light as I can on what went on in the police department, it has been my desire to render a public service. I would be a super-mentalist if I could successfully fabricate all that I have related in this story. There are too many ways to check facts, and too many witnesses who told the truth and who know the truth. The nature of my story is such that I have had to talk about myself, possibly to the point where the reader has considered me an egotist. That, however, is one of the hazards I have had to run.

It is my desire to impress one fact upon the reader's mind. When I was charged with having looted the Joint Control offices and with having stolen a check, I immediately offered to TAKE A LIE DETECTOR TEST. I ALSO OFFERED TO TAKE TRUTH SERUM.

THESE OFFERS WERE NOT ACCEPTED.

By contrast, local police officers do not hesitate to administer tests to suspected killers in a murder case.

HAVING NOTHING TO FEAR FROM THE TRUTH, AND EVERYTHING TO GAIN, I WENT TO VIRTUALLY ALL OF THE LOCAL NEWSPAPERS AND PRACTICALLY PLEADED WITH THEM TO ENLIST THEIR AID IN SECURING THESE TESTS FOR ME.

I AM STILL WILLING AND EAGER TO TAKE SUCH TESTS.

A TRICK DONE WITH MIRRORS

*"Easy still it proves in factious times,
With public zeal to cancel private crimes."*

Although the district attorney's office had told the grand jury that The People vs. Sergeant Charles Stoker was just another trial, the subsequent actions of the district attorney and his staff, including deputies and investigators, belied these words.

After a trial date had been set, following my preliminary hearing on the burglary charge, a local private investigator, who in the course of his investigation had been passing as a "bookmaker from the East," went to the office of The Los Angeles Daily News with information that he had been invited to a party. According to his report, the party was to be given by members of the district attorney's office, with the purpose of celebrating the issuance of the felonious burglary complaint against Sergeant Stoker. He explained that his acceptance of the invitation was contingent upon his taking a case of whiskey with him. This whiskey was supplied to him by The Daily News. Later, he reported the identities of those attending the party, one of whom was an investigator assigned to the Los Angeles county grand jury.

My case had been assigned to Superior Judge Charles W. Fricke's court. Judge Fricke is not only an able judge, he is learned in the law, having been a law instructor, the author of several legal volumes and a former prosecutor in the Los Angeles district attorney's office. Judge Fricke has the reputation of being "dead honest." Over the years no single doubt has been raised as to his judicial integrity.

Judge Fricke, however, is a stern judge, who is not noted for leniency towards malefactors, if they are convicted in his court. As a result of his sternness, and this is no mark of disrespect to him on my part, he is known as "San Quentin Fricke."

In a frantic desire to convict me, the district attorney's office hadn't overlooked a bet. The jury selected to hear the evidence was impaneled from communities within the county lying as far distant from Los Angeles as was possible. Evidently, this was done on the theory that residents of outlying communities were less familiar with the details of the police scandal, which had been on the front pages of metropolitan dailies for several weeks than were city dwellers.

Community newspapers in such cities as Pasadena, Monrovia, Whittier, Newhall, and Long Beach do not deal with Los Angeles news at too great length in their columns. Therefore, by impaneling jurors from outlying communities, the district attorney's office undoubtedly hoped to work toward my detriment and towards my conviction in favor of my enemies – in which category the district attorney's office belonged, if the facts may be taken as a criterion.

The district attorney's office had tried to close all doors against a possible acquittal of Sergeant Charles Stoker. Not one deputy, but two were given the responsibility of seeing to it that I didn't wriggle off the felonious hook. Moreover, one of these deputies, Clifford Crail, was accredited with being its toughest prosecutor. The relative of a former Superior court judge, Crail was in charge of the Pasadena branch of the district attorney's office when the District Attorney told him to forget his duties in that city and come to Los Angeles to *give it to me.*

In an all-out effort to "give it to Stoker," to ruin and discredit his grand jury testimony and to save the thieves and grafters in the police department, the big brass of the LAPD worked hand in glove with the district attorney towards the common goal. Of course, Chief of Police William A Worton, Assistant Chief of Police Joe Reed, Captain Cecil Wisdom, and my dear friend, Inspector William Parker, knew the date of my trial.

These conspirators had pitched a cute curve when they cited me before the police trial board on charges of "conduct unbecoming an officer." The purpose of this maneuver prior to my trial on the burglary charge, was to force my hand and make me reveal my defense. The charge that my conduct did not become a police officer was founded upon the criminal charge that I had looted the offices of Joint Control.

My attorney, Ward Sullivan, appeared before the police brass and pointed out the inconsistency, or rather the unfairness of bringing me before a police trial board before I went on trial for the burglary.

When, reluctantly, the police trial board members had agreed to postpone the date of my police trial board hearing until after I had been prosecuted on the burglary charge, it appeared that I had won a victory, however slight. But that amiable, kindly and elegant fellow, Inspector Bill Parker, wasn't through. After he had put the pressure on Chief of Police Worton, my attorney was notified that the postponement was off and that I would have to appear before the police trial board forthwith on the charge of "unbecoming conduct."

In desperation, I then appealed to a citizen's organization known as *The Citizen's Vigilante Committee*, which was composed of veterans and prominent attorneys. The creation of such an organization by prominent men is indicative of the fact that the better citizens of Los Angeles thought that something was very rotten. The word "Vigilante" connotes a day long ago in San Francisco when corruptionists had charge of the government to such an extent that the better element in the city composed a vigilante group which summarily hanged them without benefit of trial by jury.

However, members of the Citizens' Vigilante Committee made a subtle but effective demand upon Mayor Fletcher E. Bowron and members of the police commission suggesting that the trial board hearing had "better be postponed" until after my trial on the felony charge. It was.

The burglary trial proceeded, although the district attorney had no case and his aides knew it. People with no conception of the burglary, or of the burglar's identity, were subpoenaed by the state. These included the office boy and the janitor at Joint Control. Evidently the D. A. wanted to ascertain that the jury would be convinced that a "burglary" had been committed.

Two Los Angeles police officers were called, one of whom testified that he had received the burglary complaint. He explained that he had gone out and had taken a report. The other officer testified that he had gone to the scene and had made fingerprint examinations, but had failed to find any prints.

Then a police stooge of Captain Cecil Wisdom's testified that my answers before police personnel were contrary, in some respects, to my replies to questions from the witness stand during the trial. He also stated with reluctance that I hadn't been under oath when I had been questioned in Wisdom's office.

The man may have had something. I had been fully aware that neither Captain Cecil Wisdom nor anyone in his crooked office was capable of telling the truth. Consequently when I entered the sacred portals of his domain, I felt like an honest man attending a convention of chronic and pathological liars, and I answered leading questions with reserve.

You will recall that those present when I was questioned in Wisdom's office included a police captain, who, when I first went on the job and was walking a beat, had wanted me to take graft from bar owners and had magnanimously offered to share the spoils with me. Later, this individual was given the alternative of retiring on pension, or of facing charges by Chief Worton. Also present were Aldo Corsini and Chester Sharp, investigators for the district attorney's office.

That stalwart pillar of the police department – Captain Cecil Wisdom – who had filed the burglary charge against me, and who had made innumerable dictograph records of Wellpott's and Jackson's conversations and had successfully smothered them so that they were never made public, was conspicuous by his absence from the trial. Perhaps Wisdom was too embarrassed to attend, since, a few days prior to my trial, he had been indicted for perjury by the county grand jury as a result of his part in the police mess.

In his opening address to the jury, intellectual and prosecutorial Deputy District Attorney Clifford Crail, pictured cunning, conniving little Audre Davis as a woman who had loved "not wisely but too well."

According to Crail, Audre had in time perceived the monstrous villain that I was, and had finally become aware that I was using her virgin heart for fell and sinister purposes. I only wish that Audre's former husbands could have heard that peroration in sheer bathos, and that I might have listened to what they had to say in comment.

Crail cried crocodile tears of pity, his voice trembling and his body shaking as he sought to build the jury to an emotional climax in which they could see his Satanic majesty masked behind my "handsome visage." Then, taking off on a new tangent, he implied that I had an ulterior motive in testifying before the county grand jury and in revealing the mechanics of police graft and the protection of Hollywood prostitutes — namely, to cover my own illegal doings.

One can imagine the thoughts that raced through my mind as I sat on trial for a burglary that I hadn't committed — one which I didn't believe and never have believed was committed — listening to Crail's subtle implication of motive which was masterful in its cunning. The burglary had been perpetrated, so they said, during the first week of April, 1949. My trial took place in late November, 1949. Yet, nothing was said to explain what had happened in the interim.

Of course, what had happened was a full-blown police scandal, involving most of the individuals of consequence in the department. "The Good, Honest and Efficient Government — There Are No Organized Rackets in Los Angeles — We Have the Finest Police Department in the World"— umbrella of Mayor Fletcher E. (I'm Fighting the Underworld) Bowron, had been shot full of scandal-holes and was leaking slime, dirt, graft, conspiracies and whores.

Of one fact, I was certain. The district attorney's office possessed not one shred of concrete evidence to link me with the burglary at Joint Control, other than Audre's false accusation that she was with me on the night when the burglary had occurred and had waited in my car while I accomplished it.

Attorneys who had sat in the office as witnesses, expressed amazement at the bringing of the charge, and were astonished that Judge Fricke had permitted some of the far-fetched and completely irrelevant testimony to enter the record.

The district attorney's office, of course, was able to establish the fact that I had had trouble with Joint Control, whose services I had employed in relation to the construction of a duplex; and with the cabinet maker, who had tried to bilk Ruggles and me. The fact was also established that I had called at Joint Control on the day of the burglary. Still, that didn't add up to burglary.

In all fairness to the district attorney's office, which was very unfair to me, I will say that it established that I had a possible motive for the crime, the recovery of the controversial check.

To digress for a moment, let me state that, a few days prior to the trial, Audre Davis had changed her name to Mrs. Marvin Stewart, marking her fourth marriage. Of course, this marriage was *strictly for love*. Three former husbands and Sergeant Charles Stoker had broken her heart but that was all in the past.

Now, Audre ascended the witness stand and told her version of the story. She had been assigned to work with me on a case. At approximately 6:00 *o'clock* one evening, I had arrived at her home. We had then driven to an address where I left her in the car while I went in to interview a vice complainant. She said that I had returned and told her of my conversation with the complainant, explaining that the actual working of the case would be set for another day. She said that during the drive to her home, I had mentioned having received a complaint in Hollywood, and that she had asked if she might go along for the ride. At *about* 8:00 *p.m.*, she said, I had called for her at her home, and had then driven her to Hollywood.

According to her testimony, I had told of having received a complaint regarding a large house containing probable prostitutes. She said that I wasn't certain of the address, but that I had been given a description of the house, which was on the west side of the street, either in the first block north or south of Sunset Boulevard.

Audre stated that we had arrived in the vicinity of this address *between* 8:00 *and* 8:30 *p.m.*, had searched the neighborhood and had found the house in question. Then, being unable to determine if anyone were at home, wanting to know the type of persons living in the dwelling and fearing recognition if I exposed myself, I had suggested that she go to the door on some pretext and get a description of the person who answered.

Audre said she had followed my suggestion, but that no one was at home. Then, at *about 9:00 p.m.*, I had gone to the house next door and had questioned the neighbors for a few moments while Audre waited in the car, *after which we had driven directly to a street one-half block west of the Joint Control offices at Beverly Boulevard and Alvarado Street.*

Continuing her story, she said that, during the ride I had stopped to make a telephone call of approximately *three minutes' duration*, in a curb telephone booth. She stated that, when we arrived at the street *a half block* from Joint Control, I had made no explanation to her other than that I would park, after which I *immediately* left the car, telling her that I would be back within a few minutes.

I was *gone for approximately thirty to forty-five minutes* after leaving her in the car, Audre added, and when I returned, she noticed that I was perspiring profusely and was breathing heavily. She said that I had climbed into the police car without saying anything, and had driven away. She had noticed something bulging in my cheek, she testified, and had remarked that I spoke incoherently. (I suppose she meant unintelligibly.) She had then asked what I had in my mouth.

It should be noted here that, according to the time element established by Miss Davis, *this would have occurred at about 10:00 o'clock.*

Audre stated that she was wondering what was in my mouth because of my incoherency, when she had held out her hand and I had spat an object into it, after which we had engaged in no further conversation until we had reached her home, *which was approximately five miles from Joint Control offices, or another drive of fifteen minutes.* This would have happened at about 10:15, according to her testimony.

Now, here is an interesting bit of psychology. Miss Davis is a woman with a woman's reactions. Yet, she testified that she was puzzled at seeing me return to the car with something in my mouth that caused my cheek to bulge, and which made my vocal offerings unintelligible. She said that I spat the object into her hand, and that she was curious as to its nature. She implied that we had no conversation during the balance of the drive to her home, and that she had *made no examination of the object* I had spat into her hand.

She had squelched her womanly curiosity until we had reached her home and had gone inside. Then she had a first glimpse of the object in her hand. What did she see? The remnants of a wad of paper, which, she stated, had been a check. Strange? Very!

She then testified that I had confessed to her that I had burglarized the Joint Control office to recover the check, inasmuch as I was fearful of being charged with forgery. Then, out of love for me, she admitted having dried the wet check out in the oven of her gas range. Once the check was dry, she said, she had torn it to bits and had placed the remains in an ashtray. She had then lit a match to the bits of paper and had flushed the ashes down the toilet bowl. Had her story been true, it appears to me that she went to a great deal of trouble, too much trouble, don't you think?

Dramatic, huh? Yet, on cross examination, Miss Davis couldn't remember the size of the check, its color, the color of the ink, or any distinguishing features.

She said that, on *the following day*, I had given her the shoes I had worn the previous evening — the night of the alleged burglary — and had asked to take them to a shoe repair shop to have the heels changed, inasmuch as I was fearful that I had left my footprints at the scene of the "crime."

Then, in fear that alterations were insufficient to hide their original contours, she stated that we had driven to a section of Los Angeles and had thrown the shoes into the bushes.

It is worthy of note that, while Miss Davis had exhibited an excellent and detailed memory (or shall I say imagination?) of everything that had transpired from the time I had picked her up, including the investigation of the suspected vice house near Sunset Boulevard, our trip from there to the street one-half block west of Joint Control offices, the bulge in my cheek, our silent ride home, et cetera, her excellent memory proved very poor indeed on cross examination by my attorney, Ward Sullivan.

ALTHOUGH SHE HAD BEEN BORN AND RAISED IN LOS ANGELES, AUDRE COULD REMEMBER NEITHER THE LOCATION OF THE SHOE SHOP WHERE, PURPORTEDLY, THE SHOES WERE DISGUISED, NOR THE SPOT WHERE SHE SAID I HAD THROWN THE SHOES.

Moreover, the district attorney's prosecutors and investigators had made no effort to locate the shoe repair shop, or the shoes in question, although they certainly had had an advance run down on what their witness, Audre, was going to state.

In a fair trial, an all-out effort would have been made to find both the shoe repair shop and the shoes inasmuch as they would have furnished evidence in support of Miss Davis's story of the burglary and would have proven a "clincher" in the jurors' minds, if they could have been produced.

Miss Davis had stated vaguely that the shoe shop was located on Beverly Boulevard. I have since made an actual count of the shoe shops located on Beverly Boulevard. They total SIX – from one end of the thoroughfare to the other.

"Are you certain that Stoker gave you the shoes – and not some other person?" my attorney queried Audre.

"Definitely, it was Stoker," she replied, adding that she had never received any man's shoes from anyone else.

It was now my turn to take the witness stand in my own defense. I testified that on the afternoon of April 5, the day in question, I had received two complaints, one of which was from a telephone receptionist for a major broadcasting studio, who complained that an unknown man had been calling her repeatedly and making lewd suggestions over the telephone. She explained that she had arranged a tentative date with the mysterious caller and that she wanted me to substitute Policewoman Davis, who had been assigned to work with me. I testified that, prior to interviewing the woman, another complaint had aroused extreme suspicion in my mind, for, although I occasionally worked in Hollywood division on my own initiative, I had received no complaints from that division.

Complaints originating in the Hollywood area ordinarily went to the Hollywood vice squad, or to administrative vice. But my commander explained that this complaint had come directly from *Deputy Chief Thad Brown, who specifically wanted me to make the investigation.* This had occurred on what was supposedly my night off. But a plain clothes officer has no nights off if his superiors want him to work.

This complaint, I testified, was to the effect that a mysterious house with barred windows, located in Hollywood, was occupied by numerous loud women, suspected of being prostitutes. My testimony conformed with Miss Davis's testimony, except as to the time element she had outlined. I testified that I was in no position to argue with orders from the City Hall, so *at approximately 6:00 p.m.*, on the night of April 5, 1949, I had taken Miss Davis to the home of the first complainant. I had entered and had returned, with the explanation to Miss Davis that I had another complaint in Hollywood.

I gave Miss Davis the meager details, without telling her where the complaint had originated. I had driven to the vicinity of the Hollywood address which had been given me, arriving there at *approximately 7:00 o'clock*, had sent Miss Davis to the door as she had testified, and had then gone to the next door neighbor's between *7:30 and 7:45* at the latest.

I had talked only a few minutes. *Approximately nine or ten elderly ladies were present at what seemed to be a women's party.* When I had discussed my business, one of the women in the group volunteered that she thought that the woman owner of the suspected house was also the owner of a local cocktail lounge, which I knew to be a hangout for Lesbians, or female "queers."

I was given the descriptions of parties that were held in the house until the small morning hours; and I concluded that they were Lesbian brawls or orgies held by degenerates. I talked to the neighbors for about ten minutes. These persons informed me they had complained to the police on various occasions. I gave them my card and assured them that

I would make an investigation. I left *shortly before* 8:00 *p.m.*, in contrast to Miss Davis's testimony that the time was 9:00 p.m.

I was driving Miss Davis home from that address, when I stopped at a telephone booth to call Officer Jimmy Parslow. I was still wondering why I had received the assignment for the investigation. I was aware that some high police brass were at that time engaged in the scheme to disband the Hollywood vice squad. I told Parslow of the circumstances surrounding the complaint and its assignment to me, and of my suspicions regarding them. I suggested that he meet me at 10:30 p.m., and work with me on the investigation into the suspected Lesbian abode. I had obtained the name of the woman who was the owner of the house in question, and Parslow stated that he knew her to be the owner of a bar.

The closing hour for Hollywood bars, as elsewhere, is 2:00 a.m. Parslow and I had agreed that we would watch the house for a probable party from 11:00 p.m., until 3:00 a.m., to be on the safe side. Upon receipt of the complaint earlier in the evening, I had called my regular partners, Officer Jack Ruggles and Rookie Officer Lynn Selby. I had asked Ruggles to come to work, telling him to meet me at Central Police Station at 10:00 p.m. We had agreed that we would quit work not later than 4:00 a.m. if no arrests were made, and that the officers could have another day off.

Officer Selby told me that he had wrecked his automobile several days earlier and that, inasmuch as this was his day off, he had planned no way of getting to town from his home in Monterey Park, quite some distance from downtown Los Angeles.

I told Selby that I would call for him at his home at 9:30 *p.m.*, and asked him to be ready. I drove Miss Davis home, leaving her at approximately 9:00. From Miss Davis's house, I drove all the way across the City of Los Angeles to Officer Selby's home in Monterey Park, arriving there at *approximately* 9:30 *p.m.*

I testified that I had gone into Selby's house, and had spoken to his wife. Then I had driven with Selby to Central Division, approximately fourteen miles distant. Driving through the traffic, we had arrived at *exactly* 10:00 *p.m.*, at Central Division, where we expected to meet Officer Ruggles.

After waiting a few minutes, we had received a telephone call from Ruggles, who asked that he be allowed to have his night off inasmuch as he had an engagement. Since we had Parslow to work with us, Selby and I thought that we could get along without Ruggles, and agreed to his request. Selby and I then drove from Central Police Station to Hollywood, where we picked up Parslow. We then went to the vicinity of the suspected Lesbian lair, and waited until approximately 3:00 a.m. No lights appeared in the house. We dropped Parslow off in Hollywood; and I then took Selby home and went home myself, arriving at approximately 4:00 a.m.

I testified that, on the day prior to April 5, the important date in the state's case, Audre Davis had told me that she had left some clothing at a dry cleaner's which I also patronized, in the vicinity of her residence. She explained that she was short of money and asked if I would have her cleaning placed on my account so that she could call for it. She said that, after she was paid on April 5, she would return the money to me. I agreed to this small favor.

On the morning of April 4, I had stopped by the cleaner's en route to court, having in my possession some cleaning to be done and a pair of shoes to be re-heeled. Inasmuch as I was in a hurry to get to court and since Miss Davis was intending to call for her clothes that day, I told the cleaner to charge Miss Davis's bill to my account. Then I handed him the pair of shoes – the shoes that later figured in the court testimony – and asked if he would turn them over to Miss Davis and have her leave them at a shoe repair shop when she called for her cleaning.

It must be noted that this had occurred on April 4, THE DAY BEFORE THE BURGLARY WAS SUPPOSEDLY COMMITTED. You may recall that, on cross-examination, Miss Davis had testified positively that she never had received a pair of shoes from anyone else to take to a repair shop. In direct contradiction to her testimony, the cleaner and his sister testified that I had left the shoes in his shop, and had asked him to mark Miss Davis's bill "paid" and to charge it to my account.

The cleaner also testified that I had directed him to hand my shoes to Miss Davis, and to ask her to leave them at a shoe shop for heel-repairing. He explained that he was compelled to leave his place of business later in the morning and that his sister came to relieve him. He had instructed her to give the shoes to Miss Davis when and if she called for her cleaning.

TO ASCERTAIN THAT HIS SISTER WOULDN'T FORGET, THE CLEANER TESTIFIED, HE HAD MARKED "PAID" ON THE CLEANING RECEIPT ATTACHED TO MISS DAVIS'S CLOTHING AND HAD WRITTEN ON THE RECEIPT: "TAKE STOKER'S SHOES TO REPAIRMAN."

The sister substantiated the above testimony and further testified that Miss Davis had called for her clothing and that she had given the shoes to Miss Davis and had told her what was to be done to them.

TO CLINCH THIS EVIDENCE, THE CLEANER AND HIS SISTER PRODUCED THE DATED RECEIPT, WHICH BORE THE NOTATION REGARDING THE SHOES.

The prosecution's only witnesses in support of Audre's testimony were a Mr. and Mrs. James Christian, who were friends and next door neighbors of the policewoman. My friend in the police personnel bureau had informed me that these two persons were under subpoena by the district attorney's office and were going to testify that they had seen Miss Davis and me arrive at her apartment at approximately 10:00 p.m., on the night in question, April 5, 1949.

After my testimony, three elderly women, ranging from sixty-five to eighty-seven years of age, were called by my attorney. These three ladies testified that, *at exactly 7:45 p.m.*, on the night of April 5, I had come to their door and had inquired concerning the neighbors occupying the suspected Lesbian lair. They were certain of the day and of the time because they were holding a prayer meeting that night, as had been their custom for years. Nine or ten women had attended the meeting which *began at 7:30 p.m.* They had just begun their prayer when I knocked on the door. They stated that I had left their home *shortly before* 8 p.m. They testified that a DIARY WAS KEPT ON EACH MEETING.

The district attorney's office didn't subject my witnesses in prayer to cross-examination.

You will recall that Miss Davis had testified that we left that area *at* 9:00 *o'clock* and *went directly* to the offices of Joint Control, where I allegedly committed the burglary. The district attorney's office had slipped up. Conflicting evidence was given by an employee of Joint Control, who testified that he had worked in the office *until 8:30 p.m.*, at which time he had locked the doors and had departed.

My witnesses, three of them, had testified that I had left their home at 8:00 p.m. Audre Davis had set the time at 9:00 p.m. If my witnesses were correct, and they had a diary to support their testimony, I would have arrived at Joint Control offices at approximately 8:15 p.m., while the employee of the organization was still working inside.

Officer Lynn Selby then testified that I had arrived at his home shortly before 9:30 *p.m.*, on the night of April 5, after which he substantiated the balance of my testimony.

According to a law in the State of California, one cannot tamper with a state's witness. Inspector William Parker, a lawyer himself and presumably acquainted with that statute, cannot plead ignorance. Nor can Captain Cecil Wisdom. Yet, this law didn't keep them from trying to persuade Officer Selby to change his testimony which had been favorable to me. Selby had worked the night before he testified, and upon finishing his testimony, had driven straight home. Shortly after he arrived home, he had received a telephone call ordering him to report immediately to personnel. There, he was interviewed by Parker and Lieutenant John Jesse.

"Surely, you've made a great mistake in your testimony," they told him. "We have a man outside, an officer, who will prove that you were wrong. This man worked with Officer Jimmy Parslow on the night in question. You are a young officer and you are making a mistake. We knew your father well. He was a fine man. (Selby's father was a retired police department officer who had achieved the rank of major in World War II.)

Selby was told to go home, sleep over his story and return to personnel the following day — the idea being that he should return to court and change his story. Selby's testimony had been an alibi for me, *proving that I could not have committed the burglary.*

My friend in the personnel division learned of the maneuver and telephoned me, whereupon I immediately phoned personnel and asked for Inspector Parker. He wasn't in. I told the personnel secretary that, if Parker and Jesse persisted in their attempts to tamper with witnesses giving testimony, I would appear before Superior Judge Fricke, the trial jurist, and seek complaints against both of them for the offense.

The following morning, when Selby appeared at the personnel office, Parker and Jesse did not attempt to talk to him further — they knew that they had hold of a hot potato and they quickly dropped it.

Then Officer James Parslow corroborated the testimony already given by Officer Selby and me.

In his summation to the jury, Deputy District Attorney Clifford Crail, the Pasadena hot-shot brought in by the prosecution to scuttle and sink Sergeant Stoker, could in no particular break down the testimony given by the defendant, and his witnesses. So, in lieu of factual ammunition, Crail resorted to pure rhetoric and slander. In closing the state's case, he told the jury that Officer Jimmy Parslow *would testify to anything.*

Despite these words, it must be noted that Parslow had never been charged with any crime and that his veracity had never before been impugned.

When Deputy Crail made this slurring comment regarding Parslow and his testimony, he neglected to state to the jury that the chief prosecution witness — Policewoman Audre Davis - was a SELF-CONFESSED PERJURER. For motives which can have only one interpretation, Miss Davis had confessed that her testimony at the attempted pandering trial of Prostitute, Brenda Allen, had been perjured.

Yet, Crail, who had failed to mention that Audre was a self-confessed perjurer, had exhibited no reluctance to brand Parslow a liar. Perhaps he had something else in mind, about which I may refresh his memory.

Officer Parslow had testified under oath before the grand jury that he had accompanied an investigator from the district attorney's office on a tour of Hollywood's vice dens, which he had pointed out. Parslow had suggested that the district attorney's ferret raid the places in question, which were in the county and outside of his own jurisdiction, and had assured the investigator that he would assist him if he wished to undertake such a raid.

The investigator had replied: "If I raided these places, it would cost me my job!" In the presence of Deputy District Attorneys Fred Henderson, Arthur Veitch and Adolph Alexander, and Assistant District Attorney Johnny Barnes, Parslow had given the investigator's name to the grand jury.

These "outstanding" exemplars of prosecutorial zeal and integrity evinced no interest in this testimony involving the district attorney's sleuth. Parslow has never been refuted.

Let us return to Mr. and Mrs. James Christian, , two other star witnesses of the prosecution. Shortly before my trial began, Mr. Christian had been arrested for kidnaping while driving Policewoman Audre Davis's car and for using a pistol belonging to Audre's father, retired Deputy Chief of Police Homer Cross. This arrest had occurred in a neighboring city outside the jurisdiction of the LAPD, and although efforts had been made by members of the department to "blow down the beef," the deputy sheriff who had made the arrest of Christian would have no part of it.

Consequently, Mrs. Christian had been obliged to engage an attorney to defend her husband on the kidnaping charge. This man confided to my attorney, Sullivan, that Mrs. Christian had been watching the proceedings in the Stoker trial, and that she was fearful. She confided that certain people wanted her to testify that after 10:00 p.m., on the night of April 5, 1949, she had seen me in the company of

Audre Davis, but that she had actually seen us shortly after 8:30 p.m. The way things were stacking up at my trial, she said that she was desperately afraid that she would run into a perjury rap if she testified in the manner suggested by her friend, Policewoman Audre Davis, and certain officers in the Los Angeles police department.

HER ATTORNEY ADDED THAT HE HAD ADVISED MRS. CHRISTIAN NOT TO PERJURE HERSELF AT MY TRIAL, BUT ON THE CONTRARY, TO TESTIFY TO THE TRUTH. SIGNIFICANTLY, MR. AND MRS. CHRISTIAN WERE NOT CALLED AS WITNESSES FOR THE PROSECUTION - ALTHOUGH THEY WERE UNDER SUBPOENA BY THE DISTRICT ATTORNEY'S OFFICE.

While Christian was in jail on the kidnaping charge, some crank had telephoned Mrs. Christian and had told her that he could help her husband. This was a great occasion for Inspector William Parker, who announced portentously to newspapers that prosecution witnesses in the Stoker trial had been threatened — (implying that I was behind the call) — and that the "police department would bend every effort to protect them."

Judging from what Mrs. Christian told me after the trial was concluded, Parker had envisioned a possible re-trial of the charge against me and was hoping that Mrs. Christian would be instrumental in sinking me on perjured testimony.

He had suggested to her that "while she was in peril," she live in his, Parker's home.

Parker had instituted a twenty-four hour guard for Mrs. Christian, presumably to protect her from me. Yet, strangely enough, after her husband had been freed on bail and had then died of heart failure, Mrs. Christian had asked me to aid her in preparation for the funeral. When she left Los Angeles, I assisted in the matter of getting her husband's body on the train.

The story Mrs. Christian told was typical of the machinations of the police department's big brass, the district attorney's office and

Policewoman Davis, who was obviously a part of the conspiratorial cabal.

Mrs. Christian admitted that she had known nothing about the burglary in question when Audre Davis first approached her.

"Audre told me she was in trouble. She asked me to say that I'd seen her and Stoker at approximately 10:00 p.m., on April 5, 1949, if anyone came to question me," was her explanation.

Mrs. Christian had been questioned by agents of police personnel and, although unaware of the circumstances, had kept her word to Audre. After she had talked to personnel agents the story broke involving me in the burglary and the agents returned with a typewritten statement for her to sign. This statement was to the effect that Mrs. Christian and her husband had not only seen Audre Davis and Stoker at 10:00 p.m., on the night of April 5, but that Stoker had confided in them that he had committed a burglary. In conclusion, it asserted that Audre Davis was so fearful of Stoker that she had been afraid to stay alone and had been sleeping in her (Mrs. Christian's) house.

This is indicative of how far certain police officers will go in framing an enemy or someone of whom the department wants to rid itself, and it is a part of the mechanics of "convicting the innocent."

When Mrs. Christian and her husband had refused to sign the statement, she said that they were taken to Captain Cecil Wisdom's office, where THEY WERE INFORMED THAT IT WAS A MISDEMEANOR OFFENSE TO MAKE A FALSE STATEMENT TO THE POLICE DEPARTMENT. Thus, was police pressure applied to the Christians. After having made these admissions, Mrs. Christian agreed to accompany me to a local attorney's office, where she repeated her statement in the presence of the barrister, his secretary and an officer friend of mine. This was of little assistance however as the trial was over at the time.

In a criminal prosecution, the defense has the legal right to ask for and to receive from the judge permission to exclude all witnesses — prosecution and defense — from the courtroom. Deputy District Attorney Clifford Crail, however, had succeeded in obtaining permission for District Attorney's Investigator, Chester Sharp, to remain in the courtroom.

Obviously, this was done so that Sharp, hearing the testimony of prosecution witnesses, could transmit their statements to witnesses not already called, in order that the state's testimony would not conflict on essential points.

Things looked bad for the prosecution, when, after summations by the prosecution and defense, a short recess was taken. Crail then asked permission to call the sanctimonious Sharp as a rebuttal witness.

I had testified that I had gone *voluntarily* to the district attorney's office on the morning of April 6, 1949, the day following the supposed burglary, to lodge a complaint of extortion against the cabinet maker who had attempted to defraud me.

Sharp contradicted my testimony, stating that on the morning of April 6, he and Aldo Corsini, another investigator, had checked and found that I was testifying in Division Seven of the Municipal Court. He testified that he had personally called Division Seven and was told that I was on the witness stand, testifying in a vice case. As soon as my testimony was completed in this case, I was *ordered* to report to the district attorney's office.

The expression on the jurors' faces signified that Sharp's testimony had been exceedingly damaging to me. Immediately afterward, the case was given into the hands of the jury, and its members retired to deliberate. A short while later the jury reassembled in the jury box and asked the court to reconvene. The judge was asked by the jury to recall Investigator Sharp to the witness stand, for the purpose of having him repeat his testimony.

Sharp was co-operative. He repeated the testimony virtually as he had previously given it. BUT HERE, THE DISTRICT ATTORNEY'S OFFICE HAD SLIPPED A COG, FOR INVESTIGATOR SHARP'S TESTIMONY WAS COMPLETELY FALSE AND WAS PERJURED.

The police records showed that I had been *scheduled* to testify in a vice case in Division Seven of the Municipal Court, on the morning of April 6, 1949. Investigators for the district attorney's office, possibly including Chester Sharp, had checked the police records and had found this schedule.

SCANNING THE POLICE RECORD, INVESTIGATOR SHARP HAD ASSUMED ARBITRARILY THAT I HAD TESTIFIED IN DIVISION SEVEN AS SCHEDULED. BUT IF HE HAD CHECKED FURTHER THE COURT RECORD WOULD HAVE SHOWN THAT THIS CASE HAD BEEN SETTLED PRIOR TO APRIL 6, 1949, AND, CONSEQUENTLY, THAT THERE HAD BEEN NO COURT ACTION INVOLVING IT ON THAT DAY.

BUT THE JURY WAS UNAWARE OF THESE FACTS. WARD SULLIVAN, MY ATTORNEY, AND I FACED A TOUGH DECISION. WE COULD EITHER CHARGE SHARP WITH PERJURY AND ASK FOR A MISTRIAL OF THE CASE, OR PERMIT THE CASE TO GO TO THE JURY, IN WHICH EVENT THE JURORS WOULD BELIEVE THAT I HAD LIED REGARDING A MOST IMPORTANT FACT IN MY DEFENSE. HOWEVER, WE TOOK THE GAMBLE AND LET THE CASE GO TO DECISION BY THE JURY.

I had a reason for wishing to hasten conclusion of the trial. I had not paid Sullivan for his services, since I had no money with which to pay him. Yet, because he believed in my innocence, he had given of his time and effort without stint. The police mess had been dragging out a long time. I could not conscientiously ask Ward Sullivan to go to the additional trouble of defending me at a retrial of the case.

The banker who had loaned me the money to build the duplex – Mr. Keith Krug – had appeared for me as a character witness, and had testified that he knew me personally and that he believed me to be honest and trustworthy.

On cross-examination, Crail had inquired of Krug: "If you knew that Sergeant Stoker had forged his commanding officer's signature to obtain his discharge from the Army, would you still believe him to be honest and trustworthy?"

Previous to that assertion, there had been no scintilla of doubt that my discharge from the Army had been anything other than honorable.

At the very moment when Crail had asked that devious and twisted question, I was A COMMISSIONED OFFICER IN THE ARMY RESERVE CORPS! Imagine my fury and frustration when, through objections by the state, I was not given the opportunity to wipe out that slurring and vicious slander. What is wrong with laws wherein a prosecutor, acting maliciously and without foundation, can fabricate an insinuation of that kind and get away with it? I now wonder why Crail didn't say to Mr. Krug: "You know, don't you, that Sergeant Stoker is a murderer?" In light of the first question, the second would be just as justified for there never were, and never will be, any facts to support either question.

After the trial was over, some local attorneys pounced on Clifford Crail for what they declared were his unfair tactics in attempting to brand me as a forger of Army discharge papers. Crail's caustic reply, typical of an intellectually dishonest prosecutor serving a corrupt district attorney, was that he was "testing just how far Krug would go for Stoker."

Crail said that it was "merely a hypothetical question," yet, he had been fully aware of its implications to the jury; of its impact on their minds. Whatever his excuse, and he can neither have a legal or honorable one, he had asked that question in order to erect doubt in the jurors' minds as to what manner of man I was, for the sole and exclusive purpose of convicting me of a felony that I hadn't committed. That was why he had been brought in from Pasadena where he normally was assigned, and why he had done his dead level best to carry out the sinister purpose of the men who had given him orders, District Attorney William E. Simpson and Assistant District Attorney Johnny Barnes.

These are the true facts pertaining to my trial for burglary — a trial predicated upon and fashioned out of police contrived perjury, a trial for which conviction depended upon the testimony of a SELF-CONFESSED PERJURER!

CONDUCT UNBECOMING OFFICERS

"For forms of government let fools contest;
What'er is best administered is best."

I had been fired from the police department for conduct unbecoming an officer, a technicality predicated upon the fact that I had appeared before the Los Angeles County grand jury without the permission or the sanction of my police superiors.

Now, I shall relate a few incidents which will shed light on the charge of "conduct unbecoming an officer"— a charge that is frequently employed as a weapon by police brass against persons whom they do not like, or upon whom they are seeking revenge; and against police officers who have thwarted their will, or who have imperiled their official positions by either exposing, or threatening to expose, police rottenness, graft and corruption.

In the following instances involving "conduct unbecoming an officer," you will note that no official action was taken against the individuals whom I had caught "dead in the door." These men are still on the police department. The only logical deduction is that these officers enjoy the approbation of police big brass and that, because this is so, derelictions committed by them are overlooked.

While my trial was in progress, a Mrs. Irene Stanley was operating a small bar, or cocktail lounge, on Beverly Boulevard, in Hollywood. This woman was widely known as an entertainer, having been in the show business for years. Her husband was a former deputy sheriff of Ventura County. She had a grown son. They had opened their bar, *The Little New Yorker*, on a shoestring.

The *Little New Yorker* had precipitated another police scandal when, during the winter months of 1948, its proprietors and certain vice squad officers, controlled by Lieutenant Rudy Wellpott (the chief muckypoo of administrative vice), had engaged in a dispute.

Mrs. Stanley had protested to Chief of Police C. B. Horrall and Assistant Chief Joe Reed that one of Wellpott's hirelings had visited her bar and had then gone to the kitchen and told her husband that he noticed that it was doing a nice business. "He said that if we wanted to continue prosperous," she quoted the officer, "we'd have to kick loose from some juice." (This is a euphemism for money paid for police protection.)

Chief Horrall and Assistant Chief Reed scoffed at the story. They did not call the officer in to confront them, despite the fact that the woman's grave accusation reflected upon the honesty and rectitude of the officer as well as of the department.

The Stanleys then went to see Inspector Anthony Collins, who, I want to make clear, is an honest police executive with no blemish on his escutcheon. Inspector Collins listened carefully to the story told by the Stanleys. Then, impressed by their seeming honesty and sincerity, he explained that their complaint was outside of his jurisdiction, but that he would take them to the proper officer to investigate and handle it.

Inspector Collins then accompanied Mr. and Mrs. Stanley to the office of Captain Harry Lorenson, Chief Investigator for Mayor Fletcher E. Bowron's rubber stamp police commissioners.

Lorenson was advised by Inspector Collins of the nature of the complaint made by the Stanleys, adding that he was impressed by their story regarding the alleged shakedown attempt. He adjured Lorenson to "take care of the case and to handle it honestly."

Lorenson escorted the bar owners into his inner office and listened to their story. Then, pursuing a course in direct contravention to Inspector Collins's suggestions, he brushed the complaint lightly aside, indicating that he didn't believe it. In effect, he told the Stanleys to "go on about their business." They had received no satisfaction from Captain Lorenson, who was to make newspaper headlines later, when he was indicted in the Alfred Marsden Pearson beating.

Awaiting future developments, Mr. and Mrs. Stanley remained quiescent. Shortly thereafter, the same administrative vice squad officer who had attempted to make the original "touch," returned to The *Little New Yorker*. He was followed by other vice squad officers.

At this point, perhaps I should explain that if any vice squad officer remains in a bar for a sufficient length of time, he can eventually find infringement of the law to act upon.

The administrative vice squad officers began to give the interior of The *Little New Yorker* a plethora of attention — attention which, I can testify, was merited by nothing untoward that took place there. I can name any number of bars operated by racketeers in the Hollywood area which merit police attention but do not receive it. In my opinion, these bars fail to receive police attention for the reason that their owners have complied with the wishes of vice squad officers, or in other words, have proven themselves co-operative.

The *Little New Yorker* had an entertainment license, and Mrs. Stanley, who had an excellent voice, participated in the shows which were not sexy, tawdry or cheap. Patrons went there to hear her sing. No more than two entertainers were on the bill at any one time. The food was excellent.

The administrative vice officers, after having given the Stanleys' place a great deal of unwarranted attention, told them that they had better be co-operative, or the interior of the *New Yorker* would resemble a police squad room.

One can appreciate the Stanleys' indignation when they received a notice that their entertainment license had been revoked. This action was attributable to Captain Harry Lorenson of the police commission, one of the leading police "wheels" in Mayor Fletcher E. (I'm Fighting the Underworld) Bowron's administration.

The Stanleys were notified to appear before the police commission to show cause why their license should not be permanently revoked. Unquestionably, the action had been taken because the Stanleys HAD REFUSED TO BE SHAKEN DOWN BY THE ADMINISTRATIVE VICE SQUAD.

At the police commission hearing, the Stanleys were told that their license had been revoked because the PLACE ATTRACTED HOMOSEXUALS.

Present at the hearing were those two doughty and "incorruptible officers of the law," Chief of Police C. B. Horrall and Assistant Chief Joe Reed, who listened to Stanley's testimony that The *Little New Yorker* drew customers of the types generally found in cafes, with an admixture of prominent socialites and celebrities, some of whom were well known in the show business.

"Our customers are decent, law-abiding people," said Stanley, "and my wife and I have had very little trouble in conducting our business."

Ponderous Chief Horrall, who, during all of his years as Los Angeles police department officer and executive, had performed no feats that were noticeable other than his ability to say "Yes" to Mayor Bowron — then transfixed Stanley with an ophidian eye, and inquired: "Do you know a *homosexual* when you see one?"

Could anyone have asked a more ridiculous question?

Stanley replied: "No. As a cafe owner and as a businessman, I do not consider it incumbent upon me to become an expert in the field of sexual aberrations."

"Well, if you can't," snapped Horrall, "I don't believe you are entitled to a cafe entertainment license."

This declaration, in its essence, was akin to obligating the witness or any other cafe owner to buttonhole each man and woman entering the door, and to inquire: "Are you a homosexual?" It is quite true that some homosexuals exhibit the stigmata of their perversion so that it is unmistakable, but contrariwise there are many who do not.

During my career as a vice squadder, I arrested as many homosexuals as the next man. Police records should tend to qualify me as an expert in such arrests. To my knowledge, homosexuals are engaged in the making of motion pictures. Actors and actresses, subject to sexual abnormalities, appear daily on screens throughout the United States. As residents of Southern California, they frequent the swank restaurants and night clubs in Los Angeles, where they are wined, dined and entertained.

It is noteworthy that the opera bouffe Chief of Police Horrall, while he had directed the affairs of the Los Angeles police department, had displayed no zeal whatsoever in taking action against the entertainment licenses of better class places where many of these homosexuals were wont to foregather. Contrast this inaction with his determination to abrogate the entertainment license of The *Little New Yorker*, a modest cocktail lounge serving excellent food.

Dr. George Uhl, the city health officer, was called by the Stanleys as a character witness and to testify regarding his knowledge of The *Little New Yorker*. A friend of the Stanleys, Doctor Uhl, testified that he frequently went to The *Little New Yorker* to dine, and that he had observed no occurrences there that, in his opinion, would justify extraordinary police attention. He maintained that the food was good, the entertainment was clean and that, insofar as he knew, nothing warranted the opinion that The *Little New Yorker* was a gathering place for homosexuals.

Still, the administrative vice squad officers, under Lieutenant Rudy Wellpott, aided and abetted by Captain Harry Lorenson of the police commission, who in turn obviously had the support of Chief of Police Horrall and Assistant Chief Joe Reed, continued to frequent The *Little New Yorker*. They employed bulldozing and intimidating tactics on the owners and the clientele until a point was reached at which the business was ruined.

During this period, the Stanleys petitioned the police commission for a re-hearing to regain their entertainment license. When their campaign proved fruitless, their son went to a superior court judge whom the family knew, and explained that he had been approached by a local attorney who had informed him that he could "fix things up" for the Stanleys and "get their license back" for the sum of five hundred dollars.

The friendly Superior court judge advised the young man to take the matter to the district attorney's office.

District Attorney William E. Simpson wasn't at his office so the young man went to his home. He wasn't at home. Young Stanley then decided to contact H. Leo Stanley (no relation of course) chief investigator for Simpson, at his home.

In the course of their conversation, young Stanley told the district attorney's investigative chief that an officer working for me, Sergeant Charles Stoker, had made an arrest of a homosexual in The *Little New Yorker*.

Prior to this declaration, H. Leo Stanley had evinced but small interest in the young man's protestations, but at mention of the name, Stoker, his face lit up, his ears twitched and he urged, "Tell me more."

But when the young man explained that, on the night following the homosexual's arrest, I had returned and apologized for my officers and for any trouble that had been caused the owners. H. Leo Stanley's spirits seemingly dropped, according to young Stanley.

TO MAKE MATTERS WORSE, WHEN YOUNG STANLEY WAS DEPARTING, HE DROPPED A QUARTER IN ONE OF THE SLOT MACHINES REPOSING IN THE GREAT MAN'S DOMICILE - AND HIT THE JACK POT.

But the Stanleys were doomed to disappointment. Nothing happened as a result of their son's protest to Chief Investigator H. Leo Stanley of the district attorney's office. Finally, the young man went to the city editor of The Los Angeles Daily News, whose scribes exerted pressure on the fire and police committee of the city council.

At about this time, I had been charged with burglary by the police department and the machinery to discredit me was in full motion. My "ear," or informant in Captain Cecil Wisdom's office, had told me that the file on the "homo" arrest made by my officers at The *Little New Yorker* had been removed from the police records. He said that officers from personnel were planning to appear before the city council's fire and police committee and would "turn the switch," that I, Stoker, had precipitated The *Little New Yorker* "beef," the idea being that I was the villain in the piece. Although the hearing was set, I had not been informed of the date or subpoenaed, obviously a purposeful "oversight" on the part of the police and fire committee. But again, my informant gave me the time and date of the hearing. Before the committee, Mr. and Mrs. Stanley and their son related the attempts by police to shake them down. The officer in question flatly denied their accusation. Dr. George Uhl and other persons at the hearing supported testimony that The *Little New Yorker* was a decent place and an average Hollywood cocktail lounge.

Much to the discomfiture of the police, I, too, was present at the controversy. I spoke to the Stanleys' attorney, telling him I would be ONLY TOO HAPPY TO TESTIFY AS A WITNESS.

I testified that I had been told by Sergeant William Madden, night commander of Central Vice Squad, to LAY OFF AND REFRAIN FROM ENTERING THREE NOTORIOUS BARS IN LOS ANGELES.

"These three bars catered to nothing but homosexuals," I testified. "Anyone entertaining these bars can count homosexuals by the dozens." I then gave the names and addresses of the places I had mentioned.

I explained that I had observed Sergeant Madden's order to refrain from entering these bars. Nevertheless, I had stayed outside and watched the departure of homosexuals from them. I had followed many of these "queers" and on one night had arrested some thirteen homosexuals as they left a bar near the intersection of Third and Spring Streets, exactly two blocks from the City Hall and three blocks from the headquarters of Central Vice, at First and Hill Streets. I testified that five of these defendants had been released the following day, and that the remainder had pleaded guilty.

"On the occasion of the arrest at The *Little New Yorker*, I had followed a homosexual from one of the bars that Sergeant Madden had instructed me to ignore," I continued. "If I had not followed this homosexual, I would not have known that The Little New Yorker was in existence. In other words, the homosexual whom I had arrested in The Little New Yorker, had journeyed there from a bar which obviously had enjoyed POLICE PROTECTION."

I testified that, following this arrest, Sergeant Madden, my superior, had exhorted me to "Give The *Little New Yorker* hell!"

"Sergeant Madden's exhortation aroused not only my curiosity, but my suspicions as well," I continued. "I could not imagine why a mild, homey spot like The *Little New Yorker* should be subjected to a police 'roust,' while bars where homosexuals knowingly congregated ENJOYED POLICE IMMUNITY.

"After observing the customers in The *Little New Yorker*, I could not but conclude that the place was clean and free of homosexuals and that Madden's orders to 'roust' it were unjustified on the basis of the facts," I added. "Hence, I never returned to the place again."

Neither Assistant Chief Reed nor Sergeant Bill Madden *came forth at this time to deny my testimony*, but a stooge from Captain Wisdom's office stepped into the breach to run interference for the corruptionists.

"I want to tell the city council," said this police idiot, "that Sergeant Stoker had no business at *The Little New Yorker. It was outside his jurisdiction.*"

The "boys" really jump up and down embracing "technicalities" if their tails are caught in a gate. It is indeed remarkable how concerned certain officials in the police department can become regarding the technicalities of police procedure and law enforcement when something shady in the way of graft, or attempted graft, is connected with investigations.

Mr. and Mrs. Stanley testified that their conversations with the vice squad officer, and his dickerings for protection money, had been held in the kitchen of the establishment. Stanley said that when he spoke to the officer, the latter had declared: "Now, if you want to eliminate what happened a few nights ago, you'd better play ball with us, 'Juice' eliminates all that."

Irene Stanley testified that the officer had told her, "You know, a little 'juice' can take care of everything. You want to run, don't you? Well, we let a few places in this town operate. We let some of the people run."

"What do you mean?" she had asked. "What are we doing here that is not legitimate?"

"Well, you'd better make up your mind what you are going to do," was the answer. *"We can take away your license; and you can't run without a license."*

Questioned by the attorney for the Stanleys, this officer couldn't very well deny having been there on numerous occasions, nor could he deny having gone into the kitchen with the Stanleys. He stated that he had gone into the kitchen with them, and had told them that he had heard that the place was putting out juice.

It is significant to note that this vice squadder's duties consisted of enforcing vice laws. He was not an investigator for the police commission which has jurisdiction over licenses, nor was he an investigator for the police personnel division, nor was he an employee of the state board of equalization, which issues liquor licenses.

HOWEVER, THIS RAISES A QUESTION. TECHNICALLY AND OFFICIALLY, HE WASN'T CONNECTED WITH THE POLICE COMMISSION OR WITH POLICE PERSONNEL; BUT ACTUALLY, FACTUALLY, PERHAPS HE WAS. THE CIRCUMSTANCES-AND THE RESULTS OF HIS VISITS- INDICATED THAT HE HAD AUTHORITY FROM PERSONS IN THE POLICE COMMISSION AND IN PERSONNEL TO ACT AS HE DID.

No explanations were made as to his frequent visits to The *Little New Yorker.*

I would like to point out here that the conduct of the Stanleys was contrary to that of dyed-in-the-wool racketeers. Had they been running a racket joint, had they been doing anything illegitimate, they wouldn't' have "hollered." Instead,they would have pursued the course that racket people follow in similar circumstances. They would have "paid off."

It was obvious that perjury had been committed by someone. The witnesses, remember, were all under oath. The Stanleys had testified that attempts had been made to shake them down. The police department had denied that any police officer had made such an attempt. The city council, aware that perjury had been committed either by the Stanleys, or by police officers, had recommended that the police department make an investigation into the lying.

A few weeks later, the city council received a letter from Police Chief William A. Worton's office. My friend in police personnel obtained a copy of this missive prepared for the chief and his signature. Excerpts from the letter were furnished me. I quote:

"It would be logical for such officers to inquire into the possible payment of protection money, but it would not be logical for such officers to attempt to sell protection as the primary responsibility for vice enforcement rested with the geographical division and not with the administrative vice squad."

This statement, written by Parker for Chief Worton, was a bald-faced lie and no one knew that better than Parker. Parker had written that responsibility for vice law enforcement was a divisional matter, and had said that administrative vice was not responsible for vice law enforcement in the confines of The Little New Yorker, implying that the Hollywood vice squad, in which division the cafe operated, was responsible.

To those who have followed this story closely, *the lie is apparent.* The purpose of setting up the administrative vice squad and the manner in which it functioned, was to effectuate a setup that would permit the squad to work *in any division* throughout the City of Los Angeles. Hence, if a divisional squad leader started playing footsie with vice entrepreneurs and took money from them for protection, administrative vice would be in a position to step in and enforce the laws that the divisional vice squad had been holding in abeyance.

Let us return to the letter:

"In conformity with the findings in this case, it is recommended that the city council be informed that the testimony reflected in the transcript, coupled with other pertinent facts, does not constitute an adequate base upon which to instigate criminal action for perjury upon the part of any of the persons whose testimony appeared in said transcript, and that the city council can be further advised there is not sufficient evidence to indicate improper conduct on the part of any police officer concerned in this matter *with the exception of Officers Jack D. Ruggles and Charles F. Stoker and that their activities will be subject to further investigation by this department.*

"Respectfully,
"W. A. Worton, Chief of Police."

The letter offers a fair insight into the workings of the "legal" mind of Inspector William Parker — as well as of his investigative accomplishments into the personnel of the police department — and also discloses the support of Parker's casuistry by Chief of Police William A. Worton. At the time when Worton had signed the letter written by Parker, he had never seen or talked to me. I had been convicted of NO crime; I had not been convicted of any offense of any kind.

Yet, at Parker's behest, Worton was attempting to saddle me with the mud growing out of a shakedown attempt on the owners of The Little New Yorker.

Let me repeat the line which reads: "There is not sufficient evidence to indicate improper conduct on the part of any police officer concerned in this matter with the exception of Officers Jack D. Ruggles and Charles F. Stoker and their activities will be subject to further investigation by this department."

To what activities does the writer refer? I testified for the owners of the cafe. Neither Ruggles nor I had been involved in the attempted extortion. The Stanleys named the police officer attached to the administrative vice squad, who had tried to shake them down.

Paradoxically, you will note that the officer in question was NOT INVESTIGATED BY THE POLICE DEPARTMENT, AND THAT HIS GUILT WAS SHIFTED ONTO RUGGLES AND ME. LET WORTON AND PARKER EXPLAIN THAT FACT - IF THEY CAN.

Further information had been forwarded to the city council in reference to the arrest that my officer had made in The *Little New Yorker*. My agent in personnel had informed me that the police file regarding this case had been snatched by someone.

"Anent this arrest, it does not appear that an arrest was made," the city council had been told, evidently to cast suspicion on me. But the police cuties had slipped up again. I had retained a copy of the arrest report which I still have. Too, I was present in court when the homosexual was convicted and sentenced by the judge. He had asked for probation; and in this connection, I am acquainted with the probation officer who handled the matter and who can testify as to what happened.

Let Worton and Parker explain that.

In reference to my testimony regarding the thirteen arrests I had made on one night, the police department informed the city council that a check of the police files disclosed that the arrests had been made in the vicinity of Third and Spring Streets.

If, at this late date, anyone is concerned with the truth or the falsity of this statement, it should be recalled that I testified before the city council that I HAD BEEN TOLD TO STAY OUT OF THE BAR AT THIRD AND SPRING STREETS, AND THAT I HAD REMAINED OUTSIDE THE BAR AND HAD ARRESTED HOMOSEXUALS AS THEY EMERGED; MEN IN WOMEN'S CLOTHING AND WOMEN IN MEN'S CLOTHING!

Chief Worton and Inspector Parker did not allude to this, however.

The police reports will bear out the FACT THAT I MADE THE THIRTEEN ARRESTS WITHIN ONE HOUR'S TIME.

In truth, my testimony before the city council in The *Little New Yorker* affair involving police protection, was not startling, or of world shaking importance. There are always vice squad officers who will attempt to cut a corner and to make a fast dollar. At times, police protection comes cheap, on some occasions, however, it comes high.

The letter that Chief Worton sent to the city council pointed out that I had testified that my orders had come from Assistant Chief Joe Reed. However, the letter had neglected to point out that these "orders" had come to me second hand from Sergeant William Madden, a Reed man. A police executive does not personally give orders to subordinates, such as Madden, to relay to officers working under his command, of which I was one.

In the confines of Los Angeles are innumerable places known in police parlance as "Black and Tan" joints where whites and blacks intermingle sexually, for the purposes of enjoying homosexual relations, smoking marijuana, or for reasons of general debauchery, and in this connection the whites are no better and no worse than the Negroes and vice versa.

These places are hard for the police to find. Their proprietors, generally Negroes, engage or lease large houses frequently located in exclusive residential sections, where well-to-do white women engage in sinful liaisons with colored males. Of course, it is necessary for these women to hide from husbands and friends. "Black and Tan" joints operate without police permits. Such places masquerade as meeting spots for "friends," although all known debaucheries go on inside them.

However, most "Black and Tan" spots are found in the Negro Belt in the police precinct known as Newton Division. Within this division, vice laws were enforced by the Newton Street vice squad and by Lieutenant Rudy Wellpott's administrative vice squad.

When I returned to the police department from the Army, numerous prostitutes whom I had arrested told me of the existence of a "Black and Tan" joint on Adams Boulevard, just east of San Pedro Street. It was incorporated within an old mansion, which at one period in the city's history had been owned by a prominent man. However, with the degeneration of the neighborhood, it had lost its pristine glory and had become just another old mansion in the Black Belt.

Leased by a Negro racketeer (a known homosexual), who bore the underworld sobriquet of "Little Brother," this house had one distinction. It catered to a clientele that could pay well – the silver fox and mink coat trade – which included Hollywood celebrities of varying stature – actors, artists and musicians having homosexual bents.

From many sources of information, I had formed a complete picture of the place and the nature of its "after hours" operation. It would get into full swing after legitimate cocktail places had closed at 2:00 a.m. I knew that the only way in which I could enter the "joint" would be through a "repeat" or steady customer.

I found the spot completely dark one night. However, many parked cars outside furnished the tip-off that the place was "alive." I had heard, and I believe correctly, that the place had been in operation, not for days or weeks, but for years and that it had never suffered police molestation.

I knew that the place had no city permit for running a business, no entertainment license and no liquor permit. In fact, it was without a license of any kind, legal, moral or logical. I observed the spot closely, giving thought to the possibility of entering the place and making an arrest, or arrests, that would stand up in court and eventuate in convictions. From a covert place across the street, I saw couples enter, and noticed that they were carefully checked at the door. I had heard that this was done to insure that guests were "right," or known, and to keep out "riff-raff." "Little Brother" didn't want bums without money in his clientele.

I devised a scheme. I secretly obtained the voluntary off duty services of Policewoman Alice Houghton and had her work with one of my men. We watched the house. Finally, as we knew would happen, a tipsy couple drove up in an expensive car. Both were congenial and were laughing as only hilarious drunks can laugh.

Miss Houghton and her police partner walked up to them. Miss Houghton threw her arms around the woman, while the police officer slapped the man on the shoulder, shook his hand and exclaimed: "Gosh, Bub, we're glad to see you again!"

By the time they had reached the front door, the four were "buddies" and had known each other for years. I had instructed Miss Houghton and the officer that, once inside, they were to put their best feet forward and to turn on all the charm possible to the end that they would become acquainted with all the help in the place as well as the proprietor, "Little Brother." My purpose was to enter later on.

I had been attending part-time courses at the University of Southern California, and had become quite friendly with a young colored man in one of my classes. We worked out an agreement whereby he would permit me to take his wife along with Miss Houghton and the police officers into "Little Brother's" place the following night.

That night, Miss Houghton addressed the doorman by name, and we were given a hearty welcome.

I have seen countless vice spots during my police career, but nothing to compare with the saturnalia presided over by "Little Brother." Several candles around the massive room furnished the only illumination. One candle stood atop a piano played by a colored pianist. Entering the house was like walking into a darkened theatre from a sunlit street. At first, we were blinded but our eyes soon became accustomed to the dark.

The place was heavily draped and thickly carpeted. Drinks were placed on low tables on the floor. The room abounded with pillows. Couples lay in corners of the room, in which smoke from marijuana resembled the Los Angeles atmosphere on a smoggy day.

"Little Brother" and his waiters were clad in costumes which reminded one of a scene from The Arabian Nights — baggy silk pants, embroidered blouses and turbans wound around their heads. A homosexual, obviously under the influence of marijuana, was swishing about the room while beautiful white women snuggled in the arms of their Negro paramours and vice versa.

We stayed a while, made friends with everyone, and then departed. The following night, I was ready for the knockover. I sent Miss Houghton in with the same officer, supported by a second officer. I had furnished them with marked money, instructing them that, after the money had changed hands, Miss Houghton was to come outside where I would be waiting with two other officers. Then I would raid the joint.

Things went off smoothly as planned; and much to the surprise of the operators and customers, all of whom had been assured that the place operated under police protection, I went in and placed the joint under arrest. "Little Brother" was highly indignant. He immediately wanted to make a telephone call which I would not permit. I counted eighty-four people in the joint after I finally pulled them from under beds and dragged them out of closets and upstairs rooms. I arrested "Little Brother" and his retinue, all of whom immediately bailed out.

THE CASE WAS NEVER TRIED. THE DEFENDANTS VOLUNTARILY PAID VERY SMALL FINES.

Evidently, "Little Brother" thought ours was merely a routine, or "programmed" raid, for he immediately resumed operations.

A "programmed" raid is a raid on a protected vice den to provide insulation for the police department in the event of a public inquiry into such things. Smart, grafting police officers always keep a weather eye out for the breaking of vice and gambling scandals. They know that, at any time a grand jury may breathe down their necks and ask such embarrassing questions as: "Why has this place never been raided?" That's where the "programmed" raid comes in handy. Police officers and police executives on the pan require an "out" in such instances. If a programmed raid has been made on a protected vice den, they fish out and produce police records to "prove" to the grand jury, or to newspapers, that police action had been taken against violators of the vice laws.

A "programmed" raid is generally collusive, with the arresting officers and the operators of vice dens in agreement regarding its conditions. The operator agrees to furnish so many persons for the police to arrest. If the protection links include the city attorney's office and the courts, those arrested are given nominal fines and are told to "go and sin no more." Like "Little Brother," most vice habitues follow such advice by immediately going back into action.

But the raid I conducted on "Little Brother's" place was not a programmed raid. I could only arrest him and his helpers, and let the courts handle the case from that point onward. Evidently, the person or persons taking the pay-off from "Little Brother," had assured him that he wouldn't be raided again, for he reopened quickly.

But I wasn't through with "Little Brother" as he was yet to learn. I waited a few days until he had become sure of himself, then I employed the same technique again — with the exception that I switched policewomen. On this occasion, I used the policewoman who was fired when I tried to have her assigned to Hollywood, to work on the Brenda Allen investigation. I have since concluded that this policewoman was fired before expiration of her probationary period on the police department because she had worked a few cases with me. The big brass knew that. Anyone on the department who had exhibited any friendliness for Stoker was suspected of knowing too much and automatically became anathema.

On the night I had scheduled to send my officers in to make the arrests, Sergeant William Madden, my immediate superior, called me into his office and told me that he understood that I was planning to again arrest "Little Brother." He then warned me to "lay off." I asked him why.

"Well, for one thing, you're out of your district; and for another, you are creating animosity between the various vice squads," he replied. "That sort of thing ISN'T LIKED IN THE CITY HALL. WE HAVE TO HAVE CO-OPERATION BETWEEN DIFFERENT DIVISIONS. THE NEWTON STREET VICE DIVISION WILL TAKE CARE OF 'LITTLE BROTHER'," Madden concluded.

"It hasn't been taking care of him," I retorted. "Until I arrested him, 'Little Brother' ran for years without police interference. And, by the way, Madden," I continued, "Why the great to do over who arrests law breakers in vice and gambling? That's the objective, isn't it — to keep the city clean of these people and their operations?"

"You know there is police jealousy," Madden replied.

"I'm not jealous of any police officer who arrests a malefactor," I said.

Although I had listened to Sergeant Madden's instructions, I had no intention of letting "Little Brother" go. I sent my policewoman and two officers into the house, while another officer and I parked down the street in a police car. I waited for the policewoman to come out and give me the signal.

THEN, OUT OF THE DARKNESS, SERGEANT MADDEN WALKED OVER TO MY CAR.

Madden asked what I was doing there. I told him that I had decided to raid "Little Brother" again and chance the animosity of the City Hall. Then the policewoman came out and gave the signal. The other officer, a former Newton Street division patrolman, and I entered the place together.

"I'm going along," Sergeant Madden exclaimed.

Under ordinary circumstances, inasmuch as Madden was a sergeant and I was a patrolman at that time, he would nominally have been in command. But I had no intention of stopping on the sidewalk and arguing with him. Until that time, I had been a squad leader in charge of investigations.

I kicked the door open and was met by a colored individual and a police officer from Newton division, whose wife was secretary to the captain commanding that division. The colored man, who identified himself as a reporter for a Central Avenue newspaper, demanded to know what was going on.

I informed him that "Little Brother" was going to jail.
He told me that, as a reporter, HE WAS IN ASSISTANT CHIEF JOE REED'S OFFICE DAILY, REPORTING ON THE CONDUCT OF POLICE OFFICERS IN NEWTON STREET DIVISION.

He declared that everyone there, including himself, had, come at the invitation of Mr. Brother; and that, inasmuch as they were guests and club members, I had no jurisdiction to raid the place.

He introduced the officer to me, and informed me that the officer and his wife were also guests and members of the club.

"You'd better get your --- out of here, or you'll be in jail," I told the Newton Street officer.

I advised the colored reporter that if he stayed, he'd be able to report to Assistant Chief Reed that he had a bump on his head.

Sergeant Madden, standing unhappily by, then began to admonish me —"You might be wrong. Mebbe you hadn't better go through with it!"

I told Madden that, if he wanted to give me an order to refrain from making the arrests, I would accept the order; otherwise he was not to interfere.

The officer, who had accompanied me, walked into the place at the sound of commotion inside. I darted after him. He was being verbally berated by the police captain's secretary, who in a loud voice ejaculated: —"Evidently, you've turned into a stool pigeon — since you've been working with Stoker — Well, I'll tell you one thing, everybody in Newton division will hear about this!"

This woman was typical of many young women and girls who serve the police department in clerical capacities, some of whom marry police officers; or fraternize with them, thus arrogating to themselves an importance not merited by the positions they occupy.

"Little Brother" then stepped up and told me that he would like to speak to me in private. He confided that a police sergeant from the detective bureau was in one of the other rooms with his girl friend, and asked if it would be all right to let them out through the back door. I walked in, took a look and verified the statement. Then I permitted the couple to exit via the back door before the lights were turned on.

THIS CASE, LIKE THE OTHER, DID NOT GO TO COURT.

Soon afterwards, however, I became involved in the Brenda Allen investigation and force of circumstances required me to cease giving unwelcome police attention to "Little Brother."

At this writing, I can assure my readers that "Little Brother" is still operating, albeit with a change of address. He is now located in the 4200 block of South Central Avenue. Obviously, he cannot function without the help accorded him by certain members of the Los Angeles police department, assigned to vice activities.

I made a full report of the above arrests and of the circumstances surrounding them to my superior, relating Sergeant Madden's demand that I allow the arrested persons to go to the police department in their personal care. As stated in the report, I had acquiesced to Sergeant Madden's demand that "Little Brother" be permitted to drive to the booking office in his new Cadillac.

A separate and individual report was also submitted in reference to the officers present and to the aforementioned secretary to the captain of the Newton Street division.

NO ACTION WAS EVER TAKEN AGAINST THESE INDIVIDUALS.

Would you consider their conduct as officers *unbecoming?*

Before I close this chapter, I want to cite and delineate a few of the strange paradoxes, or anomalies that have gone on in the police department since I left there almost a year ago.

One of the first proclamations of Chief Worton, made when he was appointed Chief of Police, was that from then on no police officer would accept gifts or gratuities of any kind. Shortly afterwards, a young police officer was reported to have taken a bag of groceries from a neighborhood chain market. Worton immediately held an investigation, which was conducted by a Lieutenant Kenneth MacCauley, who was at that time working with Lieutenant John Jesse and directly under Inspector William Parker, in command of the new and powerful Bureau of Internal Affairs (BIA).

This man MacCauley had been Captain Cecil Wisdom's first in command when Wisdom was in charge of the old Personnel Division. MacCauley directed the so-called investigation into the crime with which I was charged, assisted Wisdom in filing the charges against me, and was appointed "Trial Advocate" at my police trial board.

Investigation of the young officer was conducted and he was charged with the criminal offense of theft, and was in turn tried by the courts at which time the manager of the market testified that it was a habit of this officer to keep the store under surveillance during the period of time that daily money receipts were being tallied. It had been the policy of the store to give the officer whatever few groceries he wanted for this additional service.

The manager said the complaint against the officer had been made without his knowledge. The officer was acquitted by the criminal courts. However, he was cited before the justice of the police trial board. He was dismissed from the police department for conduct unbecoming a policeman.

There was no getting around the fact that he had accepted a few groceries, worth not more than three dollars.

Lieutenant MacCauley was promoted to the command of the BIA when Inspector Parker was promoted by Chief Worton to the position of Deputy Chief of Police. Shortly after Parker's promotion, MacCauley was promoted to rank of Captain. He was transferred to the detective bureau, in charge of the Bunco and Pickpocket Division. This unit apprehends swindlers, gyp artists, pickpockets and bunco men of all classifications.

Lieutenant John Jesse, the other favorite of Deputy Chief Parker, *was given command* of the BIA, replacing MacCauley.

All of the old "head-hunters"— as they are called by police officers — from Wisdom and MacCauley's clique stayed with Jesse as his assistants.

In a small neighborhood in Los Angeles there dwelt a sharpy who was always out for a fast buck. His reputation could most assuredly classify him as a bunco artist. One of his methods of operation was to rent store space in an established business district, have a telephone put in under a fictitious firm name, and then take the classified section of the City directory and call numerous television stores, giving his business address and telephone number.

He would then bunco his listeners into believing that his was an established television sales outfit operating by selling outmoded sets or repossessions on a percentage basis. Not too long ago, this man was arrested for receiving stolen property. The thief of the property was apprehended and immediately pleaded guilty.

Although this man's home was filled with the stolen property, he was tried before the judge who had also heard the cases of Wellpott, Wisdom, Jackson, Horrall and Reed, and found not guilty. To this day, the officers that made the arrest are still shaking their heads, wondering what happened.

At any rate, for what it's worth, here's the letter I sent Worton at the time when Seman was being investigated by the D. A.'s office for the suspected swindle of an aged Los Angeles widow.

"In re Mr. George Seman, whose suspect activities are now under investigation by the District Attorney of Los Angeles County, and his association with Captain Kenneth MacCauley, Commander, Bunco-Fugitive Division, Los Angeles police department.

"Mr. George Seman has, for years past, been well known in law enforcement circles, having a police record, and as a small-time bunco artist.

"For the past several years, since the advent and popular acceptance of television, Mr. Seman has, according to information personally received from reliable sources, employed the following profitable modus operandi.

"Carefully and warily selecting a respectable, well established business district, he would pay rental deposit on vacant store or office space. He would hurriedly embellish this rented space with all earmarks of a bona-fide business — a suitable if fictitious firm name, and, sometimes, a girl 'secretary.'

"Mr. Seman would immediately make closely-spaced calls to the smaller television merchants located throughout Los Angeles County. Sometimes in addition, he contacted loan companies that might possibly have repossessed television sets on hand.

"He would inform recipients of his telephone calls that he was operating an outlet for television sets that were finding a sluggish market. He would inform his intended victims that he was in a position to easily dispose of any and all outmoded or slow moving television sets at a profitable price, and offer to sell any such sets they had on hand for a percentage of the profits.

"Many merchants and loan companies contacted by Mr. Seman, eager to accrue profit from the dead merchandise, accepted his offer of profitable disposal. These were informed that a truck would be dispatched to pick up the available television sets.

"True 'suckers' for Mr. Seman's bunco 'build-ups,' few intended victims bothered to check back on him. Those who did were apparently satisfied with the facts that he had a 'legitimate' business address and telephone.

"Operating his own truck, Mr. Seman's next step was to collect the drug-on-the-market television sets in person. This done, he sold the sets at extremely cut prices wherever opportunity offered. Needless to say, the victimized merchants and loan companies never saw their surrendered sets again.

"And, now, about Captain Kenneth MacCauley, LAPD.

"As you should know by this time, if there is any honesty among your personnel investigators, two of the most expensive of the television sets obtained through his bunco ruse by Mr. Seman from a Southside business establishment were, not too long ago, installed free of all charges, in the Sunland home of Captain MacCauley.

"It is quite possible that you do not know that Captain MacCauley has also accepted other gifts from Mr. Seman.

"Here is a list of such additional gifts. It may be only a partial list.

"Mr. Seman gave Captain MacCauley two horses. One was a very young colt. Captain MacCauley used an official Los Angeles Police Department car as a conveyance to transport this colt to his Sunland home.

"Mr. Seman gave Captain MacCauley clothing and perfume.

"Mr. Seman gave Captain MacCauley two expensive table lamps for his home.

"The latter gift was made by Mr. Seman and accepted by Captain MacCauley AFTER action was taken in the suspected swindle of Mrs. Johnson and on the SAME day that Mr. Seman left Los Angeles for Cleveland, Ohio, where, at this writing, he is still located.

"Since Mr. Seman's departure from Los Angeles, he has twice been contacted at Cleveland, Ohio, via long distance telephone by Captain MacCauley.

"Upon each and every occasion, Mr. Seman, who is no fool when it comes to protecting himself against any back lashing by police officers he has favored, had a witness to his purchase of, his presentation to and Captain MacCauley's acceptance of the gifts he has listed above.

"These witnesses will appear and truthfully testify at the set date and time of any *open and public hearing*.

"Who are these witnesses?

"Well, there is the man who installed the television set in Captain MacCauley's home. There is the merchant who can identify the sets as the ones taken by Mr. Seman from his store.

"There is the man who accompanied Mr. Seman when he purchased the horses for Captain MacCauley, and the man who was present when Captain MacCauley loaded the colt into an official Los Angeles police car for the purpose of transporting it to his home.

"Need I remind you, Chief Worton, that Mr. Seman has an unsavory police record filed in the Record Bureau of the Los Angeles police department?

"Need I remind you that this record shows that Mr. Seman has avidly followed the profession of bunco artist?

"Need I remind you that Captain MacCauley is in charge of the Fugitive-Bunco Division — and thus should have been acutely aware of Mr. Seman and his police record? Especially, since Mr. Seman was, within the last ninety days, defending himself in a local court action.

"Need you be asked, as Chief of Police, if you can ignore the pertinent fact in the current District Attorney's investigation of

Mr. Seman and his suspect activities that the neighbors of Mr. Seman are quite aware of frequent and apparently friendly visits paid upon Mr. Seman by Captain MacCauley?

"And can there be any answer to or refutation of these facts, Chief Worton?

"That the complainant against Mr. Seman ignored the Los Angeles Police Department, preferring the District Attorney's office, in making his complaint against Mr. Seman, because he was aware of the friendly association between Captain MacCauley and Mr. Seman?

"That, though the investigation of Mr. Seman and his past actions by the office of the District Attorney is now days old, there has been no publicly reported action in the case on the part of Captain MacCauley, or the men under his command.

"That, though the press, from information gleaned from the District Attorney's office, has reported the possible involvement of a police officer and a police department captain in the Seman case, there has been no publicly reported action taken by officials of the police department?

"That it is, as the light publicly shed upon the Seman case grows brighter and brighter, going to seem quite odd that a Captain of Police whose specific duties include the investigation and apprehension of such suspected felons as Mr. Seman should be the recipient of gifts from such a suspect?

"That any attempts to ignore the facts, or cover up the facts, concerning the relationship between Captain MacCauley and Mr. Seman should be of great interest to a Grand jury?

"I know, Chief Worton, that being informed of the facts contained in this letter you may be depended upon to take prompt and proper action in the matter.

"Respectfully,
Charles F. Stoker."

Although that letter was sent registered, special delivery to Chief Worton and mailed July 15, 1950, and it is now August 7, 1950, it has been met only with a great and studied silence.

When these facts, which were indisputable, were brought before Worton, he assigned Lieutenant John Jesse to make the investigation, and to make a report as was to be expected.

Later, Worton stated that he was of the opinion that "the boy" had just used bad judgment.

It should be remembered that the only crime Officer Parslow committed concerned some old copies of arrest reports he had made, which were readily available to everyone, and were found in the house of a man who had a minor police record. Parslow's excuse was reasonable and it was never even remotely suggested that Parslow gained any compensation for these reports. For a fact, his conduct at the most could have been construed only as "careless," or as "lacking in judgment." Yet, Parslow was brought before a police trial board and discharged from his job.

He was not given a slap on the back by Chief Worton and told to use better judgment in the future. Now, I am opposed on principle to making a sinner of one and a saint of another, particularly when the circumstances are such that the sinner should be made the saint — if anything — and the saint the sinner. Accordingly, although I am no longer a member of the police department, I still am a citizen and a taxpayer in good standing, and I believe it to be incumbent upon me to call the attention of Chief Worton to these inconsistencies, if not worse. I wrote him the following letter under date of July 15, 1950, and I not only failed to receive an acknowledgement of it, but nothing happened to indicate that he had received it, or that it had made the slightest possible ripple on the placid surface of Mayor Bowron's police administration.

By this time I believe that my readers, if there are any left, will have formed one opinion at least and perhaps a question growing out of the opinion. Well they might ask:

"Stoker, haven't you any sense of humor?"

If they do, I must retort: "No, I guess that I haven't but I should have one."

Captain MacCauley voluntarily appeared before my police trial board and voluntarily stated that he, as head of Police Personnel, felt that I should be terminated from the police department.

COPS AND ROBBERS

*"There is a method in man's wickedness,
It grows up by degrees."*

During my court trial, a grand juror, unofficially, had asked my opinion regarding the Los Angeles Police Department as a whole.

I told him that, considered as a whole, the personnel was very high. I pointed out that the department was composed largely of men who had seen service in World War II, many of whom had held positions of responsibility as officers in the armed services before they had joined the department.

The grand juror had asked why, if what I said was true, so many crimes, particularly murders, had been left unsolved in Los Angeles. I had previously told him that hundreds of police officers were constantly seeking to improve themselves by attending university and extension courses, and that many were majoring in criminal science to improve their knowledge and efficiency in police work. I had pointed out that there existed no definitive, bang-up examination for detectives, while a very tough examination was given would-be motorcycle officers. Seemingly, detectives were appointed on the basis of their ability to fill in with older groups of detectives who, for years, had made it a policy to connive with crooked bail-bondsmen and scheming criminal attorneys, more interested in loot than in police efficiency or justice.

Moreover, I explained that the bailbondsmen in Los Angeles included scabby, criminal-minded men, who exercised great powers, despite their seemingly innocuous profession of liberating prisoners for cash. I told him that many bondsmen had criminal records, having been involved in city and county rackets for years.

The best police officers are not always appointed as detectives. In demand are officers who will not threaten the "status quo," i. e., the liaisons between criminals and racketeers and the law enforcement agents and their authorities.

"Any police officer who threatens this setup," I explained, "will not long remain in a position to threaten it. In truth, some intelligent, better class men are appointed to detective units, but they are strictly controlled and their presence is merely to do the onerous work that is necessary in order to permit other officers to continue their practical studies in the great game of grand larceny."

"How does the bail bondsman operate to lessen police efficiency — and to spread crime and rackets?" asked the juror.

"Suppose a man is arrested for possession of narcotics or burglary," I replied. "He may have been caught in the act by a uniformed patrolman. After making the arrest, the patrolman states the facts of the case in his arrest report, which is turned over to the detective bureau handling that type of crime.

"Two detectives, assigned to the case, interrogate the prisoner, learning the names of his relatives, or close friends, and determining his pecuniary, or financial standing, whether or not he has money. The prisoner's offense may be bailable. Let us suppose the bail is set at five thousand dollars.

"If the detectives are crooked, this information is turned over to a bailbondsman with whom they are in league. The latter contacts friends and relatives of the prisoner and arranges to post bail for him — the premium being about ten per cent of the bond. If the bail is five thousand dollars, the premium will be five hundred dollars.

"This profit is shared by the bondsman and the detectives. The bondsman, meanwhile, having wormed his way into the confidence of the prisoner's friends and relatives, suggests that it would be 'wise' to hire a certain attorney to represent the men. Frequently he states that this certain attorney is on friendly terms with the detectives handling the case and that they — out of friendship — may forget to come up with some vital evidence at the trial which virtually would insure acquittal. The attorney, of course, is part of the ring of connivers for cash.

"Stepping into the picture, he ascertains that the prisoner's friends, or relatives, can raise several thousand dollars for the defense. Let us say that they can raise three thousand dollars. The attorney contacts the detectives handling the case, and apprises them of the fact that three thousand dollars can be made if the charge is quashed, or reduced. If the circumstances permit, the detectives then find that there exists 'insufficient evidence' to convict the prisoner.

"They make their recommendations to their immediate superior, usually an inspector or captain, who may or may not be in league with his aides in the pay-offs, but generally is. He recommends that the prisoner be discharged, or that he be charged with a misdemeanor instead of a felony, the money then is paid over to the attorney who shares it with the detectives and bailbondsman.

"On the other hand, if the prisoner has money but is stubborn about paying-off, the detectives will present their evidence to the district attorney's office. A felony complaint is then issued against the prisoner, and a preliminary hearing is scheduled.

"Perhaps, he has now seen the light and does not want to risk prosecution in court. If the deputy district attorney handling the prosecution is in league with the police officers and the bondsman, and if the prisoner is willing to pay a large amount of money in order that the charge be dropped, 'insufficient evidence' to bind him over for superior court trial will be produced at the preliminary hearing and the charge will be dismissed."

The present system which permits bailbondsmen to intrude themselves into the areas of law enforcement and prosecution, by virtue of their linkage with corrupt police officers and prosecutors, constitutes the greatest menace to honest and efficient law enforcement in Los Angeles County.

Although the State Insurance Commission is supposedly obligated to issue bonding licenses only to men of proven rectitude and honesty, many bailbondsmen have committed offenses ranging from murder down the scale.

The conduct of the bail bond racket in California is indefensible and inexcusable. Many with long criminal records easily obtain licenses to put up bail bonds for persons under arrest.

Men who have engaged in every kind of racket known to the American underworld — many of whom are still in these rackets — are engaged in this parasitical business. One firm was prominently mentioned in the California Crime Commission report and its owner was accused of being in league with the underworld and its rackets.

Frequently bailbondsmen, in perfecting and extending their techniques in grand larceny, pose as agents of the Superior and Municipal Courts in Los Angeles County whenever they believe they are dealing with someone so ignorant that he does not know any better. Relatives and friends of men and women in jail are conned, buncoed, hoodwinked and financially clipped by these vultures operating under a state license.

The bail bond business is parasitical through and through. Its operators collude with shyster attorneys and conspire with law enforcement agents.

The bail bond pitch is not a business — it's a racket and its representatives, for the most part, are men whose police records before they got into the bail bond business can't stand honest scrutiny.

If anyone is to profit out of the misery of those who go to jail — and the misery of those who are trying to get them out — it should be the State of California, or the counties and municipalities of California, and not the *bailbondeer*.

The grand juror had proven particularly interested in gambling in Los Angeles and specifically in gambling as it existed in Chinatown. Its members had been profoundly shocked to learn that the vice officers were aware of such gambling. One of the jurors asked if a gambling squad had been assigned to work the Chinatown area.

"There is such a squad," I told him. "However, it's merely a front. Actually the officers on this squad are not paid; they are young vice officers who, in most cases, know little about the techniques of gambling law enforcement. When these officers are first sent to Chinatown, they are completely out of their element and scarcely know where to start their investigation. To the average Caucasian, all Chinese look alike."

I explained that the Chinese way of living and working differs greatly from the Caucasian, and that, although an officer may be a fairly proficient poker player, or crap shooter, he may know nothing of the Chinese manner of gambling, or of the finer nuances of Mah Jongg, Pi Que or Fan Tan.

The Chinese employ intricate systems of hiding their gambling. They have cunning ways of stationing lookouts to warn them of the approach of police, and deceptive methods of covering places where gambling is being conducted. Months elapse before a raw gambling squad begins to find its way around Chinatown, to learn the locations of gambling games, to spot lookouts and to differentiate one game from another.

When officers reach this point in experience and knowledge, they are transferred for the "good of the department," the old technique used by department heads for their ulterior aims. Perhaps, they are given better positions, such as assignments to the detective bureau, so that they will have no reason to squawk.

The case of Officer Edward Hill shows how even the best of plans will occasionally slip up. Hill, a new policeman in the department, had been a master in the merchant marine with command of his own ship. He had traveled all over the world. Stopovers in many seaports had taught him all the holds and angles regarding gambling and general sin. At the outset, however, let me say that Hill was an honest copper and one of the most intelligent men I had met on the police department. In his years before the mast, he had made gambling his hobby. The shrewdest non-professional gambler I've ever seen, his ability stemmed from the fact that he was a quick mathematician with an alert mind. He knew all about percentages and played them constantly.

The police big brass made a grave mistake when they placed Edward Hill in charge of a gambling squad. They thought him another big country bumpkin who had wandered into the police department. Noting that he was being left alone, Hill at first supposed, as do most young coppers on the job, that there was no such thing as vice and corruption, that is, protected vice and corruption.

Hill thought it best to act the part of a dumb copper until he became thoroughly oriented in his new detail. However, he lost no time in learning the actual setup with regard to police-protected Chinatown. Hill wasn't an eager beaver out to reform the police department. He needed his job to support his family; nonetheless he began to bear down on Chinese gamblers.

The police department feared Hill. It had selected the wrong man for the job of enforcing the city's gambling laws in Chinatown, if gambling was to flourish in Oriental sectors. Consequently, it had a bear by the tail and didn't know what to do with him, especially after certain Chinese made the mistake of informing him that they were paying for police protection. Because Hill had been bothering and arresting them, these Chinese threatened to get rid of him. Hill, having less water in his blood than most officers, advised his Chinese protagonists to tell their friends that he didn't intend to be gotten rid of. As a matter-of-fact, he liked the Chinese gambling detail.

At about this time, a woman by the name of Patricia (Pat) Connors contacted Hill. She wanted to open a gambling joint, and said that everything was fixed to go — except Hill. She said that she wanted to be sure "the fix" was on all the way around before she started to operate. Hill informed Miss Connors that she might "fix" other people, but that he wasn't on the "take," and that if she opened a joint, she could expect to get knocked over, in so far as he was concerned. It was rumored that Miss Connors had accepted the money with which to launch the project from backers, whom she had assured that everything was fixed.

Despite Hill's warning, Miss Connors proceeded with her plan. On her opening night, she found herself in jail. Hill had been true to his word.

A few nights later, the press received word that Miss Connors had been shot. Lieutenant Rudy Wellpott, who has stalked through these pages with an uncanny, sinister persistence, had accompanied her to the receiving hospital and had given news releases attendant upon Miss Connors's wounding.

According to Wellpott, the woman had been shot in the hip, but wasn't seriously hurt, having sustained a minor flesh wound. The shooting had occurred on the east side of Los Angeles, near Brooklyn Avenue, and some fifteen miles from her motel. The story given to the press was that she was in the habit of supplying information to Lieutenant Rudy Wellpott's vice squad. Oddly enough, Lieutenant Wellpott's information was invariably gleaned from people engaged in the rackets and in actually breaking the laws that Lieutenant Rudy Wellpott was supposed to enforce.

Watching the operations of Lieutenant Wellpott and his aide, Sergeant Elmer V. Jackson, I always felt that some system of identification should inform other officers who is who in the police-vice-crime picture. It was always confusing to determine which side was up when Wellpott had administrative vice.

Wellpott's report to the press was designed to cover the truth. Miss Connors hadn't been kidding Officer Hill and me. We knew that she had taken money from her backers on the presentation of a scheme to make gambling money; we also knew that she had given them the impression that everything was fixed, even though she couldn't fix Officer Hill. Evidently, this conniving dame had assumed that Hill would not incur the wrath of corrupt police officers by upsetting her little racket boat.

Hill and I were playing a friendly game of cribbage when we heard about the shooting. Later, when we read Lieutenant Wellpott's explanation of what had happened, we had a big laugh. The department found Hill too hot to handle. They had taken his needling because they were uncertain about how much he knew.

The thieves were afraid that, if they brought some trumped up charge against him; such as "conduct unbecoming an officer," the general ruse, Hill might spill what he knew. He had let everyone know that he liked his job and intended to stay on it, at least until the sergeant's examination was held. In fact, Hill knew that he was well qualified for a sergeancy and intended to make the grade.

Since it was necessary to discredit Edward Hill in the eyes of other police officers, the thieves would have to effectuate a situation in which Hill would want a change of scenery. They could then place him in a position in which he could no longer imperil police graft.

Among coppers, particularly those working vice and gambling, it's a common practice to get together in locker rooms and hold friendly poker and dice games during off-duty hours — even though ambitious vice officers, as we know, occasionally go out and arrest elderly people for playing penny ante, much to the political annoyance of Mayor Fletcher E. Bowron.

Off duty, Hill came out of Central station, at 326 West First Street, one evening. He was approached by one of Rudy Wellpott's super-sleuths, who greeted him in an overly friendly manner. The boys in administrative vice were having a little game in the back room, Hill was told. He was invited to join in.

When Hill walked in, the crap game was in full progress. Eight or ten coppers were shooting dice. All of them worked in Wellpott's vice and gambling details.

Although Hill and I had played in many police station backroom poker and crap games, we had never seen an outsider participate in them. Yet, who was present upon this occasion but MR. NATHAN BASS, THE SOUTH MAIN STREET BAR OWNER.

You will remember that Inspector Bill Parker had informed me that Bass was the agent on Main Street for Lieutenant Rudy Wellpott.

Hill got into the game and made a few passes with the dice.

Suddenly, Bass reached out and grabbed the dice from the table. He stepped into the next room for a moment and then returned. In a very dramatic manner that would have done credit to a ham actor, Bass yelled:

"Hill is a crook! He's taking money from his buddies with crooked dice!"

"In all my days I've never seen a pair of dice as phony as those Bass produced," Hill told me in describing the scene. "A man who'd stick those dice into a crap game — particularly a crap game between gambling squad cops – should have his head examined. They must have been bought in a novelty store."

As a result of this "friendly" game, one rotten copper, who undoubtedly had been coached in his lines, threatened to shoot Hill. All that Hill could do was to beat a hasty retreat.

A few days later, Hill's transfer came through, first to traffic and later to San Pedro, proving that crooked coppers not only frame citizens at times, they frame each other, or, let's put it right – crooked coppers will frame honest ones, whereas an honest copper would never think of framing anyone.

San Pedro is the most distant precinct outpost in the Los Angeles police department and is known as "Siberia," or the Fog Belt. Hill never squawked. He is still with the department.

Lieutenant Rudy Wellpott's friend—Nate Bass—boss of the Main Street B-Girls, had cleverly accomplished the undoing of Officer Hill, a feat that his police enemies were obviously afraid to tackle. Lacking the guts to do anything to Officer Hill himself, Wellpott had left the dirty work to one of his allied friends. Such are the men who control vice and gambling law administration in Los Angeles, under Mayor Fletcher E. Bowron's "finest police department in the world."

If the slogan has become a little nauseating, don't blame me – blame Mayor Bowron.

Now, let us flash back to Pat Connors, the woman who had wanted to operate a gambling joint on East First Street – the woman who had opened her joint only to have it knocked over the first night of its operation.

Keyes was a young, naive officer on the police department. He and his partner had stopped two youthful Mexicans one night to shake them down at Temple Street and Grand Avenue as suspected burglars. One of the Mexicans, Augustine Salcido, had grabbed the officer's gun and as a result Keyes's police partner was shot, whereupon Keyes shot Salcido dead.

Communist agents entered the mess, charging that it was a proven instance of police brutality wherein a sadistic officer had unjustifiably shot down and killed a member of a "minority group." The Communists succeeded in having Keyes charged with manslaughter. Pending disposition of the charge, Keyes was transferred to the personnel division, presided over by that great friend of the Los Angeles taxpayers, Captain Cecil Wisdom. One night, Keyes received a telephone call.

The caller was a woman, who was obviously drunk. She said that she wanted to talk to Captain Wisdom and asked for his home telephone number. Keyes replied that he couldn't give her the number; however, after much argument over the phone, he agreed to take her telephone number and see to it that Wisdom received it. He wrote the number down and thoughtlessly stuck the paper in his pocket. He forgot about the incident, having concluded that the caller was merely a dizzy, drunken dame.

Later, Keyes's wife found the name and telephone number in his pocket. Suspecting the worst, she dialed the number and asked for Pat Connors, the name on the slip of paper. When his wife became enraged, Keyes decided to telephone the girl and explain his wife's call. Miss Connors, now sober, told Keyes that she wanted to meet him. Keyes assented.

Miss Connors, meanwhile, had taken aboard another quantity of the gay and frisky, or whiskey, before the meeting. She was very outspoken as to her reason for wanting to see Captain Wisdom.

"I was shot because of the Los Angeles police department," she informed Keyes. "Rudy Wellpott is to blame for it. He was supposed to fix it with the police department for me to open a gambling joint. I told my backers I was sure of the fix; but we got knocked over on opening night and the people lost their bankroll. That's why I was shot, not because I was a stool pigeon for the vice squad, as Wellpott said."

Untutored in the ways of police corruption, Keyes thought that he would be doing Lieutenant Rudy Wellpott a favor by informing him of what Pat Connors had said. He telephoned Wellpott, who arranged to meet him the next day at the police academy in Elysian Park. Keyes then called Captain Wisdom and again related what he had heard, laboring under the belief that Miss Connors was simply nuts and that he, Keyes, was doing both Wellpott and Wisdom a favor.

To Keyes's great surprise, Captain Wisdom called him out into the hall the following day. "You'd better forget about what that woman told you," said Wisdom. "If you don't, I'll see that you go to San Quentin."

This was the young officer's reward for having tried to help Wellpott, Wisdom and the police department. He was considerably disillusioned.

Later, Keyes ran into Wellpott in the City Hall. Wellpott inquired why Keyes had not met him at the police academy as he had promised. Keyes explained that he had talked to Captain Wisdom.

"What did Wisdom say?" inquired Wellpott.

"He told me I'd better keep my mouth shut, or I'd go to San Quentin," Keyes replied.

"You'd better take his advice," Wellpott remarked unctuously.

Soon after this conversation, Keyes became ill and went to the Veterans' Hospital in West Los Angeles. While he was there, the police scandal involving Brenda Allen, Sergeant Elmer V. Jackson and me broke in the newspapers. Believing that someone should be informed of his knowledge of the police mess, Keyes went to the Santa Monica police department. He had been drinking a bit, and in a fearful frame of mind, had chosen this neighboring city because it had its own police department.

Keyes confided his fears and his knowledge to several Santa Monica policemen. Of course, they had all read that Sergeant Howard Robinson and Captain William Wingard of Hollywood station had been working with me when I had arrested Brenda Allen. The Santa Monica officers, arriving at the erroneous conclusion that Robinson and Wingard would be on my side in the controversy and scandal, called Hollywood station and got hold of Sergeant Robinson.

They told Robinson about Keyes's sudden appearance in the Santa Monica station, and detailed what he had related. Robinson said that he would contact Wingard and that they would drive to the Santa Monica station and talk to Keyes. He directed the Santa Monica officers to have Keyes wait. A short while later, Sergeant Robinson entered the station and informed Keyes that Captain Wingard was outside waiting in the car. Keyes accompanied Robinson to the car. Captain Wingard was there *as was also* Captain Cecil Wisdom.

Inasmuch as he had made embarrassing disclosures about Los Angeles police to a neighboring police department, Keyes was charged with "conduct unbecoming a police officer." Having had enough of "Good, Honest and Efficient Government" under Mayor Bowron and Chief of Police Horrall, Keyes decided then and there that he wouldn't contest the charges before a police trial board. He resigned.

The details of this story of police conniving and graft were presented to the county grand jury before whom I had described corrupt conditions regarding Chinese gambling, bookmakers who had been paying graft, bar owners who had been shaken down and myriad other violators of the law. My testimony should have provided ammunition for an all-out investigation of corruption in Los Angeles.

The district attorney's office had promised the grand jury that such an investigation would be made, that witnesses and participants would be called to testify under oath, and that I would be recalled to testify.

Do you know what became of the material I supplied? Absolutely nothing.

The district attorney's office had cleverly stepped aside. Moreover, its "embattled" agents, deputies and investigators, who had promised that malefactors would be brought to book and that evil would be exposed, had gone fishing — fishing, no doubt, for bigger and more valuable fry for those in the vice-graft cabal.

But I ask you — should their conduct have been startling to anyone?

"LOVE SENDS ITS LITTLE GIFT OF ROSES"

*"All things I thought I knew: but now confess
The more I know I know, I know the less."*

A vice squad officer runs into so many strange situations, that nothing astonishes him. Indeed, if one works vice long enough, the chances are that he will become both a misanthrope and a misogynist. Sordid experiences tend to shatter one's faith in the human race; and vice squad coppers are given a kaleidoscopic picture of the seamy side of life.

In the constantly changing pattern, I recall a florist with a long record for sexual offenses. Obviously, this man had managed to avoid the penalty for his transgressions by "paying off in flowers." His floral gifts would serve to glamorize my story, were it not for the gross sexual behavior that lay behind them.

One day, I received a telephone call from a Mrs. Snively, who stated that she was the manager of the Ambassador Modeling Agency located in the world famous Ambassador Hotel on Wilshire Boulevard. She explained that she would like to talk to me, personally, and asked if I would come by and see her. I had heard of the Ambassador Modeling Agency and was aware of its good standing and reputation. It was considered the prime agency of its kind on this coast, and I had heard that to "belong" was the ultimate aim of most girls following the modeling profession.

I called on Mrs. Snively, who told me that she had a most annoying problem and desired to enlist my assistance in solving it. She explained that she had made telephone complaints to the police department, but that in so far as she knew, nothing whatever had been done in the investigative line to handle the situation.

"I've read about you in the newspapers," Mrs. Snively said. "I believe that you are energetic enough to do something about this unsavory mess."

She explained that many young girls in and about Los Angeles had been crowned Miss Grapefruit, Miss Slipper, etc., and that they had received wide publicity in the newspapers as a result. Their addresses were frequently printed along with their names.

"I continuously receive telephone calls from these girls," Mrs. Snively said, "together with calls from their indignant parents. I can only conclude that some man, giving the name of a Mr. Anderson, telephones these girls and states that he represents the Ambassador Modeling Agency. He gives them a fast line about having seen their pictures in the newspapers, congratulates them upon having been selected over a bevy of other beauties to serve as Queen of Bakery Week, or some other commercial or industrial exploitation."

Mrs. Snively said that the mysterious Mr. Anderson would make appointments with these girls, invariably at night, and that his method of procedure was to call for a girl in his automobile, drive her to a lonely spot and attempt to seduce her. In the event this failed, he would try to rape her, or to expose himself.

Frequently, he proposed indulgence in sexual abnormalities to the girls, Mrs. Snively said.

It is a fact that many girls raped in Los Angeles never report the crimes to the police department because of shame. If they are working as professional models, or in some similar calling, young women often refuse to name their attackers, or to give police information because of their fear of detrimental publicity.

Mrs. Snively told me that, although the girls had given her a description of the man, no one of her acquaintances even resembled him.

From the investigative standpoint, the problem had its drawbacks since the information and leads on the man were scanty. He was a shadowy, elusive figure.

"All we can do is to hope for a lucky break," I told Mrs. Snively. I gave her the confidential telephone number of the vice division, my home telephone number and the numbers of several officers working with me, and advised her to call me at any time, day or night, if she received a possible lead. To make matters worse, the girls and families who had called Mrs. Snively had refused to give their names and addresses. As a consequence, I had no one to interview.

I told Mrs. Snively that, if we could find a girl who actually had an appointment pending with the sexual degenerate, we would be able to substitute a policewoman. This would enable us to get the necessary evidence to make an arrest, and we would have some assurance that the depraved poseur could be jailed and put away. This, I explained, would spare any embarrassment to the models upon whom the man was seeking to prey.

The break came rapidly and unexpectedly one evening a few days later. I received a telephone call at my home. Mrs. Snively told me that she had been trying to get in touch with me. She had received a telephone message from a girl earlier in the evening.

"Please tell Mr. Anderson that I'll be late for our appointment, as I've been detained at my position," the girl began.

Mrs. Snively quickly explained the situation to the caller and then obtained her name and telephone number. I immediately telephoned the girl.

"Yes," she replied, "the man is sitting in his car outside my house waiting for me right now."

This girl's address was some twenty miles from my home, three police divisions away.

I had no possible way of arriving in time without arousing the man's suspicions. I telephoned the radio communications board, and had a police car dispatched to the girl's home with instructions to collar the man and hold him until I arrived.

When I arrived, I found the suspect sitting between two burly police officers in a squad car. One of the officers told me that when he had driven up and ordered the suspect out of his car, the man had attempted to destroy a sheet of paper by placing it in his mouth and attempting to swallow it. It bore a list of women's names, addresses and telephone numbers.

Several names had lines drawn through them, indicating that they had been discarded by the sex degenerate. Upon being asked to identify himself, the suspect gave the name, "Anderson. " I told the officers to take him to the station and hold him in the detective bureau until I arrived.

The young woman's story was much the same as that told by other girls to Mrs. Snively. She was as reluctant to have any publicity as were the man's other victims. I drove to the police station in Seventy-Seventh Street division. There, I searched Mr. Anderson. His driver's license revealed that his name was not Anderson. He was registered as RUBIN KOHN.

Other personal effects indicated that he was the owner and proprietor of a floral shop in the Wilshire District. I started to question him. He said that he was a reputable business man and that he had never been arrested. Then, to my surprise, he informed me that he was a close personal friend of Sergeant William Madden, commander of the night watch in Central Vice Division — whose name has appeared before in this chronicle of police peculiarities. He demanded that he be allowed to telephone Sergeant Madden to "report this outrage."

He informed me that certain big shots in the police department would be greatly incensed at me for treating him as I had. He then produced a card to show me proof of his friendship. This was a POLICE BUSINESS CARD, of the type furnished officers of the Los Angeles Police Department for purposes of identification and reference.

THE CARD THAT RUBIN KOHN, SEX DEGENERATE, EXTENDED TO ME BORE THE NAME OF SERGEANT WILLIAM MADDEN OF CENTRAL VICE DIVISION.

On the back of the card, written in longhand, was a short, cryptic note which read: "Any consideration shown Mr. Rubin Kohn will be greatly appreciated by the undersigned officer." (Signed) William Madden, Sergeant.

Among Kohn's personal effects was an identification card, which stated that Mr. Kohn was an honorary deputy sheriff of Los Angeles County. In a lapel button of his coat, he wore a miniature gold deputy sheriff's badge which, he informed me, had been presented to him by an executive in the sheriff's office.

As matters stood, I had nothing in the way of evidence upon which to arrest Mr. Rubin Kohn. Had I been able to place a policewoman with him in event the telephone message had reached me in time, things would have been different. Telephoning the girl, giving her a false name and misrepresenting his occupation did not constitute a crime.

I took the list of names that the officers had obtained from Kohn, and telephoned some of the numbers. Several of the girls admitted that they had "fallen" for Kohn's story, but added that they couldn't afford to suffer the publicity that would accrue to them if he were arrested and they were named as his victims.

Two girls to whom I talked, stated that they had complained to the police department after having been molested by Kohn, but that nothing had happened and that apparently nothing whatsoever had been done. This indicated to me that Mr. Kohn had an "in"; that he "threw his weight around somewhere."

These girls said that, when they had been interviewed by police officers investigating their complaints, the officers had more or less covered for Kohn and had talked in mitigation of his vileness. The officers had implied that they saw no good reason to become involved.

Disregarding Kohn's protests, I relieved him of his deputy sheriff's badge and his cards. I told him that if he wanted them back, he could receive them from the individuals who had given them to him.

Then I checked KOHN'S RECORD WITH THE POLICE DEPARTMENT, AND FOUND THE FOLLOWING DOSSIER. IF KOHN'S "FRIENDS" HAVEN'T HAD IT "PULLED" AND DESTROYED, I PRESUME THAT IT IS STILL ON FILE.

"6-22-26 — Suspicion of rape.

3-30-27 - Vag Lewd - 90 days in jail.
3-24-29– Suspicion of rape.
4-28-30– Assault with intent to commit rape.
4-13-40– Pomona, California, indecent exposure.
2-23-43 – Assault with intent to produce great bodilyharm.
7-20-46 – Long Beach – indecent exposure, molesting children, fined $600 or given the alternative of 120 days in jail. Fine paid.
5-23-48– Booked Santa Monica, Penal Code Section 288 (makes it a felony for any person to orally copulate the sexual organs of another).
9-1-49 – Assault with intent to commit rape."

Run Down: Kohn has a long record as a sexual offender in Long Beach, Santa Monica, San Bernardino and Pomona. He is registered as a sex offender, No. 8192. Officer R. W. Carter's signed report stated: "Has syphilis in advanced stages which doctors say may be affecting his sanity and which probably will affect his sanity more in the future."

I released Kohn from custody – because there was nothing else I could do– and pocketed his badge and cards. Then I placed Sergeant Madden's card in a small envelope, together with a note explaining how I had come by it, and left it for Madden. To an officer of the day watch at Central Vice, who was a former deputy sheriff, I explained the circumstances and asked if he would give the badge and the card to a deputy sheriff friend, to return to the sheriff's office. The officer assented.

The following night at about 11:45 p.m., I was parking my car in the police parking lot, when someone sitting in Sergeant Madden's automobile, hailed me in the darkness. I walked over to the car. Who should be there but MR. RUBIN KOHN!

He was overly friendly. I could distinguish the smirk on his evil kisser, as he told me that he had been driving Sergeant Madden's automobile that day and was thinking of buying it. I told him that that was splendid. Waiting in the front office was an unknown man, who identified himself as being from the sheriff's office. He told me that he would like to have Mr. Kohn's badge and card returned. He said that the badge in itself was of great sentimental value to Mr. Kohn, having been given him by the sheriff. He remarked that, although the sheriff was in the habit of passing out honorary deputy sheriff's reserve badges, this was an exception in that it was a gold miniature.

The caller then went on to inform me that Mr. Kohn held no grudge against me (it was mighty white of him), and was willing to "let bygones be bygones."

"Confidentially," he continued, "Mr. Kohn is a nice guy to know. He always furnishes the boys with bouquets. Why, whenever the sheriff gives a big blow-out, Mr. Kohn takes care of the flowers. A big bunch of roses is waiting for you in his florist shop now. Go by and pick them up."

While he was talking, I was thinking. I was wondering what I would do if I had a daughter or sister and this syphilitic degenerate attacked her.

I blew my top. I asked the man if he was aware of Kohn's record of sexual offenses.

"Oh, what the hell!" he retorted. "Those models are a bunch of God damned tramps, anyway."

I heartily disagreed with this pronouncement. Some of the finest women I have ever met were models. I told him to tell Mr. Kohn to take his flowers, and shove them in his ear or something. I then told the man what I had done with the sheriff's badge and card.

Upon hearing that the day office had these items, Sergeant Madden, who had been listening, strode majestically from the inner office and in my presence telephoned the day officer, getting him out of bed. Madden asked about the badge and card, then terminated his telephone conversation.

He told the sheriff's office representative that he would "tend to the matter."

When the man had departed, Sergeant Madden, in the presence of several other vice squad officers, called me into his office: "Stoker, I want to tell you something," he said. "Your conduct is very erratic. Fact is, you can be charged with CONDUCT UNBECOMING AN OFFICER. YOU HAD NO RIGHT TO TAKE THAT MAN'S PERSONAL PROPERTY. THOSE ITEMS WERE HIS. ACTUALLY, THE POLICE DEPARTMENT COULD CITE YOU FOR THEFT AND TAKE YOU BEFORE THE TRIAL BOARD.

"I have a God damned good notion to file a complaint against you, as it is. I want to give you a bit of advice, Stoker," he continued. "You'd better wake up and start co-operating with other police officers – especially officers from other law enforcement agencies."

I took "co-operation" to mean that I was supposed to help "blow down beefs" on syphilitic sex degenerates whenever they were caught trying to rape young girls – that is, if the syphilitic sex degenerates in question had friends among law enforcement agents.

Madden's crack aroused my Irish blood.

"Listen to me, Madden," I rejoined, "if I ever want your advice I'll ask for it – which is very improbable. If you ever offer me your advice, or if you even speak to me from now on, I'll break your damned jaw for you! If you have any doubts about that, Madden, get up and I'll proceed along those lines right now. Then, the police trial board will have cause to charge me with conduct unbecoming a policeman."

That night I concluded that my days as a Los Angeles police officer, one way or another, were numbered.

It gave me a little comfort to learn that, on the complaint of two models, Kohn had been arrested shortly thereafter on a charge of attempted rape. But his luck, or "in," again had held good, for the charges were dismissed.

In the light of the murder of little Linda Glucoft by degenerate Fred Stroble, and all of the hysteria that pervaded the scene when that gruesome crime was uncovered, one senses a prophetic note in the police report signed by Officer R. W. Carter, to-wit – "Doctors say that syphilis may be affecting Kohn's sanity and that it probably will affect it more in the future." The next girl may not be so lucky as the others.

If Mayor Bowron can, I'd like him to explain Mr. Kohn and Mr. Kohn's "connections" with members of the "finest police department in the world."

The question is fair: "How many other sex degenerates enjoy immunity in this community as well as the friendship of police officers — for A little less or more than a bunch of flowers?

LOOKING BACKWARD- AND FORWARD

"A thousand years scarce serves to form a state;
An hour may lay it in the dust."

Viewed in retrospect, it may be averred that what happened to Sergeant Stoker is unimportant. But is it? Los Angeles taxpayers shell out several millions annually to maintain their police department, and together with taxpayers in the county areas spend a comparable sum to maintain the district attorney's office. The police department and the district attorney's office should be the first line of defense against an ever increasing horde of criminals, racketeers and corruptionists.

Every organization, and especially is this true of a police group, either has morale or lacks it. Morale, like police work, is constructed out of intangibles. If the morale of a police department is low, or is non-existent, and if a department is wracked with scandals growing out of corruption and malfeasance, it becomes inefficient and worthless. Morale cannot be isolated, packaged, ordered and delivered on demand.

What happens to one individual, be he a police officer or a lay person, may be of relative unimportance. However, what happens to many persons in the realm of morale is of great importance.

No one can seriously argue that police morale was not badly shattered as a result of the Brenda-Allen-Mickey-Cohen scandal and allied police scandals involving charges of graft, frame-up and maladministration. Let anyone who attempts to argue in favor of our city administration explain why most of the police brass was forced out of office and induced to retire on pension. Let him explain why Mayor Fletcher E. Bowron thought it necessary to install an outsider, Marine General William A. Worton, as chief of police.

In radio talks, Mayor Bowron has frequently alluded to the "fact" that General Worton has "restored police morale," an admission that morale had taken a severe beating – in fact, that police morale had been shattered.

Perhaps, the mayor has no knowledge of the long years that are necessary to develop and maintain, or to restore, police department morale once it has been shattered.

Mayor Bowron's move in installing Chief Worton as a pinch-hitter for Chief of Police Clemence B. Horrall was not prompted solely by a desire to restore police morale; it was motivated in part by Bowron's determination to regain his political prestige which had waned as the result of the shocking disclosures bearing on police wrongdoing.

The synthetic reputation of the Los Angeles police department, created almost exclusively out of Bowron's verbiage, had plummeted dizzily from the empyrean heights upon which Bowron had placed it with his foundationless boasts that it was the finest police department in the United States; that it was without graft, corruption or malfeasance; and that, because of its good works, Los Angeles was free from gangsters and racketeers.

Bowron, his political foundations shaken and cracked, found it imperative to act, and he acted rapidly by bringing Worton into the scene — a fact which gained him no friends among police personnel. In all fairness to Worton, it must be admitted that he had been placed in a difficult spot. Yet, it would be untrue to state that Worton wrought miracles, restored police morale, or created an efficient department out of the remains of an inefficient organization.

Although Worton wrote and signed some one hundred odd transfer lists of police personnel, I defy him and Bowron to prove the effectiveness of these transfers in getting to the source of the trouble. At this writing, no morale exists in the police department. The personnel is disgusted, and many officers are not working, having declared their intention of "sitting on their hands" to await the blowing away of the storm.

It would seem that the Los Angeles police department is at a lower ebb today than it was when Horrall, Reed, Wellpott, Wisdom and Jackson were riding high, wide and handsome. A spirit of demoralization is abroad in the department, and the personal ambitions of Deputy Chief of Police William Parker, which have come to fruition, have not served to lift or restore morale with the prospect of inspired leadership.

In my opinion, only five men in the police department have the respect and confidence of police personnel. They are Inspectors Jack Donohoe, Anthony Collins and Lee German, and Deputy Chiefs of Police Thad Brown and Arthur Hohmann. The latter was the first selected Bowron chief of police, having passed the civil service examination with a mark above ninety-nine per cent. He was relegated to Deputy Chief for reasons which were never clearly explained and since that time, Hohmann has kept his head down, remained out of sight, and just punched the bag.

Thad Brown and Bill Parker are reputedly at loggerheads. Brown has one of the best detective brains in California. An old homicide man, he knows sleuthing procedures backwards and forwards. Donohoe is kaput for the reason that every copper knows he is the best all-around sleuth on the West Coast and knows more about the police "racket" than any five men in the department. For this reason, he will never get anywhere higher under the Bowron regime. An additional reason is that Donohoe will genuflect to no one; nor will he turn towards Mecca nine times each day if he thinks he is right which he generally is on all police matters.

Donohoe is a "copper's copper." Bowron and his sycophants know that Donohoe cannot be deceived and, because he is impeccably honest as well as smart, the city administration no doubt wishes he would retire on pension and go lose himself. Snide politicians hate retainers who can see through them and Donohoe is the police department's "Banquo's ghost."

Lee German, able as they come, keeps his mouth shut, lets no one know what he thinks, and hoes his own row of corn. Collins, just as capable, and honest as they come, views the police panorama with an Olympian detachment fulfilling his duties the while with a minimum participation in police politics.

But what of police morale? The writer's experience in combating corruption was not lost on hundreds of young police officers. This is not merely wishful thinking on my part. Many have expressed this opinion to me in confidence. In fact, if Mayor Bowron and the police brass, what's left of the old regime, could hear what these young officers state in totality, they would not speak so glibly about police morale.

Intelligent young men, today's officers are sufficiently realistic to know that the rewards of honesty, hard work and diligence in law enforcement are not promotion and pay on the Los Angeles police department, as it is presently constituted. They are aware of the fact that the soft berths and retirements on pension went to the sinners, connivers, incompetents, grafters and corruptionists who had permitted evils to flourish without interference, whereas several honest officers were charged with the commission of felonious crimes as a result of the late scandal.

Chief of Police Horrall, Assistant Chief Reed and Captain Cecil Wisdom were charged with perjury. Lieutenant Rudy Wellpott and his aide, Sergeant Elmer V. Jackson, were charged with perjury and bribery, and were indicted by the Los Angeles County grand jury, which had refused to indict me. I was falsely charged with burglary in a complaint issued by the district attorney's office, which is politically compatible with the city administration.

A bribery charge lodged against a police officer is considered a serious and aggravated crime. Yet, contrast the treatment I received with that given the others. Within one hour after Captain Wisdom had obtained the felony complaint against me, I had been booked, fingerprinted, stripped of my badge and gun, locked in the county jail and suspended.

I was "mugged," or photographed; and the record of my arrest and the charge were immediately forwarded to the F. B. I., at Washington, D. C., for incorporation in its files. The F. B. I. automatically assigned me a "criminal number" for reference purposes in the future.

While Horrall, Reed, Wisdom, Wellpott and Jackson were indicted by the county grand jury, none of them was SUSPENDED FROM THE POLICE DEPARTMENT PENDING DISPOSITION OF THE CHARGES AGAINST THEM. They lost no pay. They were never arrested, booked in jail, or fingerprinted, CONTRARY TO THE WRITTEN LAW ON THE STATUTE BOOKS. There is no record of their arrest, and no "permanent" record in files of F. B. I. hangs over their heads to dog them the rest of their days.

While he was representing me, Attorney S. S. Hahn wrote a letter to Chief of Police Worton, wherein he compared the treatment I had received with that meted out to the others. "This is not the American way of doing things," Hahn wrote. When the newspapers protested as well, "The Great" Worton, contravener of the law and flouter of the Constitution and fair play, declaimed: "I'm not going to be STAMPEDED into anything." What did he mean – stampeded? – with the law clear and not ambiguous as to his obligation. The law stipulates and sets the course of action. Worton, by this declaration, had placed himself on record as having no respect for due process of law, or for the Constitution and its statutory provisions and requirements. If he refuses to respect the law, think of the example he sets for police officers under him! Why should they, or anyone else for that matter respect it?

Defendants in the Horrall clique were not assigned before tough Superior Judge Charles W. Fricke as was I. Superior Judge Stanley Barnes heard their cases before a jury, and gave the jurors NO OPPORTUNITY TO PASS UPON THE EVIDENCE. Although the county grand jury, in its indictment of the five, had clearly indicated that it considered the evidence sufficient proof that perjury had been committed, Judge Barnes arbitrarily dismissed the case for what he termed "lack of evidence."

During the "trials" of Horrall, Reed, Wisdom, Wellpott and Jackson, lawyers in the courtroom had remarked that the prosecuting deputy district attorneys appeared to be defending the defendants. They considered the proceedings a legal farce.

To prosecute me, the district attorney had imported one of his ablest men – Clifford Crail – from the Pasadena branch of the office.

Yet, despite Crail's all out effort to convict me on a trumped up charge, spawned in perjury by Policewoman Audre Davis, he had failed to convince the jurors of my guilt.

Chief of Police Worton had lost no time in suspending me from the police department, his actions throughout clearly indicating that he was on the side of the officials. This, despite the fact that Worton had never talked to me and had never seen me. And this, too, despite the obvious fact that, as a new man in the city, he couldn't possibly have known the facts and circumstances attendant upon the police scandals.

At a press conference, Worton further displayed his prejudice and his presumptive conclusions, when he evinced a desire to smear me as thoroughly as possible for the benefit of the others. He told the scribes: "We're going to get rid of the Brenda Allens and the Stokers!" This in spite of the fact that my trial lay ahead and that a man is deemed innocent until proven guilty. By bracketing me with Brenda Allen, a convicted prostitute and panderess, in his statement to the press, Worton had demonstrated his mastery of the propaganda trick, known as "the transfer." Lump Stoker with Brenda and some of the odor will certainly rub off on him!

Worton, who may have been a Marine general, proved himself unfair, intellectually dishonest and prejudiced. If the opportunity ever arises, I will tell him so to his face.

I was never summoned before him to relate the facts I have given in this book, inasmuch as he had delegated the handling of my case to Inspector William Parker, whom he had promoted to deputy chief of police. Worton, it should be noted, had also promoted Sergeants John Jesse and William Madden, excerpts from whose police careers I have listed herein, to the rank of Lieutenant.

Unaware of the merits, or the facts, involved in the police scandals, Worton had been in Los Angeles only a few days when he waxed eloquent in praise of Chief Horrall and Assistant Chief Reed, neither of whom he knew from Adam. Until Reed's retirement, he served as Worton's assistant.

From these facts, but one conclusion can be drawn. Obviously, Worton had taken his cue from Mayor Fletcher Bowron, prime motivator of the police scandals, who had evidently informed him that I was an "evil" man and that Horrall, Reed, Wisdom, Wellpott and

Jackson were "fine, upstanding, honest police officers who had done no wrong – who could do no wrong."

This panorama of chicanery and injustice was not lost upon hundreds of police officers in the department. The factual demonstration of "justice," conducted by Bowron, Worton and District Attorney William E. Simpson, once it was engraved on the minds of young officers, caused them to formulate the catch phrase —"*Don't do a Stoker!*"

Forgetting, if you can, the writer's prejudicial interest, contrast such abstractions as truth, justice and right with the chronographic facts as I have related them. What were the practical results of the various investigations made by the police department and the district attorney's office as a result of the police scandals? That graft, corruption and maladministration were involved, as well as perjury and politics, was substantiated by the roiling ferment of indictments and enforced retirements of police executives and personnel.

Predictions were freely made in Los Angeles that "nothing would come of it all," that none of the big brass would be convicted of anything; and that the only persons who would suffer as a result of what had occurred, would be Sergeant Charles Stoker and Vice Squad Officer Jimmy Parslow. That was the consensus of opinion among the initiate (police officers, the district attorney's staff and the newspapers), and it came out exactly as they had predicted. HOW DID THEY KNOW?

This prophecy, which was common knowledge around the Civic Center and Hall of Justice, while exceedingly strange and significant, was too pat. The pattern of the "blow down," discernible at the outset, was obvious throughout. The scandal was "blown down" by those who had handled it and who had power over it.

An unpleasant situation, threatening many persons in high places, the scandal was bound to have deleterious political repercussions in certain quarters. Consequently, those who had rendered it innocuous and had processed it through the grand jury and courts were determined that it should not get out of hand. Prominent persons caught in the maelstrom had no intention of paying the penalty.

The individuals primarily and fundamentally responsible for the police scandal, went home free and unharmed. Many were rewarded for their sins, being retired on fat pensions at the expense of the public, whose police department they had used in such an indefensible manner.

We are living in a cynical era. Situations that would have aroused public fury several decades ago today pass unnoticed by the populace. Graft and sin have become so commonplace that a large segment of the public reacts to them with apathy, or not at all. Congressmen convicted of stealing from the United States Government are sentenced to prison, where they continue to draw salaries and pensions. Yet, we hear no public outcries of indignation. Morality — public and official -is dead. Rewards no longer go to the virtuous individual; they go to the sharp, slick, dishonest connivers whose motto is: "Get elected to public office; steal; and if you get caught, retire on pension."

Malleable young police officers, seeing the persecution of diligent and honest individuals while the sinful grow sleek and comfortable, can be expected to follow the adjuration: "When in Rome, do as the Romans do."

On September 26, 1938, Fletcher Bowron took office on a "reform" platform with the flamboyant promise to drive out the underworld and to end organized racketeering in the city. Did he? Whatever your answer, the F. B. I. quarterly crime reports showed that in respect to felonies, Los Angeles' Police Department under the late Chief of Police James Edgar Davis, had the lowest crime rate per capita in the nation. This despite Bowron's accusation that Jim Davis had presided over a police department that was corrupt and racket-ridden. How do apologists for Mayor Bowron explain this paradox in Los Angeles crime?

Prior to Bowron, Los Angeles had no racketeers comparable to Mickey Cohen. Bowron maintains that Cohen doesn't operate in the city, that he operates in county territory; yet, Cohen shot and killed a man in the city on May 16, 1945, and it is generally conceded by those who know that the major portion of Cohen's racket revenues is derived from the City of Los Angeles rather than from the County.

Despite Bowron's talk and fanfare anent Cohen, the city administration has done nothing about him for ten long years. The police have obviously failed to curb him. Cohen's charge that Wellpott and Jackson had tried to shake him down for large amounts of money indicated that some Los Angeles police officers were on terms of easy familiarity with the mobster. That Cohen frequently wined and dined police officers at expensive eateries in Hollywood is common knowledge. The people of Los Angeles have been given myriad reasons and excuses for police failure to suppress Cohen's racketeering and mob activities. But words, disconnected from facts, are mere rhetoric, shadow without substance.

It is my opinion that Mickey Cohen, aside from his obvious sins and transgressions, has been used as a political whipping boy by the city administration. When for political reasons it is necessary to conjure up a devil, *Mickey is it.* Or, barring Mickey, the remote, shadowy national crime king, Frank Costello, holds the spot. According to Mayor Bowron, Costello is "always about to descend on Los Angeles." The implication is clear. With Bowron as Mayor, Costello will remain in New York. Without Bowron, Costello will come to Los Angeles. In what way, I ask, could the presence of Costello worsen the local situation?

Replying to questions of a Los Angeles newspaper photographer in New York, Costello expressed no intention or desire to come to Los Angeles, despite Bowron's maunderings to the contrary.

"Who believes Costello?" you ask.

I reply that, when one considers the actions, inconsistencies, contradictions, evasions, distortions and dissimulations of Bowron, why should anyone accredit the mayor with greater veracity than the gangster?

Mayor Bowron's public performance, in connection with the grand jury and its investigation into the police scandal, should be sufficient reason to place him on the same parity in so far as truth is concerned.

Here we find a situation where for years the mayor has prated of the honesty, integrity and efficiency of the Los Angeles police department under Chief C. B. Horrall. In his weekly radio broadcasts over a period of years, Bowron has rarely failed to assert that "Los Angeles has the finest police department in the United States."

When, for good and sufficient reason, the county grand jury began an investigation into police corruption, the professional politician, Bowron, publicly declared himself to be "devoted to honesty and clean government." Accepting his protestations of piety, one would have expected him to assist the county grand jury in the uprooting and exposing of evil within the police department.

But with the facts threatening to expose him, Bowron saw that such a helpful attitude on his part would be incompatible with his political interests and with his determination to remain mayor at any cost. Far from being co-operative, we find him antagonistic, obstructive and critical, baying loudly that the warranted grand jury investigation was POLITICALLY INSPIRED, always the refuge of the trapped office-holder. Bowron cast aside his perennial pose of being eager and willing to ferret out evil. Words, he knew, could no longer insulate him from the encroaching facts.

So, what did Bowron do? He immediately accused the grand jury of "playing politics." When the newspapers purposely held out the scandal story of the police mess until AFTER MAY 31, 1949, AND AT BOWRON'S BEHEST, THAT WASN'T POLITICS. HAD THAT STORY BROKEN, BOWRON KNEW THAT BOWRON WAS THROUGH.

Then Bowron charged that the grand jurors and their leaders were in "league with the underworld."—THE VERY THING FOR WHICH THEY WERE INVESTIGATING HIS POLICE DEPARTMENT. Bowron then shouted that the grand jury was criminis particeps in a plot to discredit the city administration. With his great talent for misdirection, he implied that the grand jury was linked in a plot to aid and abet the candidacy of City Engineer Lloyd Aldrich. Aldrich had had the temerity to run against the MIGHTY MIDGET.

A whispering campaign pictured me as a part of this dark plot against Bowron. Rumor spread that I had testified before the grand jury because I had effectuated an agreement with Aldrich, whereby I would be promoted if he were elected mayor and might even be elevated to the office of chief of police. This, despite the fact that I had never spoken to Aldrich or any of his agents.

The spuriousness of Bowron's purely political defense of his perquisites was apparent to anyone of intelligence. One would have had to take a great leap mentally to connect the facts of the police scandal with Lloyd Aldrich's candidacy and underworld interests. Aldrich *wasn't* mayor. Bowron *was*. Aldrich *wasn't* directing the police administrative vice squad; Lieutenant Rudy Wellpott and Sergeant Jackson, who enjoyed the friendship and support of Assistant Chief Joe Reed, operated that outfit. Aldrich *wasn't* accepting graft or protecting Brenda Allen's houses of assignation. *Sergeant Jackson was.*

Moreover, it was the sworn obligation and duty of the grand jury to investigate graft, corruption and malfeasance in office within the police department if the jurors had reason to believe they existed. Formerly a presiding judge of the Superior court, Bowron had utilized county grand juries himself in a vain effort to effect the political undoing of former District Attorney Buron Fitts. Consequently, he was well aware of the facts involved and of the technic of grand jury procedure. He couldn't then, and he cannot now plead ignorance.

Yet, acknowledge of the mechanics of law enforcement didn't prevent this professional politico from crying "political frame-up" and "underworld plot." To the end, Mayor Bowron described Chief Horrall as the "finest police chief in the United States," and then peremptorily slit his official throat when he saw that the jig was up. Deciding that it was politically expedient to get rid of Horrall, he forced him to retire on pension. No thread of honesty, or ring of sincerity, highlighted Bowron's performance in connection with the police scandals. Through and through, Bowron played the scene politically straight and for all that it was worth in his own interests and in his own defense. He defended police malefactors, silently if not vocally, until he could no longer defend them and until the facts forced him to act against them.

How can any intelligent citizen reconcile Bowron's shabby political performance with his plaintive cry of "Good, Honest and Efficient Government?"

Moreover, his chickens were coming home to roost. Mayor Bowron who had created the hydra-headed monster of police corruption when he dishonestly and illegally elevated Captain Joe Reed to the office of Assistant Chief of Police, had been warned of what would accrue by Police Commission President Van M. Griffith. Griffith had told Bowron that this action would create unrest and dissatisfaction in the police department; that men outranking Reed would strenuously object to having Reed jumped over their heads. Griffith's prophecy was borne out by the facts; for, when Bowron insisted on promoting Reed, although he lacked rank and civil service qualifications, Griffith quit in disgust.

Two deputy chiefs of police resigned, bearing out Griffith's warning.

I have cited innumerable names of police officers and others who were eye and ear witnesses to the facts that unraveled as the result of the investigation into the Brenda Allen case and the involvement of administrative vice officers. There isn't the shadow of a doubt that Sergeant Jackson was connected with Madame Allen in a manner that wouldn't bear public scrutiny; there isn't the shadow of a doubt that District Attorney William E. Simpson and Mayor Bowron worked hand in glove to abort, thwart and blow down the police scandal and to save those culpable from suffering the penalties for their wrongdoing.

The grand jurors, for their pains, were insulted, vilified and accused of having ulterior and sinister motives. This was the "reward" they received for neglecting their businesses — this and two dollars a day and ten cents a mile one way from their homes to the Hall of Justice.

The mayor and the district attorney had resorted to the old trick of the criminal attorney with a guilty client. They had tried the innocent and accused the accusers to divert the spotlight from the guilty. They had found it necessary to discredit Sergeant Charles Stoker and Officer Jimmy Parslow, and discredit them they did.

This maneuver caused many persons to remark: "I don't know about Stoker. Maybe he isn't as clean as he says he is. Maybe he was involved in the graft, too." The purpose was accomplished for there are many persons to this day who, when talk of the police scandal is revived, still state that they "are not certain of Stoker either."

Once again, let me point out that I stood ready at all times to take any test that the probers might care to order, including scopolamine (truth serum), the lie detector test, or psychological tests. It is noteworthy that none of the others involved in the police scandal made a comparable offer.

I did this not out of bravado, but with the knowledge that I was innocent and consequently had nothing to fear.

The treatment accorded Policewoman Audre Davis after she had "confessed" to having perjured herself in the Brenda Allen pandering trial, and after she had accused me of a burglary that I hadn't committed, was worthy of mention. The red rug was rolled out for her; large sums of money were expended for her entertainment, board and room, and she was given a police guard to "protect" her from me, when, in reality, I needed protection from her. She was taken to the Del Mar race track near San Diego, and was housed at the finest hotel there.

Why? Because Audre was a "friend" of the police, whereas Stoker was an "enemy," having exposed police corruption. At this point in my story, you may wonder what can be done to obviate and make impossible a recurrence of similar police scandals.

It is my studied conclusion that the indiscriminate arrest of prostitutes in the City of Los Angeles is a futile waste of time and of taxpayers' money. This is the prevailing opinion among honest vice squad officers. There is no way of ascertaining how many prostitutes are active in Los Angeles. If I were guessing, I'd say at least ten thousand. That is an Army in scarlet.

I want to point out that there are all kinds and gradations of prostitutes. Literally thousands of salesgirls, car hops, secretaries, stenographers, typists, waitresses and clerks could be classed as semi, or part time, prostitutes — girls and young women who supplement their legitimate incomes by resorting to illicit sexual adventures for money or something else of intrinsic value. Morally and legally, I see little difference between the girl who permits one man to pay for her clothes and apartment, while permitting him sexual concessions, and the girl who accepts hard cash from many men for the same privilege.

In Los Angeles, as elsewhere, the price of sexual favors is often a dinner, a show, drinks and a good time. I venture to say that an ordinarily good looking young man with the necessary cash can enter any one of a thousand places in Los Angeles, including first class hotel bars and Main Street joints, and within an hour or two arrange an evening adventure in sex which will cost him little or much, depending upon the circumstances and the girl.

With the lowering of the sexual barriers, the whole picture of prostitution has changed in the United States, within the past thirty years. Formerly, there were red-light districts where prostitutes plied their trade, legally or illegally. Today, these districts have virtually disappeared and few can be found in our cities. From the practical point of view, in restricting and outlawing the red-light districts, the people have merely scattered the inmates to all points in urban centers rather than to have confined them to a specific place.

As a result of the changed view of sexual morality, professional prostitutes are faced with a situation that did not confront their sisterhood years ago — the so-called "amateur competition." The percentage of girls reaching the age of eighteen with their virginity intact has decreased immeasurably during this period. Whereas a girl who had pre-marital sexual experience was designated as a "lost soul" and a "social outcast" in grandmother's day; such experience is not a signal for social disapproval today.

It is possible that the change in sexual standards and morality is the aftermath of two world wars, involving great social, economic and political upheavals. Whatever the reason, lowered standards of morality exist; and lamenting or praising them will not alter the situation.

In the light of world events during the past several decades, it occurs to me that the present laws against prostitution are archaic and dated. Daily and nightly, Los Angeles police officers arrest scores of prostitutes. Yet, the number arrested comprises but a small part of the whole; and these arrests scarcely affect the totality of the scarlet industry in Los Angeles.

I believe that vice squad officers, instead of concentrating on the arrest of prostitutes, should expend their zeal on the arrest of pimps, panderers and procurers who are, in my estimation, the chief contributors to the professional prostitution evil.

Whenever one finds a dyed-in-the-wool prostitute, who is selling her body for cash, somewhere in the picture will be a man who has induced her to enter the scarlet way of life. Of course there are exceptions, but they are few. In my opinion, police effort should be concerned with the jailing and convicting of these vermin, who should be given long penitentiary sentences by way of discouraging members of their profession.

Lieutenant "Honest John" Stewart used to regale me with stories about an old time Los Angeles vice squad officer, during whose tenure houses of assignation were police-protected. This veteran squad copper couldn't stand pimps or procurers. He thought it bad enough that some girls and women became prostitutes, but much worse that some men should aid and abet their conversion from decency to sin. Accordingly, any time he ran across a pimp or procurer, he would soundly whack him. This veteran officer wore pigskin gloves to keep his knuckles from becoming skinned.

"Might get an infection," he would say.

The Los Angeles municipal ordinance known as the "resorting law," passed when the city was small in population, whereby any unmarried man and woman who repair to a hotel or rooming house for purposes of illicit sexual diversion, are guilty of a misdemeanor punishable by a five hundred dollar fine or six months in jail or both, is outmoded, unjust and unfair and should be abolished and repealed. Many a single man and woman (not a prostitute) fall afoul of this ordinance and are arrested, shamed and unnecessarily injured and humiliated by its enforcement.

Many comparatively innocent men and women are arrested under this ordinance, thrown into jail, hauled into court, fined and humiliated merely to build up records of great activity on the part of the police department. The figures look wonderful to a chief of police who submits them to a mayor for approval; but from the practical standpoint the arrests are meaningless and are known in police vice circles as "louse pinches."

Decent police officers often refrain from making such arrests, but sadistically inclined officers with twisted mentalities take delight in inflicting needless pain and grief on minor law breakers who may come under the prohibitions of the resorting ordinance.

It is my belief that our methods of enforcing the prostitution laws in Los Angeles, for the most part, merely provide an ideal spawning ground for police graft, and for the enrichment of bailbondsmen and shyster criminal lawyers who follow the police vice circuit for a livelihood.

The present hit-and-miss, helter-skelter method of vice enforcement in Los Angeles is no particular advantage to the taxpayers who pay the salaries of several dozens of officers engaged in this type of police work. The enforcement of the vice laws is particularly degrading to police officers assigned to these details, specifically to men who are congenially weak in resisting environmental conditions. Many officers assigned to vice details have neither their hearts nor their convictions in the work and especially is this true of young men from the armed forces who have taken their "fun where they found it" in places all over the world. Men of intellectual honesty have said to me: "I hate to arrest someone for doing what I've done myself."

Most of these, however, salve their consciences and misgivings by reminding themselves that "it is the law," and many, not believing in the law or in its enforcement, believe they are committing no grievous wrong when they participate in graft from prostitution. They act on the theory that such money, when shuffled with other money, is not identifiable and has no scarlet aura.

I have often wondered wherein lies the moral difference between the beautiful actress who sells herself for a fur coat and the Main Street B-Girl, or trollop, who accepts five dollars from a sex-hungry truck driver? Perhaps, there is a line of demarcation – but I can't see it.

Futhermore, there is no equal enforcement of the vice laws. Police do not exercise the same zeal in tracking down the high-class prostitute, who manages to stay inside the line of respectability by virtue of a synthetic public position, that they employ in tracking down and arresting her sleazy Main Street prototype.

I am well aware of the fact that the problem of prostitution has been attacked by better minds than mine, for the problem is as old as mankind, and thus far has proven insoluble. The question now arises: What is the best way to handle it?

There are only a few alternatives. At the outset, let me say that, as long as crooked coppers work vice enforcement, there can be no equity in enforcement, viz.: a prostitute working under a Brenda Allen with either complete or nearly complete police protection, bought and paid for, has all the best of it in escaping the law's penalties, when compared to her sister prostitute who is doing a scarlet solo out of her room in the Skid Row district. The dishonest vice squad cop will molest the latter and will protect the former.

The dishonest cop is not alone in preying on the girls in the prostitution racket. They are fair game for crooked bailbondsmen and shyster attorneys, many of whom consistently "finger," or stool on prostitutes to police for various reasons, mainly pecuniary.

Everyone will concede that the public will not permit the return of red-light, or segregated districts, where prostitutes can be licensed, medically inspected and policed. The descendants of those well-meaning men in another era who wrote the laws prohibiting prostitution, would fight the return of the red-light district with every weapon at their command. Churches and social organizations, as well as thieving coppers, politicians, pimps and procurers, would stand shoulder to shoulder with them.

This is a paradox — a situation involving legal and social consequences, wherein the PURE and the SINFUL intermingle freely on a common ground with unified INTENT, but for DIVERGENT and CONFLICTING reasons.

If red-light districts are OUT; if police-protected whore houses are OUT; and if the present method of handling prostitution is worthless, inefficient and futile, what can be done? My suggestions are fourfold: (1) The arrest, prosecution and conviction of pimps, panderers and procurers should be enforced mercilessly and without let-up; (2) organized prostitution rings should be relentlessly pursued, tracked down and broken up; (3) houses devoted to prostitution wherein several or more girls are "working" at the racket, should be raided and arrests made; and (4) police vice squads should develop and encourage a closer working liaison with agents of the Federal Bureau of Investigation, in tracking down and prosecuting men who transport girls and women across state lines for immoral purposes. The latter violation subjects offenders to the penalties provided in the Mann Act.

The present sporadic method of vice law enforcement places the emphasis on the prostitute, rather than on the pimp, panderer and procurer. If that policy were reversed, some progress could be made in controlling and mitigating the problem of prostitution. What good does it do to send a prostitute to jail for thirty days, or to fine her fifty or one hundred dollars and then turn her loose?

To illustrate this point: Brenda Allen boasted that she had been arrested eighteen times for prostitution in the City of Los Angeles, and had never served a day in jail.

Brenda knew the "angles." She knew how to stay out of jail. Until I had convicted her of attempted pandering, Brenda had received help along the line — from fixers, from shyster lawyers who had "influence" with judges, from bailbondsmen, from prosecutors, from politicians — and, yes, from police officers. She had made a mistake in boasting that she had never served a day in jail. When these boasts were quoted in the newspapers, the courts had to take official cognizance of them — and of her record.

The policy and the spirit of an organization are established by its top officials. Police department policy is inaugurated by the mayor of the city and is reflected downward through the executive branch of the department and into the ranks. This is true of spirit, as well. If the man at the top has no set convictions regarding policy, if he is merely an opportunist, possessed of a desire to retain his office, the police department will have neither policy nor spirit. That is the situation today.

Bowron's sole policy is to do anything to retain office. While he takes credit for non-existent accomplishments, Bowron has done nothing constructive for the City of Los Angeles in all the twelve years he has been mayor. I defy him to list any worthy contributions he has made toward city betterment. Taxpayers have nothing tangible to show for the money poured into his coffers for city administration other than incinerators that won't work and sewage disposal plants that are worthless, or nearly so. Nothing would please me more than to subject his record of "accomplishment" to the cold-blooded factual scrutiny of persons free from prejudice, partisanship, politics and parties with axes to grind. An honest analysis, conducted by a group of non-citizens having no economic or political interest in the outcome, would be revealing to say the least.

Years of false claims and assertions, born of selfish motives and bolstered by the media of propaganda in Los Angeles, have long maintained this artful and cherubic political confidence man at public expense.

Who is behind Bowron? A group of men whom you've never seen — and of whom you've seldom heard, comprising sharp attorneys for large corporations, newspaper executives, some of whom hold powerful positions on various city commissions under Bowron, professional politicians who carefully hide their identities and their motives for supporting Bowron, and, last but not least, political-minded ministers of the gospel.

Bowron was politically inept when he assumed office in September, 1938. However, listening to a galaxy of scheming, and plausible advisers, he has managed to weather many a storm and to spread the word over the radio and in the press that "he is honest."

What is honesty — as applied to Mayor Fletcher E. Bowron? The newspapers may have furnished a definition of honesty when they carried the following story, datelined March 20, 1950: "City councilmen yesterday unanimously disregarded Mayor Fletcher E. Bowron's objections, and voted to kill the job of assistant police chief which has been vacant since retirement of its last incumbent, Joe Reed."

Was Bowron honest when he created the job of assistant chief of police for Joe Reed, contrary to city charter provisions? Was he honest when he jumped Reed over the heads of inspectors and deputy chiefs of police who were rightfully entitled to the position, if it had to be created, on the basis of rank and merit? Was Bowron honest when he accused the 1949 grand jury of plotting with the political underworld because it had dared to investigate his corrupt, dishonest and inefficient police department on the basis of revealed facts?

Bowron always stages a convincing act, with the help of canny advisers, dramatizing himself as the victim of an unkind fate, a man badly put upon and persecuted, an honest office holder fighting the underworld single-handed, and the target of a deep plot dreamed up by Gangster Frank Costello.

Beleaguered, criticized and cornered in the late police scandal, Bowron had trotted Costello out once again and had publicly whipped him. Yet, Costello has had nothing to do with the events leading up to it.

The dark shadow of Costello's underworld wings directs public attention away from paint contracts, airport land deals, macadam paving contracts, oil agreements, zoning, rezoning and building permits. Bowron knows that Costello is a far more impressive and dramatic figure to wave before the voters than a bucket of paint, an airport, or a street traffic signal.

An apocryphal story has gone the rounds. When the chief of police under the Shaw regime which preceded Bowron was in office and the rackets were running wide open, and the administration was under heavy fire for laxity in law enforcement, the police chief called in an aide, whom he asked to go to the public library at Fifth Street and Grand Avenue. He told the aide to read up on Communism. The aide did as he had been directed and reported back. He said:

"It appears to me that Communism and the border bum blockade are excellent devices to distract public attention from whore houses, books, gambling joints and slot machines."

Does Bowron know, as all politicians know, that the hand is quicker than the eyes and minds of voters — and that voters' eyes can be redirected and their minds mesmerized until all connection with realities has been severed?

To prove that public attention can be redirected, confused and lost, I shall cite several instances which, in the moving crush of events, may have been forgotten. But not by me.

You will recall that the administrative vice detail under Lieutenant Rudy Wellpott and Sergeant Elmer V. Jackson had placed dictographs in Michael (Mickey) Cohen's home. This was done at the time the home was built. There, recordings were made over a period of months, during which time state agents, police officers and members of the district attorney's staff were entertained as guests of the gangster.

J. Arthur Vaus, who went to work for Mickey, told his employer that he would make recordings of the attempts of Wellpott and Jackson to shake him (Mickey) down for huge sums of money. When Jackson and Wellpott arrested Harold (Happy) Meltzer on the charge of carrying a concealed weapon, Meltzer and Cohen immediately yelled frame-up, stoutly declaring that Meltzer had carried no pistol on the night he was stopped with Mickey on a Hollywood street. They charged outright that the gun had been planted in the car.

During Meltzer's trial, the defense attorneys and Mickey announced that they had dictograph records to prove the asserted shakedown attempts by Wellpott and Jackson and records of Jackson's extracurricular activities with Madame Brenda Allen.

The political din was terrific. At this juncture, Attorney- General Fred N. Howser, wondering what the shouting and the tumult were about, assigned an investigator, Harry Cooper, to Los Angeles and to Mickey Cohen. The 1949 county grand jury was breathing on the necks of many police officers, and peering down the throats of several public officials. These individuals had reason to worry. Mickey Cohen had spread thousands of dollars around Los Angeles City and County in the operation of his rackets.

"HOW MUCH IS MICKEY GOING TO SPILL?" was the question in many minds. The first public intimation that recordings had been made by Wellpott and Jackson came when Cohen and his attorneys announced in open court that Mickey has purchased one set of the recordings, when Mickey thought the shakedown process was going too far. Meltzer's arrest on the gun charge, after Cohen had refused to meet the financial demands of Wellpott and Jackson, caused Cohen to holler "bloody murder."

WITH COHEN'S INTENTION EVIDENT, MANY LOS ANGELENOS WERE IN GRAVE JEOPARDY. IF COHEN WERE TO HAVE TOLD ALL HE KNEW ABOUT PROTECTED VICE AND GAMBLING PAYOFFS AND TO HAVE NAMED THOSE WHO HAD TAKEN HIS MONEY, ONE CAN WELL IMAGINE WHAT A SCANDAL WOULD HAVE RESULTED.

Nor did Attorney-General Howser's assignment of Agent Harry Cooper to look into the mess create tranquillity in the minds of those who were vulnerable. These individuals concluded that it was possible that Cohen had already told State Agent Cooper *everything*, in which event Cooper was also a menace.

At 3:00 on the morning of July 20, 1949, M. Cohen and his entourage, including Neddie Herbert, New York gangster, who had moved out West as Cohen's No. 1 man; Agent Cooper; Actress Dee Davis whom Cooper later married; Newspaper Columnist Florabel

Muir and several others walked out of Sherry's cocktail lounge on the Sunset Strip.

Sherry's was owned and operated by former New York detective Barney Ruditsky, the man whose office figured in the Brenda Allen wire tappings.

Directly across the street was a vacant lot, the level of which was below Sunset Boulevard and the front of which was bolstered by a concrete retaining wall about four feet high. Hidden behind this wall were gunmen, armed with shotguns loaded with Double 00 buckshot, the type of buckshot used in police riot guns. The assassins let go and Cohen, Herbert, Cooper and Actress Dee Davis went down under the barrage.

Herbert died several days later in a hospital. Although painfully wounded, Miss Davis and Agent Cooper, the latter shot through the stomach, recovered. Cohen was wounded in the right shoulder.

It is my opinion that the assassination of Herbert and the attempted assassination of Cohen and Agent Cooper were committed by police officers or by persons acting at their investigation because COHEN HAD THREATENED TO SPILL EVERYTHING.

The police had sufficient motive to kill Cohen. Inasmuch as the assassins had attempted to kill State Agent Cooper, it was apparent that someone believed that Cohen had exposed the ramifications of graft in police circles and considered it necessary to seal Cooper's lips before he could relate what he had learned to the attorney-general.

The slaying of Herbert and the attempted assassination of the others was a hurried affair which bore none of the earmarks of a typical gangland ambush. The Sunset Strip, where the ambuscade occurred, is closely patrolled by deputy sheriffs of the Fairfax Boulevard sub-station and its channels of ingress and egress make a getaway very difficult. The men who had manned the guns had taken a big gamble.
However, their determined try had come within a hair's breadth of succeeding.

Denying all knowledge of the recordings made by the administrative vice squad in Cohen's mansion, high police officials never appeared.

The Los Angeles Times and The San Francisco Chronicle simultaneously broke the story that the recordings existed; and news stories in both papers hinted at the identification of some of the people involved.

The district attorney's office immediately stated that a thorough investigation would be made into the history of the recordings and that every effort would be expended to locate them for grand jury investigation.

Some Los Angeles newspapers reported that the wife of Sergeant Jackson had done some of the transcribing of notes made from the recordings. Others stated that the recordings had been left in a police car and were stolen from the machine by some interested party.

Asked for an explanation, Chief of Police Worton had none. After much hemming and hawing as to why the higher brass of the department had not been apprised of the fact that the recordings had been made, Worton, referring to Rudy Wellpott said "The boy was keeping the recordings to *protect* himself."

Protect himself from what?

Upon being informed that Attorney-General Fred Howser had wondered why no executive of the police department knew anything about the recordings, Wellpott replied:

"I do not *trust* the attorney-general."

To which Howser commented: "Wellpott apparently doesn't even trust his superiors or himself." Off the record, he added: "I guess Wellpott only trusts Sergeant Jackson. Maybe he has to trust Jackson."

After this there followed complete silence. The district attorney's office forgot its avowed promise to probe into the mystery surrounding the recordings. The business of finding out what happened to the recordings was shelved. The subject was not mentioned in the presence of the 1949 county grand jury. In fact, all talk about the recordings was verboten. What happened to the recordings, and there were recordings without doubt, is a mystery to this day.

J. Arthur Vaus, who, while working for Mickey Cohen, had promised to make recordings of the attempted shakedown by Wellpott and Jackson, was obviously frightened. Although he had promised to sell The Daily News the recordings he had made from Brenda Allen's tapped telephone conversations, he never came through. Vaus had dummied up.

Significantly enough, Cohen now went on a clambake, ceasing his threats to "expose the police department and police department graft." Cohen had learned that he possessed no magical charm that would protect him from bullets, whether they were gangster or police inspired bullets. Like Vaus, he also decided that silence was golden, and that it possessed certain perquisites of life insurance.

In connection with the recordings made in Wellpott's home, Vice Squad Officer Jimmy Parslow was fired from the police department for "conduct unbecoming an officer": to wit, he had permitted police department records bearing on prostitution arrests he had made in Hollywood to get out of his hands. Parslow had gone to the office of United States Attorney James Carter, now a Federal judge, with information bearing on Federal Mann Act violations he had run across as a Hollywood vice officer. Carter had introduced Parslow to a man having no official status. Like Parslow, this man had been furnishing Carter with information bearing on a criminal investigation. Because Parslow had met the man in Carter's office, he had no reason to be suspicious of him. When Parslow had to go to court, he asked the man if he would take care of his brief case containing the arrest reports of prostitutes. The man agreed and they made an appointment to meet later. Parslow went to court.

Meanwhile, investigators working under Inspector Bill Parker were busy investigating the man who had Parslow's brief case — but not for that reason. Parslow and his newly found "friend" missed connections on their appointment; and the man took Parslow's brief case home with him. There, Inspector Parker's officers conducted a raid for no apparent reason and found Parslow's brief case.

Parslow's reports involving the prostitutes contained no information which would have placed the security of the United States Government in jeopardy. But Parslow had incurred the animosity of Inspector

Parker, and here was the golden opportunity to fire him — and fire him they did.

These minor police reports were the subject of much commotion, in contrast to the utter lack of commotion regarding the highly explosive wire recordings made by the administrative vice geniuses in Mickey Cohen's home.

It is interesting to note that neither Jackson nor Wellpott were suspended, upbraided, investigated or fired for having "lost" the Mickey Cohen wire recordings, whereas Parslow, who had entrusted his arrest reports to a man whom he had met in the office of the Federal District Attorney, was fired.

Perhaps, Mayor Bowron, Chief Worton, or Deputy Chief Parker, can render an explanation of these incidents and can explain why an allout investigation was never made of the Mickey Cohen wire recordings and why the man who had made and had opportunely lost them WAS NEVER FIRED FROM THE POLICE DEPARTMENT.

I know the answers — but I doubt that either Bowron or Worton or Parker will furnish them.

While raiding the ménage of Brenda Allen, I had obtained the names, addresses and telephone numbers of one hundred and fourteen girls in her employ, and had given copies of the list to the district attorney's office, the police department and a local newspaper. None of these girls was called in and interviewed by the district attorney's office, although some of them could have furnished valuable information bearing on Brenda Allen's operations and her association with Sergeant Elmer V. Jackson.

In addition, I had furnished the name of a prostitute, serving a sentence in Tehachapi Women's Prison, who had told me of the relationship between Sergeant Jackson and Brenda Allen. I was confident that she would retell the story because of her dislike of Brenda and her officer friend. She couldn't duck investigators due to the fact that she was safely in prison. This woman was never contacted.

The district attorney's office and the city administration wanted to get Brenda Allen out of the county jail before she spilled everything she knew. Both offices knew that if Brenda talked, so many officials would be involved that the "beef" couldn't be squelched, particularly if members of the 1949 county grand jury fastened their fangs in it.

When Policewoman Audre Davis testified that she had PERJURED HERSELF IN THE BRENDA ALLEN PANDERING TRIAL, a newspaper reporter asked Deputy District Attorney Adolph Alexander what the district attorney's office intended to do about her confession to a felony under oath.

"I am sure the district attorney's office will deal appropriately with Audre Davis at the proper time," was Alexander's retort. But the "proper time" never came. Apparently, Alexander meant that the district attorney's office would wine and dine Audre for two solid months at the Ambassador Hotel and other swank hostelries, take her to the Del Mar race track and keep her under armed guard to protect her from a non-existent threat from me.

The City Charter, under Section 202, provides that any police officer accused of misconduct shall have "an unprejudiced, unbiased and fair trial before a police trial board of rights."

That's what the City Charter says, but Chief of Police Worton was not bound by the charter's provisions; rather he believed in kangarooing those whom he disliked. On October 13,1949, Chief Worton addressed a select group of citizens at a luncheon held in the Gold Room of the Ambassador Hotel. In attendance were Mayor Fletcher Bowron members of the city council and the police commission, radio representatives and representatives of the metropolitan and district press.

On the following day, I was slated to be tried by a police board of rights on a charge of "conduct unbecoming an officer." Because this was so, Worton was prohibited by the City Charter from saying anything that would prejudice my impending trial, yet he said:

"Now to be frank — in the final analysis the police scandal has resolved itself into the word of a suspended sergeant of police and a madame of a brothel, against the word of two police officers, a lieutenant and a sergeant. The case against the lieutenant has been dismissed. Certainly, the AMERICAN SENSE OF FAIR PLAY will eventually come to the front (I hope so), for it does not make common sense to blame, or even insinuate that all police officers are crooked, EVEN IF ONE IS WILLING TO ACCEPT THE WORD OF A BRENDA AND A STOKER."

A friend in the personnel division told me that Inspector William Parker had written Worton's speech. Notwithstanding its authorship, you will note that Worton bracketed me with Brenda Allen, the madame, whom I had arrested, prosecuted and convicted. Despite Worton's accusation, I have never stated that ALL POLICE OFFICERS ARE CROOKED.

Worton failed to state that I had been assigned to the Allen investigation by superiors, a number of whom had had control over me at all times in respect to the investigation, and that these superiors included Captain William Wingard, commander of Hollywood station; Captain Cecil Wisdom, head of the police personnel division; and Sergeant Guy Rudolph CONFIDENTIAL AIDE AND ASSISTANT TO CHIEF OF POLICE C. B. HORRALL. Nor did Worton allude to Captain Wingard's statement, made in the presence of several officers, that Sergeant Jackson was a pimp and a crook and should be sent to San Quentin.

Worton's statement was a studied and premeditated effort to discredit me and my works, irrespective of justice and of the facts. By making the statement prior to my trial board hearing, he virtually ordered the three officers sitting on the trial board to fire me, an act contrary to the provisions of the City Charter.

The following excerpts are quoted from Chief Worton's speech of October 13, 1949, with the addition of my own asides.

"Has there been organized crime and vice within this city?"

(Why ask the obvious?)

"Yes, there has been a certain amount of organized vice and crime: bookmaking, prostitution, extortions and abortions."

(What are you going to do, or what have you done, about it?)

"Is there organized official corruption within the Police Department of this city?"

(Yawn)

"Is there organized prostitution in this city?"

(Yawn)

"Fortunately, within the Los Angeles Police Departmentthere are certain key officers whose honesty and attention to duty I have learned to rely on, and they are of much assistance to me now in straightening out the affairs of this Department."

(Who are, or were, these officers? Assistant Chief Joe Reed, Inspector William Parker, Captain Cecil Wisdom, Captain William Wingard, Lieutenant Rudy Wellpott and Sergeant Elmer V. Jackson, may I ask?)

"I have sought and received the co-operation of the district attorney's office of this county."

(That is not surprising. So had Mayor Fletcher Bowron and many others in the Los Angeles Police Department, before you arrived in the city to become chief.)

On April 15, 1950, a friend in Indiana sent me the following newspaper clipping from "The Farmer's Exchange" — an exquisite, divine thing wrought out of sheer gossamer. After reading it, I will be surprised at nothing that happens in my life. I quote:

"MOB SCIENTIST HITS THE SAWDUST TRAIL. FINDS REAL HAPPINESS AND IS NOW APPEARING ON YOUTH FOR CHRIST PROGRAMS IN NORTHERN INDIANA.

"Gangland's one-time top electronics engineer, Jim Vaus, recently told how mere curiosity led him into an evangelist's tent and conversion to Christianity on the night of last November 6.

"Vaus is a science graduate of UCLA and has been interested in radio since he was a youngster. He is now thirty and during the war, when he served as a Signal Corps captain, he became interested and thoroughly grounded in electronics. In this limited field, as an electronics consultant, he met Mobster Mickey Cohen and got into the big money. The gambler asked him to find a 'bug' in his house. He suspected there was a microphone hidden there, and Vaus found it and removed it. This was a year before transcription of recordings set off Los Angeles' big police scandal.

"From then on Vaus was in the pay of Cohen. The underworld, in order to cope with modern police and FBI methods, hires scientists when it can.

" 'I liked the cushy living, the big car I drove, the nice house I was able to buy for my wife and two kids,' Vaus said. 'I made up to three thousand dollars a month and didn't have to work hard.

"'I drifted into the big tent of Evangelist Billy Graham out of curiosity,' Vaus said. 'I had read in the newspapers that Stuart Hamblen (Hollywood luminary and man-about-town) had become converted and I wanted to see what it was all about. I didn't have the slightest intention of hitting the sawdust trail that night, but I did. Subconsciously, I realized that there was no satisfaction in my way of living. It was inwardly that I was dissatisfied. What I had failed to realize was that life in Christ is a new way of living. I caught part of this that night and when I hit that sawdust trail, here is what I prayed to God: 'If You can straighten out this mess I've got myself into, I'll give You my life and everything I've got, full time.' Well, in the weeks that have followed I have found joy. I plan to dedicate my life to work especially among young people before they are side-tracked into seeking the easy way, with the attitude that quick money spells success.'

"Vaus said he had wronged and gypped a lot of people and after becoming converted he looked them all up and made amends.

"It cost me about fifteen thousand dollars in cash,' he said, 'and I lost my home and fine car. But I feel that I am an Ambassador of God, the mightiest force in the world. We hear so much about life, liberty and the pursuit of happiness. Well, I don't have to pursue happiness. I've found it.'

"Vaus is being brought to this area for a series of meetings from March 27 through April 5, under sponsorship of Youth For Christ."

Upon reading the newspaper clipping relating the conversion of J. Arthur Vaus, I guess I should have been impressed. However, I couldn't forget this minister's son and his words, when he had smirkingly told me how he had used religion to get out of the Federal penitentiary. Vaus had said that he had gypped certain individuals out of fifteen thousand dollars which he had repaid in cash. Maybe I am skeptical, but I would like to see the receipts, or talk to the people he had victimized before accepting Vaus's word.

Many men before the birth of J. Arthur Vaus had learned that God and religion are excellent cloaks with which to hide skullduggery. I recall the words of an American Revolutionary patriot, who said: "Some of the greatest scoundrels hide in the folds of the Flag."

As I near the end of this personal history and look through newspaper clippings bearing upon the "Great Los Angeles Police Scandal," one screamer catches my eye:

"VILLAINS COULDN'T BESMIRCH LAPD NAME!" From the Los Angeles Daily News, a paper which has supported the administration of Mayor Fletcher E. Bowron, the article reads:

"Mayor Fletcher Bowron fairly chortled last night over the radio as he reviewed the 'crudely executed campaign' to discredit the police department, a plot that 'proved to be a prize dud.'

"Pointing out that the last of the criminal charges preferred by indictment was thrown out of Superior court and that the man who started the whole mess (that was I) was discharged from the force, Bowron said in his radio address:

"'I verily aver that the scheming minds of those who were responsible for the utterly unsubstantiated charges were those of persons with ulterior and sinister motives (I'm included in that category) and not good citizens with a worthy purpose of doing something for the public good and in the interest of the city.'

" 'Perhaps it was a good thing that the grand jury indictments were preferred,' he mused.

" 'The good names of the police officers were cleared,' he said, 'and the spotlight has been turned on the mobsters and racketeers.'

" 'But this is not the-time for complacency,' he warned.

" 'The fight to hold the line against organized crime, commercialized, syndicated gambling, and other rackets must be continuous,' the mayor said.

" 'So long as there is a chance, merely the glimmer of hope, though the odds may be long, the same old crowd that has been trying to gain control of our Police Department will keep trying.'"

There you've got it straight from the mayor's mouth.

Personally, I think that Mayor Bowron's fears are groundless – he still has Wellpott, Jackson and Brenda on his side. They have proved far more potent than I. And as long as Frank Costello remains in New York, Bowron has an issue for the people. You must remember that Bowron's not my choice: he's not your choice: he's the PEOPLE'S CHOICE.

And now, before parting, I again want to point out that the only villains in this piece: the only persons still remaining under a cloud since the "good name of the police department and its officers have been restored," are Charles F. Stoker, James Parslow and the members of the 1949 county grand jury.

Villains in the story books always get their just desserts – and we, the members of the 1949 county grand jury, and I – can only hope that justice and virtue will triumph in the future. In the words of the poet, Young, "Tomorrow is a satire on today, and shows its weakness."

For days, I wondered how to close this story. I wanted to write something impressive, emphatic and important. I prayed for inspiration, and God heard my prayers. On the morning of April 1, 1950, I picked up the 9:00 a. m. edition of the Los Angeles Times and on the front page read the following story.

It delineates better than anything I have written the sad state of the Los Angeles police department and of the district attorney's office of Los Angeles County. I quote:

"Willis Oscar Shipley, a fifty-year-old transient, was puzzled in court yesterday.

"He was charged with escape, a felony, and didn't know why.

"Officers said Shipley was arrested on a drunk charge last September, but that he escaped from the patrol wagon en route to the City Jail.

"'But judge,' Shipley explained to Municipal Judge Leroy Dawson, I didn't escape from that paddy wagon. We hit a bump, the door flew open, and I fell out, flat in the street. And they just went on without me.'

"Judge Dawson then ordered the felony charge dismissed on a motion by Deputy City Public Defender Hayes Mead."

The police report showed that Shipley was loaded, drunk, into the patrol wagon on East Fifth Street, the night of September 27, 1949. He stayed on Skid Row until the night of March 21, 1950, six months later, when he was loaded into the paddy wagon and taken to Lincoln Heights jail.

You will note that the police department, under the stentorian and militarily dramatic Marine General William A. Worton, sought a felony complaint against this poor, broken down drunken bum, and, MOREOVER, GOT IT. You will also note, that the man was taken to a preliminary hearing on the felony charge, which, if he had been bound over and convicted, could have resulted in sentence to San Quentin prison.

You will recall that I was twice turned down by the district attorney's office in the obtaining of a felony complaint for pandering against Harlot Brenda Allen. I received the complaint only when a newspaper man went along with me and after I had virtually camped out in the district attorney's office.

But why go on?

The police department and the district attorney's office should be publicly commended for their assiduity in arresting and prosecuting Skid Row bums. And no doubt they should be praised, too, for the manner in which they refuse to arrest and prosecute the bums' antitypes in the social order — the grafters, the corruptionists, the dishonest police officers and executives, the whore house madames and the Hollywood hetaerae.

The arrest of the bum calls to mind Shakespeare's lines in King Lear.

"Thou hast seen a farmer's dog bark at a beggar,
And the creature run from the cur: There,
There thou might'st behold the great image of authority;
A dog's obeyed in office.

SEQUEL

The foregoing part of this manuscript was completed on June 9, 1950. Immediately thereafter, a copy was registered with the Screen Writers' Guild.

It was the intent of the author to have this work – The Stoker Story – published by August 1, 1950. However, due to myriad difficulties involving the vagaries of publishers, and the indecision of many persons who were anxious to see the story published in the interest of public welfare, but who were aware of the highly explosive contents of the work and feared possible repercussions upon them, publication of The Stoker Story was unavoidably delayed.

Finally, after all difficulties in regard to publishing had been surmounted and the story was typographically ready in its final form, several months had elapsed. During that period, many things, indubitably germane to the story, had occurred in the City and County of Los Angeles.

This final chapter will be devoted to those incidents which, I believe, support the general thesis of this volume and are confirmatory evidence of the allegations and accusations already made herein.

In relating this addenda, the author will try to refrain from gilding these cold, hard facts in any particular. They have appeared in the daily press. They are, therefore, outside the realm of highly frescoed buncombe and illusions. They speak for themselves. Here they are.

Since this book was started, the citizens of Los Angeles voted on the question of recalling Mayor Fletcher E. Bowron at the general election, November 7th, 1950. Bowron won, employing the same tactics which have stood him in good stead politically for twelve years – to-wit, he was "fighting the underworld." He proclaimed his honesty, as did his supporters, from the housetops, the newspapers, and the pulpits.

Yet, Mayor Bowron and his aides and supporters, including many prominent attorneys who ostensibly "contributed their services gratis in THE CAUSE OF GOOD GOVERNMENT," did everything in their power to forestall the recall election until they felt assured that it would fail. They dragged the matter through the courts, much to the open disgust and annoyance of members of the appellate court, who, rightfully and in unmistakable language, ruled that the gang of schemers had no legal right to abort and short circuit the will of the people to bring a suspected official to book via the recall.

But, in the final analysis, Bowron and his coterie of schemers and advisers won the contest for, through delaying tactics, they stalled the recall until the general election on November 7th, and much more importantly, by stalling it, they made it a "SUDDEN DEATH AFFAIR," as the proponents of the recall, when it was finally validated by the courts after the city clerk had been threatened with contempt if he failed to comply with the law, had only three weeks and two days in which to marshal their facts and put on a campaign against Mayor Bowron. It was too late and the betting was four to one that the recall would fail.

The newspapers fell right in line behind Mayor Bowron, as they had done on May 31st, 1949, when he was re-elected, BEFORE FACTS RELATED IN THIS BOOK HAD BECOME PUBLIC KNOWLEDGE. The newspapers set up their usual cacophony that the recall was "just another underworld plot against Mayor Bowron, that he was honest, and that underworld interests were behind the attempt to unseat him."

Despite all the innuendo and propaganda, avalanched in Bowron's behalf, not one solitary fact or the name of any underworld personage of importance was demonstrated in truth to have been behind the recall. It is significant that neither Mayor Bowron, nor his newspaper supporters, or sycophants, alluded once to any of the facts reported in this book. Also ignored was the scandal which had rocked the police department and made him send out an S. O. S. for a retired Marine General who was given the responsibility of restoring, not only police department morale, but of re-shoring the foundations of Mayor Bowron's city administration.

Coincidentally, just before the ballots were cast on November 7th, 1950, Mayor Bowron entered a local hospital for treatment of a gall bladder ailment. He was still in the hospital when the votes were counted. Newspapers carried photographs of him being showered with congratulatory telegrams. He said, in effect, that once more truth and right had triumphed and that the forces of darkness had been vanquished.

Indeed, these sentiments must have been echoed by the parasitic gambling fraternity in Las Vegas, Nevada, and Tijuana, Mexico, for, in its opinion, there is "no better mayor in the United States than Fletcher E. Bowron." He is always engaged in the great Protean role of "fighting the underworld," which, in truth is not their underworld. Their underworld is out of his jurisdiction, but nevertheless has more than a tenuous working agreement with him.

At a meeting of ministers of various churches and in the presence of a number of newspaper reporters, Mayor Bowron in a pre-election speech, declared: "Charles Stoker was a member of a plot to oust me as Mayor of Los Angeles. The plot to oust me began at a meeting of the Coin Machine Institute in Chicago. This seminar of crime was told that the removal of Governor Warren and myself was essential to the expansion of pinball and slot machine operation.

"The program planned was a simulated scandal in the Police Department. They assigned Sergeant Stoker the job of promoting this scandal. My opponent in the election offered Stoker the position next to the Chief of Police if he defeated me. He was to have direct charge of the Vice Squad.

"When that plot failed with my election, those persons who planned the affair were not satisfied, so they organized the recall. Mickey Cohen is also linked to the recall. Sam Rummel, last attorney of record for Cohen, agreed to raise twenty-five thousand dollars for the recall.

"If anybody wants to sue me for libel, let them do it, and I will take depositions that will split this thing wide open."

After that speech was made, I, Charles Stoker, immediately sued Mayor Bowron, charging slander and libel. I reiterate that I have never had any traffic with the slot machine business other than to arrest persons whom I caught operating machines. I had no part of the May 31st, 1949, election. Nor was I ever promised anything in the nature of intrinsic value by anyone.

You will note in the last paragraph of Mayor Bowron's speech, he stated that he "would take depositions and bust this thing wide open in the event he was sued for libel." In that connection, he hasn't taken my deposition yet although several months have elapsed since I filed the suit. On the contrary, his attorney, former Assistant District Attorney Grant B. Cooper, whose mother-in-law, Mrs. Albine Norton is Mayor Bowron's secretary, has twice requested continuances of three weeks in connection with answering my complaint. At this date, December 31, 1950, the complaint has not been answered.

Either Mayor Fletcher E. Bowron is telling the truth and Sergeant Charles F. Stoker is lying, or vice versa. I have thrown down the gage of battle and I stand ready and willing to face the consequences in the full knowledge and faith that the cause I espouse, and have espoused, is honest, factual and right.

At 1:30 a.m., on December 11, 1950, Attorney Sammy Rummel, long identified as a "mouthpiece" for leading racketeers in Southern California, was murdered on the steps of his Laurel Canyon Boulevard home. The assassin used a sawed-off shotgun to kill Rummel whose body was found several hours later.

Rummel, as you have noted elsewhere in this book, appeared as attorney for Michael (Mickey) Cohen, top Hollywood gangster and for Harold (Happy) Meltzer, who was arrested by administrative vice squad officers for carrying a concealed weapon, a pistol, which in his case, inasmuch as he was an ex-convict, was a felony.

Several days after Rummel's murder, which occurred in the Hollywood police district in the City of Los Angeles, Mayor Bowron "threatened" a grand jury investigation which, he said, "might" show that Rummel was a leading figure in the recall movement against him.

This obviously was newspaper "skam" designed to buttress the political fortunes of Mayor Bowron. Several weeks have elapsed since

Bowron made the "threat" to show that the underworld was behind the recall, the implication being that Rummel was connected with the underworld, either as an attorney or otherwise, and of that there is little doubt. However, Mayor Bowron has produced no single scintilla of evidence or fact to prove that Rummel was interested in Bowron's political fate.

Police investigated the theory that Rummel had collected money to finance the recall and had "gone South" with it — and that this larceny angered those who had put it up (underworlders of course), and for that reason he was slain. Nothing has been found to support this theory, or suspicion, and at this writing the motive for Rummel's murder remains as obscure as it was on the morning his body was found.

Rummel is dead and, perforce, cannot talk. Consequently, from the standpoint of any shabby politician, all innuendoes or unsavory hints directed at his corpse are safe from rebuttal.

Readers of this treatise on the maladministration of the city government of Los Angeles will remember that, earlier in this tome, we related the fact that Rummel had defended Harold (Happy) Meltzer on the felony gun-toting charge. They will also remember the questions asked Lieutenant Rudy Wellpott and Sergeant Elmer V. Jackson by Attorney Rummel, and their answers. At that point in our story we left Meltzer "hanging on a limb" as the jury was unable to decide his guilt or innocence.

We will now report the conclusion of the Meltzer trial, using a clipping from the Los Angeles Times of December 7th, 1950.

"Harold (Happy) Meltzer, 39-year-old jeweler and former Mickey Cohen associate, yesterday was acquitted of felony gun possession charges.

"A jury of eleven women and one man returned the not- guilty verdict after three hours and ten minutes of deliberation.

"Meltzer was arrested February 15th, 1949, when vice- squad police charged that he, an ex-convict, was armed with a 38-calibre pistol while acting as bodyguard for Cohen.

"Meltzer, in return, charged that he was 'framed' and that the pistol was 'planted' by the arresting officers.

"Cohen, who testified at the trial, charged that the arrest was in retaliation for an unsuccessful attempt by two of the arresting officers, Lieutenant Rudy Wellpott and Sergeant E. V. Jackson, to extort fifteen thousand dollars from him ...

"The trial was sparked by the defense charges that Wellpott and Jackson were wined and dined many times at exclusive West Side night spots, at Cohen's expense.

"Under cross-examination by Defense Attorney William B. Beirne, both officers admitted that they had 'eaten free' at these restaurants, but said that they didn't know just who paid for their meals, liquor and entertainment.

"A previous trial earlier this year, ended in a mistrial with the jury deadlocked evenly on the question of Meltzer's guilt or innocence."

In his closing address to the jury, nodding to Lieutenant Wellpott and Sergeant Jackson, Attorney Beirne for Meltzer said, in part, "You can take these men for whatever you wish, extortionists, thieves, or what have you," alluding to Cohen's story that the reason for Meltzer's arrest lay behind Cohen's refusal to pay Wellpott and Jackson fifteen thousand dollars.

Despite the verdict of innocence on behalf of Meltzer, the state's case, in factual, direct and circumstantial evidence was overwhelming. The state at great expense brought a little old lady from Shreveport, La., who testified that she had sold the gun to a New York criminal, who unmistakably had been linked with Meltzer. The inference is fair that even though the jury may have believed that the pistol belonged to Meltzer, the jury also believed that Cohen's story as to the motive for Meltzer's arrest was true.

So much for Happy Meltzer.Now for that noble purveyor of flowers, Florist Rubin Kohn, 47-year-old sexual degenerate, with a penchant for young and beautiful models. You will recall how Rubin evaded the clutches of law by virtue of his largesse of posies to law enforcement officials and their agents, despite a record for sexual offenses stretching back through the years.

I am happy to report that, despite my unsuccessful efforts to bring Rubin to book, he finally ran out his string. You remember the story, so I'll not bore you with detail. I'll merely print the item which appeared in the *10-Star Final* of *The Daily News* on September 20, 1950.

"Florist Rubin Kohn, 47, today drew an aggregate of 360 days in county jail on six misdemeanor charges of misconducting himself with two girls he had lured into acting as his dancing instructors.

"Kohn was sentenced to serve 180 days on each of two counts and drew three years' probation on the remaining charges from Municipal Judge Joseph L. Call.

"The judge, in passing sentence, commented that Kohn has a record of arrests and convictions for sex offenses dating back 25 years.

"Kohn, operator of a florist shop at Sixth Street and Vermont Avenue, was convicted on the testimony of Miriam Kitterman, 23, professional dance teacher, and of a 17-year- old girl.

"He filed notice of appeal and said he would post a $3,000 appeal bond."

Dan Bechtel, 71-year-old public relations counselor, indicted by the Los Angeles County grand jury for accepting large sums of money from abortionists on the pretense that this money would be utilized in paying off law enforcement officers whose duty it is to arrest and prosecute abortionists, soon will face prosecution. Yet, *up to now, there has been no visible evidence that an investigation has been made of any suspected law enforcement officers having to do with this type of investigation.*

Let us return briefly to Attorney Sammy Rummel. Five hours before Rummel was murdered, he had met two men at his office – Captain Carl Pearson, hitherto head of the sheriffs anti-vice and gambling squad, and Deputy Sheriff Lawrence C. Schaffer. Police learned later that Rummel had had a conference with two mysterious men at about eight p.m., the night of December 10th, 1950. There was great to-do as to the identity of these men. Two days later, it developed that the men were Pearson and Schaffer, both of whom were mixed up in the Guaranty Finance multi-million dollar bookmaking probe.

Because of their tardiness in identifying themselves as the two mystery men who had conferred with Rummel shortly before his assassination, Sheriff Eugene W. Biscailuz fired Captain Pearson and suspended Deputy Schaffer. When interviewed by police, they told conflicting stories. Schaffer stating that Captain Pearson told him that he had made the appointment with Rummel for that fatal Sunday night, while Pearson told police that Rummel had made the appointment with him and Schaffer. *A mere question of veracity!*

In the Brenda Allen investigation you will remember that Sergeant Guy Rudolph, right hand aide of the then Chief of Police Clemence B. Horrall, came into the picture. You will also remember that Captain Pearson, after we had apprised him of the presence of Brenda's bordello (we then thought in county territory) on Cory Street, called in Sergeant Rudolph after informing me that Sergeant Jackson was connected with the Queen of all Hollywood whores. Then, you may recall, before the county grand jury, Captain Pearson testified that *I had brought* Sergeant Rudolph into the investigation and had *told him that Sergeant Jackson was involved.*

It was the other way around. *Just another question of veracity.*

Late comers to this story on municipal government in Southern California may not know that Guaranty Finance was a money lending outfit located on Florence Avenue in county territory which, in reality was a front or cover-up for the largest bookmaking operation in Los Angeles county. A Lieutenant James Fiske of the Los Angeles police department, then working vice and gambling, jumped over his jurisdiction one night, "prowled" the offices of Guaranty Finance and tried to do something about it.

Captain Al Guasti, retired, latterly a prominent figure along "policy lines" in the sheriff's office, called the then Assistant Chief of Police Joe Reed and told Reed to keep his policemen, meaning Fiske, out of county territory. Subsequently Guaranty Finance became a number one topic in Governor Earl Warren's California Crime Commission's report and lethargic Los Angeles county officials got into action with the result that several leading figures in the outfit were indicted and convicted.

There was reputed to have been a $108,000 pay-off for police protection, or sheriff's office protection, which showed on the books and stood unexplained.

Police subjected Captain Al Guasti to a severe grilling in the Rummel murder, as well as his ex-aide, or stooge, Captain Carl Pearson.

At this writing, the 1950 Los Angeles County grand jury is still engaged in investigating the Guaranty Finance setup. Moreover, the Senate Committee investigating nation-wide crime and its ramifications, known as the Kefauver Committee and headed by the Senator of that name from the State of Arkansas, is scheduled for a return engagement in Los Angeles.

The appointment of temporary Chief of Police William Worton ended July 21st, 1950, and there were two leading candidates for the job —Deputy Chiefs of Police William H. Parker, who has frequently appeared in these pages, and Thad Brown. Rumor had it that the police rank and file favored Brown and didn't like Parker, but the issue was to be decided by the Los Angeles Police Commission of five members, of which Mrs. Curtis L. Albro, was one. Mrs. Albro, a clubwoman, purportedly favored Brown.

In the nick of time and to the detriment of Brown and the good fortune of Parker, Mrs. Albro dropped dead with the result that Parker received the appointment on August 2, 1950.

If this sequel to The Stoker Story seems disconnected, so are the facts, which are merely set forth herein to fill gaps in the continuity which are now bridged by additional facts. Audre Davis, the policewoman, and Brenda Allen, the prostitute, both played leading roles in the events herein related. Accordingly we must read from the Advance California Reports of cases determined by The California Supreme Court, published September 7, 1950. I quote:

"Justice J. Shenk — By this proceeding in habeas corpus the petitioner (Brenda Allen) is seeking her release from the custody of the sheriff of Los Angeles County. She alleges that her conviction was the result of perjured testimony on the part of members of the police department of the City of Los Angeles and that thereby her constitutional rights were unlawfully invaded.

"On July 7,1949, Audre Davis appeared before the grand jury and was subjected to direct and cross-examination concerning certain matters that had taken place during the course of the prosecution of the petitioner. She was a policewoman in the police department of the City of Los Angeles and was one of the principal witnesses on behalf of the prosecution against the petitioner. At the hearing before the grand jury she stated that she had sworn falsely at the petitioner's trial. She also stated that Charles Stoker had committed perjury at the trial and had influenced her to swear falsely. Stoker was a sergeant in the police department and was the officer to whom Audre Davis was required to report in the performance of her duties.

"After the testimony of Audre Davis before the grand jury became known to her, the petitioner filed an application for a writ of habeas corpus in the District Court of Appeal, 2nd., Appellate District, basing her application upon the same grounds set forth in the present petition. That application was denied on August 3, 1949. On August 10th, she filed her application for a writ of habeas corpus in this court and the writ was issued. Upon the return to the writ a reference was ordered. The Honorable William F. Traverso, judge of the Superior Court in and for the City and County of San Francisco, was appointed to take testimony bearing upon the following questions and to make findings of fact thereon:

"1. Did any witness who testified at the trial of Marie Mitchell, also known as Brenda Allen, on the charge of attempted pandering, a felony, in action No. 119980 in the Superior Court, Los Angeles County, commit perjury as defined in Section 118 of the Penal Code; that is, did any such witness give false testimony as to any material matter which he or she knew to be false?

"2. In the event that any such witness so falsely testified, did any representative of the State of California responsible for the presentation of testimony, including any police officer, cause or suffer such testimony to be introduced knowing that such testimony as given was false?

"On the basis of all of the evidence introduced, the referee made 14 specific findings of fact to the effect that the testimony of Audre Davis and Charles Stoker given at the petitioner's trial WAS TRUTHFUL ...

"EVIDENCE ON THESE ISSUES OF FACT WAS TAKEN AT THE HEARING BEFORE THE REFEREE. AUDRE DAVIS WAS CALLED ON BEHALF OF THE PETITIONER. SHE REFUSED TO ANSWER PERTINENT QUESTIONS ON THE GROUND THAT THE ANSWERS WOULD TEND TO INCRIMINATE HER AND SHE WAS EXCUSED. CHARLES STOKER, CALLED ON BEHALF OF RESPONDENT, TESTIFIED TO THE TRUTH OF HIS TESTIMONY AT THE PETITIONER'S TRIAL AND DENIED THAT HE HAD DONE ANYTHING TO INFLUENCE AUDRE DAVIS TO TESTIFY FALSELY AT THE TRIAL. STOKER'S TESTIMONY BEFORE THE GRAND JURY WAS INTRODUCED IN EVIDENCE. IN HIS TESTIMONY THERE, STOKER ALSO ASSERTED THE TRUTH OF HIS TESTIMONY AT THE TRIAL AND DENIED INFLUENCING AUDRE DAVIS'S TESTIMONY.

"IT IS ENOUGH TO SAY THAT SERGEANT STOKER'S TESTIMONY BEFORE THE REFEREE WAS ALONE SUFFICIENT, IF BELIEVED, TO SUPPORT THE REFEREE'S FINDINGS. THE MOTIVES OF AUDRE DAVIS IN TESTIFYING AS SHE DID BEFORE THE GRAND JURY SERVED GREATLY TO DISCREDIT HER, AND THE TESTIMONY OF STOKER BEFORE THAT BODY ALSO REFLECTED ON HER CREDIBILITY.

"*The writ is discharged and the petitioner is remanded to custody.*"

It is comforting to the author to know that in the matter of his own veracity and that of Miss Davis, the California Supreme Court gave him the benefit of the doubt.

After the Guaranty Finance multi-million dollar book- making scandal hit the front pages with full force, and slammed into the integrity of law enforcement agencies purportedly devoted to see to it that such outfits do not operate, District Attorney William E. Simpson saw fit to remove his chief investigator, H. Leo Stanley, from control of the district attorney's vice squad.

On December 6, 1950, the newly created vice squad, secretly sneaked into the swank Hollywood residential section, kicked in a door and arrested ex-policewoman Audre Davis for bookmaking. The investigators then called members of the Los Angeles police department and had Audre carted away to jail.

At the time of her arrest, Miss Davis stated to the arresting officers that she was "only visiting." Not trusting the Los Angeles police department, this upstart, invading vice squad submitted the seized bookmaking markers (betting notations) and took them to a handwriting expert for analysis. He in turn stated that it was his professional opinion that the seized markers were in the handwriting of Miss Davis. As a result of evidence and testimony, Miss Davis was held on three counts of bookmaking — a felony — at a preliminary hearing. At this moment of writing, she is awaiting trial.

Chief Investigator H. Leo Stanley of the district attorney's office has issued an ultimatum that, unless control of the vice squad is returned to him, he will tender his resignation to the district attorney.

According to newspaper accounts, Miss Davis will be defended by a former Deputy City Attorney whose wife was the secretary to the convicted president of Guaranty Finance. This secretary was indicted but the charge was subsequently dismissed.

Within the month attorneys for the author of this book will start suit in an effort to regain his position as a sergeant of police — a position he lost because he had the temerity to fight organized graft and corruption inside the Los Angeles city administration of Mayor Fletcher E. Bowron.

FINIS

2011 Addendum

LAPD-Then and Now: A Footnote to History:

In 1949, immediately after his testimony before the Grand Jury as a whistle-blower on police graft and corruption, LAPD Sgt. Charles Stoker was ordered before a police trial board and summarily fired for CUPO (Conduct Unbecoming a Police Officer). The Reason for his firing?

Even though he was under secret subpoena by the Grand Jury, the Department claimed he, "failed to obtain official police department permission prior to testifying."

Fast forward sixty-years.

On November 2, 2010 a story appeared in the *Los Angeles Times* under the headline:"L.A. County jury awards $4 million to former LAPD officer." *The award was based on the jury's conclusion that the officer was fired in retaliation for testifying against the Department in a labor dispute.*

The article, written by *Times* investigative reporter, Joel Rubin, went on to state that officer Richard Romney, an 18-year veteran had testified against the LAPD regarding what he believed to be Department violations of the *Fair Labor Standards Act.*

"Days after he took the stand, LAPD officials opened an investigation into Romney, alleging he had admitted in open court to violating the Department's written policies on overtime."

Then LAPD police chief, William J. Bratton, rejected a recommendation that Romney be given a light, one-day suspension, and instead, called on a discipline panel to fire Romney. The panel agreed, and Romney was kicked out in February, 2009.

Additional civil lawsuits are pending against LAPD and the lawyer representing the officers indicated that, *"the potential payout in verdicts or settlements could cost the city between $100 million and $150 million."*

INDEX

"Outlaw" Grand Jury, 215, 217
Abortion Ring, 134, 135, 141
Addison, Chuck, 12
Albori, Marco, aka Albert Marco, 6
Albro, Mrs. Curtis, 376
Aldrich, Lloyd, 145, 171, 172, 343, 344
Alexander, Adolph, 218, 245, 280, 360
Allen, Brenda, aka Marie Mitchell, aka, Marie Balanque, "The Los Angeles Express", 218, 222, 223, 224, 232, 251, 255, 323, 351, 355, 359, 361, 366, 376
Ambassador Hotel, 252, 325, 360
Ambassador Modeling Agency, 325, 326
Anderson, Mr., 326, 327, 328
Audrain, Dr., 134, 135
Ball, Bill, 139
Banquo's Ghost, 336
Barnes, Johnny, 57, 217, 218, 219, 220, 245, 280, 285
Barnes, Stanley, 338
Bass, Nate, 56, 164, 165, 321
Bechtel, Dan, 141, 374
Becker, Mr., 144
Berman, Jack, 153

B-Girls, xv, 56, 163, 164, 176, 321
Biltmore Hotel, 107
Black and Tan, xv, 298
Black Dahlia Murder, 100
Blair, Ed, 135
Blair, Edwin, 67
Bledsoe, Ben, 9
blowdown, 218, 340
boat ride, 216
Bowman, Lt., 91
Bowron, Fletcher, 2, 3, 14, 15, 17, 104, 120, 198, 199, 339, 341, 360, 362, 364
Brenda Allen, aka Marie Mitchell, aka, Marie Balanque, "The Los Angeles Express", 3, 4, 18, 22, 26, 30, 36, 37, 39, 44, 45, 48, 52, 54, 55, 56, 68, 69, 75, 78, 80, 82, 85, 90, 103, 108, 109, 119, 120, 122, 124, 127, 146, 161, 167, 174, 177, 178, 180, 181, 183, 185, 187, 188, 189, 217
Brown Derby, xv, 175
Brown, Thad, xv, 199, 230, 274, 336, 376
Builders Control, 147
Burns, Willie, 133, 170
California Crime Commission 1950, 4, 18, 316, 376

California Supreme Court, 376, 378
Cap, 143
Carbo, Frank, 15
Caress, Zeke, 6, 10, 12, 50, 53
Carter, James, 358
Chandler, Harry, 6, 9
Chapman, Abe, 215
Chinatown, 65, 185, 186, 219, 316, 317, 318
Christian, Mr. & Mrs. James, 280
ChristianMr. & Mrs. James, 277
Churchill, Winston, 53
Citizen's Vigilante Committee, 267
City of Angles, 31
Clark, David, 108
Clinton, Clifford, 3, 13, 16, 17
Cohen, Mickey aka Michael "Mickey" Cohen, 22, 39, 56, 130, 132, 160, 167, 168, 175, 178, 179, 220, 221, 224, 248, 341, 342, 355, 357, 359, 362, 370
Coin Machine Institute of Chicago, 370
Collins, Anthony, xv, 287, 336
Connors, Patricia "Pat", 318, 321, 322
Conterno, Dominic, 10, 108
Convicting the Innocent, 155, 239, 282

Cooper, Grant B., 371
Cooper, Harry, 204, 248, 355
Cop Set Up, 166
Corsini, Aldo, 152, 153, 246, 268, 283
Costello, Frank, 31, 49, 342, 353, 365
Crail, Clifford, 266, 268, 279, 282, 285, 338
Crawford, Charles aka, "The Gray Wolf", 6, 9, 10, 50, 108
Creel, George, 13
Criminal Complaints Committee, 52, 161, 209
Cross, Homer, 54, 104, 201, 280
Cryer, George, 5, 6, 9
CUPO (Conduct Unbecoming a Police Officer), 380
Daugherty, Attorney General, 153
Dave's Blue Room, 175
Davis, Dee, 248, 355, 356
Davis, Victor, 191
Dawson, Leroy, 366
Dockweiler, John, 13, 16
Donaho, Jack aka Jack Donahoe, xv, 199
Dr. Pollom, 143
Eleventh Commandment, 33
Fan Tan, 317
Farmer Page, 20, 50, 53
Farmers Exchange, 362
Ferguson, Vernon, 168, 175

Fiske, James, 375
Fitts, Buron, 13, 16, 344
Flamingo Hotel, 15
Fog Belt, 321
Forrester, Anne "Black Widow", 2, 3, 18
France, Anatole, 41
Fricke, Charles aka "San Quentin Fricke", 141, 265, 338
Frontier Club, 14
Gali-Gali Bar, 124
Gans, Robert (Bob Gans), 6, 10
Garrison, Phil, 228
German, Lee, xv
Gestapo, 232, 256
Glucoft, Linda, 332
Gold Room, Ambassador Hotel, 360
Goldie, Bob, 153
Goldie, George, 153
Governor Warren, 370
Graham, Billy, 363
Greenberg, Big Greenie, 15
Griffith Park, 52
Grossman, Mr., 141
Guasti, Al, 375, 376
Hahn, S. S., 244, 338
Haight, Raymond, 50
Hall of Justice, 114, 246, 340, 345
Hamblen, Stuart, 363
Harding, Warren G., 153
Harris, Roland, 95

Henderson, Fred, 218, 245, 280
Herbert, Neddie, 56, 204, 248, 355
Hill, Edward, 317, 320
Hohmann, Arthur, xv, 336
Hollywood Vice, xiv, 104, 228
Hoover, J. Edgar, 47, 160
Horrall, Clemence, 53, 66, 85, 120, 161, 171, 240, 335, 375
Houghton, Alice, 249, 252, 257, 299
House of Murphy, xv, 175
Howser, Fred, 357
impulse indicator, 74
Jack Swan, 129
Jackson, Elmer, 56, 91, 197
Jackson, Robert, 32
Jacobs, Tommy, 10
James, G. A., 178
Jesse, John, 187, 189, 191, 193, 194, 241, 253, 255, 257, 258, 260, 278, 305, 306, 311, 339
Jesus Christ, 46
Johnson, Mr. & Mrs., 122
Joint Control, 147, 148, 149, 150, 151, 152, 154, 156, 157, 183, 234, 264, 266, 267, 269, 271, 272, 278
Juice, 36, 287, 293
Julian Petroleum Corporation, 153
Justice J. Shenk, 376
Kent Kane Parrott (also spelled Parrot), 5, 54

Keyes, Officer, 321, 322, 323, 324
Kincaid, Clarence, 3
Kirk, Eric, 137, 141
Kitterman, Miriam, 374
Kohn, Rubin, 328, 329, 330, 373, 374
Krug, Keith, 147, 284
Kynette, Earle, 12, 13
L.A. County Board of Supervisors, 380
L.A. Daily News, 12
LAPD Intelligence Squad, xiii
Lee German, 336
Lewis, Roy, 159, 177
Lincoln Heights Jail, 129, 366
Little Brother, xv, 298, 299, 300, 301, 302, 303, 304, 305
Lorenson, Harry, 128, 287, 288, 290
Los Angeles Daily News, 118, 223, 228, 265, 291, 364
Los Angeles Times, 6, 9, 170, 240, 357, 365, 372, 380
Lubin, Eli, 129
M.V.D. Russian Secret Police, 256
MacArthur, Douglas, 52
MacCauley, Kenneth, 305, 307, 308
MahJongg, 317
Main Street Bar, 56, 166
Mann Act, 351, 358

Marie Mitchell, aka Brenda Allen, 377
Marsden, Alfred, 128
Marsden, Alfred, 287
Martel, Pierre, 153
Masquerading, xv
Mayfair Hotel, 231, 258
McAfee, Guy, 2, 4, 6, 9, 12, 13, 15, 20, 50, 53, 54, 56, 104, 108
McAleer, Owen, 54
McNeil Island Fed Penitentiary, 4, 131
Mead, Hayes, 366
Means, Gaston, 153
Meltzer, Harry "Happy", 133, 159
Menuhin, Yehudi, 31
Mitchell, Marie aka Brenda Allen, xii
Mitchell, Marie, aka Brenda Allen, 18, 68, 69, 71
Mix, Edward, 146
Murder Inc., 15
Negro Belt, xv, 298
Ninety-One Club, 14
Ogul, Dave, 129
Ostervik, Allan, 164
Ottiger, August, 190
Outlaw Grand Jury, 214, 215
Page, Stanley, 12
Parker, William H., aka Bill Parker, 56, 125, 126, 161, 199, 209, 210, 228, 240, 249,

253, 254, 257, 266, 278, 281, 296, 305, 335, 339, 361, 362
Parrot, Kent Kane (also spelled Parrot), 2
Parslow, James, 95, 124, 279, 365
Parslow, Jimmy, 56, 124, 126, 161, 210, 228, 231, 257, 275, 278, 279, 340, 346, 358
Pearson, Alfred, 168, 287
Pearson, Carl, 85, 88, 374, 376
Pi Que, 317
Piccadilly Restaurant, xv
Pinker, Ray, 94, 99, 100
Pixler, Dr., 141
Pollom, Dr., 141
Porter, John C., 10, 11
Programmed Raid, xv, 301
Racketeer from the East, 23
Ramlow, Jerry, 223, 226
Raymond, Harry, 12
Reed, Joe, 52, 53, 54, 57, 66, 86, 91, 120, 163, 173, 196, 223, 226, 229, 240, 266, 287, 289, 290, 297, 344, 345, 353, 362, 375
Resorting, xv
Richardson, Friend, 16
Rist, Jimmy, 129
Robinson, Curly, 17
Robinson, Howard, 81, 323
Rodell, Fred, 41
Roland Harris, 124, 228
Roll, Ernest, 119

Rosenbloom, Maxie, 58
Ruditsky, Barney, 56, 86, 205, 224, 356
Rudolph, Guy, 55, 85, 91, 100, 132, 161, 223, 224, 227, 228, 361, 375
Ruggles, Jack, 56, 87, 107, 185, 228, 238, 259, 263, 275
Rummel, Samuel, 175
Russell, William, 178
Ruth, Raymond Russell, 191
S.C. Lewis, 153
Salcido, Augustine, 321
San Francisco Chronicle, 357
San Quentin, 10, 13, 33, 51, 78, 79, 93, 105, 108, 130, 141, 144, 174, 228, 261, 265, 323, 361, 366
Sasso, Augustus, aka "Chito", 10
Saturnalia, 103, 300
Schaffer, Lawrence, 374
Scherer, Tutor, 12, 20, 50, 53
Scott, Robert, 218
Selby, Lynn, 275, 278
Seman, George, 307
Seventy Seventh Street Division aka 77th Street Division, 328
Shannon, Izzy, 16
Sharp, Chester, 152, 246, 268, 283, 284
Shaw, Frank, 10, 11, 13, 16, 17, 18, 198
Shaw, Joe, 11, 13, 225

Ship Café, 10
Shipley, Willis Oscar, 365
Siberia, 321
Siegel, Ben aka "Bugsy", 15
Simpson, William, 16, 52, 115, 119, 213, 250, 285, 291, 340, 345, 378
Slack, Tom, 168
SlapsieMaxie's, xv, 175
Small, Joe, 139, 141
Snively, Mrs., 325, 326, 327, 328
Snyder, Meredith (Pinky), 6
Spencer, Herbert, 108
square apple, 35, 58
Stanley, H. Leo, 181, 218, 220, 245, 291, 379
Stanley, Mrs. Irene, 286
State Attorney General, 41, 355
State Board of Equalization, 249, 250
State Insurance Commission, 315
State Medical Board, 133, 134, 135, 136, 141
Steffens, Lincoln, 44
Stewart, John, 23, 58, 63
Stewart, Marvin, 55, 106, 124, 125, 201, 234, 236, 270
Stralla, Anthony aka Tony Cornero, 2, 18
Stroble, Fred, 246, 332
Sullivan, Ward, 267, 272, 284
Syndicate, 2, 10, 11, 13

tank job, xv, 216
Teapot Dome Scandal, 153
The Little New Yorker, 286, 288, 289, 290, 291, 292, 293, 294, 295, 296, 297
Traverso, William, 377
Trent, Meta "Chubby", 223
Tucker, Horace, 162
Tulley, Mr., 141, 142, 143
Uhl, George, 290, 292
Utley, James, 2, 12, 18
Van Griffith, 52
Vaus, J. Arthur, 56, 72, 87, 88, 130, 131, 132, 177, 179, 181, 206, 220, 221, 225, 354, 357, 363, 364
Veitch, Arthur, 161, 280
Wellpott, Rudy, 55, 56, 63, 75, 78, 86, 88, 91, 116, 120, 121, 127, 139, 146, 159, 163, 168, 173, 174, 175, 179, 197, 199, 218, 223, 225, 226, 231, 240, 261, 286, 290, 298, 318, 319, 320, 321, 322, 337, 344, 354, 357, 362, 372, 373
William H. Parker, aka Bill Parker, xv, 166, 230, 232, 267, 376
Wingard, William, 56, 81, 84, 223, 226, 323, 361, 362
Wisdom, Cecil, 56, 57, 90, 110, 121, 123, 127, 146, 154, 188, 196, 223, 232, 241, 244, 253,

266, 268, 278, 322, 324, 337,
361, 362
Wobblies, 9

Worton, William, 171, 183,
195, 199, 230, 241, 245, 257,
266, 296, 334, 366, 376

www.ingramcontent.com/pod-product-compliance
Lightning Source LLC
LaVergne TN
LVHW051617040325
805106LV00031B/407